By WILLIAM L. SHIRER

Love and Hatred: *The Troubled Marriage of Leo and Sonya Tolstoy*
20th Century Journey: *A Native's Return: 1945–1988*
20th Century Journey: *The Nightmare Years: 1930–1940*
Gandhi—A Memoir
20th Century Journey: *The Start: 1904–1930*
The Collapse of the Third Republic
The Sinking of the *Bismarck*
The Rise and Fall of Adolf Hitler
The Rise and Fall of the Third Reich
The Consul's Wife
The Challenge of Scandinavia
Stranger Come Home
Midcentury Journey
The Traitor
End of the Berlin Diary
Berlin Diary

# Love and Hatred

## THE TROUBLED MARRIAGE OF
## OF
## LEO AND SONYA TOLSTOY

# William L. Shirer

SIMON & SCHUSTER
New York   London   Toronto
Sydney   Tokyo   Singapore

**SIMON & SCHUSTER**
Rockefeller Center
1230 Avenue of the Americas
New York, New York 10020

10  9  8  7  6  5  4  3  2  1

Library of Congress Cataloging-in-Publication Data

Shirer, William L. (William Lawrence), 1904–1993
   Love and hatred : the troubled marriage of Leo and Sonya Tolstoy / William Shirer.
     p.   cm.
   Includes bibliographical references and index.
     1. Tolstoy, Leo, graf, 1828–1910—Marriage.   2. Tolstaia, S. A. (Sof'ia Andreevna), 1844–1919—Marriage.   3. Authors, Russian—19th century—Biography.   4. Authors' wives—Russia—Biography. I. Title.
PG3388.S5  1994
891.73'3—dc20
[B]          93-38849          CIP
ISBN: 0-671-88162-0

Grateful acknowledgment is made to the following publishers for permission to reprint material in their control.
   Doubleday, a division of Bantam Doubleday Dell Publishing Group, Inc., for excerpts from V. F. Bulgakov, The Last Year of Leo Tolstoy, translated by Ann Dunnigan.
   Hippocrene Books for excerpts from The Final Struggle: Being Countess Tolstoy's Diary for 1910, translated by Aylmer Maude, published by Octagon Press, 1980.
   Random House, Inc., for excerpts from The Diaries of Sophia Tolstoy, translated by Cathy Porter; English translation, introduction, and commentary copyright © 1985 by Jonathan Cape, Ltd.
   Charles Scribner's Sons, an imprint of Macmillan Publishing Company, for excerpts from Tolstoy's Letters, translated by R. F. Christian, English translation and editorial matter copyright © 1978 R. F. Christian; and for excerpts from Tolstoy's Diaries, translated by R. F. Christian, English translation and editorial matter copyright © 1985 R. F. Christian.
   Yale University Press for excerpts from Alexandra Tolstoy, The Tragedy of Tolstoy, translated by Elena Varneck, copyright 1933 by Yale University Press.

*To my wife Irina Alexandrovna Lugovskaya
and to the brilliant young cardiologist
John R. Levinson, M.D., Ph.D.,
of Massachusetts General Hospital in Boston.
    Her decisiveness and care and his wisdom and
boldness enabled me to survive the three years
it took to finish this book.*

# Contents

## BOOK THREE
*The Last Year* • *1910*

# *Foreword*

This book began as an inquiry into why Leo Tolstoy's long and productive life ended as it did: strangely, irrationally, and in tragedy. The very last days, in a forlorn place, were terribly lonely.

This is not, strictly speaking, a biography of the great Russian novelist and moral preacher. Nor of his formidable wife. With the exception of the English translation of two firsthand works written by Russians more than three quarters of a century ago, no book in English, so far as I know, has focused on why the last years of this towering literary genius and his gifted but troubled wife were so tormented and led to such a sorry end.

All historians and biographers build on the works of their predecessors, and I am indebted to a number of them, but this book is based largely on primary sources—the diaries, notebooks, and letters of Leo Tolstoy and his wife; of their daughter Tanya; of Dr. Dushan P. Makovitsky, the resident family doctor; of Valentin Bulgakov, the youthful last secretary of the great writer—and on the firsthand testimony of the Tolstoy children, Sergei, Ilya, Tanya, and Alexandra. And Vladimir Chertkov, the devious, scheming close friend and disciple of Tolstoy in the last third of the writer's life and an implacable enemy of Countess Tolstoy, has left his dubious recollections.

For years Tolstoy's biographers saw the Countess, as Aileen Kelley, a Tolstoy scholar, has noted, "through his eyes." But all this changed when her diary appeared in a definitive Russian edition in

1978, forcing all who write of Tolstoy to drastically alter their view of his wife, who had been depicted as a Xanthippe, the shrewish wife of Socrates, and the source of all of Tolstoy's torments. "It would be unthinkable," R. F. Christian, the British Tolstoy scholar, has remarked, "to write a serious biography of Tolstoy without drawing on Sonya's diaries extensively, and nobody but his wife could have written about him with such intimate knowledge and frankness."

I have drawn on them considerably, mindful, though, of what obviously are distortions, exaggerations, and, once in a while, downright lies. But not until 1985 was a complete edition of Sonya Tolstoy's diary available in English—that translated by Cathy Porter—though Alexander Werth, an old colleague of mine in Europe among the foreign correspondents, had brought out an abridged edition in 1928 and 1929. It broke off, however, in 1897, thirteen years before the tensions between Tolstoy and his wife reached their unhappy climax. The Soviets had not yet finished publishing her diaries in Russian.

It was because no English-language translation of her later and most important diaries existed that I took up the study of Russian in order to read them—a task that in the end proved beyond my abilities, though I achieved a rudimentary ability to read the language. But my wife, Irina Lugovskaya, is Russian and she was able to help me with translation as well as to give me a sense of Russian culture, which in so many ways is beyond the grasp of a foreigner.

The papers of Leo Tolstoy, including all his literary works, his diaries and letters, were published by the Soviet Union in ninety volumes in a massive jubilee edition which came out throughout the 1920s. A large selection in English of the diaries and letters, translated and edited by R. F. Christian, appeared in 1978 and 1985.

An invaluable source in English is *The Final Struggle*, edited by Aylmer Maude, the English translator, friend, and biographer of Tolstoy, and by Sergei Tolstoy, the eldest son. This book contains not only long extracts from the diaries and letters of Tolstoy and his wife for 1910, the last year of his life, but also letters and diary entries from those who were close to Tolstoy at the end. Hundreds of footnotes by Sergei Tolstoy, revealing and explaining many events and relationships, are especially valuable.

The diaries and notebooks of Leo and his wife are unique in

literature and unique as sources of information for their lives, their thoughts, and their troubled relationship. No others that I can remember, with the possible exception of the confessions of Augustine and Rousseau, are so brutally frank and forthcoming. Day after day, year after year, they put down their innermost and increasingly bitter thoughts about the other. And for years they left what they wrote for the other to read—it was a perverse form of communication between them.

Sometimes they repented of the hurt their diaries inflicted on the other, saying that they had written such things when they were out of sorts, and didn't really mean them.

Toward the end of 1894, for instance, Tolstoy wrote Chertkov to destroy all copies of his diaries for 1884 and to return the original to him. That year he had been severely critical of his wife and his sons. Reading over his journal by chance, aroused in him, he said, "a very painful feeling of shame, remorse and fear for the grief which a reading of these diaries may cause to the people about whom such bad and cruel things are said."

> It's unpleasant—more than unpleasant, it's painful—that these diaries have been read by people other than you—even by the person who copied them—painful because everything that was written in them was written under the impression of the moment, and was often terribly cruel and unjust, and furthermore because they speak about the sort of intimate relations which it is vile and odious of me to record, and still more odious to allow anyone except yourself to read. . . . I am horrified by the thought of the use which enemies may make of words and expressions in this diary directed against persons mentioned here.

Sonya, too, regretted a good deal that she had written of her husband—at least in the early years of their marriage. She conceded that she took up her journal only when she was depressed or resentful. "It makes me laugh," she confided to her diary in 1868, six years after their marriage (it is the only entry for that year), "to read my diary. What a lot of contradictions—as though I was the unhappiest woman! But who could be happier? Could any marriage be more happy and harmonious than ours? . . . I always write in my diary when we quarrel."

Still, as time went by, and they became gradually more incompatible, they continued to put down in their diaries thoughts increasingly critical of the other. And their journals reflected more and more their true feelings.

"The diaries are me," Tolstoy said, and his wife might have said the same thing of hers.

There are gaps in each of the diaries. In 1865, for instance, Tolstoy abandoned his for thirteen years, not resuming it until 1878. It was the period when he was writing his two masterpieces, the novels *War and Peace* and *Anna Karenina*. He had no time or energy for anything else.

Sonya, too, abandoned her diary for long stretches—once for two and a half years after her favorite son Vanechka died in 1895 at the age of seven and she could not get over the loss, which had devastated her.

Yet, aside from the gaps, Tolstoy's diaries cover a span of sixty-three years, from the first entry on March 17, 1847, when he was eighteen, to November 3, 1910, when he was eighty-two and lay dying in a strange place. Sonya started a diary when she was sixteen and began a new one on October 8, 1862, two weeks after her marriage, and continued it to November 9, 1910, the day Tolstoy was buried—a span of forty-eight years, though she continued her daily notebooks for another nine years to October 19, 1919, a fortnight before her death. In all, her diary and notebooks come to some half a million words.

The two diaries, especially Tolstoy's, consist of much more than their outbursts against each other. Tolstoy used his to jot down his thoughts about everything under the sun, especially the meaning of life and death. They are full of notes about developing what he was writing and ideas for future novels, short stories, essays. And they tell of a writer's eternal struggle to write and, in Tolstoy's case, of the struggle within himself, with his doubts, his weaknesses, his lustful appetites, and his contradictions.

Sonya's diaries also give us a picture, as no one else can, of the daily life of the growing Tolstoy family in Moscow and especially in Yasnaya Polyana, where the two spent most of their lives. It tells of her problems in running the estate, raising children, putting up relatives, friends, and Tolstoyans, supervising the house and the education of the children and of the joy and burden of copying and recopying Tolstoy's long manuscripts, with their handwriting that often only she could decipher. And she discloses how it was—never easy but often rewarding—to live with a genius. Sonya Tolstoy, while far from being the literary genius that her husband was, turned out to be an extremely expressive writer.

A few words about procedures.

Throughout the book I have used the dates of the Julian calendar (Old Style) which was in use in Russia in Tolstoy's time. The Julian calendar during the nineteenth century was twelve days behind the Gregorian calendar (New Style) used in the West, and thirteen days behind in the twentieth century. Thus January 1, 1901, in Russia was January 14 in the West. The difference in calendars has sometimes caused confusion, as mentioned on page 19. Since all the dates recorded by the various characters in this book were in Old Style, I have thought it logical to conform. (The Soviet Union adopted the "New Style" in 1918, after the Bolshevik revolution.)

Russians address each other and speak of others formally by their first and patronymic names. Thus everyone except relatives and close friends would address Countess Tolstoy as "Sofya Andreyevna," meaning "Sofya, daughter of Andrei." Tolstoy was "Leo Nikolayevich," "Leo, son of Nikolai." "Ovich" and "yevich" and "ovna" and "yevna" in Russian are the masculine and feminine patronymic endings, respectively. But this form of address and way of referring to others sounds awkward and monotonous in English and I have often dropped the patronymic. Russians invariably use diminutives of first names when addressing or speaking of relatives and close friends. Alexandra becomes "Sasha," Marya is "Masha," Leo becomes "Lyovochka," and Sofya "Sonya." One Russian intellectual who read the manuscript abhorred the use of "Sonya" for Sofya, but Sonya is what Tolstoy called his wife and I have retained it. However, I have followed the Russian custom of calling her Sofya whenever her patronymic is used.

There are no universally accepted rules for the transliteration of Russian names and words into English. The Russian *e*, for example, after a vowel or a soft, or palatalized, consonant or as the first letter in a word is pronounced *ye*, and I have followed that practice. Finally, the last names of women in Russian have a feminine ending. Thus Sonya Tolstoy would be known as Sonya Tol-staya. But again this is confusing in English and I have called most of the Russian women by their fathers' or husbands' family name.

Mention is occasionally made of sums in Russian rubles. In Tolstoy's time the ruble varied in value from 74 to 79 cents in American currency. A dollar then was worth $13.50 today.

"Nobody will ever understand me."

        —TOLSTOY


"He has never taken the trouble to understand me, and does not know me in the least."

       —COUNTESS TOLSTOY

# Flight!
# October 28, 1910

I N THE CHILLY predawn darkness of October 28, 1910,* Leo Tolstoy, eighty-two, at that time probably the most renowned writer in the world and acclaimed by millions at home and abroad for his concern for the poor and as a Christian apostle of nonviolent resistance to evil, stole out of his ancestral home at Yasnaya Polyana, abandoning his wife of forty-eight years, to seek a little peace and quiet he knew not where.

Ten days later, in the lonely cottage of the stationmaster across the tracks from the railroad station at Astapovo, a village that few Russians had even heard of, he was dead. His erratic flight from his wife had come to a sudden end in this forlorn place, where he had been forced to leave a train heading south. Exposure to the cold in the drafty, unheated, smoke-filled third-class railroad cars† had inflamed his lungs; pneumonia had developed and brought to an abrupt conclusion his long and productive life.

To many, especially to millions of Russian peasants, freed from centuries of serfdom only forty-nine years before, and also to workers and students, he was almost a saint. A good many people from all walks of life, in Russia and abroad, including the United States and Canada—they called themselves Tolstoyans—had tried

* Old Style, i.e., according to the Julian calendar. October 28, Old Style, would have been November 10, New Style. Normally, by November 10 in central Russia, the first snows fall and the temperature drops below freezing.
† Like Gandhi, Tolstoy, actually a wealthy Russian aristocrat and landowner, usually in his later years traveled third-class. From early middle age on, he had worn peasant dress—always the long loose peasant blouse.

to follow his moral precepts. To Mohandas K. Gandhi, just beginning his labors for the oppressed Indians in South Africa, Tolstoy had been one of the great inspirations of his life. From the Russian author, who wrote to him directly, had come the basic idea that eventually he would use to help gain independence for India: nonviolent resistance as a social and political weapon. Gandhi had called his commune Tolstoy Farm.

Finally, to millions of readers all over the world, Tolstoy had been the towering author of *War and Peace, Anna Karenina,* and other novels and works.

The press around the globe, shocked by the news from Yasnaya Polyana about Tolstoy's flight, put the story on its front pages. "TOL-STOY QUITS HOME, HIS REFUGE UNKNOWN," said a headline at the top of the middle column on page 1 of *The New York Times* on the morning of November 12. A three-part subhead told more of the story. And the dispatch began:

> *Special Cable to* THE NEW YORK TIMES
> LONDON, NOVEMBER 11—A special to the London Times from Moscow says . . . that Count Tolstoy has left Yasnaya Polyana for an unknown destination, saying he intends to spend his last days in seclusion.

The dispatch also quoted Prince Dmitri Obolensky, a son-in-law of the writer, as saying that Countess Tolstoy "was in despair."

What was the explanation for Tolstoy's precipitous flight? What had brought on such a drastic and fatal act?

Even two of his sons did not know for sure.

Four years later, Ilya Tolstoy, his second son, would write that "from the moment of my father's death till now, I have been racking my brains to discover what could have given him the impulse to take that last step."[1]

Sergei, Tolstoy's eldest son, also years later, asked: "Why did he go? And why had he not gone sooner? It is not possible to give a simple and categorical reply to these questions." And Sergei observed that Vladimir Chertkov, Tolstoy's closest friend at the end and his most ardent follower, agreed. He quotes Chertkov: "No investigation, however careful, can exhaust all the outer and inner circumstances receding into an endless past, that have brought about the event. Besides, even in the domain of Tolstoy's personal life which admits of inquiry, the direct and indirect causes of his 'going away' are so numerous and many-sided that it is beyond the power of a single individual to make an exhaustive enumeration of them."[2]

Chertkov does not mention that he himself was one of the "causes." But he was. For this somewhat sinister and devious man, a former aristocratic guards officer who turned Tolstoyan and suffered exile in England for his devoted efforts on the great writer's behalf, himself played a key role in the breakup of Tolstoy's long marriage and his desperate flight from his wife. He became Countess Tolstoy's mortal enemy and did his best to persuade her husband to leave her.

To understand Tolstoy's death, we first have to try to understand his life. It was dominated by two titanic struggles, aside from the struggle every author has to write. One was with himself and the other with his wife. The last he himself called "a struggle to the death." He might have said the same about the first: the lifelong wrestling with himself, with his conscience and his enormous doubts and contradictions. One critic has described Tolstoy's flight as "a final, futile effort to escape his contradictions: a wife he loved but could not endure, a celebrity he courted but could not abide, a life of aristocratic privilege he was born into, yet found a source of shame."[3] One could add the contradiction of a renowned novelist who later regretted having written novels, even his greatest ones, and who, after a midlife "conversion," turned from them to writing mostly religious and moral tracts. A tragic folly, many thought it, but for Tolstoy, it was the road to salvation.*

His early years were happy enough. He seems to have been one of the few great writers who could look back on a happy childhood, about which he wrote so charmingly in his first three, short autobiographical novels, *Childhood, Boyhood, Youth.* Though he was orphaned at nine—his mother died when he was two and his father

---

* Martine de Courcel in a charming, very Gallic biography, *Tolstoy: The Ultimate Reconciliation,* has written a whole book to try to show that Tolstoy stole away from Yasnaya Polyana so that he could resume writing novels, his true calling which he had all but abandoned with contempt years before. But that could hardly be. It was too late for that. He was too old and spent. His greatest works lay behind him, his greatest fiction written thirty, forty years before.

seven years later—there apparently were none of the scars that come from the early life of so many other authors, often with lasting psychological consequences. "Happy, happy times of childhood . . ." he exulted, looking back at twenty-four.[4] He was treated with love and understanding by his parents and later by caring relatives who finished the job of bringing him up.

It was his fateful marriage, when he was thirty-four, that dominated the rest of his life—at first for the better, allowing him to settle down after years of dissipation and aimlessness, raise a family, and write, in succession, his two masterpieces, *War and Peace* and *Anna Karenina*, and then for the worse, leading to a marital life of utter misery ultimately for both partners, and finally, after forty-eight years, to his sad end when, in desperation, he ran away from it.

· BOOK ONE ·

# The Years Before

## 1828–1879

ONE

# The Trials
# of Early Marriage

*I*T IS DIFFICULT to tell exactly when the marriage of the Tolstoys began to break down. Some believe that the trouble started about ten years after their wedding in 1862. Others say twenty years, that is, after Tolstoy underwent his midlife "conversion" or "crisis," drastically changing his way and view of life but failing—to his bitter disappointment—to induce his wife and children to follow him.

Mirsky, in his *History of Russian Literature,* wrote that the first fifteen years of Tolstoy's marriage were "exceptionally and shamefully happy."[1] Tolstoy's oldest daughter, Tanya, who of all the children retained the best balance in judging their parents, thought that "because of the great love that united them, the seeds of discord already present in the earliest days of my parents' union remained dormant for about 20 happy years of marriage—until the moment of Tolstoy's religious crisis."[2]

Sonya herself—as Tolstoy preferred to call his wife, who was christened Sofya—thought that "the first nineteen years we spent at Yasnaya Polyana was the happiest time of our lives."[3] Leo Tolstoy in a diary entry on May 26, 1894, says, that "it began that time fourteen years ago, when the string snapped and I became aware of my loneliness." That would have been in the seventeenth year of their union.

In truth, their diaries show, it began at the very outset of their marriage. Two strong-willed individuals, fiercely independent, seemed bound to clash. Though the bride was only eighteen and innocent of life, she proved to be a match for the worldly thirty-four-year-old Tolstoy, who—mistakenly, as it turned out—believed that he could shape his young spouse to his rather old-fashioned ideas of what a wife should be. On this score, he became disillusioned quite quickly, like Levin after three months of marriage to Kitty in *Anna Karenina*. Levin is very much an image of Tolstoy, his creator.

> Levin had been married three months. . . . At every step he found that he was disappointed in his former dreams. . . . Levin was happy, but he saw that it [married life] was not at all what he had imagined.

Levin had never imagined that he and Kitty could possibly quarrel.

> . . . but all of a sudden in their very early days they had such a violent quarrel that she had said to him that he did not love her, that he only loved himself. . . . They made it up. . . . But that did not prevent new collisions . . . and very frequently too, for the most unexpected and trivial reasons. This first period of their marriage was a trying one. . . . Altogether their honeymoon, that is, the first month after the wedding . . . remained in the minds of both . . . as the most trying and humiliating time of their lives.[4]

It was somewhat similar with the Tolstoys.

On October 8, 1862, only a fortnight after her marriage, Sonya Tolstoy began a diary of her adulthood—she had kept one as a child. This first entry runs on for several hundred words.

> Ever since yesterday, when he told me he didn't trust my love, I have been feeling truly terrible. . . . He loves to torment me and see me weep. . . . What is he doing to me? Little by little I shall withdraw completely from him and poison his life. . . . Today I began to feel that we were drifting further and further apart. And I thought how vulgar this kind of relation was. And I began to distrust his love too. When he kisses me I'm always thinking, "I'm not the first woman he has loved."

The next day, she writes that they opened their hearts and that she feels much better. But two days later, on October 11:

> I am terribly, terribly sad, and withdrawing further and further into myself. My husband is ill and out of sorts and doesn't love me. . . . I could never imagine it would be so terrible.

In the meantime, Leo Tolstoy was confirming in *his* diary their somewhat shaky start. In an entry covering the last five days of September—their first week of married life at Yasnaya Polyana—he wrote:

> Today there was a *scene*. I was sad that we behave just the same way as other people. I told her she had hurt me with regard to my feelings for her, and I wept. . . .
> October 2, 3, 4: We've had two more clashes: (1) because I was rude and (2) because of her n* . . . there have been difficult moments.

On December 23 the couple returned to Moscow, where Sonya's family lived and where they had been married exactly three months before, for a stay of some weeks.

> December 27, Moscow: . . . I was very displeased with her, compared her with other people, almost repented of it. . . . We had words over the doll; she wanted to show off her simple tastes in front of me. Now we've got over it. We went to the theater; it was wasted on *her* too.
> December 30: . . . Sonya moves me with her tears. The mere difference between us hurts me. . . .

Even before they departed for Moscow, Sonya was in despair. The atmosphere at Yasnaya Polyana she found more and more depressing. "There is never a happy voice to be heard, as if everyone had died. . . . There is nothing here but deathly silence," she wrote, among her other complaints, on November 13.

> November 23: Today I ran out of the house because everyone and everything disgusted me—so I just slipped out and ran

* It is not clear what word was intended by this initial.

off alone, and I wanted to laugh and shout for joy. . . . I went out simply because I was bored.

But it was more than that.

> He gets impatient and angry. Let him. . . . He will not talk to me. It's terrible to live with him. My husband is not mine today, he will not talk. . . . He is a stranger to me.

By the time they got to Moscow, Sonya found that she was pregnant. But this did not help matters, nor did the fact that they were starting a new year. In their diaries, at least, Leo did most of the complaining.

> January 8: In the morning—her clothes. She challenged me to object to them and I did object . . . tears and vulgar explanations. . . . We patched things up somehow. . . . Over dinner the patch came off; tears and hysterics. . . . I felt depressed with her.
> January 15: . . . at home I suddenly snarled at Sonya because she wouldn't leave me alone. . . . I still have the fear that she's young and can't understand or love much in me. . . .
> January 25: Yesterday we had a quarrel, allegedly over the big room but really because we are both idle. . . . I'm more convinced than ever that in life, as in all human relationships, the basis of everything is work.
> March 3: [They have returned to Yasnaya Polyana.] Twice we almost quarreled in the evening. Almost. Today she feels bored and hemmed in. . . . I'm afraid of this mood more than anything in the world.

On August 5, in the midst of the harvesting at Yasnaya, Tolstoy sat down to write a long entry in his diary. He wanted to describe the birth of his first child, Sergei, on June 28. But he broke off in the middle of a sentence to change the subject.

> Her character gets worse . . . with her grumbling and spiteful taunts . . . her unfairness and quiet egotism frighten and torment me. . . . I've looked through her diary—suppressed anger with me glows beneath words of tenderness. . . . If this is so,

and it's all a mistake on her part—it's terrible. . . . I'm terribly depressed.

He claims that he was in good spirits when he met the Countess in the morning, but that she was in a bad temper and began to nag not only him but everyone else in the household.

"I can't endure it calmly," he says, "because it's not simply bad but terrible. Like Mashenka [his sister], she has the same trait of morbid and capricious self-assurance and submission to what she imagines to be her unhappy fate."

The new year did not cheer Sonya up either. In her first entry of 1863—on January 9—she notes that she has never felt so wretched. She is full of remorse. She has been treating her husband badly. But two days later, on January 11:

> I am calmer now because he's being a little kinder to me.
> But my unhappiness is still so fresh that every little memory of
> it brings on a terrible physical pain in my head and body.

Part of her trouble, she admits, is her selfishness and jealousy. "I have been feeling out of sorts," she goes on, "and angry that he should love everything and everybody, when I want him to love only me." She also feels that her husband resents her because of her pregnancy. On April 29, with the baby due in two months, she wonders why Leo should be so "unkind" to her, "as if it were my fault that I am pregnant."

> May 8: My pregnancy is to blame for everything. . . . As far
> as Lyova is concerned I do not exist. . . . If he is occasionally
> kind to me it is more a matter of habit. . . . He does not love me
> any more . . . that is all over now.
> May 22: I feel cold and dreary—afraid that our past has
> died. . . . There is not a drop of love in him. . . . As for me, I have
> no life of my own, although I used to have one, when I loved him
> and comforted myself with the thought that he would love me
> too. What a fool I was to think so.

When their first child arrives on June 28, Tolstoy is furious that Sonya does not breast-feed him. He pays no attention to the doctors, who try to explain to him that Sonya has mastitis, that she herself cannot nurse the child and that they must get a wet nurse. "It wasn't that I did not want to," Sonya explains. "I longed to; it was what I wanted more than anything else." She quotes a letter "full of tenderness and remorse," which Leo wrote her apologizing for his attitude, "but in a moment of rage with me he crossed the lines out."[5]

As the summer at Yasnaya Polyana progresses, things do not get better. Her diary harps on it, day after day.

> July 23: I have been married for ten months and my spirits are flagging; it's terrible. . . . Leo is murderous.
>
> July 31: What he says is *so banal*. I know things are terrible, but why should he be so angry? Whose fault is it? Our relations are frightful, and at such a painful time as this too. He has become so unpleasant that I try all day to avoid him. . . . Now I feel everything is over. . . . I have just been reading his diary. . . . "These past nine months have been practically the worst in my life," he wrote—to say nothing of the tenth. How often he must secretly have asked himself why he ever got married.

At the beginning of August, apparently Leo is still complaining about her not nursing the baby. He keeps "torturing" her about it, she says.

> August 3: He wants to wipe me off the face of the earth because . . . I am not doing my duty. . . . How can one love an insect which never stops stinging?

The first anniversary of their marriage approaches.

> September 22: It will be a year tomorrow. Then I had hopes of happiness, now only of unhappiness. . . . What does he need my love for? It was just an infatuation. . . . What despotism! "This is what I want," he says, "don't you dare say a word."

She comes back to the subject on November 13.

> I am left alone morning, afternoon and night. I am to satisfy his pleasure and nurse his child. I am a piece of household furniture. I am a *woman*.

"I am a *woman*"! Was that why Leo hated her so?

She had read the lines in the opening pages of his diary in which at eighteen he had expressed his disdain for women as women. "Regard the society of women as a necessary unpleasantness of social life, and avoid it as much as possible," he had written.

> From whom indeed do we derive sensuality, effeminacy, frivolity in everything and a multitude of other vice, if it is not from women? Who is to blame for the fact that we lose our inner feelings of boldness, resolution, judiciousness, etc., if not from women? . . . They are worse than us.[6]

Sonya would learn soon enough of her husband's low esteem for marriage as he sat down a few months later to write *War and Peace*. Making a fair copy each evening of what Tolstoy had scribbled in his terrible handwriting during the day, Sonya came across some lines that reflected her husband's view. It is a much quoted scene from the early pages of the novel. Over dinner one evening Prince Andrei Bolkonsky turns to the young idealist Pierre Bezukhov just as the prince's wife has left them: "Never, never marry, my dear fellow . . . My wife is an excellent woman . . . But, my God! What wouldn't I give now not to be married."

Pierre is taken aback by such talk, but his friend goes on:

> "Tie yourself up with a woman, and like a chained convict, you lose all freedom . . . If you only knew what women in general are! Egotism, vanity, silliness, triviality in everything. That's what women are when they show themselves as they really are . . . No, don't marry, my dear fellow. Don't marry!"[7]

That first year of their marriage Leo and Sonya Tolstoy sowed the seeds of discord that their daughter Tanya mentioned as originating "in the earliest days" of the marriage. The seeds did not lie dormant, as Tanya believed. They caused much suffering and sorrow to both and got their marriage, in which they had had such high hopes, off to a rocky start. But they did more than that. The constant quarreling took its toll. Leo noted it in his diary as early as January 15, 1863, some four months after their wedding.

> The last squabble has left some small traces—or perhaps time has. Every such squabble, however trivial, is a scar on love.

A momentary feeling of passion, vexation, self-love or pride will pass, but a scar, however small, will remain forever on the best thing that exists in the world—love.

Sonya realized it too. In a diary entry two days later on January 17, she wrote, "He is right, our quarrels make a *cut*."

It seems almost unbelievable after such a recital of bickering, disappointment, and disillusionment by both over their first year of marriage that their diaries should also be full of passionate declarations of love for each other. But such are the contradictions in these two impetuous newlyweds.

To take Tolstoy's diary first: Back at Yasnaya Polyana after the Moscow wedding, Leo writes on September 25, "Unbelievable happiness. . . . It can't be that this will last as long as life itself."

> September 26–30: I love her just the same, if not more.*
> December 30, Moscow: [The last entry of the year.] I will always love her.

Tolstoy began the new year of 1863 with a passionate and poetic declaration of love for his young wife.

> January 5, Moscow: Family happiness completely absorbs me. . . . I love her when I wake up at night or in the morning and see her—she looks at me and loves me. . . . I love it when she sits close to me and we know that we love each other as much as we can, and she says: "Lyovochka" and stops—"why are the pipes in the stove so straight?" or "why do horses live such a long time?" etc. I love it when we are alone for a long time and I say: "What are we to do today, Sonya, what are we to do?" And she laughs. I love it when she is angry with me and suddenly in the twinkling of an eye, her thoughts and words are sometimes harsh: "Leave me, I'm tired of you": and a minute later she's already smiling kindly at me again. I love her when she doesn't see me and doesn't know I'm there, and I love her in my own

---

* In a letter to Countess Alexandra A. Tolstoy, a distant relative, whom in his younger years he'd thought he would like to marry if she hadn't been eleven years older—they remained close friends all their lives—Tolstoy wrote on September 28, 1862, from Yasnaya to tell her of his bride, "whom I love more than anything in the world. . . . I've lived to the age of 34, and I didn't know it was possible to be so much in love and so happy." (*Tolstoy's Letters*, Vol. I, p. 169.)

way. I love it when she is a girl in a yellow dress and sticks out her lower jaw and tongue; I love it when I see her head thrown back and her serious and frightened and childlike and passionate face; I love it when . . . [Tolstoy himself breaks off.]

Sonya, whose diary that first year is so full of bitter comments about her husband, can wax as lyrical about her love as he. The new year of 1863 finds her in a better mood, "wretched with remorse" for having treated her husband so badly.

January 9: I love him deeply, he has never been so precious to me, and I have never felt so . . . loathsome. Yet he is never angry with me and he still loves me, and his face is so gentle and saintly. A man like this could make me die of happiness and humility. . . . How could I have treated him so badly? I cannot love him any more than I do, for already I love him to such excess, with all my heart and soul, that there is no other thought or desire in my mind apart from my love for him, nothing. There is absolutely no evil in him, nothing I could reproach him for . . .

March 3: I am now happy in the knowledge that he loves me and loves me constantly.

March 26: Lyova gives me so much happiness. I love his cheerfulness, his moroseness, his good, good face, his gentle kindness. . . . Images of him pass through my mind as I imagine him from every angle and all the expressions that cross his face. Writing all this down is only a pretext for absorbing myself in him and dreaming about him. I always feel sick with happiness when he returns home. . . .

April 10: What a wonderful man he is!

# TWO

# A Narrow Escape
# from Matrimony

THE WOMAN LEO Tolstoy fell in love with toward the end of 1862 and made up his mind, so long hesitant, to marry at once was no stranger to him. He had known her and her family since her childhood. As a boy he had imagined himself so madly in love with her mother, who was only two years older than he, that in a fit of jealousy he pushed her off a balcony, injuring her. They remained good friends, and after she married she sometimes visited Yasnaya Polyana to see her close friend, Tolstoy's erring sister Marya.

She had a curious background. Christened Lyubov Alexandrovna Islenyev, she was the daughter of a wealthy landowner, Islenyev, who was rapidly gambling away what was left of the family's considerable fortune. He had made a secret marriage with a lady already married, and when that union was annulled, the six children they had had, among whom was Lyubov, became legally illegitimate and were forced to alter their name to Islavin.

This put a damper on their hopes of marrying into the nobility. At sixteen Lyubov married Andrei Behrs, a court physician in Moscow of German descent, and eighteen years older than his bride. A strong family man, or so Tolstoy thought, the good doctor had a certain eye for women—he had once had a love affair with Turgenev's mother. But he was genuinely devoted to his children. Eight of the thirteen born to the couple survived, of whom three were daughters. Tolstoy was fond of all three—he had watched them grow up from little tots. In the summer of 1862 Lisa, the eldest, was nearly twenty; Sofya (whom Tolstoy would ultimately prefer to call Sonya) was eighteen and Tanya sixteen. When, during the previous year, Tolstoy began to show a great deal of interest in the sisters, the parents had expected him, as was the custom in their circles, to propose to the eldest, Lisa. At first Tolstoy considered her.

Returning from his second trip to Western Europe in the spring of 1861, he wrote in his diary for May 6: "I've forgotten the pleasant days at Behrs'; but I daren't marry Lisa." In September, he was in Moscow and visiting the Behrses, and on the twenty-second he scribbled in his diary: "Lisa Behrs tempts me, but nothing will come of it . . . there's no feeling."

That had been Tolstoy's problem with a young woman he almost married six years before. No feeling.

On March 20, 1851, when Tolstoy was twenty-three, he noted in his diary: "I came to Moscow with three aims: 1, to gamble, 2, to marry, 3, to obtain a post."

His gambling, he decided, was "bad and mean." It had landed him deeply in debt and he was going to have to sell part of his property, he said, "to remedy" his affairs. As for getting some kind of government job, that was "impossible," though he did not say why. About marrying: "I've put it aside until I'm forced to it either by love or reason or even fate."

And he had put it aside year after year. There were the two years with the army between 1852 and 1854 in the Caucasus during which, besides taking part in raids against the Tatar tribes, he found much time for gambling, drinking, and "wenching," as he called it. But also for writing. There were the months of bitter combat at the siege of Sevastopol in the Crimean War in 1854 and 1855, where he served as an artillery officer. But again he found a good deal of time for writing. By the time he resigned from the army in 1856, he had published a considerable body of work: the first two of the three novelettes, *Childhood, Boyhood, Youth;* two long pieces of brilliant reporting from the front—*Sevastopol in December, Sevastopol in May*—and several short stories, including *Recollections of a Billiard Maker, The Woodfelling, The Snow Storm, Two Hussars,* and *A Russian Landlord.* Though he was only twenty-eight, critics were already accepting him as one of the major Russian writers. In Moscow in

1856, while still in uniform, he had posed for a photograph with some of his fellow contributors to the literary magazine *The Contemporary*, founded by Pushkin and now edited by the brilliant poet Nikolai Nekrasov. They were Grigorovich, Turgenev, Goncharov, Druzhinin, and Ostrovsky—already big names in current Russian literature.

It was time, he decided on returning to civilian life, to settle down, take charge of his run-down estate, press on with his writing, find a wife and start building a family. With this in mind, he returned to Yasnaya Polyana in the middle of June 1856, tried in vain to free his peasants from serfdom—apparently they thought it was a trick and turned his offer down—set up a school nevertheless to teach their children how to read and write, sought to improve the primitive farming on the place, and became infatuated with a pretty twenty-year-old girl who lived on a neighboring property. Perhaps it was love—he could never quite be sure. But it was serious enough. For soon he would be talking with her of marriage.

His closest friend, Dmitri Dyakov, who visited him in the middle of June, strongly advised it and Tolstoy confided to his diary: "Listening to him it seems to me too that this is the best thing I can do." That very afternoon Dyakov rode halfway with Tolstoy to the young lady's home in Sudakovo, hoping that his friend would see in her his future wife and tell her so. But for Tolstoy, not yet. "A pity she has no backbone or fire," he wrote in his diary that night. "Just like noodles."

The object of his attention was no stranger to the returning master of Yasnaya Polyana. Valerya Vladimirovna Arsenyev had been orphaned two years before, and Tolstoy had become the guardian of the children—Valerya, her two sisters, and a brother. But now, in the summer of 1856, when he was twenty-eight and she twenty, he had suddenly seen much in her that he had not noticed before—or remembered. She might have the solidity of noodles but, as his diary reveals, he began to see other qualities in her that attracted him. She was pretty, sweet, and kind, he noted, and obviously falling deeply in love with him.

Still, her imperfections weighed on him and in letters of inordinate length and surprising conceit, he began to point out what they were and how she might correct them if she wanted to become his wife and raise a family. Twenty of his letters to her survive, none of hers to him.

Rarely has an innocent young woman been so put down by a suitor. And rarely has a suitor been so confused and inconsistent. It all comes out in his diary and in his lengthy letters to her.

> June 18, 1856: Valerya chatted about clothes and the coronation.* Frivolity with her appears to be not a transient but an enduring passion.
>
> June 26: Valerya in a white dress. Very sweet. Spent one of the pleasantest days of my life. Do I love her seriously? And can she love me for long? Those are two questions I'd like to solve for myself but can't.
>
> June 28: Valerya is terribly badly educated and ignorant if not stupid.
>
> June 30: Valerya is a wonderful girl, but I definitely don't like her.
>
> July 12: Valerya was nicer than ever, but her frivolity and lack of concern for anything serious are horrifying.
>
> August 10: Valerya and I talked of marriage; she's not stupid and is unusually kind.

The Arsenyevs, chaperoned by their French companion, Mlle. Jenny Vergani—a formidable lady who was formulating the strategy by which Valerya could hook Tolstoy in marriage—left for Moscow two days later and the absence seemed to make Tolstoy's heart grow fonder. Away in Moscow for the coronation festival, the young lady seemed more attractive to him than ever. When she returned on September 24, Tolstoy hastened over to Sudakovo to see her. Again he was disillusioned. "Valerya is sweet," he recorded in his diary, "but alas, simply stupid." The next day, Valerya came over to see Tolstoy. Again he found her "sweet, but limited and impossibly trivial."

This did not prevent him from spending the next few nights at Sudakovo. On September 29, while still there, he woke up at nine, he says, in a bad temper.

> Valerya is unfitted for a practical or an intellectual life . . .
> I was angry. The conversation was steered around to Mortier, and it turned out that she was in love with him.

The young landlord was not only angry but jealous, though without reason. His sweetheart had not fallen in love with Mortier,

* Tsar Alexander II was crowned in Moscow that summer.

her piano teacher in Moscow. Tolstoy's jealousy only increased his affection. "For the first time," he wrote in his diary, "I experienced something like a feeling for her."

Back at Yasnaya Polyana two days later, the ardor cooled. "Thought less about Valerya, thank God. I'm not in love." But he thinks that someday he will experience it "with terrible force, and God forbid it should be for Valerya. She is terribly shallow, without principles and cold as ice."

> October 19: Spent the evening and the night at the Arsenyevs. Looked more calmly at Valerya. She's grown terribly stout and I definitely have no feelings for her.

Five days later he records that he did have feelings for her after all. "October 24: Went to a ball. Valerya was charming. I almost fell in love with her." He felt the same, he says, when he saw her at Tula on October 31. This despite the fact that he didn't like her hairstyle. "Terrible," he wrote down in his diary. And he'd begun to feel uneasy about having gotten himself into a situation with Valerya from which there seemed no escape but marriage. "Quite involuntarily," he noted on October 24, "I've become a sort of fiancé. . . ." The "constraint" vexed him "more and more." By the end of the month he felt desperate enough to seek a drastic solution. Suddenly, on November 1, he lit out for Moscow.

Once away from her, he missed her and felt the old pangs of love. "Thought only of Valerya on the journey," he noted in his diary as soon as he arrived in Moscow. The next day, November 2, he wrote Valerya a long letter—it went on for several pages. It was full of expressions of love and of his doubts. What he called the "foolish man" in him wanted to go right back to Sudakovo "and never to part from you again." In contrast, the "good man" in him was skeptical and had not been truly happy with her. He felt that he had given in to the foolish man's impulses just before he left. "I could say nothing to you except foolish words of endearment, of which I am now ashamed. . . ."

Still—"I already love in you your beauty, but I am only beginning to love what is eternal in you and forever precious—your heart, your soul. Beauty one can get to know and love in an hour, and cease to love just as quickly, but the soul one has to learn to love." Having given his advice on love, Tolstoy added a little on how she should behave.

> Please *go for a walk* every day whatever the weather. And wear a corset, and put on your stockings yourself, and generally make various improvements of that kind in yourself.

On November 7, Tolstoy moved on to St. Petersburg, greatly increasing the distance between him and his loved one. But now he thought he had reason to *hate* her. Part of the reason—perhaps the principal reason—for his hurried departure from Moscow was that he had heard from a friend there that Valerya, when in the city to attend the coronation, had indeed fallen in love with her piano teacher, Mortier de Fontane, that she had visited him every day and was now corresponding with him.

On November 8, in Petersburg, Tolstoy, out of his mind with jealous rage, sat down and wrote Valerya a letter so harsh and brutal that he dared not send it. "I no longer respect you . . . I don't believe you." He demanded to know how far the relationship had gone with the Frenchman.

He got off a second letter, somewhat toned down. "I am furious with you because I can't help loving you." Never again could he have that feeling of respect and trust he had once had for her. "On no account will I see you until I feel . . . that I can trust you as absolutely as before." Still smarting from jealousy, he asked her to tell him "the whole history of your love for Mortier." For a parting shot, he told her he had seen some of her relatives and friends in Petersburg, and "it's incomprehensible how you can live with these people without being disgusted."

His put-downs of her now filled his letters. He seems to have been unconscious of how arrogant they were, and insensitive to the effect they would have on her. He writes from Petersburg on November 9 that he is sending her a new book of tales by Turgenev and wants her opinion of them "however absurd it may be." He makes some point about getting the truth and adds, "Well, yes, for you this is still incomprehensible." And he goes on: "You haven't lived yet: you haven't experienced enjoyment and suffering, but only gaiety and sadness." He asks her to make her letters more responsive to his. "However, to tell the truth—my hand on my heart—I'm already thinking of you much less now." After all this, he adds: "But at any rate, you're really a terribly nice person." He doesn't close there. He has to tell her: "I know many women more intelligent than you, but I've never met one more honest. . . . You see, I so ardently wish to love you that I am teaching you how to make me love you."

No wonder Valerya takes her time to answer. He cannot understand why. "Do write me for goodness sake," he admonishes her on November 11. "Why don't you write? Goodbye, dear lady, and Christ be with you." By November 13 she has not responded and he gets off a letter saying, "I'm writing to you for the last time. What's the matter with you? Are you ill? Whatever it is, write me a line." He wants her to know the consequences of her silence.

> At first I was affectionate, then I was angry, and now I feel that I'm already becoming indifferent, and thank God! Some instinct has long been telling me that nothing will come of this except your unhappiness and mine. It's better to stop in time.

But he can't. Finally Valerya begins to answer his letters. She had been hurt by them and he hastens to apologize. "I felt sorry to have hurt you," he writes on November 19. But they must recognize that there are differences between them that are "terrible for our future." For instance: "the fact that a great part of the intellectual interests which are the main ones of my life will remain alien to you, despite all your love."

But it is not only her mind that is lacking, he now advises her, but her character. "Your principal defect is weakness of character and all the other minor defects that come from it." He gives an example: "Alas! You are deluding yourself that you have taste. That is, you may have, but you haven't any tact." But he really means *taste,* because he goes on to criticize her clothes, especially "a pale blue hat with white flowers, that better suits a lady riding a trotter in English harness or walking up a staircase with mirrors and camellias." For her, such a hat is "ridiculous." He tells his loved one about the joys of having read Goethe's *Iphigenia* and adds: "It's impossible for you to understand . . . the indescribably great pleasure one feels from understanding and loving poetry."

As late as December 7, Tolstoy assures her that "our objective, besides that of loving, is also to spend our lives together and fulfill all the obligations that marriage entails." But there creeps into his last letters a growing feeling that they'll never achieve that objective, that he doesn't love her enough to marry her, and that a union with so superficial, scatterbrained, and provincial a young woman would be a disaster for them both.

On December 12 he finally makes up his mind and breaks the news to her as gently as he can. He readily takes the blame, he says, for perhaps having led her on. "Try to forgive me, and let's remain good friends. Love and marriage would bring us both only suffering, but friendship, I feel, would be helpful to us both." And he who had just written his brother Sergei that he was a "family man by nature" tells Valerya: "It seems to me that I wasn't born for family life."

Though he is jilting her, he closes his letter by proclaiming his love. "Of all the women I've known, I've loved and still love you the most, but all that still is not enough. . . . Goodbye; Christ be with you, dear Valerya Vladimirovna."

In case his sweetheart did not fully realize that he was throwing her over, Tolstoy wrote another farewell letter on January 14, 1857. He has now returned to Moscow. Again he takes the blame for having misled her. He claims he hasn't changed his attitude toward her. "I'll never cease to love you *the way I did* [he underlines the words], i.e. with friendship. . . . My heart is not and has never been attracted to any other woman as it has been to you. But . . . I'm not capable of giving you the same feeling as your fine nature is prepared to give to me. I've behaved badly to you—I was carried away."

And then abruptly—and coldly—he pens the words that must have stunned the jilted young lady. "In a few days I am going to Paris and when I shall return to Russia—goodness only knows." (As we shall see, he knew very well when he was returning.)

Goodbye dear Valerya Vladimirovna, thank you a thousand times for your friendship and please forgive the pain that I perhaps caused you. . . . Really and truly I feel and know that you will bring happiness to some fine man, but as far as the heart goes, I am not worth your little finger, and would only bring you unhappiness.

> Goodbye, dear Valerya Vladimirovna, Christ be with you; you and I both have a long and splendid road ahead of us and God grant that it may lead you to the happiness that you deserve 1,000 times over.

Leo Tolstoy certainly had a long and splendid road ahead of him. But Valerya? Finally convinced that she had lost Tolstoy for good, she soon thereafter married a young man who would eventually become justice of the peace in Oryol.

On the same day as his farewell letter to Valerya, Tolstoy got off a cheerful note in French to Aunt Toinette, a distant relative who had helped to raise him and whom he adored, at Yasnaya Polyana:

> You probably understand, dear Auntie, why I don't want to—and ought not to—come to Yasnaya, or rather to Sudakovo now. I seem to have behaved very badly toward Valerya, but if I were to see her now, I would behave even worse. As I wrote to you, I am more than indifferent towards her, and feel I can't deceive either myself or her anymore. . . . Not only have I never had, but I shall never have, the slightest feeling of true love for Valerya. . . . I expect to return to Russia in July.

The day Tolstoy jilted Valerya for good, he wrote nothing in his diary. There is a brief entry for the next four days—January 15, 16, 17, 18: "Can't remember what happened each day. Oppressed by loneliness, idleness and the absence of women." No mention of Valerya.

# THREE

# Two Very Different Kinds of Love

TOLSTOY REACHED PARIS February 9, 1857, and immediately fell in love with the luminous city. Turgenev, who lived there most of the year in an unhappy relationship with Mme. Pauline Viardot, the singer, greeted him and immediately took him out, exhausted though he was from the long journey, to a ball. Soon the younger Russian writer was engulfed in the social life of the gay capital, high and low, for he was still lusting for "a woman" and sometimes found one on the boulevards or in the cafés. Paris was full of Russian aristocrats and Tolstoy spent most of his time with them. If he saw few French, he tried to take in all the tourist sites—the Louvre, the Bibliothèque National, Notre Dame, Sacré-Coeur, the Cluny Museum. At the Invalides, gazing on Napoleon's tomb, he was disgusted. He felt only hatred for the man who had invaded Russia and destroyed Moscow. "Deification of a villain," he muttered in his diary. "It's terrible."

The more he saw of his once idol, Turgenev, the less he liked him. But, as with Valerya Arsenyev, and others, he blew hot and cold. Turgenev had taken hold of him from the moment he arrived in Paris and had done his best to show him the city, take him to one festivity after another, and introduce him around. But to no avail. Tolstoy poured out his resentments—and contradictions—in his diary. February 17: "Dinner with Turgenev. He is quite simply vain and petty." February 21: "Spent another pleasant evening with Turgenev." February 24: "Turgenev called in the morning. . . . He's kind and terribly weak."

Next day they set off for Dijon together. February 25: "Turgenev doesn't believe in anything, that's his trouble: he doesn't love, but loves to love." February 26, Dijon: "Had dinner. Played chess in a café. Turgenev's vanity . . . is nice." March 1, Dijon: "Turgenev is a bore. . . . Alas, he's never loved anyone. . . . We almost quarrelled."

Relieved to be back in Paris where he did not have to spend each day and each evening with his friend, Tolstoy nevertheless continued to see him frequently. March 4: "Called on Turgenev. He's a bad man in that he's cold and useless, but he's very clever artistically and does nobody any harm." The very next day, March 5: "Called on Turgenev. No, I must avoid him. I've paid enough tributes to his merits, tried every possible way of making friends with him, but it's no use." March 7: "Turgenev called at 5, and seemed to look guilty. What can I do? I respect, value and even love him, I suppose, but I feel no sympathy for him and that's mutual."

It was. Turgenev, as we have seen, who had been among the first in Russia to take up the young, unknown writer and praise him to the skies, who was the first man of letters to befriend him in Moscow, had finally concluded that they could never really be friends. "I cannot establish any lasting friendship with Tolstoy, our views are too different," Turgenev wrote a friend. "No; after all my attempts to get along with Tolstoy, I have to give up," he wrote another friend. "We are put together too differently. . . . I cannot relax with him. . . . He lacks serenity, and yet he also lacks the turmoil of youth. As a result, I don't know how to take him. But he will develop into a remarkable man and I shall be the first to applaud and admire him."[1]

Despite their incompatibility, Turgenev was a great enough man to freely acknowledge that his uncongenial friend was destined for greatness in literature.

Young Tolstoy—he was twenty-nine—may not have been mature enough to appreciate Turgenev as a man but he was growing up, sometimes deeply regretful that the passage of time was also changing his relationships, even with his elder brother Sergei, who visited him now in Paris. In their youth they had been very close, and later Tolstoy would recall that he was "enraptured by Sergei, copied him, adored him and wanted to be like him. I was enraptured by his handsome appearance, his voice (he was always singing), his drawing, his spirits and in particular (though it seems an odd thing to say) the spontaneity of his egotism."[2]

Now in Paris, both on vacation and relaxed, they became bored with each other. With some hurt Tolstoy noted it in his diary, March 7:

> Dined with Seryozha and saw him off. Impossible muddle and helplessness. Our development is so different that we can't live together, although I am very fond of him.

Sergei returned to his estate at Pirogovo, where he was living with his Gypsy mistress, Marya Shishkin, and begetting one child after another. He retained his affection for his younger brother to the end.

There now occurred in Paris a commonplace event that would haunt Tolstoy the rest of his life. It made of him at once a lifelong enemy of capital punishment and it engendered in him a hatred of the State for its cruelty to human beings that made him an anarchist of sorts. It also hastened his departure from Paris. For the first and last time in his life he saw a man guillotined.

His diary for March 25: "Got up at 7 feeling ill and went to see an execution. A stout, white, strong chest. He kissed the Gospels and then—death. How senseless! . . . Feel unwell and depressed. . . . The guillotine kept me awake a long time and made me reflect."

Indeed, almost twenty-five years later, when he wrote *Confession*, he was still reflecting on the guillotining he had seen on that gray morning in Paris. And he was still wildly indignant.

> When I saw how the head was severed from the body and heard the thud of each part as it fell into the box, I understood, not with my intellect but with my whole being, that no theories of the rationality of existence or of progress could justify such an act. . . . I knew . . . that it was wrong.[3]

The day before the execution Tolstoy had begun a letter to a literary friend in Petersburg, V. P. Botkin, urging him to come to Paris and telling him that he was having the time of his life. He had been in the French capital, he said, for nearly two months and he did not plan to leave for another two months.

Tolstoy broke off and decided to finish the letter the next day.

> I wrote this yesterday and was interrupted and today I'm writing in a completely different mood. I was stupid and callous enough to go and see an execution this morning. . . . I've seen many horrible things in war and in the Caucasus, but if a man had been torn to pieces before my eyes it wouldn't have been so revolting as this ingenious and elegant machine by means of which a strong, hale and hearty man was killed in an instant. In war it's not a question of the rational will, but of human failings of passion; but in this case it's cold, refined calculation, and a convenient way of murder. . . . It is the insolent, arrogant desire to carry out justice.

The crowd surrounding the guillotine was "repulsive," and Tolstoy saw one father "explaining to his daughter the convenient and ingenious mechanism."

> The law of man—what nonsense! The truth is that the State is a conspiracy designed not only to exploit, but above all to corrupt its citizens. . . . I will never serve any government anywhere.

The beginning of Tolstoy as anarchist.

Two days later, still sickened by his experience, he abruptly departed for Geneva. A distant cousin of his was staying there and he decided he very much wanted to see her.

On his first day in Geneva he called on her. "Alexandrine," he wrote in his diary that evening, "delightful." Next day, March 31: "Alexandrine has a wonderful smile."

The delightful woman with the wonderful smile was Countess Alexandra Andreyevna Tolstoy (the daughter of Leo Tolstoy's grandfather's brother). From 1845 to 1856, the year before their encounter in Geneva, she was lady-in-waiting at the imperial court in Petersburg. When Tolstoy saw her in Geneva in 1857, she was in attendance on the Grand Duchess Marya Alexandrovna, the daughter of Tsar Alexander II, with whose education she had been entrusted by the royal family. Later she held various posts at the court until her death in 1904. Though she seems to have been an attractive woman of some beauty, cultivated and highly intelligent and, to Leo Tolstoy, the most wonderful woman he ever met, she never married.

Judging by his letters and his diaries, Tolstoy at times thought quite seriously of marrying her. On April 29 in Geneva he wrote in his diary: "To the Tolstoys'. [Alexandra's sister is] staying with her. . . . Went with them to Saleve. Very enjoyable. I'm ready to fall in love. It's terrible. If only Alexandrine were ten years younger!" She was forty; he was nearing twenty-nine. So once more he hesitated, as he had with Valerya Arsenyev, though telling himself in his diary that he was falling more and more in love with his cousin.

May 12: "Love is suffocating me." He finally pulled himself away from her to start the journey home, but on July 16 wrote her from Baden-Baden, where he had lost his last kopeck at roulette, asking for a loan of two hundred francs. He also implored her: "Only don't stop loving me." Back home at Yasnaya Polyana, he wrote her on August 18: "I now see that of all my life abroad, it's the memory of you that is the sweetest, dearest and most serious one for me, and I long to write to you—to imagine more vividly and intimately. . . . There's so much I would like to say to you that might offend your modesty. . . . My friendship for you has grown here into such a vast and unwieldy friendship. . . ." One gathers that he is dying to tell her that he is feeling for her more than a friendship but does not dare for fear of distressing her. But already, to himself, he is calling their relationship *"une amitié amoureuse."*

Perhaps for a short time, the winter of 1857, it was even more than that, at least to him. They met again in Petersburg, toward the end of October. October 22: "Evening at the Tolstoys'. Alexandrine is charming—a joy and a comfort. I've never seen a woman who holds a candle to her." November 6: "Alexandrine is charming. She is definitely the woman who charms me more than any other. Talked to her about marriage. Why didn't I tell her everything?"

That he was truly in love with her? But he continued to hesitate, even though on December 1, as the memorable year neared its end, he felt a surge of love. "Alexandrine has me on a string and

I'm grateful to her for it. However, in the evenings I'm passionately in love with her . . ."

There is evidence that Alexandra was hesitant too and that she herself drew back when Tolstoy grew too ardent. "Leo sometimes reproached me," she wrote in her *Reminiscences*, "for not letting him into the innermost recesses of my heart and for not confiding to him what personally concerned me . . ."[4] Yet she could write to him, as she did at the end of that first summer (August 29, 1857), "All that I love in life disappeared when I left Switzerland."

So, for forty-seven years, until her death in 1904, six years before his, they remained the closest of *"amoureux"* friends, exchanging letters frequently (two hundred of them have survived) and seeing each other occasionally, mostly in St. Petersburg. They are wonderful letters, each writer confiding completely in the other. To no one else, not even to his wife, did Leo Tolstoy pour out his heart and soul and mind as he did to Alexandra in his letters to her.

There is one especially poignant one, dated October 17, 1863, a year after Leo Tolstoy had married. In it he summed up more clearly and frankly than ever before the scope and depth of his love for his cousin. He asked her to destroy it. They had not written to each other for some time, so Tolstoy began by giving Alexandra his news.

> Now I'm a writer with all the strength of my soul, and I write and think as I have never written or thought before. . . . [Tolstoy had begun to write the opening chapters of *War and Peace*.] I am a happy and tranquil husband and father. . . . You, I love less than before . . . but still more than all other people (and how many there have been!) whom I have met in my life. I have always reproached you with one thing, and I still have that reproach in my heart. . . . In our relations you have always shown me only the *general* side of your mind and heart, you have never spoken to me of the details of your life, of the simple, tangible, private incidents of your life. . . . I don't even know what is most intimate and precious to you in your life. . . . I would like you to lead me, not into your sanctuary, but into the everyday interests of your life. . . . After an evening with you, I remember, I always used to have an *arrière-goût* of something delicate, fresh and fragrant, but I always wanted something more substantial. . . . It seems to me that we could have entered

into these more essential relations. Can this really have been lost forever?

The next two and a half lines were carefully erased, as if Tolstoy did not dare to go any further, as much as he wanted to and started to: "I beg you not to show this letter to anyone and tear it up."

They did have their quarrels—mostly over religion. The Countess was deeply religious and, unlike Tolstoy, a staunch believer in the Orthodox Church and its orthodoxy.

"Good Lord! How you do go on at me!" Tolstoy wrote her once. She had criticized him sharply for his "ignorance and pride" in matters of religion. She was especially concerned at his failure to confess and take Communion at Easter. They nearly broke off relations for five years in 1882 and again in 1897 when they had what turned out to be their last meeting in Petersburg. But they always resumed their correspondence and preserved their great friendship.

In the summer of 1908, as Tolstoy was turning eighty, he mused one day in his "secret" diary* about what the biographers would say of him. "They're all writing my biography," he exclaimed, but he was sure none of them would write of his transgressions against the Seventh Commandment. "There won't be any of that terrible filth of masturbation and worse from 13 or 14 to 15 and 16 (I don't remember when my debauchery in brothels began)." And it would be the same, he added, with "my liaison with the peasant woman Axinya—she's still alive. Nothing of this . . . will appear in the biographies."

He was wrong about Axinya, as he was about his early sowing of wild oats. He apparently forgot that he wrote about them himself in his diaries (and often thinly disguised in his fiction), thus providing firsthand confirmation. He had set down at the time, for instance, how madly in love he was with this "peasant woman Axinya," his mistress for three years, from 1858 until he married, and the mother of his first child. Now, nearly half a century later, he was looking back at her with interest and affection—to the enragement of his long-suffering wife, herself now sixty-four, who was

* On July 2, 1908, at Yasnaya Polyana, Tolstoy wrote: "I'm starting a diary for myself—a secret one." This entry is for July 9.

driving him to such despair that he was on the point of clearing out, despite his age, and leaving her.

The object of young Tolstoy's passions in the three years before his marriage was a fiery, buxom peasant girl of twenty-three with flashing black eyes, whose peasant husband had been conscripted into the army. Her name was Axinya Bazykina. Her status as serf and married woman did not prevent the master of Yasnaya Polyana from carrying on with her. In 1858, when the liaison began, the peasants of Russia were still serfs,* the property of their masters. A peasant girl had no rights, no protection, if her owner wanted her. But from what little is known of Axinya, she was not reluctant to become her master's lover.

Tolstoy's diary tells briefly the story of his love. May 13, 1858: "Caught a glimpse of Aksinya. She's very pretty. I've been waiting for her for the last few days in vain. Today in the big old wood. . . . I'm a fool. A beast. Her neck is red from the sun. . . . I'm in love as never before in my life. I've no other thoughts. I'm tormented. *Tomorrow—every effort.*" He underlined the words. "June 16: Had Aksinya . . . but I'm repelled by her."

He was not repelled for very long. The relationship—and the passion—continued. May 26, 1860: ". . . She was nowhere about. I looked for her. It's no longer the feeling of the stag, but of a husband and wife."

But Leo Tolstoy's class consciousness at that time was much too strong to permit him to marry the passionate peasant girl, love her though he said he did as his wife. He was unlike two of his brothers, one of whom, Dmitri, had a prostitute as a common-law wife, and the other, Sergei, who after many years and many children with his Gypsy mistress married her. Leo still hoped to find a wife from his own upper class.

Even while pursuing Axinya and fathering his first child with her,† he kept looking for a partner in the upper circles of Moscow

---

* The serfs were liberated on February 19, 1861, by Tsar Alexander II.
† His name was Timofei (Russian for Timothy) and he lived with his mother in a village not far from the main house at Yasnaya Polyana, where she often worked. After the boy grew up he worked first in the stables, then as a woodsman, eventually ending up as a coachman for Tolstoy's brother Sergei. Like his mother he probably was illiterate and remained so. Tolstoy, despite his great love for the peasants and the peasant way of life, never tried to educate him, even to rescue him from illiteracy. And he was coy about recognizing Timofei as his illegitimate

and Petersburg. At one point he thought of marrying the daughter of Tyutchev, a poet friend of his, but concluded that she was too cold.

For a time he considered two daughters of another friend, Prince Lvov, but gave up on them, too. On New Year's Day, 1859, he wrote in his diary rather desperately: "I must get married this year—or not at all."

Perhaps he was still too much in the grip of his passion for Axinya to seriously search for a wife. Part of her attraction to him seems to have been not only her great sensuality, but the fact that she represented to him the whole peasant way of life which appealed to him so strongly. It would not be very long before he was adopting peasant dress and spending more and more time in the fields with his peasants, helping with the sowing and harvesting of the crops and talking about his desire to live and work as a peasant.

"I often dreamed," he confessed in his diary at that time, "about a life of farming—of eternal labor, eternal Nature and, for some reason, some gross voluptuousness always entered these dreams. A heavy woman with callused hands, firm breasts and bare feet always worked in front of me."[5] It seems most likely that the voluptuous Axinya, with the red neck and bare feet, was the one he thought of for the rest of his life for filling that role.

His obsession with her carried over into his fiction. Someone like Axinya appears in several of Tolstoy's short stories, especially in *The Devil*, in which the kind of animal passion she inspired in him comes out and drives the hero to a tragic end. The story was not published in Tolstoy's lifetime but his wife read it and copied it, as she did almost all his writings. Perhaps out of his feelings for her, he did not publish it during their long life together. But neither did he forget the peasant lover who inspired it.

son. At eighty Tolstoy wrote in his diary: "They say that Timofei is my son, and I have never asked his pardon." Tolstoy knew perfectly well that the boy was his son; his wife nagged him about it constantly, never letting him forget it.

# FOUR

# A Whirlwind
# Courtship

THE FIRES that stoked Tolstoy's love for Axinya had not died out that summer of 1862, until toward its end when he began to fall in love with the eighteen-year-old Sofya Andreyevna Behrs. Though her family was, socially, several rungs below the Tolstoys, she was, to Leo, marriageable. He felt comfortable with the three Behrs daughters as they began to grow up, entertaining them with tales of the Caucasus and the battles he fought in Sevastopol. But being much older—nearly as old, in fact, as their mother—he had not thought of them as prospects for marriage. Until, that is, he returned from his second trip to Western Europe in 1861 and began to revisit the Behrs family in Moscow and at their summer place outside the city. His thoughts, as we have seen, had turned first to Lisa, the eldest, whom, it soon became clear to him, the parents hoped he might marry. But Lisa had struck him as lacking in feeling.

Even to her sisters, Lisa seemed cool, aloof, and overly intellectual. They called her "the scholar." Still, Tolstoy was not ready to count her out. A year later, after a dinner at the Behrses', he noted in his diary on September 8, 1862: "Lisa seems to be quietly taking possession of me. My God! How beautifully unhappy she would be if she were my wife."

By this time he had fallen in love with Sonya. Their love had ignited suddenly in August when her mother decided to take her three daughters to visit her father at Invitsi, and to drop in at Yasnaya Polyana, which was close by, ostensibly to see Marya,

Leo's sister, but mostly, it seems, to give Tolstoy a further opportunity to make up his mind as to which of the three daughters he wished to propose to. Sonya has left a lengthy account of the visit, written half a century later, two years after Tolstoy's death.[1]

According to her, Leo began to pay special attention to her soon after the family arrived. The three girls were assigned to the "room under the vault," which Tolstoy would shortly use as a study when he began to write *War and Peace*. Sonya found it "poorly furnished." Beds were made up on the leather sofas but, as they were one short, Sonya offered to sleep on the chair.

"Well, I'll make up a bed for you," she remembered Leo saying, as he was "clumsily unfolding a sheet." Sonya says she felt embarrassed, "but there was something lovely and intimate about making up beds together." When they returned to the living room her sister Lisa, she adds, stared at them "inquisitively." While the others gathered for supper, Sonya went out and sat on the balcony to savor her exalted feelings. "I felt such happiness, and such an extraordinary sense of boundlessness," she says.

Leo came out to call her to supper.

"No thank you, I don't want anything," she told him. "It's so lovely out here." Leo went back to the dining room, she says, "but returned to the balcony to see me without finishing his supper. I don't remember exactly what we talked about, I just remember him saying to me: 'How simple and serene you are,' which pleased me very much." She fell asleep that night with a "new feeling of joy in my young soul."

A few days later, when the Behrses went off to visit Lyubov's father, Leo followed them on horseback the next day. It was obvious by now that he wanted to see more of Sonya. And the climax of the visit, which both swore for the rest of their lives actually happened, shows them drawing closer together. Yet the incident they describe is hard to believe.

After an evening of dancing, the mother had ordered her children to go to bed, when Leo interrupted. Sonya tells what followed.

"Wait a moment, Sofya Andreevna!"
"What is it?"
"Will you read what I am going to write?"
"Very well."

"I'm only going to write the initials—you must guess the words."

"How can I do that—it's impossible! Oh, well, go on . . ."

He brushed the game scores off the card table, took a piece of chalk and began writing. We were both very serious and excited. I followed his big red hand, and could feel all my powers of concentration and feeling focus on that bit of chalk and the hand that held it. We said nothing.

"Y. Y. & Y. N. F. H. T. V. R. M. O. M. A. & I. F. H."

"Your youth and your need for happiness too vividly reminds me of my age and incapacity for happiness!," I read out.

My heart was pounding, my temples were throbbing, my face was flushed—I was beyond all sense of time and reality; at that moment I felt capable of anything, of understanding everything, imagining the unimaginable.

"Well, let's go on," said Leo and began to write once more.

"Y. F. H. T. W. I. A. M. & Y. S. L. Y. & Y. S. T. M. P. M."

"Your family has the wrong idea about me and your sister Lisa. You and your sister Tanechka must protect me," I read the initials rapidly.

She says it did not surprise Leo. "It all seemed quite natural. Our relation was such that we soared high above the world and nothing could possibly surprise us."*

That night in the vaulted bedroom, Sonya sat down on the floor, lit the stump of a candle, and wrote it all down in her diary. "I grew vaguely aware," she says, "that something of great significance had occurred between us—something we were now unable to stop."

The Behrses stopped for a day again at Yasnaya Polyana on their way back to Moscow. Somewhat to the surprise of the rest of the family, but not to Sonya's, Tolstoy insisted on coming along with them to Moscow, sitting on top of the stagecoach for the two-day trip to the city. According to Sonya, her suitor visited them nearly every day at the Behrses' summer place at Pokrovskoye, a dozen miles outside Moscow, where they settled in for the rest of the summer. "Leo and I had long walks and talks together [but] . . . there were no romantic scenes or confessions," Sonya says. "We had known each other for so long."

* The reader may be surprised, as was this author, that anyone, even Sonya falling dizzily in love, could instantly make out the words to those initials.

Early in September the Behrs family moved back to their cramped apartment in the Kremlin, and Sonya says Tolstoy continued to visit them daily there. By this time both were confessing to someone close that they were in love. Sonya announced it one day to her younger sister, tomboy Tanya, who had asked her why she was going around in such an emotional state.

"I'm afraid I love the Count," she told her.

And on September 7 from Moscow, Tolstoy wrote his beloved Alexandrine: "Toothless old fool that I am, I've fallen in love."*

Tolstoy, who had hesitated for so long to take the plunge into matrimony, now moved with unaccustomed swiftness. In fact, he was desperate. And, as usual, confused. This is plain from his diary entries that first fortnight in September. After a visit to Sonya at the Kremlin on the evening of September 10:

> September 10: More in love than ever before. . . . I'm beginning to hate Lisa as well as pity her. Lord, help me, teach me. Mother of God, help me.

The next day, he says, he didn't "dare" to go to the Behrses'. But on the twelfth, he gets up the nerve. He calls at the Behrses'. He talks to Sonya.

> September 12: I'm in love as I never believed it possible to love. I'm mad, I'll shoot myself if it goes on like this.

"Tomorrow morning," he says, he'll go to the Behrses' and propose. He curses his timidity for not having done it sooner. "I was timid. I should simply have spoken . . ." On the thirteenth he confesses he went to Sonya but "nothing happened." He was again tongue-tied. "I'll go tomorrow as soon as I wake up," he promises his diary, "and say everything, or I'll shoot myself."

But again his timidity freezes him. He cannot speak the words. Finally, desperate, he decides to write Sonya a letter.

> September 14, 4 A.M.: I wrote her a letter. I'll give it to her tomorrow, i.e., today, the 14th. . . . Happiness, and such happiness seems impossible, my God, help me.

---

* Though he was only thirty-four, Tolstoy had lost most of his teeth.

He carries the letter to her on the fourteenth but he cannot bring himself to deliver it. Somehow he feels more confident, though, that she will accept him. He still finds Sonya "strange" but thinks that "the situation has become clearer. . . ."

Perhaps so, but on the next day, September 15, he still hesitates. "I didn't speak," he notes in his diary at the end of that day, "but said there was something to speak about."

When Leo arrived on Saturday the sixteenth at the Behrses', the three sisters were entertaining a group of young cadets, friends of their brother Sasha. The young people were so exuberant and loud, and apparently having such a good time, that Leo found no opportunity to speak alone to his beloved. He hung around the house the whole day, desperately looking for an opening. Finally, his patience exhausted, he asked Sonya if she would mind coming with him to her mother's room, which he found unoccupied.

"I wanted to say something to you," Sonya quotes him as saying, "but I haven't been able to, so here is a letter which I've been carrying around in my pocket for several days now. Please read it, and I'll wait here for your answer."

Sonya says she "seized it" and "tore" downstairs to the bedroom the sisters shared.

Moscow 14 September, 1862

Sofya Andreyevna,

It's getting more than I can bear. For three weeks I've been saying every day: today I'll tell her everything; and I'll go away with the same anguish, remorse, fear and happiness in my soul. And every night, as now, I go over the past, torment myself and say: why didn't I speak? What should I have said? And how? I'm taking this letter with me in order to hand it to you, in case, once again, I'm unable to, or haven't had the courage, to tell you all.

Your family's false attitude towards me* consists in the fact, as it seems to me, that I am in love with your sister Lisa. This is unjust. . . .

But both then and afterwards I lied to myself. Even then I could have broken everything off and gone back to my monastery of solitary work and enthusiasm for my job. Now I can do nothing; and I feel I've spread confusion in your family, and that the simple precious relations I had with you as a friend and

---

* The underlining throughout the letter is Tolstoy's.

honest woman have been destroyed. I can't go away and I daren't stay. Tell me, as an honest woman, your hand on your heart—without hurrying, for the love of God, without hurrying—tell me what I must do. . . . Tell me as an honest woman, do you wish to be my wife? Only say yes if you can do so fearlessly, with all your heart; otherwise better say no, if there's a shadow of a doubt in your mind.

For the love of God, question yourself carefully. It will be terrible for me to hear "no," but I foresee it and I'll find the strength to bear it; but if I should never be loved as a husband as much as I love, that would be even more terrible.

"I didn't read the letter all the way through," Sonya says, "I merely skimmed through it to the words: 'Do you want to be my wife?' I was just on the way upstairs to say yes to Leo when I ran into my sister Lisa in the doorway, who asked me, 'Well, what happened?' "

" *'Le comte m'a fait la proposition,'** I answered hurriedly." Sonya does not say what her elder sister's reaction was. But according to Tanya, Sonya's younger sister, Lisa was beside herself, screaming, "Refuse him! Refuse him instantly."[2] Apparently Lisa believed to the last that Tolstoy would respect tradition and propose to the eldest. Then Mrs. Behrs appeared. She, too, had believed Lisa would get the offer. But she adapted quickly to the situation, whatever her disappointment, took Sonya firmly by the shoulders, and turned her toward the door. "Go to him," she said, "and give him your answer."

Sonya needed no prompting. "I flew up the stairs on wings," she says, "tore past the dining room and drawing room and rushed into my mother's bedroom. Leo stood in the corner, leaning against the wall, waiting for me. I went up to him and seized both his hands."

"Well, what's the answer?" he asked.
"Yes—of course," I replied.

Having procrastinated for so long and then having, to his own surprise, made up his mind so quickly to propose, Tolstoy insisted

---

* "The Count has proposed to me." Like most women of her class, Sonya spoke French a good deal of the time with her family.

that the wedding take place at once. When Mrs. Behrs protested that she would need several weeks to prepare a proper trousseau, Tolstoy brushed her off. "She's got enough clothes," he said, "and she looks good in them too."

"Leo was in a terrible hurry to get the wedding over," Sonya says. "My betrothal lasted only a week."

That was long enough for Leo Tolstoy to do something that his wife bitterly resented to the end of her days, and that almost wrecked the marriage before it began. Tolstoy did it out of a sense of decency and honesty, but Sonya never quite recovered from it.

On September 15, the day before he got up courage, finally, to propose—by letter—Tolstoy wrote in his diary that if Sonya did accept him and they were married, there must be no secrets of the past between them. "She will read everything." He would not hide from her, an innocent, sheltered, young eighteen-year-old, his dissolute past. He would not marry until he came clean with her.

One evening, three or four days before the wedding date, he brought his diaries to her and insisted she read them. She did, and they shattered her. This is the word she herself uses. "I remember how shattered I was by those diaries," she wrote, "which out of an excess of honesty he made me read before our wedding. It was very wrong for him to do this; I wept when I saw what his past had been."

The bitterest pill of all for so sheltered a young woman were references in his diaries to his passionate love for Axinya, his recording at one time that they were so close as to make him feel they were "man and wife," and the revelation that her fiancé had an illegitimate son with the peasant woman. The horrible references stirred up in Sonya something that even her mother and her favorite sister, the ebullient Tanya, had not suspected: a fierce, overwhelming jealousy, a poison so strong that it eventually would help doom the marriage. In a few days, Sonya told herself, she would be moving to Yasnaya Polyana, where she would be the mistress of the house. But lurking in the shadows would be this peasant "wench" (and perhaps even her bastard son by Leo)—this barefoot peasant hussy who had brought forth such love from the man who was about to be her husband. What if she should meet this creature?—apparently she still worked in the house. Sonya was afraid she would kill her. She says she actually dreamed that she would kill her child.

Aside from Axinya, what was it in her fiancé's past that so shocked and repelled her? Plenty, as she kept turning the pages of his diary. Chiefly Sonya was shocked that Leo had had such a dissolute youth, taken up largely with his gambling, his drinking, and his "wenching," as entry after entry kept calling it.

Some entries that he made while with the army in the Caucasus, aged twenty-two to twenty-five, were typical.

> July 3, 1851: [He had sworn off card playing, but . . .] I got carried away and lost 200 rubles of my own, 150 of Nikolinka's [his brother] and 500 borrowed—a total of 850. . . . Rode over to Cherylennaya, got drunk and slept with a woman. . . . Wanted a woman again yesterday. Luckily, she refused. How loathsome! But I'm writing it all down to punish myself.

On August 22, he notes that he has a birthday coming up on the twenty-eighth. "I shall be 23." He celebrates it in advance.

> August 25: Yesterday I had a cossack girl in my place. I hardly slept all night.
> August 26: Roamed around the village in the evening eyeing the wenches. . . . In the morning—write my novel, do some trick riding, study Tartar and go wenching.

As the new year, 1852, began, Tolstoy told himself that he was now convinced "that it was possible to be virtuous and also not unhappy." On the last day of February, he promises to do something about three evil passions he says dominate him: "Gambling, sensuality and vanity." But by midsummer he is in trouble again. He has gone to a spa near Pyatigorsk to take the waters.

> July 22: Got up at 6 . . . and was sure that I'd caught syphilis again. God's Will be done. All is for the best.

Nevertheless, he is relieved when his doctor tells him the next day that he hasn't got syphilis. Apparently it's only a recurrence of his old clap.*

"I cannot recall those years," Tolstoy would write later in *Confession*, "without horror. . . . I was a fornicator and a cheat."[3]

---

* The very first entry in Leo Tolstoy's massive diary, on March 17, 1847, when he was eighteen, tells of his sojourn in the hospital being treated for a venereal disease. "I caught gonorrhea," he wrote, "where one usually catches it," meaning a brothel—in Kazan, where he was living and studying at the university.

# FIVE

# Marriage at Last—
# Despite the Doubts

*I*T CANNOT be said that matters that frantic week between the engagement and the wedding of Sonya Behrs to Leo Tolstoy got off to a very auspicious start. Besides the devastating effect on Sonya of reading her fiancé's early diaries, she had to cope with his last-minute doubts. On the day of the wedding, September 23, 1862, Tolstoy, though custom forbade such a visit on that day, dropped by for a moment to see Sonya. Servants had finished packing their bags. They would be departing from the Behrses' home for Yasnaya Polyana right after the wedding ceremony in the nearby Church of the Nativity of the Blessed Virgin.

"We sat down together on the valises," Sonya remembered, "and he started tormenting me, questioning me and doubting my love for him. The thought occurred to me that he wanted to run away, and that he might have sudden fears of marriage."

Her thinking was correct. In a curious diary entry covering very briefly September 20 through 24, Tolstoy writes: ". . . jealousy of the past, doubts about her love and the thought that she's deceiving herself. . . . On the wedding day, fear, distrust, and the desire to run away."

That evening, as the bride waited anxiously in her home in the Kremlin for Leo's best man to come, as was the custom, to tell her that the bridegroom was waiting in the church, the man failed to appear at the appointed hour. A quarter of an hour passed, a half hour, an hour, and, as Sonya later reported, "no one came."

"It flashed through my mind," Sonya says, "that he had run

away—he had been so odd that morning after all." Finally, Tolstoy's manservant, not his best man, arrived out of breath to inform the bride that Leo had been held up because he couldn't find a clean shirt. They had all been packed away in the bags piled up in the Behrses' hallway. Tolstoy, the valet said, had gone out and tried to buy one, forgetting that it was Sunday and all the shops were closed. Alexei, the servant, finally found a clean shirt in one of the suitcases. But, to Sonya, "another age elapsed" while he took the clean shirt back to the bridegroom at his hotel and Leo put it on and set out for the church.

One would have thought that, with the last hitch resolved, the participants in the wedding, especially the bride and her immediate family, would be filled with joy. But just the opposite! "Everybody," says Sonya, "was plunged into gloom" by the impending separation. The Behrses had been such a closely knit family. How could the brothers and sisters and the parents bear losing their darling eighteen-year-old Sonya? How could *she* bear leaving them? "I'll die of grief without you," sobbed Tanya, her favorite sister. Sonya says she herself "sobbed all the way to the church." Was this an augury, even before the ceremony began, of how the marriage would fare?

Tolstoy himself, Sonya says, seemed puzzled and dismayed at all the weeping and wailing. This was a marriage, after all, not a funeral. At one moment after the ceremony, when lamentations continued, Tolstoy turned to his bride, she relates, and said he "could see I didn't love him very much if it hurt me so to leave my family."[1]

Putting down her memories of the marriage half a century later, Sonya notes that her husband had "described our wedding beautifully in his account of Levin and Kitty's wedding in his novel *Anna Karenina*." She thought it was of special value because in describing Levin's thoughts, Tolstoy was revealing his own, which neither she nor anyone else knew that day.

If so—and it is almost certainly true, for Tolstoy put a great deal of himself in most of his novels, and especially in the character of Levin—then the bridegroom's last-minute fears for their marriage were much more pronounced than we learn from his diaries or from his wife's account.

During the afternoon of the wedding day—the ceremony in

*Anna Karenina*, like that of Sonya and Leo, would take place in the evening—Levin was suddenly filled with doubts.

> A strange feeling came over him. He was overwhelmed by fear and doubt. . . .
>
> "What if she doesn't love me? What if she is only marrying me because she wants to get married? What if she doesn't know herself what she is doing? She might come to her senses and only after she is married realize that she doesn't love me and never could love me."
>
> And strange and most evil thoughts about Kitty began to come into his mind. . . .
>
> He leaped to his feet. "No, this won't do!" he said to himself in despair.
>
> "I'll go to her and ask her. Say to her for the last time: 'We are free and don't you think it's better than everlasting unhappiness, disgrace, infidelity?' "
>
> In despair, he drove to her house despite the orthodox custom that a groom not see his bride on the wedding day until they met at the church for the ceremony. He found her in one of the back rooms, sitting on a trunk, giving her maid orders for packing. She was surprised to see him.
>
> "Darling, I mean why are you here? This is a surprise."
>
> She dismissed the maid and turned to him.
>
> "What's the matter, darling . . . ?"
>
> "Kitty, I'm terribly unhappy and I can't be unhappy alone. I've come to say that there's still time. We can still put a stop to it all and put it right."
>
> "Put what right? I don't know what you're talking about. What's the matter with you?"
>
> "I've said it a thousand times. . . . I mean, that I am not worthy of your love. You can't possibly consent to marry me. Think it over. You've made a mistake. . . . You can't love me . . . if . . . I mean, you'd better say no. . . . Better now, while there's still time."
>
> "I don't understand. Do you mean you want to retract . . . that you don't want to . . ."
>
> "Yes, if you don't love me."
>
> "You're mad!"[2]

In the novel, Tolstoy goes on to describe the delay of the ceremony because the groom didn't have a clean shirt. He has already told how Levin insisted on Kitty's reading his diaries. He then gives what he failed to give in his diary—as did Sonya in hers—a detailed description of the Orthodox wedding ceremony, closing on a skeptical note. Some of the women at the church have been discussing why Levin and Kitty chose an *evening* ceremony. A princess remarks that a wedding in the evening "is the sort of thing tradespeople would do," to which a Mrs. Komsumsky responds.

> "It's prettier. I was married in the evening too," said Mrs. Komsumsky, and sighed as she remembered how sweet she had looked that day, how absurdly in love her husband had been with her, and how different things were now.

The newlyweds left that same evening by a *dormeuse* (sleeper) coach Tolstoy had bought, pulled by six horses. It took two days to cover by coach the 130 miles from Moscow to Yasnaya Polyana. Sonya admits she cried the whole way. They stopped for the night at Biryulevo, a way station, and went to a hotel where Sonya says they were given "the royal suite."

"I huddled in a corner of the sofa," Sonya says, "and sat there silently as though condemned to death."[3]

Early the next evening, they arrived at Yasnaya Polyana, driving past the two whitewashed pillars at the entrance and up the driveway between rows of birch trees to the main house. There at the entrance, Aunt Toinette greeted them, holding the icon of the Mother of God. Leo's brother Sergei was at her side offering, in the traditional Russian sign of welcome, bread and salt. Sonya, still shy and frightened, bowed low to each of them, crossed herself, kissed the icon, and embraced the two. Then she and her husband went inside, joining the others for supper.

It was to be their principal home for the next forty-eight years, the place where Tolstoy would write *War and Peace, Anna Karenina,* and most of his other works, where most of their thirteen children would be born and all of the ten surviving ones raised, and the scene of a tumultuous and troubled marriage that, despite their bickering from the outset, gave them much happiness and fulfillment at first, and then slowly but inexorably disintegrated into an unbearable hell for them both.

# SIX

# Yasnaya Polyana, Sonya's Jealousies, and War and Peace

THE HOUSE at Yasnaya Polyana to which Leo Tolstoy brought his bride that late September evening of 1862 was much smaller than the thirty-six-room mansion he had inherited fifteen years before. To pay his gambling debts, Leo had sold the main part of the house and it had been carted away, leaving two modest-sized wings, one of which was occupied by Tolstoy's school for peasant children and the other by Aunt Toinette, now sixty-seven, and himself. The eighteen-year-old bride, a city dweller all her life, found it far from palatial.

With the exception of the living room, the rooms were small and dark. One is struck by that even today, though the house was subsequently enlarged on both sides as Tolstoy's royalties grew and the necessity for more room for more children increased. They were also austerely furnished, the furniture being simple and hard—only the divans were upholstered. There were few rugs or carpets, and none at all in the bedrooms. Apparently, Tolstoy expected people to avoid freezing their feet on the cold bare bedroom floors in winter by wearing felt slippers or bast shoes.

Sonya was puzzled that very first night at her husband's insistence on sleeping on an old, worn, red leather pillow that looked as if it had been extracted from an abandoned stagecoach. He did not like softer pillows or any kind of pillowcase. At night, instead of oil lamps the rooms were lit by candles, which left a certain odor lingering through the house. The next day, when Sonya took her first tour of the grounds as mistress of Yasnaya Polyana, she was surprised that there were no cultivated flowers growing in the gardens, that the paths were not swept, and that the spacious "lawn" in front of the house that sloped gently down to the road was a mass of ugly, tall weeds (as it is today, more than a century later). She must have been appalled to notice that the servants tossed all the refuse of the house onto the weeds where once, in the days of Prince Volkonsky, Tolstoy's grandfather, a real lawn had been. The house servants, she saw when she came down for breakfast that first morning, slept at night wherever they could find a spot in the hallways. Despite his professed love for the peasants, apparently Tolstoy had never thought of providing them with bedrooms.

Sonya would grow to love this country estate, especially the rolling fields, the vast woods, the ponds, the little river, though she never felt the passion for it that her husband did. For him, as he once said, Yasnaya Polyana *was* Russia. Thirty-five years later while living for a spell in Moscow, Sonya looked back at that first week at Yasnaya Polyana and remembered:

> Mud outside and dirt inside, the filthy yard, the two filthy rooms where I lived with Leo Nikolayevich, the four mousetraps which clicked mercilessly all the time and mice, mice without end!, the cold, bleak house, the grey sky, the drizzle; traipsing through the mud with a lantern from house to house and deadly silence everywhere, painful and gloomy. . . . What a painful, depressing, difficult week it was.[1]

There was something else, besides the pain and gloom of the place and the first little quarrels, that made that initial week and the weeks that followed difficult for the young countess: her fear of running into Axinya, her husband's former peasant lover and mother of his child.

It was bound to happen soon, she felt, because Axinya was brought in frequently with other peasant women to clean the house. And one day in December, it did.

When Sonya came down to breakfast, she saw a tanned, muscular, broad-shouldered peasant woman on her hands and knees, scrubbing the floor. At her side was a three-year-old boy, playing in the doorway. He struck her as being the spitting image of her husband. So this was Axinya, the peasant trollop he had written about so passionately in his diary. And this was their bastard son, Timofei. Sonya was beside herself with rage.[2] That night, she wrote in *her* diary:

> One of these days I shall kill myself with jealousy. "In love as never before!" he writes.[3] With that big, fat lump of a woman. How frightful! I looked at the dagger and the guns with such pleasure. One blow, I thought, how easy it would be—if only it weren't for the baby. Yet to think that she is there, just a few steps away. It drives me mad! I shall go for a drive. I may even see her. So he really did love her! I should like to burn his diary and the whole of his past.

Her jealousy of the peasant woman arouses her to jealousy even of the women in his short stories.

> I have been reading the openings of some of his works, and the very mention of love for women makes me feel so disgusted and depressed that I would gladly burn everything. I want never to be reminded of his past again. . . . If I could kill him and create a new person exactly the same as he is now, I would do so happily.[4]

Four weeks later in Moscow, she has a murderous dream about Axinya, or rather, mostly about her illegitimate son.

> I dreamed of an immense garden into which all our Yasnaya village girls came, all dressed up like ladies. They all went off somewhere, one after another. A. [Axinya] came last, wearing a black silk dress. I began speaking to her and was seized by such violent rage that I picked up her child and began tearing it to pieces. I tore off its head and its legs—I was like a mad woman. . . . I often torture myself thinking about her, even here in Moscow.

Countess Tolstoy never got over her fierce jealousy of Axinya. Years passed and she still resented her husband's affair with the peasant, sprinkling her diary with her bitter comments. In the spring of 1865, after they had two children, she admits being suspicious of her husband when he goes out to inspect the fields.

March 8, 1865: I got it into my head that he was going off
to see A. This thought has been tormenting me all day.

Still . . .

If it were true, how could he be so calm, open and natural
with me? It must be said, however, that as long as she and I live
in close proximity every bad mood or cold word from Lyova will
instantly reduce me to an agony of jealousy.

And she tortures herself by asking what if her husband did
return and told her he loved Axinya still? "I just felt obliged to
confess the terrible thought which dimly but persistently hovers in
my mind."

More than forty years later, when she is sixty-five, she still
cannot get Axinya, now probably eighty, out of her mind. She has
been copying some new short stories of Tolstoy's and she is a little
vexed that he is always writing about the peasants. Obviously—she
is sure—still thinking of Axinya.

January 14, 1909: He relishes that peasant wench with her
strong female body and her sunburnt legs, she allures him just as
powerfully now as she did all those years ago: the same Aksinya
with the flashing eyes, almost unrecognizable at the age of 80,
has risen from the depths of the memories and sensations of his
past. Aksinya was a Yasnaya peasant girl, Leo Nikolayevich's
last mistress before his marriage, and she still lives in the village.
It all had a rather depressing effect on me. . . . Indeed if he had
slightly more sensitivity he would not call his peasant heroines
Aksinya.

Jealousy! It seemed to spread through her like a cancer and
forever linger. She became jealous even of her most loved sister,
Tanya, who meant the world to her and was her most trusted
confidante. On May 3, 1865, Sonya noted it in her diary.

I am angry with Tanya for meddling in Lyovochka's life.
They go to Nikolskoe, or go off hunting, riding or walking. I
actually made a jealous scene for the first time in my life yester-

day. . . . The two of them have gone off to the woods alone to shoot woodsnipe and I am imagining God knows what.*

Next year Sonya found another woman who incited her jealousy. This was an attractive young intellectual named Marya Ivanova, whose husband had just been hired to manage the estate. Tolstoy was attracted to her at once and, much to Sonya's annoyance, had long conversations with her about politics, philosophy, and literature. Marya was a "radical" and a nihilist and a bitter enemy of the Orthodox Church. Tolstoy found her ideas interesting and sympathetic. For a time he could not see enough of her. Sonya considered this "quite improper. Their conversations go on far too long, and they may be flattering to her but for me they are a complete torture. . . . I have a horrible premonition that this nihilist woman will be my *bête noire*."[5]

And:

> July 22 [1866]: Lyovochka invented some excuse for visiting *that* house earlier today. Marya Ivanova told me so, and also that he had stood beneath her balcony talking to her. What reason can he have had for going over there in the rain? It is obvious; because he likes her. The very thought is driving me insane. I wish her every conceivable ill. . . . At the moment I am wild with jealousy. . . . I simply can't endure her. It enrages me to see her beauty and high spirits, especially in the company of Lyovochka.
>
> July 24: Lyovochka visited her house again today, and came back saying how he pitied the poor woman and her dull life. Then he asked me why I hadn't invited them to dinner. If I had had my way, I would never have let her in the house in the first place. Oh Lyovochka, can't you see you've been caught. Maybe he will dismiss the bailiff, and then I shall be rid of my tormenting jealousy of Marya Ivanova.

Tolstoy was now deep in his first big novel. And Sonya, despite their wrangling and her appalling jealousies, was turning out to be very helpful in his writing. Each evening, she sat up late, after

---

* Actually, Tanya had fallen in love with Sergei, Tolstoy's older brother, and on June 9, a month after Sonya had expressed her suspicions of her, she noted in her diary: "Tanya and Seryozha are to be married. They are a joy to see." The wedding was set for June 29. On July 12, Sonya wrote in her diary: "Nothing has come of it. Seryozha has betrayed Tanya. He has behaved like a swine." In the end, Sergei could not bear to part with his Gypsy mistress of fifteen years, Masha Shishkin, and their children. Tanya, in despair, tried to kill herself.

everyone else had gone to bed, making a fair copy in her neat handwriting from her husband's almost undecipherable scrawls. She was, for all her faults, extremely intelligent, well read, and full of not only admiration but also understanding for what her husband wrote. As she copied page after page not once but often half a dozen times, for he was constantly revising, she began to realize that this was a major work, something altogether bigger and deeper and more ambitious than he had ever attempted before.

"All this winter," she wrote her sister Tanya in 1867, "Leo has been writing in a state of emotion that often goes as far as tears. In my opinion, his novel *War and Peace* is going to be something quite out of the common run." Everything she had copied up to then, she added, had moved her to tears.[6]

She was more than just a faithful copier. As the novel moved into its sweeping historical sections, she proffered her own advice. Tolstoy himself had been wrestling with the problem of blending the fictional part of the book with the historical. Later, some critics would feel that he never quite solved it.

"Dear Sonya," he wrote to her. "I shall never forget how one day you told me that the whole historico-military side of *War and Peace*, over which I had labored so hard, was coming out badly, and that the best part would be the psychological side, the characters and the pictures of family life. It couldn't have been truer, and I have not forgotten how you were able to see that and tell me."[7]

Just making clean copies of Tolstoy's manuscript was a considerable job in itself. Apparently no one else in the house could make out his almost illegible handwriting. And making one clean copy was never enough, for Tolstoy would rewrite it and hand it back to her for copying again. Sonya once said she had copied the novel seven times. Since it runs to 1,453 printed pages in my edition, that means that her fair copy came to at least 3,000 manuscript pages. So she must have written down in her own careful handwriting 21,000 pages. And this does not include countless pages that Tolstoy, as his daughter Tanya noted, threw away.

Then there were the proofs. When they came back from the publisher for corrections, Tolstoy, as anyone who has looked at them can testify, would scribble a whole new version on practically every page. His publisher, P. I. Bartenyev, though a good friend, finally balked.

"God knows what you are doing!" he wrote Tolstoy indignantly. "If you go on like this we will be correcting and resetting forever. Anyone can tell you that half your changes are unnecessary. But they make an appreciable difference in the typesetting costs. I have asked the printer to send you a separate bill for corrections. . . . For the love of God, stop scribbling!"[8]

Aside from copying the manuscript seven times and urging him to go easy on the long, historical diversions, Sonya's greatest contribution to helping Tolstoy with *War and Peace* was to persuade him to discontinue serializing it in the monthly periodical the *Russian Herald* and start publishing it at once, volume by volume, as a book. The review had paid him a tidy sum for serial rights, but Sonya believed they would make more money in the long run if the work came out forthwith in book form. Tolstoy agreed, perhaps partly because the publication of the serialized second part had not aroused much enthusiasm among the reviewers or the readers.*

It was not the kind of book that adapted well to serialization. The sweep was too grand. There were no "teasers" at the end of each installment to tempt a reader to buy the next issue to see how things turned out.

In this instance, at least, Tolstoy was a better businessman than he (or Sonya) admitted. He made an arrangement with a Moscow printer and with his friend Bartenyev, who was a distinguished historian, librarian, and editor of the journal *Russian Archive,* to publish the book for a ten percent cut. Tolstoy himself advanced the printer forty-five hundred rubles. As it turned out, this first edition of the book, which sold for eight rubles for all six volumes, would bring the Tolstoys a small fortune.

After the first two installments had been serialized and then brought out as the first volume of the book, Tolstoy was still searching for a title for the novel. In fact, even when published in book form in 1867, the first volume was called *1805.* At one point, in 1866, Tolstoy wrote his friend the poet Afanasy Fet that he was going to entitle the novel *All's Well That Ends Well,* but apparently he quickly thought better of it. It was not until after the publication of the first volume that Tolstoy finally chose a title that would

---

* "The second part is weak," Turgenev wrote a friend after reading the first two installments. "How small and artificial it is. . . . Tolstoy's novel is bad. . . . The author has studied nothing, knows nothing. . . ." Later, after he read the whole work, Turgenev changed his mind.

become known throughout the world. He does not mention in his diaries or letters how he finally decided what the title would be. Apparently he got it from Pierre Proudhon, the French anarchical social reformer, whom he met in exile in Belgium during his second trip to the West, and to whose ideas he was much attracted. Proudhon came out that year with a book called *La Guerre et La Paix*. At any rate, for Tolstoy, *War and Peace* it was to be.

It is a book of prodigious imagination, a joy and a wonder to read a century and a quarter after it first saw the light of day.

The same, almost, can be said of the book that followed, *Anna Karenina*. This was more of a traditional novel—a tale of two love stories set in the present, one ending in tragedy, the other in family happiness. In fact, Tolstoy, who sought for years for a proper title, at first called his new novel *The Story of Two Marriages*. His struggle to write *Anna Karenina*, and especially to finish it, was long and frustrating. After getting the first germ of an idea for it, he dropped it in order to write another and quite different book. An entry in Countess Tolstoy's diary for February 24, 1870, sheds light on his dilemma.

> Today, after many doubts and hesitations, L. has at last got down to work. Yesterday he said that after serious consideration he had realized that it was the epic genre which suited him best at present. . . .
>
> This morning he covered a whole sheet of paper with his close handwriting. The action begins in a monastery, with a large crowd of people, including all the main characters.

This was the novel about Peter the Great, which Tolstoy had been thinking about even before he started *War and Peace*. He had spent a good deal of time reading up on Peter and his time. Actually, he took most of the next three years trying to launch the book. But, somehow, it would not go. He wrote twenty-seven versions of the first chapter and still was dissatisfied. He could not understand why he had developed a writer's block. Perhaps it was because in the back of his mind there lurked the idea for quite a different work of fiction. Sonya referred to it in the diary entry above. Having recounted how he started to work on the Peter novel, she added quite a different note.

Yesterday afternoon he told me he had had the idea of writing about a married woman of noble birth who committed adultery. He said his purpose was to make this woman pitiful, not guilty, and he told me that no sooner had he imagined this character clearly than the men and the other characters he had thought up all found their place in the story.

# SEVEN

# Anna Karenina

*T*HIS IS the first mention we have of the idea for *Anna Karenina,* which Tolstoy put aside to struggle with Peter the Great. Three years later, on January 31, 1873, Sonya noted his continuing frustration: "He is still reading documents. . . . He has written about ten different opening chapters. Yesterday he said, 'The machine is all ready, now it must be made to work.' But he could not make it work. The day before, he had written his friend Fet that it was 'frightfully difficult' and, on March 17, he wrote him: 'My work is not progressing.' "[1]

But two days later, on March 19, Sonya noted this in her diary.

> Last night, L. suddenly said to me, "I have written a page and a half, and it seems good." I assumed this was yet another attempt to write about the Peter the Great period, and didn't pay much attention. But then, I realized that he had, in fact, embarked on a novel about the private lives of present-day people. So strange the way he just pitched into it.

Sonya then proceeded to tell of how the new inspiration for *Anna Karenina* came, and Tolstoy confirmed it in a letter on March 25 to the noted critic Nikolai Strakhov. It came from Pushkin—especially, Tolstoy says, from a single line from the poet. Sonya had taken Pushkin's *Tales of Belkin* from the downstairs library at Yasnaya Polyana for her eldest son, Seryozha, to read. The boy had left it in the living room, where Tolstoy noticed it the next morning. He wrote to Strakhov about what happened next.

> I read it all through (for the seventh time, I think) unable to tear myself away. . . . But more than that, it seemed to resolve all my doubts. . . . There is a fragment *The guests were arriving at the country house.* Involuntarily, unwittingly, not knowing why or what would come of it, I thought up characters and events, began to go on with it . . . and suddenly all the threads became so well and so truly tied up that the result was a novel . . . a very lively, impassioned and well-finished novel with which I'm very pleased . . .

Seldom, if ever, has a great writer revealed so clearly the genesis of a novel. Tolstoy, relieved to have an excuse to abandon the Peter book, became so excited about the prospect of the new one that he told Strakhov he had written a draft of it in a week and it would be "ready" in two weeks, if God gave him the strength.[2] He was really carried away. He would soon come down to earth as hurdles—the kind every writer is bound to run into—constantly rose up to slow his progress and depress him. Actually, more than four years of hard and unceasing labor lay ahead before he would finish. He kept Sonya and his friends, especially Strakhov, informed of his torturous ups and downs. With no other book did he leave such a detailed record of how difficult it was to write.

Tolstoy could not decide what kind of persons he wanted his main characters to be. Anna, for example, who appears in early versions as Nana, Tatyana, and Anastasia, bears little resemblance to the Anna of the finished novel. She is a bit of a hypocrite, terribly sensual, and an outrageous flirt. Vronsky, her lover, who in the end is depicted as a typical dilettante guards officer, is in the early versions a poetic and artistic young man. Levin is not introduced at all in the first versions and only gradually becomes a character— very much like the author, with his creator's view of life.*

On August 24, 1873, Tolstoy wrote Strakhov that he simply couldn't finish the novel, it was so bad. On October 4, Sonya scribbled in her diary that her husband was "polishing, revising

---

* Tolstoy not only made Levin resemble himself but made him experience many of the happenings of the author's own life, such as his handing over his diary to his fiancé and the episodes of the Tolstoys' wedding. The name Levin is very close to the author's first name in Russian, Lev.

and continuing with the novel." But a few weeks later, she informed her sister Tanya that Leo had "definitely abandoned" the novel. But, of course, he had not. He bounced back quickly. Sonya explains (diary of November 20):

> All this autumn he kept saying: "My brain is asleep." But suddenly about a week ago, something within him seemed to blossom and he started working cheerfully again. . . . He silently sat down at his desk this morning, without even drinking his coffee, and wrote and wrote for more than an hour, revising the chapter dealing with Anna's arrival in St. Petersburg and Alek's relations with Lydia Ivanovna.

By the end of February 1874, Tolstoy so much liked what he had written thus far in a new version that he began to talk to Moscow printers about setting the type for an edition he would publish himself. But when the proofs came back, he did not at all like what he saw. In fact, he found it "horrible and disgusting"—so much so that he decided to destroy the printed plates, pay off the printers, and begin all over again—for the third time.

This time, it was to prove successful. By December 1874, he was far enough along to begin negotiations with Mikhail Katkov, editor of the *Russian Herald*, for serial rights to *Anna Karenina*, which he sold for twenty thousand rubles,* a tidy sum.

Sonya thought that once the serialization of the novel had begun, her husband would find it difficult to delay any longer getting to the end of it. But after sending in a couple of installments, he again dallied. For one thing, he wrote Strakhov, he was busy "managing 70 schools" that had been opened in his district. And, in June, he set off with his family, as he often did, to spend the summer on an estate he had bought in Samara.

It may have been that several deaths in the family contributed to his inability to get on with the novel. They upset him, and yet his reaction to some of them struck his family as strange. On November 9, 1873, his youngest son, Petya, fifteen months old, died of the croup. Sonya was beside herself with grief. "What a bright, happy little boy—I loved my darling too much and now there is nothing," she wrote in her diary.[3] And she went on to express her suffering. Her husband was briefer. He wrote to his brother Sergei: "Petya is

* Approximately $202,500 today.

dead and has just been buried. . . . This is new for us, and very painful, especially for Sonya."[4] Then he broke off to write about the typesetting for *Anna Karenina*. The abrupt change of subject strikes one as almost cold-blooded. A few days later, he explained to his friend Fet: "This is the first death in the family in eleven years, and the thing is extremely hard for my wife. There is some consolation in the fact that of the eight of us, his death was certainly the easiest for us all to bear." But his wife, he added, "could not reason and is plunged into grief."[5]

On June 20, 1874, Tolstoy's beloved Aunt Toinette, who had looked after him as a child and a youth, and remained in his household to that day, died at seventy-nine.* She was his last link to the past at Yasnaya Polyana and, in his curious way, he mourned her going. He wrote of her death to his beloved cousin Alexandrine.

> Yesterday, I buried Auntie Tatyana Alexandrovna. . . . She died almost of old age, i.e., she had faded away little by little, and had already ceased to exist for us three years ago, so much so that (I don't know whether this was a good or bad feeling) I avoided her and couldn't see her without a feeling of agony; but now that she's dead (she died slowly and painfully—like a childbirth), all my feeling for her has returned with a still greater force. She was a wonderful creature. . . . She lived here for fifty years and never did anything unpleasant to anyone, let alone any evil. . . . I lived with her all my life; and I feel frightened without her.[6]

The sorrows at Yasnaya Polyana continued into the next year. On February 16, 1875, in a letter to Strakhov, Tolstoy told of living through the winter "in a strange and awful state." There was a "family sorrow."

> The family sorrow is the terrible brain disease of our nine-month baby [Nikolai, the Tolstoys' seventh child]. For three weeks now he has been going through all the stages of this hopeless disease [meningitis]. My wife is feeding him herself and is in despair one minute that he will die and the next, that he will live and be an idiot.

---

* After his wife's death, Leo's father had proposed marriage to Aunt Toinette, hoping she could help him raise his five young children. She turned him down, but remained at Yasnaya Polyana to help rear the children. She took a special liking to Leo.

The boy died a few days later. That fall, again in a letter to Strakhov, November 8–9, Tolstoy wrote that for two weeks he had been looking "after a sick wife who gave birth to a stillborn child and has been at death's door." All through that year, not only Tolstoy but his wife fell deeper and deeper into depression. Sonya told about it in a lengthy entry in her diary on October 12, the only time she wrote in it in 1875. She was fed up with her distinguished husband and with her life at Yasnaya Polyana.

> This isolated country life is becoming intolerable. Dismal apathy, indifference to everything, day after day, month after month, year after year—nothing ever changes. . . . Besides, I am not on my own. I am tied to Lyovochka . . . and I feel it is mainly because of him that I am sinking into this depression. It's painful for me to see him when he is like this, despondent and dejected for days and weeks on end, neither working nor writing, without energy or joy. . . . It is a kind of emotional death, which I deplore in him. Surely, it can't go on much longer. It may be vulgar and wrong of me, but I feel oppressed by the terms of our life which he has laid down—by this terrible monotony and solitude which reduces us both to such apathy. . . . Lyovochka is far too apathetic and indifferent to be of any help to me, for nothing touches his heart.

No doubt they had grown closer in the years that he was toiling on *War and Peace* and, now, struggling with *Anna Karenina*. She had borne him—in twelve years—eight children, of whom five survived. She had been an ideal helpmate for his writing, copying in her own clear hand the various versions of his books, helping him with the business arrangements for serializing and publishing both works, and encouraging him to press on when he felt discouraged and blocked. And Sonya had been very proud of the success of the first book and now of the parts of the new one that had appeared in the *Russian Herald*. She found herself married to the most famous writer in Russia. But the strains of his struggles with *Anna Karenina*, his great depressions, his quick temper with her and the children, his indifference to her, were putting new stresses on the marriage, which, for all the love it had generated, had been difficult from the very first.

Back from Samara in the fall of 1875, Tolstoy wrote Strakhov that he was "tinkering" with his novel "with no success." By November, he was telling Strakhov: "If only someone would finish *Anna Karenina* for me!" On April 15, 1877, he finally finished it himself.

Or so his publisher thought. For there, at the end of the last chapter of Part 7, Anna Karenina lay dead, crushed under the wheels of a train before which she had thrown herself.* But Tolstoy wished to tack on, as he had done with *War and Peace*, a final part in which he would express his ideas about a war—in this case the war between Russia and Turkey which had broken out on April 13, 1877, as he was finishing his novel. He bitterly opposed the war, much to the disgust of his publisher, Katkov, who refused to publish the final section, Part 8, arguing that the novel ended with the death of its heroine.

Even at that time, a publisher wanted to tell a writer, no matter his fame, or that he was a genius, how to finish his novel!

Tolstoy was indignant. He wrote an angry letter to another publication, *New Times*, revealing what his publisher had done to him—and to his readers.[7] And to Strakhov, he fumed against Katkov:

> I'm sick and tired of him, and I've told him that if he won't publish it in the form that I wish, I shall not let him publish it at all.[8]

So Tolstoy published the final section at his own expense in a special edition, and it was incorporated, along with many new changes in the entire text, for the first time into the book version that was published in June 1877.

---

* Tolstoy got the idea for the ending (and probably the name of his heroine) from an actual event that took place near Yasnaya Polyana in 1872, the year before he started the novel. Sonya wrote about it in her diary under the caption "Why *Anna Karenina* Was Called 'Anna,' and What Suggested the Idea of Her Suicide." A neighbor named A. N. Bibikov had living with him as a housekeeper and mistress a woman named Anna Stepanovna Pirogov, a distant cousin of his late wife.

"She had dark hair and grey eyes," Sonya says. "And although she wasn't beautiful, she was very pleasant looking." But one day, Bibikov hired a new governess for his children, a German woman whom Sonya describes as "beautiful" and whom, the Countess adds, he soon fell in love with and proposed marriage to. That was the reason that Anna one day put on a new dress, went to the nearby Yasenki railroad station (the railroad had just reached Yasnaya Polyana), and threw herself under the wheels of an approaching freight train. Tolstoy, though he did not know the woman, went to the inquest in a station shed, where the mangled body had been taken.

"Leo saw her lying there," Sonya reports, "her skull smashed in and her naked body frightfully mutilated. It had the most terrible effect on him." (Sonya's diary, p. 894, and footnote, p. 2001.) It also provided him with a dramatic end for the novel proper.

Turgenev had not much liked it, but Dostoyevsky thought it was wonderful. "I did not like *Anna Karenina*," Turgenev wrote a friend, "despite some truly magnificent pages (the horse-racing, the haymaking, the hunt). But the whole thing is sour, it smells of Moscow and old maids, the Slavophilism and the narrow-mindedness of the nobility. He has gone off the track. It is the fault of . . . his isolation and lack of perseverance." Dostoyevsky, though no great admirer of Tolstoy, thought this time his rival had written a masterpiece. "*Anna Karenina*," he wrote in *Diary of a Writer*, "is a perfect work of art . . . utterly unlike anything being published in Europe; its theme is totally Russian. There is something in this novel of our 'new world,' a new world that has not yet been heard in Europe, although the peoples of the West have great need of it. . . ."

When Tolstoy published his own version of the end, Dostoyevsky turned angrily against him. In opposing the war against the Turks, he wrote, Tolstoy was cutting himself off from the Russian community and "suffering a mental aberration."

Most of the book reviewers were ecstatic about *Anna Karenina*, though a few clobbered it, finding it highly immoral and, as one wrote, "devoid of a shadow of an idea." According to Sonya, her husband never read the critics. "We get neither papers nor journals," Sonya wrote in her diary. "L. says he doesn't want to read the critics. 'The critics always infuriated Pushkin,' he said. 'It is better not to read them at all.' "[9]

"What is so difficult about writing how an officer gets entangled with a woman?" Tolstoy once remarked about *Anna Karenina*. "There's nothing difficult in that."[10] That was after a great change came over him and he began to disparage his two great novels. Nevertheless, *Anna Karenina*, like *War and Peace*, remains one of the great works of the imagination, a moving tale of two very opposite love affairs, that of Anna and Vronsky, Levin and Kitty. But it is much more than that. It is at the same time an ode to life, to human courage and endurance, a plea for understanding and tolerance of those who fail and fall, a devastating critique of a cruel and corrupt society, and a deep inquiry into the questions that troubled the author all his life: Who are we? Where did we come from? Where are we going? What is the meaning, if any, of life—and death?

# EIGHT

# Tolstoy's Great Midlife Crisis

W̲ITH THE PUBLICATION of *War and Peace* and *Anna Karenina,* Leo Tolstoy had emerged as one of Russia's towering novelists, perhaps its greatest; the equal, if not more, of Dostoyevsky, better than Turgenev. The two masterpieces were bringing him a great deal of money in royalties—some twenty thousand rubles a year. His estates were netting him another ten thousand, swelling his annual income to a total of thirty thousand rubles.*

As a landowner, he was spared the worries of so many others for whom, especially after the emancipation of the serfs, the land left to them could no longer support them in their old lazy, luxurious way of life.

As a writer, Tolstoy was also spared the fears of so many writers—fears that he had once shared—of having to write for money. In fact, it seemed to Tolstoy's contemporaries that he had, at fifty, won all of life's prizes, accomplished all he wanted, and that he could justly feel he was on top of the world. Besides literary fame and fortune, the possession of considerable estates, he had an ancient name, a title, an intelligent and attractive wife who helped him in his work, a growing family (seven children by 1879) which he loved. To have a large and happy family had long been one of his great hopes—he had made it one of the themes of the two novels. He had found the time and the means to devote himself to one of his personal goals: schools for the peasant children, in which

---

* Worth approximately $303,750 in today's U.S. currency.

he had attempted to carry out his own ideas of child education. He had found time too, after the emancipation of the serfs in 1861, to serve as "arbitrator of the peace," arbitrating between the free peasants, hungry for a parcel of land, and their former owners, and doing it so evenhandedly and fairly that his avaricious fellow nobles and landowners, holding on for dear life to every acre they could, cursed him as a traitor to his class.

Tolstoy himself was well aware of how well-off he was. "From all indications," he wrote of this time,

> I should have been considered a completely happy man. This was when I was not yet 50 years old [at forty-nine he had finished *Anna Karenina*], I had a good, loving and beloved wife, fine children and a large estate that was growing and expanding without any effort on my part. More than ever before I was respected by friends and acquaintances, praised by strangers, and I could claim a certain renown without really deluding myself. . . . Moreover I enjoyed a physical and mental vigor such as I had rarely encountered among others of my age.[1]

What more could a man possibly want in life?

For Tolstoy, a lot, as it happened. After four years of struggle to write and finish *Anna Karenina*, and despite the instant acclaim that it brought him, Tolstoy became a very unhappy man, at war again with himself, displeased with where he had arrived in life, with what he had done, scornful, indeed ashamed, of what he had written up to now, feeling that in truth he had reached a dead end where life had no more meaning, where death made a mockery of life, which, as he wrote his friend Strakhov, had become, really, a joke. He turned to religion as a solution, resumed going to church and fasting, taking the sacraments, saying his prayers. But he soon found the dogmas of the Orthodox Church more than he could stomach.

He thought, in fact, that the church had ruined Christianity and denied the real Christ himself. Perhaps he could find answers in the Gospels. In order to understand them in all their purity, he taught himself Greek. But his crisis, spiritual and mental, kept getting worse. He told of it in detail and with great passion and candor in a small book he began in 1879 which he called *Confession*. It was an agonizing work of a tormented mind and soul. One biographer has called it a noble document; others have found it exaggerated, misleading, hypocritical, and in parts not even true. My own reading is that it has indeed a great nobility and a wrenching sincerity. After all, it is an inquiry into the most profound questions confronting man: Why am I here? For what? And from where? What meaning has life that inevitable death does not destroy?

To the Russian critic D. S. Mirsky, *Confession* is "one of the world's masterpieces, a work of art . . . one of the greatest and most lasting expressions of the human soul in the presence of the eternal mysteries of life and death. . . . It is the greatest piece of oratory in Russian literature."[2]

Obviously, Tolstoy exaggerated his own failures and shortcomings for greater effect in recounting the story of the midlife crisis that overcame him and, in one phase, drove him to the verge of suicide.

There were other consequences and they were drastic. His crisis changed his way and his view of life. It drove him, for the most part, to abandon writing more novels, and to curse as worthless those he had written. From now on, he would turn to what he considered much more important: writing about religion and morals, about how men could better their lives and save their souls. Some of these tracts were brilliant, passionately and beautifully written, and raised the most serious questions of life and death. Sometimes they were dressed up in fiction, but they were not the imaginative creations that had made him such a magnificent novelist.* The novelist would turn himself into a preacher—one of the greatest who ever strode this earth. Millions in and outside of Russia—Mohandas K. Gandhi, then toiling for the poor in South Africa, was one†—would follow the new prophet. But there were

---

* Still, some of the short stories and novellas he wrote after his conversion are so good that they might be considered minor masterpieces—as good as *The Cossacks*, written even before *War and Peace*.

Among them one could include *The Kreutzer Sonata*, *The Death of Ivan Ilyich*, *Master and Man*, *The Devil*, *Father Sergei*, and, of course, the novel *Hadji Murat*, begun in 1894, finished only in 1904, and not published until after Tolstoy's death.

*Resurrection*, a lengthy novel, which Tolstoy finished and published in 1899, showed a falling off of his great creativity, though many have found it a fascinating piece of fiction.

† During my stay in India at the beginning of the 1930s, Gandhi frequently talked to me of how much he was influenced by Tolstoy. In his autobiography, Gandhi wrote: "Tolstoy's *The Kingdom of God Is Within You* overwhelmed me. It left an abiding impression on me. Before the independent thinking, profound morality, and the truthfulness of this book, all the books [that I had previously read] seemed

many—Turgenev was one—who regretted that in the prime of his life, this genius of a novelist would desert literature to turn out sermons.

And finally, Tolstoy's "conversion," as some have called it, would doom a marriage that, as we have seen, had been difficult from the outset and yet had brought much fulfillment and happiness and love to both partners as the family grew, but which now would begin to become increasingly unbearable for them. Their children agreed that from this time on, the marriage of their parents began to fall apart, poisoning the atmosphere in the house and making both their father and mother more and more miserable. Sonya and most of the children, especially the boys, could not follow Tolstoy in his new path, which included renunciation of private property and copyrights on his books. They regarded it as a threat to their survival as upper-class ladies and gentlemen. And this lack of support and understanding from his family, Tolstoy resented. So Leo and Sonya began to drift further apart, becoming not only strangers but enemies—engaged, as Tolstoy was to warn his wife, in "a struggle to the death."

Tolstoy's conversion, his struggle to understand the meaning of life and death through religious belief, did not happen overnight. It had come on gradually over the years. In the very first paragraph of *Confession*, after remarking that he had been baptized and brought up in the Orthodox Church, he tells us that by the time he dropped out of college at eighteen, he had lost all belief in what he had been taught.

"At the age of sixteen," he says, "I gave up praying and quit going to church and fasting."

On March 5, 1855, when Tolstoy was twenty-seven and serving as an artillery officer at the Battle of Sevastopol, there came to him suddenly what he called a stupendous idea. It was a revelation he would go back to a quarter of a century later and make the foundation of a new religion of his own that would break completely and forever with Orthodox Christianity. He poured his thoughts into his diary that day as French shells burst around him.

to pale into insignificance." (Gandhi, *The Story of My Experiments with Truth*. Boston: Beacon Press, 1957, pp. 137, 160.)

In response to inquiries by Gandhi, Tolstoy wrote him two lengthy letters, the last of more than two thousand words, a few weeks before his death.

Today I took communion. Yesterday a conversation about divinity and faith inspired me with a great idea, a stupendous idea, to the realization of which I feel capable of devoting my life. This idea is the founding of a new religion appropriate to the stage of the development of mankind—the religion of Christ but purged of dogmas and mysticism, a practical religion, not promising future bliss but giving bliss on earth.

To hear him tell it in *Confession*, he simply had gone to hell in the days of his youth.

I cannot recall those days without horror, loathing and heart-[rending] pain. I killed people in war, challenged men to duels with the purpose of killing them, and lost at cards; I squandered the fruits of the peasants' toil and then had them executed; I was a fornicator and a cheat. Lying, stealing, promiscuity of every kind, drunkenness, violence, murder—there was not a crime I did not commit. . . .

He goes on to assail himself for his sins as a writer.

I began to write out of vanity, self-interest, and pride. . . . In order to acquire the fame and the money I was writing for, it was necessary to conceal what was good and to flaunt what was bad. And that is what I did. . . . As an artist and poet I wrote and taught without myself knowing what I was teaching. I received money for doing this; I enjoyed excellent food, lodgings, women, society; I was famous. . . .
Very strange indeed.

Getting married, he stops to say, did not improve matters.

The new circumstances of a happy family life completely diverted me from any search for the overall meaning of life. . . . My whole life was focussed on my family, my wife, my children, and thus on a concern for improving our way of life. . . . My striving for personal perfection . . . now became a striving for what was best for my family.

Fifteen married years went by, he says, which would bring him up to 1877 when he finished *Anna Karenina*.

In spite of the fact that during those fifteen years [the years he wrote his two masterpieces] I regarded writing as a trivial endeavor, I continued to write. I had already tasted the temptations of authorship, the temptations of enormous monetary awards and applause for worthless work, and I gave myself up to it as a means of improving my material situation and a way of stifling any questions in my soul concerning the meaning of my life and of life in general.

"But five years ago," he says, "something very strange began to happen to me. My life came to a stop. . . . The truth was that life is meaningless. . . ." He grew so sick of life that he contemplated leaving it. "I had to use cunning against myself," he goes on, "to keep from committing suicide."

I hid a rope from myself so that I should not hang myself from the beam between the closets. And I quit going hunting with a gun so that I would not be too easily tempted to rid myself of my life.

Tolstoy next turned to the sciences in search of answers to his questions. But in vain. "They not only had not found anything," he concluded, "but had also clearly recognized the fact that what had brought me to despair—the meaninglessness of life—was the only incontestable knowledge that was accessible to man."

He next sought understanding in philosophy. He reread the Greeks, Kant, and Schopenhauer. He found some solace in Socrates, agreeing with him that "all evil results from the life of the body," so that "the destruction of the body is good and we must wish it." But on the whole, even the philosophers disappointed Tolstoy. "They not only failed to lead me out of my despair," he says, "but rather increased it."

The philosophers having let him down, Tolstoy began to look for the answers he needed in life, hoping to find them in his fellow aristocrats, the rich nobles and the landowners. But Russia's upper classes, he quickly concluded, had nothing to offer. They were wasting away sinfully in idleness, pleasures, ignorance, and a horrible narrow-mindedness.

So, he says, he looked around at the masses of people, the

workers, and peasants. And, to his surprise, he found they had some of the answers he was seeking: "Contrary to what I saw among the people of our class, where a lifetime is spent in idleness, amusement, and dissatisfaction with life, these people spent their lives at hard labor and were less dissatisfied with life than the wealthy. . . . They knew the meaning of life and death, labored in peace, endured suffering and hardship, lived and died, and saw in this not vanity but good. I began to love these people."

He kept turning too to religion. He wanted to believe in something, to have some kind of faith, for without faith, he believed, "one cannot live." He studied the texts, he says, of Buddhism and Islam, and especially those of Christianity. He made pilgrimages to the monasteries, talked with the learned monks and Orthodox theologians. Again in vain! "What they gave out as faith," he found, "was not an explanation but an obfuscation of the meaning of life." He found himself "repelled" by the church services, sacraments, fasts, the bowing before relics and icons.

He was forced, he says, to reject the Orthodox Church in which he had been raised and to which his wife and children remained fiercely loyal. In fact, he rejected a great deal that all the Christian churches, Catholic and Protestant, held sacred. He could no longer believe, for example, in the Resurrection of Christ because he could not imagine that it had happened. Nor could he accept as fact or truth the Annunciation, the Ascension, the Pentecost, or the Intercession of the Blessed Virgin. They seemed to him now "cheap imagery unworthy of the cause of God." The churchmen had "cut up Christ into shreds and tacked their idiotic, vile explanations—hateful to Christ—on to every morsel." Tolstoy also rejected the very concept of the Trinity. He could not believe that Jesus was "the second person of God, who became incarnate in the womb of the Virgin Mary through the intervention of the Holy Ghost. To say that was God, and the second person of the Trinity," he wrote to cousin Alexandrine, a devout Orthodox Christian, "was sacrilege, falsehood and nonsense." Such heresy almost destroyed their long friendship.[3]

The ideas Tolstoy expressed in his letters were confidential, and those he expounded in his books, especially *Confession* and *Criticism of Dogmatic Theology* (1880), were withheld from the general Russian public by the Tsar's censors, who refused to allow the works to be published. But they were circulated in manuscript copies and eventually published abroad and soon came to the notice of the authorities, ecclesiastic and civil, in Petersburg. They provided much ammunition for a process that began in the mideighties: preparation for excommunicating Russia's most influential writer.

The tormented author, having rejected the Christianity of the churches, finally found what he could believe in in the Gospels. It is from these, especially the Sermon on the Mount, that he began to formulate his new version of Christianity. There was one passage particularly that hit him like a thunderbolt and became the foundation of his new religion: "Resist not him that is evil. Whosoever smiteth thee on the right cheek, turn to him the other also." This he would soon refine into a broad advocation of nonviolent resistance to evil, a concept that, as we have seen, he passed along to, among others, Gandhi, who in turn refined it further into a political movement that would free his vast country from British rule.* It also formed the basis of what would soon become the Tolstoyan movement, which attracted millions of followers not only in Russia but throughout the world.

To that precept, Tolstoy added some others from the Sermon on the Mount that he believed should guide one's conduct through life: One should not commit adultery, should not be angry, should not swear oaths (to obey, as Tolstoy interpreted it, political or religious authorities), should love one's enemies (and neighbors) as oneself.

Relieved to have discovered what he was seeking in the Gospels on which his new religion and philosophy of life would be founded, Tolstoy now tried to shed his old self and become a new and better man.

"I renounced," he says, "the life of our circle." The aristocracy, he decided, was nothing but a bunch of parasites. The luxury in which they lived made it impossible for them to understand life. Only the peasants and workers understood. Henceforth, he would try to live like them. He would adopt the dress of the peasants, work with them in the fields, scythe in hand during the mowing, behind a horse in the plowing. He would learn from the village cobbler how to make his own shoes and those of the family.

Private property, he now saw, was one of the great evils. So he

---

* Martin Luther King, Jr., who got it from Gandhi, would apply the concept of nonviolent resistance to his struggle for equality for American blacks.

would give up his ownership of the land. As a first step, he gave
Sonya power of attorney to run his estates and eventually deeded
them to his wife and children, also giving them the right to republish for their own profit (though he now regarded this as a sin) all
his literary works that had appeared up to 1881. Those to come
would be in the public domain. He gave up his property rights to
conform with his new religion, though Sonya, who could not follow
him in his conversion, noted sarcastically that he continued to live
in the luxury he claimed to deplore. She noted too that though he
now began to preach complete abstinence from sexual relations,
even between husband and wife, he kept on making her pregnant.
By 1879, for the tenth time! At times she would see it as sheer
hypocrisy, as an attempt by her husband to garner more publicity
and add to his already great fame.

> He would like the eyes of the world [she wrote] to see him
> on the pedestal which he took such pains to erect for himself. But
> his diaries cast him into the filth in which he once lived, and that
> infuriates him.[4]

Since her husband's conversion, she complains, his demands
on her have become impossible and she resents the hypocrisy of his
renouncing money and then constantly dunning her for some.

> I am expected to renounce everything, all my property, all
> my beliefs, the education and well-being of my children. . . . I try
> to keep the family together, have business relations with pub-
> lishers, get some money for Leo Nikolayevich, who constantly
> comes up to me with that air of indifference, malevolence and
> even hatred and demands that I give him more money. . . . The
> children criticize me for opposing their father and they too ask
> me for as much as they can get. . . . Oh, to leave it all behind—I
> shall leave, somehow or other. . . .[5]

Poor Sonya. Her husband's change of life baffled her. She
could not understand it and she did not like it. She could see it was
changing his whole being. It was threatening their marriage, their
children.

"It's painful for me to see him when he is like this," she had noted in her diary as far back as October 12, 1875, "despondent and dejected for days and weeks on end, without energy or joy. . . . It is a kind of emotional death. . . . Surely, it can't go on much longer." But it did.

Tolstoy abandoned his novel on the Decembrists which he had begun after finishing *Anna Karenina* and on which he had done a great deal of research and given much thought. In a letter to her sister Tanya in 1879, as she awaited the birth of a new child, Sonya had told of what the famous author was turning to.

> Leo is working, so he says, but alas! He keeps writing religious tracts, reads and thinks until his head aches and all this to prove how inconsistent the Church is with the teachings of the Gospels. There will hardly be a dozen people in Russia interested in that.

In this instance, Sonya was a bad prophet. Soon not only a dozen but dozens of thousands, and then millions, would become very much interested "in that."

The consequences of Tolstoy's conversion, then, were momentous—to himself, his family, and his marriage. To the world, too, it might be added, for the man who had just given it *War and Peace* and *Anna Karenina* now abandoned, in large part, his role as novelist.

No one has put it better than Cathy Porter, translator of Sonya's diaries into English. "The consequences of Tolstoy's long and painful conversion," she concludes, "were both deeply impressive and utterly intolerable; for Sophya it was a disaster."

It drove them apart. It poisoned their family life. It doomed their marriage. Their eldest son, Sergei, and their eldest daughter, Tanya, have testified to that.

"The discord between them," Sergei would write of his parents, "was in fact the discord between the Leo Tolstoy of the former years before the change in his outlook on life, and the new Leo Tolstoy after that change. His former views, which were shared by his wife, conflicted with his subsequent views. . . . In relation to his family, he was influenced by considerations that until about 1881 he had been a different man, and that that man—a landed proprietor and literary man—had died, and in his place had been born a new man who did not recognize property rights and did not write for money but for the good of mankind. . . . My mother did not share my father's negative attitude to the ownership of property, but on the contrary, continued to think that the richer her children and grandchildren would be, the better."[6]

Tanya Tolstoy, a favorite of her father, though she tried to maintain good relations with her mother, agreed with her brother:

> We were unable to follow him on his new path. As a family we had been brought up in certain traditions, in a certain social climate, and now our leader was suddenly abandoning the life to which we had become accustomed.

Tolstoy had spoiled his family with luxuries and the way of life of the rich and famous.

> And now he was saying that he would like his wife and children to live like peasants. Why? Why suddenly give up a life of pleasure at this stage for a life of drudgery and deprivation? That was how my mother formulated the problem in her mind. . . . The disharmony between my father and his family became particularly acute. The interests of husband and wife were becoming increasingly divergent.[7]

Worse than that.

They were leading to the bitter "struggle to the death," as Tolstoy soon realized, and which now began to unfold inexorably with increasing intensity. And they would lead to an appalling alienation, not only between Tolstoy and his wife but between him and his children.

Tolstoy would describe the latter in a letter to a friend.[8]

> I'm sad—because of the exultant, self-assured madness of the life of the people around me. I don't understand why it has been granted to me to see their madness so clearly, and they are completely unable to understand their own madness and their own errors; and we just stand opposite each other without understanding each other, being astonished and condemning each other.

He later wrote to another friend of the loneliness the alienation from his family had caused him.[9]

I suffer painfully from the awareness of my own loneliness in the family because of my beliefs, and the fact that they all in my eyes seek the truth but turn away from it. I suffer both for them and for myself. . . . I suffer because my wife doesn't share my convictions.

Living with an aspiring saint became increasingly miserable for Sonya. As she waited the birth of her tenth child, she noted in her diary on December 18, 1879:

I sit waiting for my confinement. . . . The thought of a new baby fills me with gloom; my horizons have become so narrow, and my world is such a small and dismal place.

On August 26, 1882, her despair would reach a climax. She poured the words into her diary amidst the tears. The twentieth anniversary of her wedding was approaching.

It was 20 years ago, when I was young and happy, that I started writing the story of my love for Lyovochka in this book . . . 20 years later, here I am sitting up all night on my own, reading, and mourning its loss. For the first time in my life Lyovochka has run off to sleep alone in his study. We were quarreling about such silly things—I accused him of taking no interest in the children and not helping me look after Ilya, who is sick, or making them all jackets.

But it has nothing to do with jackets, and everything to do with his growing coldness towards me and the children. Today he shouted at the top of his voice that his dearest wish was to leave his family. I shall carry the memory of that heartfelt heart-[rending] cry of his to the grave. I pray for death, for without his love I cannot survive. . . . I cannot sleep in the bed he has abandoned. Lord help me! I long to take my life. . . . The clock is striking four.

Tolstoy's conversion had cut him off from his wife, his children, his church, his class, his writing of novels, and from the life he had led up to now and which, in his new role of prophet and saint, he despised. A long, different, difficult, stormy road lay ahead. For him, and his wife.

## BOOK TWO

*The*
*Last*
*Years*

*1879–1910*

# NINE

# The Troubled Saint

*I*N HIS QUEST for righteousness, Tolstoy moved quickly to accomplish several good works. He would seek a reconciliation with Turgenev after seventeen years of estrangement; he would write the Tsar and ask him in the name of God not to hang the revolutionaries who had assassinated the Tsar's father, Alexander II. He would give away most of his land to the peasants and induce his wife and children to join him in leading a more simple and moral life, abandoning the luxuries and comforts they had enjoyed until now. He would write no more novels—he was ashamed of those he had written*—and devote his literary talents henceforth to turning out tracts to persuade mankind to give up its evil ways and follow him in living the selfless, simple life that Christ had preached. He would resume writing a diary.

"After thirteen years I want to continue my diary," he jotted down on April 17, 1878. He had been too busy writing *War and Peace* and *Anna Karenina* to keep a journal.

Actually, except for a few scattered entries, he did not really get back to writing it until 1881. From then on, to the end, twenty-nine years later, it constitutes an almost daily record of his thoughts and acts and changing relations with others, especially with his

---

* Tolstoy wrote to V. V. Stasov, a well-known critic and librarian: "Concerning *Anna Karenina*: I assure you this abomination no longer exists for me." (Ernest J. Simmons, *Leo Tolstoy*, p. 340.)
    And to Turgenev: ". . . it gives me an extremely disagreeable feeling . . . to reread what I have written . . . or even hear it talked about. . . ." (Henri Troyat, *Tolstoy*, p. 389.)

children and, more especially, with his wife. Increasingly, he noted his despair over the mounting quarrels with Sonya and their drifting further and further apart, for which, in the main, he blamed her.

The long break with Turgenev, who had befriended him early on and helped launch his literary career and with whom in the end—1861—he had quarreled so bitterly that each had challenged the other to a duel, had begun to prick his new conscience. On April 6, 1878, in the midst of his "conversion," he sat down at Yasnaya Polyana to write a letter to Turgenev.

> Lately, when recalling my relations with you, I felt to my great surprise and joy that I bore no hostility towards you. God grant the same is true of you.
>
> If this is so, then please let us extend our hands to each other and, please forgive me once and for all for everything for which I was to blame towards you.
>
> . . . I remember that I owe my literary renown to you, and I remember how you loved my writing and myself. . . .
>
> Sincerely, if you can forgive me, I offer you all the friendship which I am capable of. At our time of life, there is only one good—affectionate relations between people. And I will be very happy if such relations can be established between us.

Turgenev, in Paris, wept when he read it. Quickly he replied.

> The letter you sent me to the post office to be left until called for, did not reach me until today [May 6]. It touched me deeply and made me very happy. It is my fondest wish to renew our former friendship and I most warmly shake your outstretched hand. You are quite right to believe I have no hostile feelings towards you. If I ever did, they vanished long ago.

Turgenev could not refrain from reminding Tolstoy that he had been the first to champion him as a writer. He still remembered, he said, Tolstoy as "an author whose first works I had the good fortune to applaud before anyone else. . . . I rejoice with all my heart and soul to see the end of the misunderstanding between us."

He would return to Russia for the summer, he concluded, and proposed that they meet.

The elder writer lost no time. On August 8, he arrived at Yasnaya Polyana for a brief visit. Sonya was delighted, the children excited, at seeing such a distinguished guest. Turgenev *looked* like a great writer, they thought. Ilya Tolstoy, then twelve, still remembered years later how imposing Turgenev was, with his "tall stalwart figure, his grey silky, yellowish hair, his soft tread and his thin, little voice, quite out of character for his imposing exterior."[1] To the children their father seemed rather puny in comparison.

It was a beautiful summer day, so the two men joined the family outdoors. A seesaw in the yard attracted them and, very nimbly, Turgenev, sixty, climbed on one end and Tolstoy, fifty, on the other, seesawing up and down to the delight of the children until both men were breathless. After dinner, Turgenev read one of his short stories, "The Dog," to the family, but it was not one of his best and the reception was not very enthusiastic. Still, he did not seem to mind. Nothing could dampen his high spirits. For his part, the master of the house, wary though he still was of his old friend and enemy, was on his best behavior and tried to be friendly and genial. Later, though, when the two men adjourned for a talk in Tolstoy's study, the old edginess between them once again surfaced. In their discussion of literature and philosophy they found themselves unable to agree. Turgenev kept arguing that the most important thing in life was the worship of beauty in all the arts and in nature, and that a great writer had a duty to stick to what he did best. Tolstoy bristled at such ideas. Art was important but Christian morality and the search for God were more important.

They parted, however, on the best of terms, and in a thank-you letter Turgenev wrote Tolstoy:

> I can't help saying once more how good and enjoyable it was for me to be at Yasnaya Polyana, and how happy I am to see that the misunderstanding between us has vanished without a trace, as though it had never existed. . . .[2]

And to Fet, he wrote of his great joy at renewing relations with Tolstoy. "He has calmed down considerably and matured. We Russians know he has no rival."

But Tolstoy was not so magnanimous. He was not so sure that their misunderstanding had vanished "without a trace." When Turgenev returned for a second visit on September 2, he seemed to annoy his host, as in the earlier years of their friendship. The day after his departure, Tolstoy wrote to both Fet and Strakhov about Turgenev's visit. To Fet, he wrote, "Turgenev is the same as ever, and we have no illusions as to the degree of intimacy between us." He wrote the same to Strakhov:

> Turgenev has been here again and was just as nice and brilliant, but—between you and me, please—he is rather like a fountain of piped water. You were afraid all the time that he would soon run out and dry up.

Three years later, on August 22, 1881, Turgenev returned to Yasnaya Polyana for his third and, as it turned out, final visit. His health was failing and he had begun to feel that he had not much more time to live. The family—Sonya and her children, her sister Tanya and her children—were happy to see the great writer again. They were dancing the quadrille in his honor one evening, when suddenly Turgenev, despite his feebleness, jumped up and, as Ilya remembered,[3] put his thumbs in the armholes of his waistcoat and wildly began dancing a cancan, explaining that this was the way they danced it in Paris. The children and their mothers were thrilled at the handsome, silver-haired old man cavorting around the salon. But Tolstoy could only frown. That night in his diary he wrote: ". . . Turgenev, cancan. Sad."

Turgenev had no idea that ever since their reconciliation, Tolstoy had continued to harbor negative thoughts about him. When he returned to Paris in 1878, he had busied himself introducing Tolstoy's works to the French. They were just beginning to be published in Paris. But Tolstoy professed to be no longer interested in the books and short stories he had written, and in answer to Turgenev's efforts on his behalf in Paris he wrote a surprisingly irritable reply.

> Please don't think I am being affected, but really and truly, even a cursory mention of my writings produces an unpleasantly complex feeling in me, the greater part of which is shame and fear that people are laughing at me. . . .

Much as I owe you and believe that you are well-disposed towards me, it seems to me that you are laughing at me. So, let's not talk about my writings. . . .[4]

Overlooking Tolstoy's pique, Turgenev replied that he had never, "in the slightest degree," made fun of Tolstoy or his works. "Why should I laugh at them? I thought you had long since gotten rid of such 'centripetal' feelings."

But Tolstoy could not be appeased by such words, courteous as they were. He wrote to Fet: "Received an epistle from Turgenev yesterday. You know, I have decided to step away from him and temptation. He really is an unpleasant trouble-seeker."[5]

There was something in the chemistry of the two authors that doomed their friendship from the beginning. Each got on the other's nerves. They had never really been able to hit it off together. And during and after his conversion Tolstoy felt that their different views of life and literature could never be bridged. Turgenev, despite his magnanimity toward Tolstoy, also saw quite clearly that there could never be a harmonious relationship between them.

Ilya Tolstoy cites two letters of Turgenev to Tolstoy that he thinks shed light on the gulf between the two men. This time it is the older man who points it out. "Probably through my fault, each of us will long feel considerable awkwardness in the presence of the other. . . . Outside of our special, so-called 'literary' interests, I am convinced we have few points of contact. . . ." Ilya quotes a second letter in which Turgenev, not for the first time, chides Tolstoy for not having become "a pure man of letters. . . . I really do wish beyond all things to see you under way at last with all sails set."[6]

On his deathbed, Turgenev wrote Tolstoy in the same vein, but more passionately. Dated June 27, 1883, it is a moving, poignant letter.

Kind and dear Leo Nikolayevich. It is long since I wrote you, for I have been and I am, speaking frankly, on my deathbed. I cannot recover. There is no use thinking of it. I am writing to you particularly to tell you how glad I am to have been your contemporary, and to express to you my last, sincere wish. My friend, return to literature! The gift came to you from the same source as the rest. Oh, how happy I should be if I could think that my request would have an effect on you! I am a doomed man—even my doctors don't know what to call my malady.* I can neither walk, nor eat nor sleep. It bores me to talk about it. My friend, great writer of the Russian land, heed my request!

Tolstoy never answered the letter. Perhaps he thought he had already made it clear to Turgenev why he had abandoned literature.

Ilya Tolstoy reveals that his father was "sincerely annoyed" at one line in the letter, Turgenev's appeal to Tolstoy as the "great writer of the Russian land." He thought it was a "nonsensical expression."[7]

But when Turgenev died at Bougival, a suburb of Paris, on August 22, Tolstoy grieved. He began to reread all of his old rival's works, several volumes of them. He wrote to Sonya:

> I am always thinking of Turgenev. I was intensely fond of him and sorry for him and now I do nothing but read him. I live entirely with him. I shall certainly give a lecture on him.

He tried to be as good as his word. Invited by the Society of Lovers of Russian Literature to speak at a memorial service for Turgenev in Moscow, Tolstoy, who three years before had turned down Turgenev's urgent request that he join him and Dostoyevsky to speak at the unveiling in Moscow of a statue of Pushkin, readily accepted. Dostoyevsky had received a tumultuous ovation when he spoke at the Pushkin meeting.† Now Tolstoy's chief rival was gone. Tolstoy would be the chief speaker. For weeks he worked on his paper. But in the end he was unable to deliver it.

---

* Actually, it was cancer of the bone marrow.
† Turgenev had been extremely annoyed at Tolstoy for turning him down on his fervent request that he speak at the Pushkin unveiling—so annoyed in fact that he advised Dostoyevksy, who had intended to visit Tolstoy at Yasnaya Polyana, not to go. Tolstoy, he apparently told Dostoyevsky, was in no mood to receive visitors, as he had just learned Tolstoy was going through a spiritual crisis that might be affecting his mind. At any rate, Dostoyevsky wrote his wife: "Grigorovich told me today that Turgenev fell ill upon his return from Tolstoy's place and that Tolstoy is half mad and maybe completely mad."

Though Turgenev had also quarreled bitterly with Dostoyevsky years before, they too had had a reconciliation. With Tolstoy's withdrawal, Turgenev helped arrange for Dostoyevsky to make the principal address at the Pushkin ceremony. His speech electrified Russia.

For some time under the reactionary Tsar Alexander III, the authorities had been taking a dim view of Tolstoy's doings and, even more, his thoughts. A police informer had reported that Tolstoy was preaching the equality of men to the peasants and attacking the teachings of the Orthodox Church. In October 1883, the minister of the interior (Count Dmitri Tolstoy, no relative of Leo) asked the Tsar to take measures to restrict the rebellious writer because he was "undermining the people's confidence in justice and arousing the indignation of all true-believers."

In the meantime, the minister was told by one of his subordinates that Tolstoy was scheduled to address the memorial meeting for Turgenev. Tolstoy, he added, "is a madman, from whom one might expect anything. He may say unbelievable things and there may be considerable scandal."

The Tsarist government could not permit such a challenge from so defiant a source. The Tsar did not dare to arrest the great writer with so immense a following in Russia, but he could silence him (as he had done by censoring many of Tolstoy's recent works). The governor of Moscow "advised" the Society of Lovers of Russian Literature to postpone the memorial service for Turgenev indefinitely. Tolstoy was prevented from paying his public tribute to a great writer he had both loved and despised.

In private, Tolstoy wrote to Alexander N. Pypin, a well-known historian, about Turgenev.

> I always loved him, but only after his death did I appreciate him properly. . . . The chief thing about him is his *truthfulness*. . . . Turgenev was a fine man (not very proud, very weak, but a good and kind man) who always expressed well *the very thing* that he thought and felt. . . . Turgenev's influence on our literature was very good and fruitful. . . . I very much regret that I was prevented from speaking about him.[8]

And to Strakhov, he had written that Turgenev didn't have a flaw.[9]

Three years before, on January 28, 1881, Dostoyevsky had died and Tolstoy wept at the news. "How I should like to be able to say all I feel about Dostoyevsky," he wrote Strakhov.

> I never saw the man and never had any direct relations with him, and suddenly when he died I realized that he was the very

closest, dearest and most necessary man for me. I was a writer, and all writers are vain and envious—or at least I was. But it never occurred to me to measure myself against him, never. Everything he did was so good, so sincere, that the more he did the happier I was.

I always considered him as a friend, and was convinced that one day we would meet, and that it was my fault that we had not managed to do so yet. And suddenly he was dead. It was as though one of my supporting pillars had suddenly buckled. I was overcome, but then I realized how precious he was to me, and I cried and am still crying.[10]

Tolstoy was always deeply moved by the death of a fellow writer. As with most people, he could only speak well of the dead. Later, he was more critical. This was especially true of his feelings toward Turgenev and Dostoyevsky. Though he would never admit it, it is plain from his writings he considered them to be his chief rivals.

To Strakhov, who was a protégé, a friend (though not a very true one),* and an admirer and biographer of Dostoyevsky, he wrote in late 1883 to dampen his friend's championship of the author of *Crime and Punishment* and *The Brothers Karamazov*. "I believe you have been the victim of a false and erroneous opinion towards Dostoyevsky. This opinion, which is universal, has exaggerated the man's importance and raised him to the rank of a prophet or a saint, a man who died in the throes of a fierce struggle between God and evil. He is moving and interesting, no doubt, but one cannot set on a pedestal a man who was all struggle. . . . He is remarkably clever and genuine, and I still regret that I didn't know him."

To V. V. Rozanov, a young journalist and writer who was a fervent admirer of Dostoyevsky (he had once married one of his mistresses, Paulina Suslov), Tolstoy was even more critical of Dostoyevsky.

---

* Strakhov had written to Tolstoy that while writing a biography of Dostoyevsky, he had to fight off a "feeling of revulsion."

 . . . I cannot regard Dostoyevsky either as a good man or a happy one. He was vicious, envious, depraved and spent his entire life in a state of emotional upheaval that would have made him appear ridiculous had he not been so malicious and intelligent. . . . He was a truly wicked and truly evil man. . . . [Some friend! Some disciple!]

(Strakhov's letter, November 28, 1883, quoted in Henri Troyat, *Tolstoy*, p. 401.)

*The House of the Dead* is a fine thing, but I do not set great store by his other books. People cite passages to me. And indeed there are some very fine points here and there but on the whole it is dreadful stuff. His style is turgid, he tries so hard to make his characters original and in fact they are hardly outlined. Dostoyevsky talks and talks.

Asked if he didn't like *The Brothers Karamazov*, perhaps Dostoyevsky's finest novel, the sage of Yasnaya replied that he couldn't finish it. What about *Crime and Punishment?* "I read a few chapters at the beginning," Tolstoy responded, "and you can guess everything that's going to follow."[11]

To Maxim Gorky, Tolstoy was just as condescending toward Dostoyevsky. The young writer remembered how Tolstoy "spoke out about Dostoyevsky with evident reluctance, stiffly, evasively. . . . 'He was a violently sensual man. He felt much but he did not know how to think. . . . There was something Jewish in his blood. He was mistrustful, vain, cantankerous and miserable. It's a funny thing that so many people read him—I can't understand why.' "[12]

On the Sunday morning of March 1, 1881, Tsar Alexander II, the liberal ruler who had freed the serfs, was assassinated in St. Petersburg by a group of six fanatical nihilists led by a woman, Sofya Perovsky. The murder was so cold-blooded and ghastly that it was certain the conspirators would be quickly tried and hanged. To this the new Tolstoy was firmly opposed, though he was deeply shocked at the murder of the Tsar he so greatly admired. His new Christian belief told him that it was wrong to take lives in revenge and that the new Tsar, Alexander III, must turn the other cheek. Capital punishment, in Tolstoy's eyes now, was one of the worst crimes.

Against the pleadings of his wife, who feared her husband would only get himself into trouble, Tolstoy wrote the new Tsar a long letter, imploring him as a Christian not to allow the assassins to be hanged and suggesting that they be pardoned:

> . . . Sire! If you were to do this, to summon these people to give them money and to send them somewhere to America, and

were to write a manifesto headed by the words, "But I say unto you, love your enemies," I, a poor, loyal subject . . . would weep with emotion, as I am weeping now every time I hear your name. I know that at these words goodness and love would flow across Russia in a torrent. The truths of Christ are alive in the hearts of many. . . .

It was true, Tolstoy concluded, that the spirit of revolution was growing among the Russian people, but it would not be put down by repression.

Only one word of forgiveness and Christian love, spoken and fulfilled from the height of the throne, and the path of Christian rule which is there for you to tread, can destroy the evil gnawing away at Russia.

As wax before fire, every revolutionary struggle will melt away before the Tsar-man who fulfills the law of Christ.[13]

It was a brilliantly written letter and a passionate expression of Tolstoy's new beliefs in the attraction and power of Christianity as he understood it. But, as he must have known, it would fall on deaf ears.

One problem was to make sure that the letter actually reached the Tsar. Tolstoy sent it along to his friend Strakhov in Petersburg, asking him to give it to the man he believed was closest to the new Emperor—K. P. Pobyedonostsev, who had been the monarch's tutor and recently had become chief procurator of the Holy Synod, a post that made him the most powerful figure in government and also the boss of the Orthodox Church. Though intelligent and widely read—he was a friend of Dostoyevsky—he was a man of narrow vision and an extreme reactionary who believed that only drastic suppression could end the growing revolutionary movement in Russia.

He refused to pass the letter along to the Tsar. Instead, he wrote the Emperor that the very idea of pardoning the killers filled him "with horror." "No, a thousand times, no," he pleaded. The Emperor must not listen to the cries of "a few weak-hearted and feeble-minded individuals" asking for mercy for the murderers. "For the love of God, Sire," he concluded, "do not listen to misguided sycophants."

He need not have worried. Alexander III scribbled across his letter: "Rest assured, no one will dare to come to me with such a request, and I promise you that *all six of them will hang.*"

Tolstoy had written Pobyedonostsev a rather frank note asking him to forward his letter to the Tsar. "I know you to be a Christian," he began, "and . . . that is sufficient for me to be bold enough to approach you with an important and difficult request, namely to hand on to the Emperor a letter written by me about the recent terrible events." He went on:

> For the love of God, take the trouble to read my letter, and if you find there is nothing in it which has not been said please destroy the letter and forgive me for the trouble I have caused you. But if you find there is something new in my letter, which might attract the Emperor's attention, please hand or send it to him.

Though in his new life he was trying to give up his title, this time he pulled rank and signed the letter "Count Leo Tolstoy."[14]

And he would not be put off by the all-powerful procurator of the Holy Synod when informed by Strakhov that the minister declined to forward his letter. He appealed to the other sources he knew at court, who delivered another copy to the Tsar. The monarch did not deign to reply to him, and on April 3, 1881, the six convicted assassins were hanged. Pobyedonostsev did send an answer a couple of months later.

> When I read your letter I saw that your faith had nothing in common with mine, which is that of the Church, and that my Christ was not your Christ. My Christ is a man of strength and truth who heals the weak and yours seemed to me to be a weak man himself in need of healing.[15]

As a result of his conversion Tolstoy now, in 1881, decided that drastic changes were needed in the way he and his family lived. In a long diary entry of October 5, he set down his new ideas for a Spartan but happy family life. He would give his income from his immense estate in Samara "to the poor people and the schools"; the smaller estate at Nikolskoye, which he had inherited from one of his brothers, he would give outright to the peasants. He would keep "for the time being" his ancestral estate at Yasnaya Polyana, which he calculated would give him an income of between two and three thousand rubles a year, enough to support the family if they agreed to lead a much simpler life.

Since in his new life he was preaching sexual abstinence even between a man and his wife (though not yet practicing it), he would run the household at Yasnaya Polyana as the Shakers did in their communes.

> Live [all together]: the men in one room, the women and girls in another. One room to be a library for intellectual pursuits, and one work room for general use. And since we are spoiled, a separate room for the sick. Apart from feeding ourselves and the children and teaching them, there will be work on the estate and helping with the corn, medical treatment and instruction. On Sundays, dinners for the poor and destitute, reading and talks.
>
> Living, food and clothing, all very simple. Sell or give away everything superfluous—the piano, furniture, carriages. . . . Treat all people alike, from governors to beggars. The one aim is happiness—one's own and that of one's family—in the knowledge that this happiness consists in being content with little and doing good to others.

Countess Tolstoy and the children, as we have seen, rejected any such idea as ridiculous and absurd. They could not understand why he now regarded private property as one of the great sins, and when, a little later, he told them he wanted also to renounce the copyrights on his books, the royalties from which constituted the main source of his income, they revolted. Especially Sonya. She made it clear she would fight to the bitter end to see that the children were adequately taken care of. She would not stand for their becoming paupers.

Tolstoy himself, though he talked increasingly of giving up his old way of life and living like a peasant, never seemed to get around to carrying out his resolve. Not even in regard to sexual abstinence, for Sonya's pregnancies continued. He did begin to give up hunting, smoking, and drinking and, in time, he became a vegetarian.

Eventually, he would give his wife power of attorney to run his estates and publish his books; he would renounce all copyrights after 1883 and, in the end, turn over his estates not to the peasants but to his children. Though he began to dress like a peasant, he never succeeded in his vow to live like one. Instead, he continued to the end of his life to live like the aristocratic country gentleman he was. True, for a time he would make his own shoes, ill-fitting as they were, and spend a few summer days in the fields at harvest time swinging a scythe. But most of his time, as before his conversion, was filled with writing, reading, answering some of the hundreds of letters he received weekly from all over the world, receiving distinguished guests, and visiting the great estates of the nobility and the wealthy. Once, when he became seriously ill, he did not go to the nearest hospital, as the peasants would do if they were lucky, but took off in a luxurious private railway coach along with a considerable retinue: part of his family, some of his friends, a special doctor, and twelve servants. His destination? No peasant hut, but a great estate offered him by a friend, Countess Sofya Panina at Gaspra in the Crimea.

Sonya, most of the children, and some of the public thought him hypocritical; to others his failure to practice what he preached was simply a human foible. Whatever it was, his constant harping on reforming his family affected the Tolstoy marriage. The gulf between the two kept widening and their quarrels became bitter and more frequent.

The move to Moscow in 1881 did not help. It made Tolstoy all the quicker to complain and squabble. He hated the city.

For more than a year Sonya had been trying to get her husband to agree to spending winters in Moscow. She was tired, after nineteen years, of the monotony of living in the country twelve months a year. "The autumn had brought on my usual depression," she had written in her diary. "I sit here in silence, doggedly stitching up my rug or reading. I feel cold, dull and indifferent to everything—and ahead lies nothing but darkness."[16] And to her sister she confided a year later: "Sometimes I find this cloistered existence extremely hard. . . . It is a prison. . . . I often feel as though someone is fencing me in, shutting me away, and I want to knock . . . down and smash everything . . . and run away. . . ."[17]

Aside from Sonya's yearning to return to the city, if only for the winter, was her determination to put the children in school there. Their education in Yasnaya Polyana by tutors and their parents, she thought, had been haphazard. Sergei, their eldest son, was now eighteen and ready to enter the university. Tanya, seventeen, wanted to enroll at art school. Ilya, fifteen, and Leo, twelve, should be put in grammar school.

The very idea of returning to the wicked city, where he had spent his youth carousing, deeply depressed Leo. "I often wish to die," he jotted down in his diary shortly before their departure in mid-September. He had had his fifty-third birthday on August 28 but the family was so busy packing for the move to Moscow that no one remembered. "I could not help feeling sad," he had confided to his diary, "that nobody remembered."

The house in Moscow that the Tolstoys rented that first winter was no worker's hut. It was owned by Prince Volkonsky and was one of the most spacious residences in town, with a large garden. Grand as it was, it seemed to Tolstoy to be made of cardboard. In his huge study, the size of a barn, he could hear through the thin walls the talk and the clatter of the rest of the house. It was impossible for a writer to work there, so he sought to find a small apartment nearby where he could think and write in peace.

Back in this city of sin, which he had loved so much as a wild young man, he was utterly miserable. The first month in the huge and uncomfortable house seemed an age.

"A month has passed," he wrote in his diary on October 5, 1881 (though it was scarcely more than two weeks), "the most agonizing of my life."

He felt more alienated than ever from his family.

> They are still settling down [he wrote in the same diary entry]. When will they start to live? Unhappy people! They have no life.

By 1884, a disastrous year for the Tolstoy marriage, Leo was in agony, not only from his worsening relations with his wife, but from what he felt was his estrangement from his children. His diary that year is filled with complaints about the children and his inability to comprehend them and their ways. That spring he was particularly vexed with Tanya, then twenty, though she was the most gifted and levelheaded of the children. On the evening of March 30, he joined the family for tea but found them all "so repulsive, pathetic and degrading to listen to, especially the poor, mentally sick, Tanya" that he took to bed.[18]

He was disappointed in his two elder sons. "Among my children," he wrote Strakhov, "there will be no one to carry on my work."

> If I were a carpenter, my sons would be beside me at my bench. . . . Alas, it is exactly the opposite. One of my sons [Sergei] is finishing his studies at the university and wants to be a civil servant. The other [Ilya] will be a soldier, and his head is already turned by shoulder bars. The third—but what is the good talking about them? . . . Neither the third nor the fourth nor my daughter will follow the same path as I. . . . It would have been better for me to have had no children at all.[19]

He seemed obsessed with the idea that Tanya was becoming much too worldly, though he complained that the rest of the family was bad enough in this regard.

As his second daughter, Masha, grew up, she became Tolstoy's favorite child. "I feel great tenderness towards her," he wrote in his diary. "Her only. She makes up for the others, I might say."

Gradually, Masha assumed the role of secretary and copier of his manuscripts. These tasks had previously been the exclusive preserve of Sonya, who more and more resented being replaced by her daughter.

"I used to be the one to copy out everything he wrote," she lamented in her diary on November 20, 1890. "Now he carefully conceals everything and gives it to his daughter instead." The very thought drives Sonya into another fit of utter despair.

> He is systematically destroying me by driving me out of his life this way. There are times in this useless life of mine when I am overwhelmed with violent despair and long to kill myself, run away, fall in love with someone else. I now see . . . there is nothing in him but sensuality . . . and I see that my life is destroyed. . . . My God! he is always so unfriendly, so querulous and so artificial. . . .

A few days later, Sonya again confides to her diary her ill feeling toward her daughter. She suspects Masha has fallen in love with Pavel Biryukov, a disciple and helper of Tolstoy. At first, she violently opposes it. She says she can hardly wait until Biryukov leaves. But on the other hand:

> Sometimes I feel like letting Masha go. Why hold on to her? Let her go with Biryukov, then I can take her place beside Lyovochka. I shall do his copying and put his affairs in order.[20]

Her first diary entry for 1891 finds her still obsessed with Masha, who has become, she writes, "the most terrible cross God has sent me to bear. She has given me nothing but pain from the moment she was born."[21]

On April 4, Tolstoy woke up with a toothache and a fever and was in bad sorts. That evening, he records in his diary, he worked until one A.M. making some boots. But his mind was on the difficulties he was having with the whole family.

> It's very depressing in the family. Depressing, because I can't sympathize with them. All their joys, social success, music, furniture, shopping—I consider them all a misfortune and evil for them, and I can't tell them so. I can and do speak, but my words don't get through to them. . . . I'm surprised at their ruthlessness. They must surely see that for three years now I've not only suffered but been cut off from life. I've been assigned the role of a querulous old man. . . .

Next day, he says, he gets up feeling "jaded and sad, particularly at the sight of everyone at home. . . . Their madness is astonishing." On April 9, he notes that he began to "reprimand Tanya and was angry." Later in the day, he concludes that he ought to ask Tanya's forgiveness but can't quite make up his mind to do so. On the twenty-fourth, he bemoans in his diary: "Why can't I talk to the children, to Tanya?" He is so miserable that he keeps telling his diary he wants to die. "I long for real death," he says, and repeats it three times during the middle of the month.

His greatest despair, however, is not so much over the children as over his wife. When Sonya breaks in on a conversation he is having in his study with Strakhov, he is wildly indignant. "A mad and senseless interruption," he calls it. He tries to talk to his eldest son, Sergei, now twenty-one, but finds him "impossibly obtuse. The same castrated mind that his mother has."[22] After a further conversation with his son, he notes, "He's just like his mother, malicious and unfeeling." On May 3, he receives a letter from his wife, who had gone to the country for a few days. "Poor woman, how she hates me," he writes in his diary. Two nights later he records that he "dreamed that my wife loves me. . . . Nothing like that in real life. And it's that which is ruining my life. I'm not even trying to write. It would be good to die."

Then, on June 18, with the family back at Yasnaya Polyana, came a terrible blowup. Tolstoy became so incensed with Sonya after a petty quarrel that, despite knowing that she was due to give birth that day or the next to their twelfth child, for the first time in his life he fled from his home.

(Sonya had not wanted to have the child. She thought eleven pregnancies were enough. And since her husband had taken to proclaiming that sex, even between husband and wife, was a sin, she thought they would be open to ridicule if they had another child. So she decided for the first time in her life to have an abortion. Unbeknownst to her husband, she drove to Tula to have it done by a midwife there. But when the woman learned that she was Countess Tolstoy, she became flustered and declined to do the abortion. Sonya then tried to do it herself, taking scorching hot baths and jumping to the floor from the top of her dresser. But nothing worked.)

On the evening of June 18, as the whole family, including the Kuzminskys—Sonya's sister Tanya and her husband and children—was gathered around the big dining room table at Yasnaya Polyana, a dispute suddenly arose over some horses that Tolstoy wanted to sell. It was a trivial enough subject but, as is sometimes the case in family life, a huge quarrel burst forth from nothing. According to Tolstoy, Sonya reproached him for the way he took care of the horses. Many of them on the Samara estate, she reminded him, had died of neglect. His anger and resentment growing with every word of reproach, he finally got up and left the room without saying another word, packed a rucksack, stalked out of the house, and lit out on foot on the road to Tula, eight miles away, turning to yell to the family that he was going to America to start a new life.

Shortly after, Sonya's labor pains began. Her children tried to put her to bed but she refused, sitting on a chair in the garden waiting, she said, until her husband returned. Finally, her son Ilya carried her to bed. Just as the labor pains resumed, Tolstoy suddenly appeared out of the night. Halfway to Tula he had calmed down and had second thoughts. What was he doing, abandoning his wife at the very moment she was giving birth to their child? He turned back, but on approaching the house he flinched at the prospect of seeing his hateful wife. His daughter Tanya greeted him.

"Don't you want to see Mother?" she asked.

"No. I don't want to see her," he replied irritably, and made off to his study where he said he would sleep the rest of the night on the couch. Sometime after two A.M., Tolstoy noted in an account he gave in his diary of June 18, his wife somehow got out of bed and came and woke him up, saying: "Please forgive me. I'm in labor. Perhaps I'll die." Tolstoy said nothing, but helped her back to the bedroom and watched for a moment while her labor pains began again.

A few hours later Sonya gave birth to her twelfth child, Alexandra, whom the family quickly called Sasha and who would play a strange role in the last act of the family tragedy and then—after many ordeals, including arrest by the Bolsheviks—make her way to America and a new career over a long, long life.

If Tolstoy felt any remorse about his behavior he did not show it. Instead, he found fault with his wife for her whole attitude toward having the child. "Why is the most joyful and happy event in a family passed off like something unnecessary and depressing," he noted in his diary. . . . "If anyone governs the affairs of our lives, I would like to reproach [him]. It is all too difficult and heartless. Heartless where she is concerned. I can see that she is heading with increasing speed toward destruction and terrible mental suffering."

He concluded: "A wet-nurse has been engaged to feed the baby." To the husband this was a cardinal sin. He had objected strenuously to it with the first baby even though the doctors had insisted on it. Through twelve pregnancies, he had not changed his mind. Not to breast-feed your child at birth was a step toward perdition.

To let off steam, he wrote a friend about it.

> My wife has given birth to a little girl. But my joy has been
> poisoned by the fact that my wife, despite my clearly stated
> opinion that to hire a wet nurse away from her child to feed a
> stranger is a most inhuman, unreasonable, and un-Christian act,
> nevertheless and without any reason took a wet nurse from her
> living child. All this happens somehow without our understand-
> ing . . . I wrestle with myself, but it's hard. I am sorry for my
> wife.[23]

To add insult to injury, Tolstoy asked his wife to copy this
letter. She mentioned it in her diary: "The martyrdom was mine,
not his."

So the birth of Alexandra drove the parents still further apart.
Recapitulating in his diary the month of June, Tolstoy wrote, "I
can't say the break with my wife is any worse, but it's complete."

To his brother Sergei, who had come to Yasnaya Polyana to
congratulate him and Sonya on the birth of another child, Tolstoy
confided the extent of his rift with his wife, noting in his diary: "I
told him for the first time in my life the whole gravity of the situation."

It did not improve as the summer days went by. Sonya, still ill
from complications that followed the birth of Alexandra, and resentful of her husband's outrage at her not nursing the child, was
irritable. And he continued to find her most difficult. He kept noting in his diary her shortcomings and how she made him suffer:

> June 23: My wife is very calm and contented and can't see
> the complete break between us.
> June 24: Dreamed about going to France.
> June 26: My wife was glad of a chance to censure and abuse
> me.
> July 3: Sonya is capricious and is always talking about
> herself. It's a terrible torture.

On July 7, he noted, he came back to the house and had the
"misfortune" to speak about "nonstop tea drinking." Ever since his
conversion, he had felt that there was too much tea drinking by his
frivolous family. This time there was another scene and the famous

writer says he stalked out of the room. He had begun to feel, he says, that Sonya was trying to patch things up by tempting him with her body. A strange charge from a husband who, despite all his recent ravings against intimate relations between spouses, could hardly wait to resume them so soon after her confinement.

> She's beginning to tempt me carnally. I'd like to refrain, but I feel I won't in present conditions. But cohabitation with a woman who is a stranger to you—i.e. with her—is terribly vile.
> I'd just written this when she came to my room and started a hysterical scene—the sense of it being that nothing had changed, and she is unhappy and she must run away somewhere. I was sorry for her, but at the same time I was aware that it was hopeless. Until the day I die she will remain a mill-stone around my neck and around the children's. . . . I must learn not to drown with a mill-stone around my neck.[24]

During the night of July 12, he tells his diary, he went to her but she turned him down. There were, he says, "harsh words" between them. "I don't understand," he wrote, "how to save myself from suffering, and her from the destruction to which she is flying headlong." He adds that he prayed, but that he realized it was because he was so weak.

Two nights later, he asked his wife to come to his bed "and she refused with cold spitefulness and the desire to hurt me." In vain, she tried to tell him that it was too soon—it was less than a month since the baby had come, and there had been complications, which he knew about. The master of Yasnaya Polyana was so angry, he says, that he couldn't sleep "all night."

Result: He determined for a second time in a month to clear out and abandon his family. He had had enough. He says he packed his things and decided this time he would tell her he was leaving.

> I got ready to go away and went to wake her up. I don't know what was the matter with me—bitterness, lust, moral exhaustion—but I suffered terribly. She got up, and I told her everything, told her that she had ceased to be my wife. A helpmate for her husband? She hadn't helped me for a long time but had only hindered me. A mother to my children? She doesn't want to be. A nurse? She doesn't want to be.

He still couldn't get over his wrath that she had not nursed the child. He had one more shortcoming of Sonya's to note and it was the worst: "A companion of my nights?" he asked, and answered: "She provokes me and makes it into a game."

"I was wrong not to go away," he concludes. "I think it will happen sooner or later."

Later maybe, but not sooner. On August 9, these two mercurial individuals agreed to make up. "Came home. Sonya and I were reconciled. How glad I was. Actually if *she* were to take it upon herself to be good, she would be very good."

It was a big "if." A month later, on September 5, he encountered in Sonya, he reported, "unexpected malice. Later she came down to my room and nagged at me until she was beside herself. . . . She ran out in hysterics. I ran after her. I'm terribly exhausted."

The year before, in 1883, Tolstoy met and formed a strange friendship with a younger man who would become his devoted disciple, exert an immense influence over him in the remaining twenty-seven years of his life, turn out to be the nemesis of Sonya, and do his best to wreck her marriage, so that the closing years of the Tolstoys' lives became a hell on earth. To the deadly conflict between Tolstoy and his wife was added a murderous strife between his wife and this man.

His name was Vladimir Grigoryevich Chertkov.

# TEN

# The Advent of Chertkov

CHERTKOV CAME from the highest social circle in Petersburg. His father, who was very rich, was a general and aide-de-camp to Tsars Alexander II and III. His mother was a close friend of the Empress Marya Fyodorovna. Vladimir Chertkov himself—tall, slim, and handsome, with a finely chiseled aquiline nose[1]—had graduated from the military academy and become an officer in the elite horse guards. Like Tolstoy in his youth, he had led a dissolute life. Like Tolstoy too, he had undergone a conversion and had resigned from the guards and retired to one of his family estates to set up schools, libraries, and clinics for the peasants.

His mother, despite her high station, had abandoned the Orthodox faith to become a disciple of Lord Radstock, the English evangelical preacher, and her son had followed her. To strengthen his new faith, his mother had sent him to England, where he spent most of his time with the evangelicals of Radstock. Already fluent in English, he lived like a country gentleman in England and, though genuinely interested in bettering the lot of the poor, he joined numerous upper-class clubs and associations. Later, he would spend a long exile in England. But on this first trip, despite his religious zeal, he became somewhat disillusioned with British Protestantism. He wanted more. He sought something that would give purpose to his life and enable him to devote himself wholeheartedly to good works, to helping the poor and the oppressed.

Returning to Russia in 1880, he began to read Tolstoy. The final chapters of *Anna Karenina* moved him to tears. When he turned to Tolstoy's religious works, especially *Confession*, he felt that he had found the inspiration to begin a new life. Through friends he arranged to meet the Master.

They met in Tolstoy's home in Moscow in the fall of 1883. They took to each other at once. Tolstoy was fifty-five, Chertkov just turned thirty. Within a few months they had become close, intimate friends. In Chertkov, Tolstoy had found a fanatical follower. In Tolstoy, Chertkov had found the god he was searching for. Six months after their first meeting, the great writer noted in his diary: "He and I are amazingly one." By this time—so soon!— Tolstoy was confiding to his young friend the most intimate details of his marital and family life.*

Declaring that he wanted to tell Chertkov about himself, he wrote: "I would like to say that I'm happy and cheerful, but I cannot . . . I feel miserable." The life around him, he said, he "found repulsive."[2] On July 24, 1884, a little more than seven months after their meeting, Tolstoy wrote Chertkov from Yasnaya Polyana that he wanted to tell him something that happened to him that he hadn't "told anybody yet." He had been, he said, tempted "by the flesh," apparently by a peasant woman. He arranged a secret rendezvous with her and one day set out to keep it, a "loathsome thing" to do but he said he could not help it. As he left the house for the assignation, his son Ilya called out to him and reminded him that he had promised to give him a lesson at that very hour. "I came to my senses and didn't keep the appointment." God saved him, he said.

In the same letter Tolstoy confided to Chertkov an experience he had "lying in bed" with his wife.

> She wasn't asleep, nor was I, and I suffered painfully from the awareness of my own loneliness in the family because of my beliefs, and the fact that they all in my eyes seek the truth but turn away from it. I suffered both for them and for myself.

"Being sad and miserable," he continued, "I began to pray to God to touch my wife's heart."

> She fell asleep . . . and suddenly it occurred to me that I suffer because my wife doesn't share my convictions.

* Tolstoy and Chertkov exchanged nearly a thousand letters in all.

He admitted to Chertkov that when his wife "nagged and vexed" him, he often spoke "coldly, even in an unfriendly manner" to her.

> Not only have I never entreated her with tears to believe in the truth, but I have never even expressed to her all my thoughts lovingly and gently; yet there she is lying by my side, and I say nothing to her, and what ought to be said to her I say to God.

No wonder that the zealous disciple began to wonder about the Master's wife and whether she was fit to be married to the great man he worshiped.

Chertkov considered himself to be a disciple of the Master. But a unique disciple. He soon made himself the high priest of the Tolstoyan movement, the custodian of its purity, from which he would not allow even the Master himself to deviate one inch. He began to take over the object of his devotion.

How was this possible? Those who knew Chertkov were not surprised. For though Tolstoy was blind to his follower's darker traits of character, others were not. They knew Chertkov as an arrogant, imperious, pompous, ambitious, humorless tyrant. They knew him also to be deceitful and rude. There was something sinister about the man.

How could such a person win Tolstoy's complete confidence and inspire such an intimate relationship, inspire even a passionately expressed love? For Sonya's later charge that her husband had fallen in love with Chertkov is borne out by one of Tolstoy's letters to his young friend. On November 7, 1884, just a year after they'd first met, Tolstoy wrote him: "I would like to live with you and, if we are still alive, I shall live with you. Never cease to love me as I love you."

Sergei, Tolstoy's eldest son, cited two reasons for what he called "the exceptional feeling of my father for Chertkov." First, the alienation that Tolstoy felt from his wife and children after his conversion had left him with a feeling of great loneliness. He no longer had anyone close at hand to converse with about the new aspirations of his life. Chertkov promised to fill that void. Second, the older man took to him because he found that they had much in common: a yearning to understand God, the truth, and the meaning of life and death; contempt for aristocratic society and the authority of an autocratic, oppressive government; and a readiness to suffer for their convictions.[3]

Within a year of their meeting Tolstoy and Chertkov set up a publishing house called the Intermediary to issue inexpensive books of uplift for the masses, especially those of Tolstoy. This was a project dear to Tolstoy's heart, and thanks to Chertkov's organizing abilities and his drive, the venture was an immediate success. Within six years the company had sold twenty million copies at five kopecks apiece. Besides the works of the Master himself, those by other writers, foreign as well as Russian, were selected. Several novels by Dickens, Tolstoy's favorite English author, appeared.

In the beginning Sonya took a liking to Chertkov. She had a dim view of most Tolstoyans because they were unwashed, smelly, dirty, and slovenly. But here was a convert who was clean, rich, educated, and from the highest society. Besides, Chertkov seemed to be an attractive young man, handsome, well-mannered, and intelligent. But this favorable opinion did not last very long. Within a year she began to see that a rival had crept under the roof and was threatening her place in the house in more ways than one.

In publishing, for one thing. In 1884 she had finally wrung from a reluctant husband permission to publish his collected works. Since he had abandoned fiction writing, the income of the Tolstoys had tumbled. And the expense of a second home in Moscow had become burdensome. By bringing out Tolstoy's complete works, Sonya hoped to restore their financial situation and also to revive Tolstoy's name as a writer. She consulted the widow of Dostoyevsky, who had just brought out an edition of her husband's complete works. Then she borrowed twenty-five thousand rubles* from relatives and friends and set up business in a shed near their Moscow home. Soon the books began coming off the press and the money began to come in. Mrs. Dostoyevsky had told Sonya that she netted sixty-seven thousand rubles in two years. Sonya did even better: fifty thousand rubles† the first year.

Her husband was not pleased. Since his conversion he had regarded making money from his writing as sinful. In contrast to his materialistic wife, Chertkov was publishing his works without

* Approximately $253,125 today.
† Approximately $506,250 today.

making a speck of profit. That increased his admiration for his disciple and diminished that for Sonya and her publishing venture. Countess Tolstoy began to resent Chertkov, who she felt was coming between her and Leo. When she realized that the disciple was also taking over the Master, she became alarmed. She may have lost the love of her husband but she was still his wife, the manager of his estates, the publisher of his complete works, the mother of his children. She would not give up her place in his life to a pompous interloper without a fight. By the middle of 1885, she saw that the struggle for Leo Tolstoy would not be easy, for their incompatibility had reached such a stage that Tolstoy, in despair, was again threatening to leave her.

As Christmas approached that year, Sonya told of it in a letter to her sister Tanya.

> He came in while I was writing and I saw that his face was terrible. . . . "I have come to tell you that I want to separate from you. I cannot live like this, I shall go to Paris or America."

"What has happened?" Sonya said she asked. "He began shouting reproaches, coarse words, everything worse and worse. When he said, 'Wherever you are, the air is contaminated,' I ordered a trunk brought to me and I began to pack."

Now they were both threatening to leave. It was an ugly scene. Sonya said the four children, Tanya, Ilya, "little Lev and Masha," gathered around them and began to howl. Finally, she reported to her sister, her husband calmed down and begged her to stay. "So," she concluded, "it came to an end."[4]

But it didn't come to an end.

Tolstoy retired to his study and began to write his wife a letter in which he would describe and sum up the calamitous relations between them, as he saw them, lay down ways of making them tolerable again, and warn that if Sonya did not accept them, the only thing left would be a fight to the death. Dated Moscow, December 15–18, 1885, it is a long, repetitive, and agonizing letter—full of contradictions—and extremely egotistical. But it attempts, however one-sidedly, to get to the heart of their troubles.

> For the last 7 or 8 years all our conversations have ended after many painful torments in the same way. . . . I said: there

can be no agreement and no loving life between us until you come to what I have come to, either from love for me . . . or from conviction, and then we can go along together. I said: until *you* come to me. I didn't say: until *I* come to you, because it is impossible for me. . . . But you can try to come to something you haven't yet known. . . . I mean in general terms a life devoted to God and to other people, and not to one's own pleasures.

He repeated this argument several times in the next pages, stopping to admonish Sonya to please try to understand what he was writing. "For goodness sake, don't say this is madness. My darling, for the sake of all that is holy, listen calmly to what I am going to say. For goodness sake, contain yourself and read this calmly." And he kept harping on his change of life and how thereafter he had to live by the precepts of the Gospel and how the failure of his wife and children to understand this caused him such suffering.

"I can't help suffering, living the life we live." Whether it was in Moscow or Yasnaya Polyana, it made no difference.

The new life in Moscow has been an agony for me, the like of which I have never experienced in all my life. . . . It was no better in the country. The same disregard of me, not only by you but by our children.

The sheer unreasonableness of the great writer, now that he was letting his hair down, kept coming out. And the hypocrisy!

You reproached *me* for not bothering about money matters and the upbringing of our children, as though I could bother about money and the increase or preservation of my fortune, in order to increase or preserve the very evil from which, in my view, my children were coming to grief . . . or could bother about their upbringing, the aim of which was pride, separation from other people, worldly education and diplomas—the very things I knew to be the ruin of people.

There remained, Tolstoy informed his wife, three "choices" for them, but after stating them he rejected them all. The first was to give up his property "to those it belonged to—the workers," but this would arouse the "malice and anger" of his family. Second, "to leave the family"—but that would mean he had to give up trying to save the children. As for leaving his wife, that would be breaking "God's commandment." Third, to go on living as they had, but this would make him "suffer twice over from life and remorse."

"Is this really necessary?" he asked Sonya as he neared the end of his letter. "Is it necessary to live in these agonizing conditions until death? It isn't far away now." How terrible it would be, he said, for him to die full of reproaches for his wife, and how awful for her, left with the feeling that she could have avoided causing him such painful suffering. He could not refrain in the final pages of his letter from getting off his chest another reason for his suffering. Sonya and the children, he charged, had never appreciated him as a writer. For Sonya, who had hand-copied all his manuscripts, discussed them with him, and only recently begun to republish them with loving care, this would be the unkindest cut of all. Had she not for years urged and nagged him to return to writing novels because that was where his genius lay? Still, Tolstoy insisted:

> All my works, which have been nothing more or less than my life, have been and are of so little interest to you that when you come across them you read them out of curiosity, like works of literature, while the children are not interested in reading them at all. You think I am one thing and my writing another. But my writing is the whole of my life.

In the last page the wounded writer repeated once more:

> All our disagreements have been caused by the fateful mistake 8 years ago whereby you regarded the revolution that had taken place in me . . . as something unnatural, fortuitous, temporary, fantastic, one-sided, which there was no need to understand, but which you needed to struggle against with all your might. For 8 years you struggled, and the result is that I suffer more than ever.

And then as the letter came to an end:

> You attribute what has happened to everything except the one thing, that you are the unwitting, unintentional cause of my sufferings. A struggle to the death is going on between us.

Tolstoy did not hand Sonya the letter; perhaps he did not dare to. He left it for her on his desk as he was leaving with his daughter Tanya to spend a few days in the country. Sonya discovered it soon enough and, according to Marya, one of her daughters, she insisted on reading it to the children. On the margin she scribbled: "A letter from Leo Nikolayevich to his wife, neither given nor sent to her."

She seemed to be still in a state of shock from reading the letter when she wrote him on December 22. She wanted to appear caring but could not hide her resentment.

"I would give anything to know how you are," she began amiably. Then:

> But I'm afraid to touch these painful wounds which are not only unhealed but, it seems to me, have started to bleed again. . . . I am happy to think that away from me your shattered nerves have been calmed. . . . Give the Olsufyevs all my blessings. . . . You are comfortable with them. You don't hate and condemn them as you do me.

Two days later, on Christmas Eve, Tolstoy in his reply turned the other cheek. "I see how badly I've wronged you," he wrote. "The moment I understood this and expelled from me all sorts of imaginary grievances, and resurrected my love for you and Sergei, I felt well again."

Sometimes a sudden sorrow, shared, brought them close again. Shortly into the new year, on January 18, 1886, their youngest son, Alexei, four and a half years old, died of quinsy after an agonizing day and night of fighting for breath. Sonya was devastated.

"Can your heart imagine my sorrow?" she wrote her sister Tanya. "I buried Alyosha today."

The father reacted somewhat differently. He wrote to Chertkov that the death of the child, which he once would have thought incomprehensible and unjust, now seemed reasonable and just. It did, he added, improve relations with his wife. "Through this death," he wrote his disciple, "we have been united in a closer and deeper affection than before."

But as so often with the Tolstoys as the years went by, the feelings of love and affection did not last long. By the autumn of 1886, Sonya was again writing in her diary of her despair, cursing her husband for his treatment of her.[5]

> My God, how often I long to abandon it all and take my life. I am so tired of living, struggling and suffering. The egotism and the unconscious malice of the people one loves most is very great indeed! Why do I carry on despite all this? . . . I can't do what my husband wants (so he says) without breaking all the practical and emotional claims that have bound me to my family. Day and night I think only of how to leave this house, leave this life, leave all this cruelty, these excessive demands on me.

For the first time in her life, she feared she was losing her mind. "Last night I caught myself thinking aloud, and I was terrified that I might be going mad!"

In August of that year Tolstoy had persuaded his wife and children to join him in the fields and help with the harvest. He had fallen off a hay wagon and hurt his foot. When it became infected and turned to periostitis, he was forced to take to bed, where he remained until October, at times fearing he was near to death. Sonya nursed him day and night for three months and said she loved every minute of it. It was the one thing she felt she could do well.

Was the bearded lord of Yasnaya Polyana grateful? "Now that he is on his feet again," Sonya continued in her diary that October day, "and almost well, he has given me to understand that he no longer needs me."

> So on the one hand I have been discarded like a useless object, and on the other impossible, undefined sacrifices are demanded of me and I am expected to renounce everything, all my property, all my beliefs, the education and well-being of my children. . . . The children criticize me for opposing their father and they too ask for as much as they can get. . . . Oh, to leave it all behind—I *shall* leave, somehow or other. I have neither the strength nor the love for all this labor and struggle.

For the first time in her diary, Sonya sounded absolutely desperate, as if, at forty-two, she had given up on life. And for the first time she began to feel that her husband and children were driving her insane.

# ELEVEN

# The Kreutzer Sonata

$A$LL THROUGH that year of 1886, despite the turmoil in his household, Tolstoy was experiencing a burst of writing, and Sonya, despite her bitter resentments, was busy making legible copies for the printer of all he wrote. And for the first time in years, to Sonya's joy, Tolstoy was writing not only a philosophical and sociological tract but works of fiction: a long short story that many have felt was one of the most moving he ever wrote—a minor masterpiece—and a play that while surely not a masterpiece was a searing, haunting drama of the dark, brutal side of peasant life. It is still produced in Russia and the outside world.

The sociological piece—*What Then Must We Do?*—which he had struggled for years to finish, was inspired by his shock at observing the poverty-stricken sections of Moscow. The sixteen-room house he eventually bought for the family in the city, though luxurious itself, was situated in the midst of a factory district that included a distillery, a hosiery mill, a brewery, and a spinning mill. There Tolstoy could hear the factory whistles calling the workers, many of whom were children, for their fifteen-hour day of labor, and he could listen to the workers, most of them peasants who had been lured to the city, tell of their wage slavery and the hopelessness of their lives. But his most haunting experience had come the year he served as a volunteer census taker in the most run-down quarter of Moscow, a miserable place full of prostitutes, pimps, drunks, and beggars, all living in the stench of verminous flophouses. Tolstoy had never forgotten the experience, and now in

*What Then Must We Do?* he was describing it as only he, with his literary genius, could. And this led him to the core of the book: the spectacle of abject poverty existing side by side with the luxuries and privileges of the rich. It had to stop, the writer demanded. Poverty had to be done away with.

If it was not, he wrote in a conclusion that was more prophetic than even he realized, there would come in Russia "a workers' revolution with horrors and destruction and murder." It came only seven years after Tolstoy's death.

The short story he wrote that year was *The Death of Ivan Ilyich* and it showed that, at fifty-seven, despite abandoning fiction for ten years, ever since *Anna Karenina,* in order to concentrate on his religious, philosophical, and sociological booklets, his artistic powers were undiminished.

Tchaikovsky thought the story magnificent, confiding in his diary: "I read *The Death of Ivan Ilich.* More than ever I am convinced that the greatest author-painter who ever lived is Leo Tolstoy." And a Russian-born French biographer of Tolstoy, Henri Troyat, a sharp critic of some of the Master's writing, believed that "beyond any doubt, this double story of the decomposing body and awakening soul is one of the most powerful works in the literature of the world."

It is also an exposé of the dull and superficial world of the Russian bureaucrat (Ivan Ilyich was a judge) with its false ideas of worldly success, and other stupidities. Nothing that Tolstoy wrote in his innumerable philosophical brochures equals it in its mordant criticism of the shallowness of modern middle-class life—but also in its portrayal of the possibility of redemption for, in the end, Ivan Ilyich, after a long and terrible illness, sees the emptiness of his past life and bravely confronts God and death.

It is ironic that Tolstoy, who extolled the virtues of the peasants and tried to dress and live like them, should write in *The Power of Darkness* a drama that shows them living in filth, degradation, and flagrant sin. There is deceit, hate, envy, cruelty, adultery, two murders among them. There is little decency or humaneness in any of the characters. But the play is gripping.

Tsar Alexander III and the Empress, after listening to a private reading, liked it and asked the royal theaters in Petersburg and Moscow to produce it. But the all-powerful Pobyedonostsev took an opposing view. He found Tolstoy's play an offense to morals and good taste. "Even Zola," he wrote the Tsar, "never reached this level of vulgar and brutal realism." On reading this report, the weak-minded Tsar had second thoughts. He now found the play "disgusting." "This ignominious L. N. Tolstoy," he wrote his minister, "must be stopped. He is nothing but a nihilist and a nonbeliever." And he forbade its performance in any theater in Russia.

Early in a long entry in her diary for November 20, 1890, Sonya wrote: "Lyovochka has broken off all relations with me. Why? What can the reason be?" A few lines later she records something that would seem to answer her question though she is unaware of it.

> I secretly read his diaries in the hope of discovering how I could help him and myself. . . . He must have discovered that I was reading them, for he started hiding them away.

As her diary makes clear, he began to resent her snooping. This was a new issue between them that would further poison their relations until, in the end, more than anything else, it brought on the final act in the tragedy of their lives.

Actually, Tolstoy had never before objected to Sonya's reading his diaries, and he had always read hers. It had been from the beginning a form of communication between them. When one had a gripe against the other, they would often prefer to note it in their diaries, knowing that the other would read it. But now suddenly Tolstoy had begun to resent it. How could one, he said, honestly and frankly record his inner life if someone else was looking over his shoulder—or behind his back—to see what he wrote?

That seemed reasonable enough. It was a feeling most diarists share. But Sonya saw other motives for his wanting her to cease copying his diaries. "Lyovochka is beginning to worry about me copying out his diaries. He would like to destroy the old diaries, as he wants to appear before his children and the public as a patriarchal figure. Still the same old vanity!"

Years later, on March 27, 1895, Tolstoy explained in his diary why he would like to destroy his early entries. This entry, he said, was a testament of his wishes which he would later formalize in a will.

> The diaries of my former bachelor life I ask you to destroy, after selecting from what is worth in it, and in the diaries of my married life I ask you to destroy everything which, if published, might be unpleasant for anybody.

Tolstoy then gives his reasons.

> The diaries of my bachelor life I ask you to destroy, not because I would like to conceal from people my own bad life . . . but because these diaries, in which I only wrote down what tormented me through the awareness of my sins, produce a false one-sided impression.

Having written that, he immediately had second thoughts. "But no," he writes, "let my diaries stand as they are. At least they will show that despite all the triviality and worthlessness of my youth, I was still not abandoned by God."

It did not help matters that Sonya sometimes came across entries in later sections of his diary that shocked and embittered her.

> I copied Lyovochka's diaries up to the part where he wrote: "There is no such thing as love, only the physical need for intercourse and the practical need for a life's companion." I only wish I had read that remark twenty years ago, then I would not have married him.[1]

On February 12 of the following year, Sonya returned to the subject in her diary. "I've been copying out Leo's diary," she noted. "He took it away from me this evening. He has told me several times that he did not like me to copy it out."

Later:

> Lyovochka has virtually forbidden me to copy out his diaries, and I am furious. . . . I shall go on with it while he's not looking.

Inevitably a quarrel ensued. Sonya described it in her diary.

> Today he brought it up again and said I didn't realize how much I was hurting him; he wanted to destroy the diaries—how

Tolstoy's father, Nikolai Ilyich Tolstoy. 1820. Unknown artist. Watercolor.

Leo Tolstoy. St. Petersburg. 1849. From a daguerreotype by V. Shenfeldt.

Leo Tolstoy. Moscow, 1854. From a daguerreotype.

*Opposite top*, Sonya Tolstoy. 1863. Shortly after her marriage.

*Opposite bottom*, Tatyana Andreyevna Behrs, Sonya's sister. 1862. Time of Sonya's marriage. *Photo courtesy of M. B. Tulinov.*

*Left*, Leo Tolstoy. Moscow. 1878–79. *Photo courtesy of M. M. Panov.*

*Opposite top*, Leo Tolstoy on horseback in the yard of the house in Moscow. 1898.

*Opposite bottom*, Leo Tolstoy skating in the garden of the Moscow house. 1898. Next to him are the children of Tolstoy's cook. *Two photos courtesy of Sonya Tolstoy.*

*Below*, Sonya Tolstoy with the younger children. From left to right: Andrei, Mikhail, Alexandra, and Vanechka. Moscow, 1892. *From the Tolstoy Museum, Moscow.*

*Left*, Leo Tolstoy and Maxim Gorky at Yasnaya Polyana. November 8, 1900.

*Opposite top*, Sonya Tolstoy (in the middle) with her children at Gaspra. From left to right: Ilya, Andrei, Tatyana, Leo, Mikhail, Marya, Sergei, Alexandra. 1902.

*Opposite bottom*, Leo and Sonya Tolstoy in the study of the Yasnaya Polyana house. 1907.

*Below*, Leo and Sonya Tolstoy on the balcony of Countess S. V. Panin's country house at Gaspra in the Crimea. 1902. He was recovering from a severe illness. *Four photos courtesy of Sonya Tolstoy.*

*Opposite top*, dinner in Yasnaya Polyana in front of the house. 1908. From left to right: Dr. Dushan Makovitsky, Alexandra Tolstoy, Elizabeth Obolensky (Tolstoy's niece), Vladimir Chertkov, Leo Tolstoy, Sonya Tolstoy, grandson Misha (Mikhailovich) Tolstoy with a governess, Nikolai Gusev, Varya Feokritov. In the background—servants.

*Opposite bottom*, Leo Tolstoy's bedroom in Yasnaya Polyana. 1908.

*Below*, Sonya Tolstoy's bedroom in Yasnaya Polyana. 1908. *Three photos courtesy of K. K. Bulla.*

*Opposite left,* Leo Tolstoy riding Délire in Yasnaya Polyana. 1908. *Photo courtesy of K. K. Bulla.*

*Opposite bottom,* Leo Tolstoy and Vladimir Chertkov in the study in Yasnaya Polyana. 1909.

*Below,* Leo Tolstoy playing a game of skittles at Yasnaya Polyana, at the age of eighty-one. 1909. *Two photos courtesy of V. G. Chertkov.*

*Above,* the last photograph of Leo Nikolayevich and Sonya Andreyevna Tolstoy, taken on their forty-eighth wedding anniversary. Yasnaya Polyana, September 24, 1910. It is also the last photo of Tolstoy alive. *Photo courtesy of Sonya Tolstoy.*

*Opposite top,* the Astapovo station of the Ryazan-Ural railroad. 1910. Tolstoy, fleeing from his wife and too ill to continue his journey, was taken off the train here and put up in the stationmaster's cottage across the tracks, where he died a few days later. *Photo courtesy of S. G. Smirnov.*

*Opposite bottom,* Sonya Tolstoy standing on tiptoe, trying to catch a glimpse of her dying husband through his bedroom window in the stationmaster's house at Astapovo. She was denied permission by her children and the doctors to see him until a couple of hours before he died, after he had lost consciousness. November 7, 1910. *From the Tolstoy Museum, Moscow.*

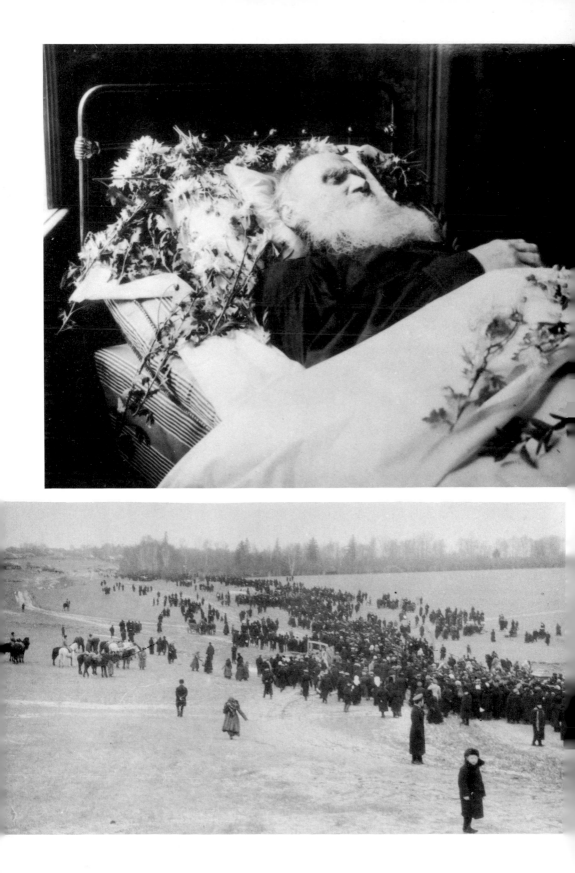

*Left,* Leo Tolstoy on his deathbed. Astapovo. November 7, 1910.

*Opposite below,* Burial of Leo Tolstoy. Procession on the road from the Zasyeka station to Yasnaya Polyana. November 9, 1910. *Two photos courtesy A. I. Savelyev.*

*Below,* Leo Tolstoy's open coffin is carried by his sons from the stationmaster's cottage across the tracks to the railroad station at Astapovo. November 8, 1910. *Photo courtesy of C. F. Smirnov.*

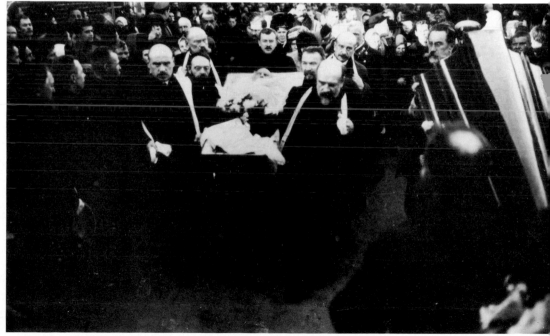

Leo Tolstoy's burial. Peasants' carts with wreaths. *Photo courtesy of A. I. Savelyev.*

would *I* like to be constantly reminded of everything that tormented me, and every bad deed. He said much more besides, to which I replied that if it all sounded so painful I was not a bit sorry for him, and if he wanted to burn his diaries, let him; but if one were to say which of us caused the other more pain, then it was he, for he hurt me *so* deeply when he published his last story to the entire world that it would be hard for us ever to be quits.[2]

She meant his long story, or novella, *The Kreutzer Sonata.** It is a hysterical diatribe against women and marriage—even against marital love and sex—and against having children, and against much else he didn't like. It is really a thinly disguised story of Tolstoy's marriage, of his life with Sonya. That the great writer and moralist should reveal to the world the most intimate details of his marital life and tell of his bitter resentment of his wife and children shocked many Russians and threw Sonya into the greatest despair of her life. She felt utterly humiliated. Her diary of February 12 describes it.

> I do not know how or why [but of course she did] everyone connected *The Kreutzer Sonata* with our own married life but this is what happened, and now everyone from the Tsar down to Leo Nikolayevich's brother and his best friend Dyakov feel sorry for me. And it isn't just other people—I too know from my heart that this story is directed against me, and it has done me great wrong, humiliated me in the eyes of the world and destroyed the last vestige of love between us.
>
> Today I decided at last to let Leo Nikolayevich know my feelings about *The Kreutzer Sonata.*

She did, and another quarrel ensued. "It is so painful," Tolstoy wrote in his diary two days later. "I spoke irritably to her and infested her with my irritation. Then I stopped thinking of myself and thought of her and we affectionately made it up."

Sonya confirmed it in *her* diary the day before. "Yesterday's discussion depressed me deeply, but it ended with a reconciliation, and we agreed to try to live the rest of our lives as peacefully and amicably as we could."

* It runs to ninety-eight pages in my edition.

It was an agreement that, strive though they might—and they did—they were simply by this stage of their lives incapable of carrying out. Their once great love had slowly died over a quarter of a century. Both reluctantly had finally faced it. On the day Tolstoy wrote in his diary that after a four-hour stretch of writing he had finally finished *The Kreutzer Sonata*, he paused to note a remark that same day of Sonya's: "Yes, I loved you very much but nothing came of it."[3]

Tolstoy had finished *The Kreutzer Sonata* in the fall of 1889, and before the Tsar's censor decided whether it could be published or not, some eight hundred copies were secretly lithographed and circulated in Petersburg and Moscow. The reaction of readers was swift and explosive. What had Russia's greatest writer done? His return to a major work of fiction after a ten-year hiatus (except for *The Death of Ivan Ilyich*) had brought forth a work unlike anything he had previously written. Some critics praised it; others thought that it was lacking in taste, immoral, and that so great a writer should not have stooped to turning out such a scandalous work. In the United States it was criticized as being pornographic and was banned in some places. In Germany it was brought out as a racy sex novel with a picture of a naked woman on the cover.

*The Kreutzer Sonata* is a tale told by a man named Pozdnyeshev whom the author has met in a railway compartment during a long train journey, and who insists on recounting at great length the story of his marriage to a woman he came to hate and in the end, in a fit of jealousy, murdered. Except for the killing and the problem that led to that end, it pretty much follows the lives of Leo and Sonya Tolstoy, their loves and hates, the quarrels that gnawed away at their marriage, and the problems they had with their children. Along the way Tolstoy avails himself of the opportunity to air a number of grievances and resentments—against women, marriage, doctors, lawyers, professors, flirtatious females who tempt and seduce innocent men, and mothers who, like the narrator's wife and Sonya sometimes, commit the terrible sin of not nursing their babies.

But the worst sin of all, which Pozdnyeshev and his wife share, is a strong sexuality that despite their mutual hatred lures them continually into bed. The celebrated author who in his two masterpieces, *War and Peace* and *Anna Karenina*, praised family happiness and the joy of having children and who had fathered thirteen himself now stepped forward in *The Kreutzer Sonata* and frantically, and, many thought, hypocritically, condemned sex between husband and wife. It is Pozdnyeshev of course who propounds these ideas, who laments all the failings of his beautiful wife, who comes to resent her and hate her, but the reader quickly realizes it is really Leo Tolstoy who, until toward the end of the story, is recounting his own life and thoughts and, like the man in the railway coach, dragging his wife through the mud.*

Even in little things, the narrator says, there often raged in him a "terrible hatred" of his wife.

> Sometimes I watched her pouring out tea, swinging her legs, lifting a spoon to her mouth, smacking her lips and drawing in some liquid, and I hated her for these things.

"We were like two convicts," he went on, "hating each other and chained together, poisoning one another's lives and trying not to see it. I did not know then that ninety-nine percent of married people live in a similar hell to the one I was in."

He then turned to another matter that had increased his resentment of his wife. Tolstoy, it will be remembered, had hated to move to Moscow during the winter when Sonya insisted on it so that the children could receive a formal education. Pozdnyeshev relates how he hated the same thing:

> Just when parents find life together unendurable, it becomes necessary to move to town for the children's education.

And he raves against city life, as Tolstoy did.

> So we lived in town. In town a man can live for a hundred years without noticing that he has long been dead.

* To Chertkov, whom he had earlier advised to marry and have children, Tolstoy now, under the spell of writing *The Kreutzer Sonata*, gave different counsel. "Let everyone try not to marry, and if he be married, to live with his wife as brother and sister. . . . You will object that this would mean the end of the human race. What a great misfortune!"

The climax and end of this story came out of Tolstoy's imagination. The husband suspected that his wife was having an affair with a musician (unnamed, as is the spouse), a violinist who often came to their home to play duets with his wife, who had studied the piano. One day Pozdnyeshev returned early from a trip, found the two together, and in a rage of jealousy stabbed his wife to death, the violinist having fled. Pozdnyeshev tells the author that he was acquitted because the court held that he was defending his honor. Given Tolstoy's imagination and creative talents, the murder scene is one of the most moving in literature.

But readers in Moscow and Petersburg were more interested in *The Kreutzer Sonata* as a story of the Tolstoys' marriage. The scenes of the quarrels between the narrator and his wife were so vivid that many readers assumed Tolstoy was really writing about himself and his wife. The outburst against sex in general and between husband and wife in particular was taken to reflect Tolstoy's own view. And, indeed, he had first propounded it in his earlier philosophical tracts, beginning with *Confession*. While he was writing *The Kreutzer Sonata* he had received encouragement for his idea from a strange source. A leader of the American Shakers had called on him and later sent him some books and pamphlets explaining the Shakers' opposition to sexual intercourse, even between spouses. Tolstoy was greatly pleased, and on April 9, 1889, he jotted down in his diary: "I read the writings of the Shakers. Perfect. Total chastity. Odd to receive this just when I am concerned with the question." This seemed to the writer to be divine support for his idea. And a few days later: "I must propose the Shaker arrangement to Sonya." But he could not bring himself to do it.

If the great writer was so opposed to sex, and thought it a sin for a wife and husband to indulge in it, why had he, by his own admission, lusted for so much of it with his wife? Why had he fathered thirteen children? The question embarrassed not only Sonya but, even more, her spouse. Sonya thought she might be pregnant again and, on August 6, 1889, Tolstoy took up the matter in his diary.

> August 6, Yasnaya Polyana: . . . Thought: What if there should be another child? How ashamed I should be, especially before the children. They will reckon up when it was conceived

and will then read what I am writing [finishing *The Kreutzer Sonata*]. And I felt ashamed and sad.

Sonya discussed it sarcastically. To a friend she said: "It's fine for Leo Nikolayevich to write and advise others to be chaste, but what about himself?"
And in her diary on Christmas Day, 1890, she confided:

> I am very much afraid I am pregnant again. Everyone will hear of this ignominy, and they will all be maliciously repeating the joke that is making the rounds in Moscow, that that is the real postscript to *The Kreutzer Sonata*.*

In St. Petersburg, the Tsar read *The Kreutzer Sonata* and liked it very much, though the Tsarina said she was shocked. Pobyedonostsev, the reactionary censor, who had banned other works by Tolstoy, surprised everyone by his reaction to the book. "A powerful work," he conceded. "If I ask myself whether I must condemn it for immorality, I cannot bring myself to say that I should." The minister of the interior, backed by the church, however, succeeded in getting the book banned both as a single publication and in a new volume of the author's complete works.

The second part of the ban upset Countess Tolstoy, who had included it in the thirteenth volume, which was being readied for the press. Against her husband's wishes, she set out alone for Petersburg to try to get the Tsar himself to permit her to include the work in the last volume.

There were two good reasons in her mind, her diaries make clear, for the venture. First, she thought that when the public learned she was petitioning the Tsar for permission to publish the book, it would conclude that she wouldn't take such action if she thought *The Kreutzer Sonata* was really the story of her own marriage. Second, she figured that inclusion of the banned book in Volume 13 would help to increase the sales of the collected works.

In Petersburg the Tsar kept her waiting. Not until twelve days after she had written asking for an audience did he consent to receive her. Once in his august presence, though nervous, Sonya

---

* In response to initial criticism, Tolstoy had hastily drafted a postscript explaining and defending what he wrote.

performed brilliantly. She described the scene at great length in a proud entry in her diary on April 22, 1891—nine days after the audience. She even wrote a heading for it: "My visit to St. Petersburg."

As she waited in the anteroom of the palace for the interview, she recounted, she was so nervous and her heart was pounding so wildly that she thought she would die. But Alexander III quickly put her at ease. He was rather shy himself, she noticed, and spoke to her "in a pleasant, melodious voice, his eyes warm and kind," and with "a friendly, bashful smile."

She began by telling a fib—or at least half a fib. She assured the monarch that her husband was abandoning his "philosophical and religious works" and was returning to literature, hoping to write something like *War and Peace*.* "Ah, how good that would be!" the Emperor exclaimed. "What a very great writer he is!" Sonya then turned to *The Kreutzer Sonata*.

"Surely though," the Tsar chided her, "you would not give a book like that to your children to read?"

Sonya sidestepped the question and remarked that "the fundamental idea [of the book] is that the ideal is always unobtainable." And she pleaded with the Tsar to allow her to publish the work in the last volume of the collected works. Alexander gracefully consented, noting that if it appeared in the collected works "not everyone can afford to buy it and it will not have a very large circulation."

Still, the Emperor asked her if her husband "could not alter it a little?"

"No, Your Majesty," Sonya says she replied. "We can never make any corrections to his works."

The ruler of Russia changed the subject, asked after the children, said he would like to have her meet the Tsarina, and bade her good-bye "very warmly." The talk with the Empress was conducted in French, which Sonya faithfully set down in a long diary entry. That interview over, Sonya hurried from the palace to her sister Tanya's house, packed her bags, and caught the 3:00 P.M. train to Moscow.

She was sure she was returning in triumph. She had persuaded

---

* Half a fib because, although Tolstoy had told his wife he hoped to return to fiction, he did not say he was going to give up his philosophical writings.

the Tsar himself to lift the ban on *The Kreutzer Sonata*. It had all, she thought, been a grand success. "I cannot help secretly exulting about my success," she wrote in her diary. Alexandrine Tolstoy, who had helped her get an audience with the ruler, wrote her that she had made an "excellent impression" on the Tsar, and another friend reported to her from Petersburg "that the Tsar found me sincere, simple and sympathetic, and that he had not realized that I was still so young and pretty."

> All this flatters my female vanity and avenges me for all the years in which my husband not only failed to promote me in society but actually did his utmost to drag me down.

Leo did not greet her very kindly on her return. He resented that she had intervened with the Emperor on behalf of a work of his. He and the Tsar, Sonya quoted him in her diary as saying, "had managed to ignore each other up until now . . . all this could do us a lot of damage, and might well have some disagreeable consequences."

In his diary on April 18, Tolstoy wrote:

> Sonya arrived about three days ago. I find it most unpleasant that she has been ingratiating herself with the Tsar. . . . I couldn't control myself and said some harsh things to her, but it has passed.

It passed, he noted, "especially because the wicked feelings of mine made me glad of her return." His "wicked feelings" may be easily imagined. Despite all his preachments of chastity, he could not stay away from her. Five days later, the same feeling. Sonya noted it in her diary.

> Tanya has just gone by my door and told me that Lyovochka asked her to tell me that he is in bed and [has] put out the candle. Innocent lips transmit these anything but innocent words. I know what they mean, and I don't like it.

Disgusted with himself, Tolstoy concluded that the only way to avoid temptation was to sleep alone, or at least in separate beds.

But Sonya declined. Despite all that she had written in her diary about her disgust at having to have so much sex with her husband, she wanted them to share the same bed, as they had for a quarter of a century. And such narrow beds! Seeing them today—both the one in Moscow and the one in Yasnaya Polyana, which are not much larger than what we would today call a small single bed—one wonders how they could have avoided what was continually happening. They keep reporting in their diaries that they can't help it and feel ashamed.

Especially Sonya. From the beginning, she claimed, she didn't like it—or rather "that," as she called it. Only a few months after they were married, she confided in her diary: "The physical side of love matters a great deal to him. That's dreadful—for it's exactly the other way around for me." A quarter of a century later, she exclaims that life "could be good *without that*. But it very seldom happens otherwise with him." A few days later, after reading more of her husband's diaries, she writes: "In Leo's diaries there is no love, as I understand it. This feeling was evidently unknown to him. He knew only sensuality."

In 1890 and 1891, just after the publication of *The Kreutzer Sonata*, her diary is filled with complaints about their intimate life. Three days after Christmas, 1890, Sonya was looking through some of Leo's early letters to her, professing his great love. "There was a time," she notes, "when he loved me so deeply. . . . But surely on his part it was nothing but a physical attraction."

A month later, on January 25, 1891:

> It occurred to me this evening as I was correcting proofs for *The Kreutzer Sonata*, that when a woman is young, she loves with her whole heart, and gladly gives herself to the man she loves because she sees what pleasure it gives him. Later she looks back, and suddenly she realizes that this man loved her only when he needed her. And she remembers all the time his affection turned to harshness or disgust the moment he was satisfied.

"He loves me," she notes on another occasion, "only at night, never during the day." One day in March 1891, Sonya noted that Leo was in "an extraordinarily sweet, cheerful, affectionate mood at the moment."

For the usual reason alas. If all the people who read *The Kreutzer Sonata* so reverently had an inkling of the voluptuous life he leads, then they would cast this deity from the pedestal where they had placed him.*

Leo did not deny his overpowering sensuality, though he seemed oblivious to Sonya's resentment of it—even when she talked to him of suicide! His diary of September 24, 1889:

At dinner Sonya spoke of how she had watched a train approaching and (like Anna Karenina) wanted to throw herself under it. I felt very sorry for her.† The main thing is, I know how much I'm to blame. I remember for example my loathsome feeling of lust just after Sasha was born. Yes, I remember my sins.

"I've sinned again," he kept writing in his diary after what he called a "bad" night. "Slept evilly," he would say. And he wrote in his notebook that he was simply unable to be chaste. "I've never betrayed my wife," he wrote in a secret diary he kept for a few days toward the end of his life. "But there was lust in my relations with her—nasty and criminal lust."

For all her claims in her diaries that she was repulsed by her husband's sexual demands, Sonya admitted that in middle age she began to like them. But she felt ashamed to concede it. In her diary of January 25, 1891, already referred to, she added a rather revealing paragraph. She muses about how as a married woman gets older, "she becomes passionate with her husband at certain times and demands that he satisfy her." It's a pity, she says, "if he can no longer satisfy her." And she goes on: "A younger woman has none of the sexual passion, especially when she is busy bearing and feeding children. Only once in every two years is she a real woman in fact! Her passion awakens only in her 30s."

---

* Sergei Tolstoy, who edited his mother's diaries for publication, cut a good deal when she wrote of her life with Tolstoy.

† The desire to emulate Anna Karenina's end began to be an obsession with Sonya. A year or so later, on December 15, 1890, in despair at what her husband had written in *The Kreutzer Sonata*, she jotted in her diary: "I've been seriously thinking of saying goodbye to everyone and then lying down on the railroad tracks."

Still, in her own case she hates to admit it. Her diary, July 27, 1891:

> Horribly dissatisfied with myself. Lyovochka woke me this morning with passionate kisses. . . . I have succumbed to the most unforgivable debauchery—at my age too! [She is forty-seven.] I am so sad and ashamed of myself! I feel sinful and wretched and can do nothing about it though I try.

After such debauched lovemaking they had a quarrel, as they often did afterward. Her diary continues:

> Ah, what a strange man my husband is! This morning after we had had that terrible *scene*, he told me he loved me passionately. He was completely in my power, he said: he had never imagined such feelings were possible. But it is all *physical*—that was the secret cause of our quarrel. His passion dominates me too but I do not *want* it, my whole moral being cried out against it, I never wished for *that*. All my life I have dreamed sentimental dreams, aspired to a perfect union, a *spiritual* communion, not *that*.

The "terrible scene" Sonya referred to was probably the aftermath of what was the biggest blowup of their lives up to then. It happened six days before and Sonya described it in great detail in her diary of July 21, 1891. What brought it about was a matter that Tolstoy had been discussing with his wife for some time. He wanted to inform the press that from now on anyone was free to publish everything he had written since 1881, including all that was in Volumes 12 and 13 of the collected works that Sonya had recently brought out. Sonya had opposed it, arguing that it would leave them financially unable to support themselves, let alone their children. The estate in Samara had not paid off, and was being sold at a loss. The income from Yasnaya Polyana was not enough. They really depended on his book royalties for most of their living. And she opposed his giving away his copyrights for a second reason. Allowing publishers to bring out his works without having to pay royalties, she argued, would only enrich the publishers—at the expense of the Tolstoy children. But on this occasion, she says in her diary, she decided to oppose him no longer and to "endure" his decision "meekly." When he brought it up on the twenty-first, however, her "immediate feeling," she admits, was one of outrage.

> I must write down the whole foolish, improbable, sad story of what happened today. . . . I feel utterly crushed, exhausted in body and soul. . . .
>
> I felt how terribly unfair he was being to his family, and I realized too for the first time that this protest of his was merely another way of publicizing his dissatisfaction with his wife and family. . . . We said a great many unpleasant things to one another. I accused him of being vain and greedy for fame. He shouted at me, saying I only want the money, and that he had never met such a stupid, greedy woman. I told him he had humiliated me all my life, for he had never learned how to behave toward a decent woman. He told me I wanted only to spoil the children with money. It ended with him shouting "Get out! Get out!"

She says she did, leaving the house and wandering about the garden not knowing what to do. The night watchman saw her crying and she felt ashamed, fleeing to the apple orchard, where she sat down in a ditch. There, she says, she signed her agreement with her husband's letter to the press abjuring his copyrights. Then she wrote in a notebook that she was going to the railroad station at Kozlovka, a nearby village, to throw herself under a train. It was getting dark. She got as far as "the footbridge over the great ravine." By this time, she says, she was "completely deranged." Suddenly she stumbled on her brother-in-law, Alexander Kuzminsky. Realizing, she goes on, that God did not want her to commit the sin of killing herself, she followed him home. On the way, though, as she passed the big pond, she thought of throwing herself in it and drowning.

One by one, the whole family, who had been out searching for her, returned to find her at home, relieving their anxieties by "laughing and chattering."

> Lyovochka was as merry as if nothing had happened. [It] had no effect whatsoever on his heart. As for the fact that I was near killing myself—he will never know about that, and if he did he wouldn't believe it anyway. . . .

Days like this are hastening my death. Something inside me has broken, and has left me feeling sad, hard, old. "Let them strike but let them finish me off quickly," I thought.

I am haunted again and again by thoughts of *The Kreutzer Sonata*. Today I again told him I could no longer live with him as his wife. He assured me this was exactly what he wanted too but I do not believe him.

Peace broke out between them, though not on the basis that Sonya had asked and he had accepted. In that, they were asking too much of themselves. On September 16, 1891, with Sonya's consent but not her approval, Tolstoy sent off identical letters to two leading newspapers, the *Russian Gazette* and *New Times*, asking them to publish a statement that he, Tolstoy, granted "to all who so desire the right to publish free of charge . . . all those of my works written by me after 1881 and printed in Volumes XII and XIII of my complete works, and similarly all my works which have not been published in Russia and which may come out again after the present day."*

Tolstoy felt immensely relieved to have finally given up making a profit from his writings, or at least those since 1881. There would be no more "sinning" in that regard. But there would be plenty of other troubles ahead. Since most of his income came from his writing, Sonya would never forgive him for depriving the children, if not herself, of this source of livelihood. In the years to come she would begin to suspect, not without reason, that Leo was planning to deliver the final blow to her and the children by giving up copyrights of *all* his works—including those published before 1881, among them *War and Peace* and *Anna Karenina*, which, with the rest of his writings, made up the thirteen volumes of his collected works that Sonya had published and which had brought the Tolstoys a considerable fortune.

Actually, despite what he did give up in 1891, he and his family continued to live in the style to which they had become accustomed. It was not so much the giving up of the copyrights that marked a new watershed in the lives of the great writer and his wife. It was rather the writing and publishing of *The Kreutzer Sonata*.

---

* He made an exception of *The Death of Ivan Ilyich*, which he had dedicated to Sonya.

Tolstoy may have felt good to have at last got off his chest in *The Kreutzer Sonata* what he thought of his wife and their marriage and their children. In his diary he admitted that the book was "negative and malicious." What he didn't seem to realize was that it had humiliated his wife and wounded her deeply. As she set down in her diary the day of the blowup, she was haunted "again and again" by the thought of the book. After its appearance there seemed to be no way to heal the growing rift between these two gifted beings, who were so richly endowed in everything but the ability to understand each other. From time to time they would make up, as they said, cease their quarreling, and profess their love. But before long they would be at each other again. After *The Kreutzer Sonata,* as that last diary entry of hers shows, Sonya gave way to a mounting hysteria, along with threats and the first attempt to kill herself. Tolstoy at first tried to feign indifference or let his temper flare up, as he did that July day and with increasing frequency thereafter. But at heart, as his diary begins to show, he grew desperate, unable to find a way to cope with his wife or even with his children. As for Sonya, as *her* diaries reveal, she began to drift down a dark and nightmarish road toward madness. The fear that she might be losing her mind, as she wrote in her diary as far back as the autumn of 1885, "terrified" her.

# TWELVE

# Conflict
# and Good Works

*T*HE WRITING of *The Kreutzer Sonata,* catastrophic though it was to the relations between Tolstoy and his wife, had what seemed, even to her, at least one good effect. It restored Leo's confidence in his writing. As he was finishing the book, he rejoiced in his diary at "the recovery of my talent."[1] And for fiction! After declaring for years—ever since *Confession*—that he was ashamed of the two big novels he had written, masterpieces in the eyes of the world, he confided to Sonya, who was delighted, that he was hoping to get back to writing another big one. He also talked to himself in his diary about it.

On January 25, 1891, as the snow piled up at Yasnaya Polyana, to which he had retreated from his hated Moscow, he wrote:

> I began to think how good it would be to write a novel, a long one, illuminating it with my present view of things. And I thought I could unite in it all the plans of mine, which I regret not having carried out.

Next day he went back to the subject.

> How happy I would be if I had written in my diary yesterday that I had begun a big work of fiction. Yes, to start now and write a novel would make so much sense. My first, early novels were unconscious creations. Since *Anna Karenina,* for more than ten years, I've been dissecting, separating, analyzing: now I

know what's what and I can mix it [all together] again and work in this mixture. Help me, Father.

All through 1890 and 1891 his diary is peppered with notes of ideas for his writing, especially his projects for short stories and novels. They offer a fascinating look into the mind of a great writer and how it begins to formulate a plot, a character, a story line that will not become a published book or even a short story for several years—until Tolstoy has completely digested it and is ready to write it down in final form (which will be revised again when he attacks the proofs and often rewrites entire pages before letting it go to press).

From the beginning of 1890 Tolstoy kept jotting down notes about "Koni's story." The idea came from a friend, A. F. Koni, a brilliant and noted liberal Petersburg lawyer, who was largely responsible for setting up the jury system in Russia and who, in 1887, had recounted to Tolstoy the details of a murder case in which he was involved as a lawyer for the defendant. A prostitute was on trial for her life before a jury, one of whose members, an aristocrat, had once seduced her and so contributed to her fall.

Tolstoy played with the story year after year. His diary for February 11, 1890, at Yasnaya Polyana: "On my walk I thought a great deal about Koni's story. Everything is clear and very good."

He thereupon lists eight points he wants to get in. The first:

> He didn't want to possess her but did so because that is what one has to do—or so he thought. In his imagination she is charming. He smiles and he feels like crying.

And more:

> February 16: Got on with Koni's story; not bad.
> January 9, 10, 1891: For Koni's story: he plays catch with Katyusha and they kiss behind a bush *And for the same story:* the first part—the maternal love: the second, the power, the beauty of pure love.

After much note taking (and there would be much more) Tolstoy had finally sat down and begun the actual writing of "Koni's story." Three weeks before, on December 15, he scribbled in his diary: "Yesterday I started Koni's story from the beginning. Enjoyed writing it very much." He had finally begun what would turn out to be his last novel, nearly as long as *Anna Karenina*. Koni's story was being transformed into *Resurrection*. It would not be finished until 1899. In between spurts of working on it, he was busy creating a surprising number of other works. Though he would often pause in his diary to note how discouraged he was with his writing, it was a period of tremendous creativity. He was in his early sixties, not in very good health and alienated—or so he felt, to his sorrow—much of the time from his wife and children. But his feverish imagination was giving birth to ideas for some of the best things he ever wrote.

One was a story, *Father Sergei*. Tolstoy's diaries note the incubation of that moving tale—the story of a monk who succumbs to the temptations of the flesh, and what the consequences were. It is at once the most penetrating pronouncement of the author's religious beliefs and a portrait of himself—or part of himself. So much so that he chose not to publish it in his lifetime.

His going back to fiction brought him closer to Sonya. She had so long hoped for it. "Talked frankly with Sonya," he noted on August 15, 1890, "for almost the first time in many years. She spoke about prayer sincerely and intelligently. . . . I am very glad." Soon another happening would help to keep their relations better than they had been for years.

In the meantime, he was not content to wrestle only with Koni's story and *Father Sergei*. He was bursting with ideas for other works, stories and, even more—a novel. And he was not neglecting his religious and philosophical works either. He had begun to write *The Kingdom of God Is Within You*, both an attack on the Orthodox Church and a plea for nonviolent resistance to evil—the book which would so impress Gandhi, and many others.

In his diary entry of January 25, 1891, Tolstoy had mentioned that he had made some progress with *The Kingdom of God*—he had finished, he says, six chapters. And then, after remarking how good it would be to get to work on a long novel, he paused to note some of the works of fiction he was turning over in his mind: "Alexander I and the Soldier," which would become *The Posthumous Papers of Fyodor Kuzmich*, a story he put off beginning until 1905 and never finished; "The Robber," which he later put into *The Forged*

*Coupon; The Settlers,* which he had begun as a novel fourteen years before and which dealt with the peasant settlers in Russia during the late eighteenth century; *Mitasha,* which never got beyond a rough draft beginning: "There was a wealthy man"; and "Notes of a Madman," which became an unforgettable short story that was never finished but is included in many Tolstoy anthologies: the fictional account of an actual happening when Tolstoy, staying overnight in a village inn, has a nightmare in which Death stalks him in his bed—the famous "Night at Arzamas." And, finally, he noted "The Nihilists," which he abandoned completely.[2]

Early in the spring of 1891, Tolstoy conceived the idea for a major novel. In a way it was to be an antidote to *The Kreutzer Sonata*—this time the story of a mother and all the sacrifices she makes to bring up her children. A mother was to be the heroine, motherhood the great subject. Tolstoy tells about its gestation in two diary entries that spring.

> March 25, Yasnaya Polyana: . . . Went for a walk and imagined very vividly, as I seldom do, a work of fiction on the subject of upbringing. Lopukhina. The mother. The problem of the mother. *Notes of a Mother.* Much that is good, artistically speaking, came into my head and is still coming.

He returned to the idea a couple of weeks later. He was going to base the book, as the earlier entry hints, on the life of a Tula woman friend, A. P. Lopukhin. He found the idea of a novel about the upbringing of children exciting—at least in the beginning.

> April 9, Yasnaya Polyana: Yesterday I began writing *Notes of a Mother.* Wrote a lot, but it only served to convince me that I mustn't write that way. I must write in the first person.

So he began again, making it in the form of a diary. He worked on it, on and off, for the next five years but could not take it very far. Perhaps his early excitement about writing of motherhood waned. Perhaps his difficult relations with his wife—and with some of his children—made it hard to remain enraptured with the idea of motherhood and family. Perhaps spells of discouragement about his writing, and his occasional lapse into his old feud with women in general, helped to account for his cooling off about it. At the same time Tolstoy laments (as usual) in his diary that he feels weak and listless, and cannot write. "Must resign myself," he notes early that spring, "to the thought that my career as a writer is finished—and be glad without it."[3]

Maybe so. Maybe, as he says, he should try to be happy to think he was through as a writer. But his diaries reveal the contrary: that the idea depressed him deeply.

> March 5, Yasnaya Polyana: Was very depressed today. . . . Wrote nothing and didn't try to.
>
> March 18: Was just thinking of starting to write but again disinclination and apathy.
>
> June 2: I am beginning to doubt the importance of what I write.
>
> June 8: Did some mowing. My writing is going badly.

He was depressed too because he could not curb his sensuality. He would soon be sixty-three and it had possessed him since he was thirteen—for half a century! "I do know for certain," he confided in his diary on May 22, "that copulation is an abomination which can only be regarded without revulsion under the influence of sexual desire. Even in order to have children you wouldn't do this to a woman you love. I'm writing this at a time when I am myself possessed with sexual desire, against which I cannot fight."

One day in June he hiked to Tula, as he records in his diary. There on one of the streets he noticed a woman, "eyes close together and straight eyebrows, seemingly on the point of tears, but plump, nice looking, pitiable and arousing sensuality. That's what the merchant's wife in *Father Sergei* should be like."[4]

Thinking of her dredged up old hang-ups about women that one would have thought he had exhausted in *The Kreutzer Sonata.* "The intellectual fashion of exalting women, of asserting that they are not only equal to men in their spiritual capabilities, but higher than them, is a very bad and harmful fashion."

> . . . To assert that the average woman is endowed with the same spiritual strength as a man . . . is to deliberately deceive yourself. . . . So to regard women as what they are—weaker crea-

tures spiritually, is not cruelty to women; to regard them as equals is cruelty.[5]

There is a curious follow-up in his diary a month later. He is summing up some of his thoughts of the summer. Number four: "The absurdity of our lives is the result of the power of women; but the power of women is the result of the incontinence of men."

Still, the Tolstoys were living in relative peace, although there were squabbles now and then. In February 1891, Sonya complained in her diary that Leo was "being stiff, sullen and unpleasant again." She was also "silently angry" with him because one night he kept her up late.

> He spent such a long time downstairs washing that I thought he must be ill, for washing was quite an event for him.[6]

He was beginning to repel her physically. He was not only dressing like a peasant but going unwashed like a peasant. "It's like pulling teeth to get him to wash!" she exclaimed. "My aversion to my husband physically these days is making me very miserable, but I cannot get adjusted to it. I shall never get used to the dirt and the bad smell."[7]

In June 1891, Tolstoy jotted in his diary that he was "depressed because of Sonya." He resented the fact that she did not like his giving up his copyrights and he was annoyed at the bickering of the family, to whom that year he was trying to deed most of his property: "All this worry about money and property and the complete failure to understand." He and Sonya began to discuss "whether a person can sacrifice his life rather than do [something] that harms nobody, but is offensive to God. She objected—words of abuse. I had evil thoughts of going away. . . . I mustn't. I must endure it."[8] That fall Tolstoy recorded one instance when "before she left [for Moscow], she talked with me so joyfully and well that I couldn't believe it was the same person."[9]

That summer an event occurred that would bring them together again. More than that. It would bring out in Tolstoy, so crabbed about his family life these days, an outpouring of compassion and generosity toward his suffering fellowmen. Suddenly a

part of Russia—the very land not far from his own Yasnaya Polyana—was stricken with famine. The great author and humanitar-
ian was at first reluctant to chip in to help, declaring that he had
always been opposed to charity. "Everyone is talking about the
famine," he noted in his diary on June 25.

> Everyone is worrying about the starving people, and want-
> ing to help them and save them. How disgusting it is! People
> who have never thought about others, about the ordinary peo-
> ple, suddenly for some reason are bursting with the desire to
> serve them. It is either vanity—wanting to show off—or fear, but
> there's nothing good about it.

He would not soil his hands in such a venture. He summed up
his half-baked ideas about the matter a fortnight later in a letter to
the writer N. S. Leskov, who had written to him asking him what
he thought they ought to do. More than we have seen up to now,
the letter brings out a quirky side of the great man that probably
had begun in his midlife crisis.

The famine, he wrote Leskov, "certainly" could not be averted
by collecting money and buying bread to feed the hungry. There
was plenty of food in Russia, he argued, but there was a famine
because it was not distributed fairly. Failure to change the system,
he went on, would produce nothing but sin.* Those who contributed to the relief of the famine, Tolstoy told Leskov, would be doing
it out of "vanity, ambition, or fear that these people might become
embittered." So, he wrote, "good deeds ought not to be done suddenly on the occasion of a famine."

> And therefore the one thing needed against famine is for
> people to do as many good deeds as possible. And a good deed
> consists not in feeding the hungry with bread, but in loving both
> the hungry and well-fed. And it's more important to love than to

---

* It was true, as Tolstoy says, that there were adequate supplies of food in Russia—the government was still exporting grain that year and the famine could have
been averted if Russia had had an adequate transportation system—true even in
the minds of many that the system, "dreadfully backward and inefficient," needed
changing. But what Tolstoy did not seem to realize was that the starving peasants—hundreds of thousands of them—could not wait. They needed food at once
in order to survive.

feed. . . . I'm not writing this so much to you as to those people
. . . who assert that to collect money and hand it around is a
good deed, not realizing that a good deed is only a deed of
love. . . . And if you ask me what you should do, I would reply:
awaken in people love for one another: not love on the occasion
of a famine, but love always and everywhere. . . .

"It's more important to love than to feed"! Leo Tolstoy, the
great sermonizer, was brought to his senses by an old friend and
neighbor, I. I. Rayevsky, who told him that the disaster was real
and asked for his help. Tolstoy had been stung by criticism in the
press of his do-nothing attitude toward the famine: Leskov had
given the newspapers extracts from Tolstoy's letter to him, and
their reaction was furious. "A heartless doctrinaire," one journal
called Tolstoy. This angry reaction upset her husband "terribly,"
Sonya noted in her diary.[10] At Rayevsky's urging, the master of
Yasnaya Polyana agreed to send his three grown sons, Sergei, Ilya,
and Leo, out to the district of Ryazan, where Rayevsky had his
main estate, to see for themselves. They soon returned and told
their father that the situation was worse than he could imagine.
Hundreds of thousands of the poor, mostly peasants, were threatened with starvation. The old man woke up quickly.

Casting his objection to charity aside, he decided first to check
the situation in the districts surrounding his brother Sergei's estate
at Pirogovo, where several crop failures had been reported. What
he saw there finally convinced him that the famine was serious, that
the government, which began to deny that there was any problem,
was not going to do much about it, and that, although it was
against his principles, he must do what he could to collect food,
firewood, and clothing for the afflicted peasants. Having once come
to a decision, he acted quickly and with vigor. He dispatched one
son, Leo, to the Samara district, where the Tolstoys owned a large
estate, and the eldest sons, Sergei and Ilya, to places in his own
Tula province, where he learned the situation was critical. Yasnaya
Polyana had been spared, but areas not far away had been hard hit
by the drought. He himself prepared to set off with his daughters
Tanya and Masha to Rayevsky's estate at Begichevka, one hundred
miles southeast of Yasnaya Polyana, the center of an area where the
famine was the worst in the country.

Sonya, who had heard her husband hold forth endlessly on the evils of charity, was still somewhat skeptical of his motives. Before leaving he said to her: "Please don't imagine that I'm only doing this to be talked about. It's just that one can't stand aside and do nothing." To which Sonya answered in her diary.[11]

> Yes, indeed, if he were doing it because his heart bled for the suffering of the starving, I would . . . give everything I had. [He had asked her to send him money to buy food.] But I don't feel, and never have, that he was speaking from the heart. . . .

Before long she would change her mind on that. And a few weeks later, in the midst of laboring day and night to set up soup kitchens and buy food for them and arouse not only Russia but the world by eloquently written appeals to the press for help, Tolstoy acknowledged that "to be sure, the wretched desire for world fame is mixed up with it." But he would try to do it, he added, "for the sake of God."[12]

Working mainly out of Begichevka, where he teamed up with Rayevsky, Tolstoy proved to be a surprisingly good organizer. Together they set up 240 soup kitchens that fed some thirteen thousand people daily. The sight of starving children moved Tolstoy deeply, and for them he established special canteens that provided food for three thousand youths. In addition, he collected firewood for the peasants to heat their huts during the winter, and gathered clothing for them. To pay for these things, Tolstoy personally raised, by his appeals in the Russian and foreign press, considerable sums of money: 150,000 rubles* in Russia, half a million dollars in America, which sent seven shiploads of grain, and 25,000 pounds in England. Back in Moscow, Sonya made her own appeal to the press and raised several thousand rubles, which she sent off to her husband to buy food.

Tolstoy was soon in trouble with the authorities, not only for giving publicity to the famine, the existence of which the government denied,† but for his appeals to the newspapers, especially abroad. For the first, the government accused the author of "rev-

---

* $1,518,750 today.
† "There is no famine in Russia," a government statement declared flatly. Actually, some 400,000 would perish in it.

olutionary agitation"; for the second, with acts bordering on treason.

When the censors forbade the Russian press to publish any more letters from the Tolstoys about the famine, Leo had arranged to have one censored letter, a bitter indictment of the government for its failure to do anything serious about famine relief, published abroad. He appealed for private contributions. When the London *Daily Telegraph* ran it, there was an outburst of sympathy throughout Britain and committees were formed to raise funds to send to Tolstoy. The government in St. Petersburg regarded this as an insult to Russian honor. One of its organs, the reactionary *Moscow News,* ran a front-page editorial denouncing the author. "Count Tolstoy's appeal," it said, "is based on a rabid, wild-eyed form of socialism. . . . He openly preaches social revolution."

In the capital, the minister of the interior ordered a special investigation of Tolstoy's activities in the famine district, and there were rumors that the government, in order to silence the great dissenter, might exile the Tolstoys or lock him up in a monastery.

Sonya wrote her husband to be careful and told him of the reports sweeping Petersburg. "For the love of God," Tolstoy wrote back, "do not trouble yourself with such things, my dear . . . I write what I think—things that could not conceivably be acceptable to the government and upper classes."[13]

The Tsar was displeased, but he did not dare arrest the crusading author. Overruling the minister of the interior, Alexander III told him: "I will ask you not to touch Tolstoy. I have no desire to make a martyr of him and provoke a general uprising."[14]

Leo Tolstoy from this time on became untouchable. No tsar, no minister, no chief of police, dared to arrest him. They would continue to censor his books, short stories, articles, and letters to the press. They would not let up spying on him and arresting his followers. Tolstoy had gained a unique place for a Russian writer; for any writer.

Rayevsky, who had first enlisted Tolstoy's help, died at his home at Begichevka on November 26, 1891. Working night and day in the cold and snow of early winter, he had contracted pneumonia. Tolstoy was grief-stricken. "I am suffering a great grief," he wrote the family on the twenty-ninth. "My friend has died, one of the best persons I have ever known. He was ill for a week with influenza and died in my arms. He and I worked together and have grown to love one another even more than before."

Rayevsky's death left Tolstoy and his daughters alone to keep up the famine relief in the district. But early in January 1892, Sonya joined her husband at Begichevka to help, sharing a sparsely furnished, ill-heated small room, going out daily with him to inspect or set up soup kitchens, scrounging around for food and for wood and clothing for the desperate. Like Leo, Sonya had been reluctant at first to get engaged in famine relief. But the anguished letters from her husband and children from the famine district had moved her. "I don't know what you'll think of my idea," she had written Tolstoy as she began in Moscow to raise funds, "but I have had enough of sitting still and doing nothing to help you."

Tolstoy was delighted to see her. For nearly a fortnight, while her daughter Tanya tended the four young children in Moscow, Sonya threw herself with abandon into the work with her husband. For one thing, she brought more order into the relief work.

> The hardest thing for us [she wrote in her diary] is having to decide which people are the neediest, who should go to the canteens, who should get the firewood and clothes that have been donated. When I made a list a few days ago there were 86 canteens. Now as many as a *hundred* have been opened.

Work on famine relief had brought the Tolstoys closer together. Leo had scarcely arrived with his two daughters at Begichevka before he was writing Sonya that he was worried about her. He hoped there would be a letter the next day. "Write in detail about yourself, your health and the children. I kiss you, my dear, and the children," he wrote her."[15]

When Sonya wrote to him about her letter to the *Russian News* and about the money that had been pouring in for famine relief after it was published, Tolstoy had been highly pleased Sonya had at last seen the light. He wrote her back: "I am sure you cannot imagine how lovingly we think and speak of you. . . . Every night I see you in my dreams, my sweet friend."[16]

Toward the end of November that year Tolstoy had returned to Moscow for a brief rest. It was a joyous reunion—something he and his wife had not experienced for years. "Joy," he wrote of his stay in Moscow in his diary on December 19 after his return to the famine district. "Relations with Sonya have never been so cordial. I thank Thee, Father. This is what I asked for. Everything I asked for has been granted." And he thanked God again.

As the famine continued into its second year, Tolstoy remained at Begichevka to carry on his relief efforts. Often that second year he thought fondly of his wife. "Yesterday," he wrote her once, "reading over your letters, I wanted with all my heart—the heart you say I don't have—not only to see you but to be with you."[17]

The new era of tender feelings and love between Tolstoy and his wife ended with the end of the famine.

Despite the fact that Sonya had helped a good deal in his famine relief work, and that his grown children—his daughters Tanya and Masha, his sons Sergei, Ilya, and Leo—had worked in the field during the crisis, Tolstoy returned home from two years of helping feed the starving peasants to rekindle his resentment at the luxurious way the family lived. That he shared that luxury to a large extent, he could not see. "Oh, this luxury!" he complained to his diary on December 22, 1893. "This commerce in my books! This ethical morass! This empty agitation!" He wanted to tear himself away from it all. His family would never understand him, especially his wife.

One evening in February 1891, the painter Nikolai N. Gay and his wife, close friends of the Tolstoys', had become engaged with their hosts at Yasnaya Polyana in a discussion about, as Sonya put it in her diary, "how much husbands suffer when their wives don't understand them."

> Lyovochka said: "You conceive a new idea, give birth, with all the agony of childbirth, to an entirely new spiritual philosophy, and all they do is resent your suffering and completely refuse to understand!" I then said that while they were giving birth in their imagination to all these spiritual children, we were giving birth, in real pain, to real live children who had to be fed and educated. . . . One's life was much too full and complicated to give it all up for the sake of one's spiritual vagaries.

Sonya says she and Leo both said much more "in the same reproachful vein."[18]

The reproaches began to wear Tolstoy down. "It has become clear to me," he wrote in his diary, "not in a moment of anger but in a very peaceful moment—that I might, and probably will, have to leave home."[19]

From then on for the rest of his life—for the next eighteen years—the idea of leaving was never far from his mind.

His growing despair was affecting his writing. Or at least his opinion of it. "Decided to stop writing," he announced in his diary. "Read through all the works of fiction which I've begun. They're all bad."[20]

However deep his pessimism about his family life and his writings, he could still record in the same entry the joy he felt about the wonders of the world, of which he was usually so skeptical. His writing, in his opinion, might have gone to pot, and his marriage, too, but life went on and, despite all its injustices and violence, it could still be good.

> Looked at a wonderful sunset as I walked towards Ovsya-nikovo. . . . I felt joyful. And I thought: no, this world is not a joke, not just a vale of trial and tribulation and a transition to a better, everlasting world but is itself an everlasting world which is beautiful and joyful. . . .[21]

The great wide world could be beautiful and joyful, but Tolstoy at this time—1893–94—could not say that of his private life. The devious Chertkov had resurfaced to spread more poison between the Master and his wife and to gain more ascendancy over the man he worshiped but wanted to control.

Back in 1890 Chertkov had tried to get control of Tolstoy's diaries, which Sonya had been recopying until her husband abruptly, as we have seen, forbade her even to look at them. That setback had been bad enough. Sonya, it will be remembered, had said she would continue to read his diaries when he was not looking. But the thought of sending these diaries, so personal about his feeling toward his wife and children, to Chertkov, as the disciple had urged and as Tolstoy had agreed, was too much for Sonya. If the great writer was going to give over his diaries to anyone, then they should go to her, who all these years had considered herself to be the faithful keeper of his papers. She let her husband know that she would fight any such transfer to Chertkov. From this moment the struggle for Tolstoy's diaries became a relentless war between them.

Tolstoy, who at first agreed to turn over his diaries to Chertkov "for safe-keeping," changed his mind—mostly to avoid another conflict with Sonya. "Chertkov is afraid," Tolstoy noted in his diary, "that I'll die and the diaries will be lost. . . . But they can't be sent . . . it would give offense."[22]

Next day Tolstoy wrote to his devoted but demanding disciple:

> I'm very sorry I can't send you my diaries. I wasn't think-ing when I wrote before. Not to mention the fact that it would upset my attitude to what I write, I can't send them without causing unpleasantness to my wife or keeping secrets from her. That I can't do.

To make amends for his broken promise, Tolstoy told Chert-kov, he would copy out extracts for him—some one twelfth of the total or "thereabouts." The high opinion Tolstoy had of his diaries we learn for the first time. "The diaries," he concluded his letter, "won't be destroyed. . . . Nothing of God's can be destroyed."[23] His diaries belonged to God.

Despite Tolstoy's loyalty to Sonya in not sending the diaries to Chertkov, she was bitter at the disciple for attempting to obtain them. She had won a temporary victory but this enemy, she was sure, would not give up his quest, just as her husband would not give up this scheming man as a close friend. Even months later Sonya was pouring her grievances against her husband into her diary.

> Lyovochka has broken off all relations with me. . . . He is systematically destroying me by driving me out of his life this way. . . . My God, he is always so unfriendly. . . . Days, weeks, months pass when we say not so much as one word to one another.[24]

Chertkov, denied the diaries, next tried to get possession of the manuscripts of Tolstoy's works, which Sonya had deposited for safekeeping in the Rumyantsev Museum in Moscow. Once again

Sonya was indignant. How dare this interloper try to take over the sacred manuscripts of the Master? Apparently this time he succeeded. One of only two entries in Sonya's diary for 1893 is dated August 2:

> I have just learned from Chertkov that most of Leo Nikolayevich's manuscripts are either with him or in St. Petersburg—with General Trepov of all people. Our children must be informed of this at once.

Years later she added a sentence to that entry, saying that "subsequently" Chertkov removed all of Tolstoy's manuscripts to Christchurch in England. She apparently was still too angry and frustrated to add any more. But in her diaries subsequently she poured out her resentment of her husband not only for being taken in by this charlatan of a Chertkov but for the way he treated her—and for much else. She had turned fifty and her nerves seemed to be becoming even more frayed than those of her husband. They irritated each other. More and more she accused him of hypocrisy and vanity. His renunciation of earthly goods she called "purely verbal."

> My husband has worn me down over the years with his coldness, and has loaded absolutely everything on my shoulders, absolutely everything: the children, the estate, the house, his books, business affairs, dealing with people, with his publishers, and then with selfish, critical indifference, he despises me for doing all this. And what about *his* life? He walks and rides, writes a little, does whatever he pleases, never lifts a finger for his family, and exploits everything to his own advantage: the services of his daughters, the comforts of life, the flattery of others . . . and fame, his insatiable greed for fame, continually drives him on.[25]

A few months later she was back on the same theme. "I cannot share my husband's ideas," she wrote in her diary on January 26, 1895, "because he is dishonest and insincere. His whole philosophy is so strained, artificial and unnatural, based as it is on vanity, the insatiable thirst for fame, and the compulsive desire for ever more popularity."

If the world only knew how he treated his family!

> Ah, how little kindness he shows his family! With us he is never anything but severe and indifferent. His biographers will tell how he helped the porter by drawing his own water, but no one will know that he never once thought to give his wife a moment's rest, or his sick child a drink of water! In 32 years he never once sat for five minutes by his sick child's bedside to let me have a good night's sleep.

The occasion for Sonya's outburst in her diary of January 26, she explained in the same entry, was that Tolstoy had just written a marvelous story, *Master and Man,* and instead of giving it to her to add to the next volume of the complete works, or even to the Intermediary, which would have published it for a few kopecks, he had given it for nothing to an attractive young lady, Lyubov Guryevich, who edited a magazine called the *Northern Herald.* Sonya was beside herself with rage—not only because she did not get the story for her Volume 13, but because, jealously, she suspected that her husband had fallen for the woman editor, probably had fallen in love. To Sonya, Guryevich, as she wrote angrily in her diary, was "that half-Jewish woman who was always buttering him up and trying to inveigle him into sending her things for her magazine. Why did he give it to Guryevich? It has made me furious and I am now trying to find a way . . . to spite her. And I *shall* find a way too!"[26]

She became so hysterical about it that Tolstoy threatened to leave her once and for all. There was a terrible blowup: the house in Moscow rocked from their shouting. Both, of course, took to their diaries to tell their side of the story. This time there was more than shouting.

It all started, Leo noted in his diary, with that "unfortunate story *Master and Man.* It was the cause of a terrible storm on Sonya's part that broke out yesterday. . . . It began with her beginning to copy out the proofs. When I asked her why . . ."[27]

Here a page is torn out of the diary—whether by Tolstoy or his wife or by Sergei Tolstoy or Chertkov, who later edited it, is not known. Leo goes on to record his thoughts about other things, returning to the big scene in his diary eight days later.

The following day things got worse. . . . She was decidedly close to madness and to suicide. The children followed her on foot and by vehicle, and brought her back home [when she ran from the house in her nightclothes]. It was the devil of jealousy, insane, groundless jealousy.[28]

Sonya's account in *her* diary was much longer and more detailed. She did not put it down in her journal until February 21, prefacing it with another angry outburst against her husband: "I am passing through yet another painful period. I don't even want to write about it, it's so terrible. . . ."

Whether she wanted to or not, she soon turned, after some bitter reproaches of her husband, to the "episode," as she called it, a little further on in her diary that day.

> . . . I was upset about his story, *Master and Man*. But I tried to keep this to myself, and worked hard on the proofs with Lyovochka. Then just as they were about to be sent off I asked him if I could make a copy for myself so I could publish it in Volume 13 of the *Complete Collected Works*.
>
> Since I didn't want to delay them being sent off to St. Petersburg, I said I would do the copying at night. For some reason, however, Lyovochka was incensed at the idea . . . angrily protesting against my copying it out, saying only that it was insane. I couldn't bear the idea of the *Northern Herald* having the sole rights; I recalled the words of Storozhenko, who said that Guryevich (the editor) must have bewitched the Count, since she's got two articles out of him in one year. I was quite determined that, come what may, I would see that my own edition and the *Intermediary*'s were published simultaneously. We were both furious and upset. Lyovochka got so angry that he rushed upstairs, put on his clothes and said he was leaving home forever and wouldn't be returning.
>
> Since I felt my only crime was wanting to copy it out, it suddenly flashed across my mind that there must be some far more serious reason why he should want to leave me, and that this was just an excuse. I immediately thought of that woman and lost all control of myself, and as he should not be the one to leave, I ran out of the house and tore off down the road.

Moscow lay deep in snow and it was cold—two degrees Fahrenheit, Sonya says—and she had taken off clad only in her dressing gown and house slippers. She says Tolstoy came "chasing" after her and that he, too, was scantily clad—"in his pants and waistcoat, without a shirt." He soon caught up with her.

> He pleaded with me to go back, but at that point I had only one wish and that was to die, never mind how.

Obviously Sonya got her ideas of how to depart this world from her husband's fiction. Previously, she had threatened to throw herself in front of a locomotive, as Anna Karenina had done. Now she was thinking of perishing in the cold and snow, as one of the two characters in *Master and Man* had done—this way was fresh in her mind from reading the story they were now quarreling about.

> I remember I was sobbing and shouting: "I don't care, let them take me away and put me in prison or the mental hospital!" Lyovochka dragged me back to the house. I kept falling in the snow and got soaked to the skin. I had only a night dress on under my dressing gown and nothing on my feet but a pair of slippers, and I am now ill, demented and choked.

"Somehow or other," Sonya goes on, they "smoothed things over." But, as happened so many other times—not for long!

> The next morning I again helped him correct the proofs for the *Northern Herald*. He finished them after lunch and was about to take a nap. "Well, I'll make a copy now, if I may," I said. He was lying on the sofa but when I said that, he leapt up, glared at me and again refused to let me do it, without giving any reason. (I still don't know what it might be.) But I didn't lose my temper, and merely begged him to let me copy it out.

Sonya says she had tears in her eyes and could hardly speak. She promised him she wouldn't release her publication of the story without his permission.

> I was only asking him to let me copy it out. He didn't refuse me in so many words, but his anger stunned me. . . . Why were Guryevich and her journal so precious to him that he wouldn't let his story be published simultaneously in the *Intermediary*? Feel-

ings of jealousy and rage, the mortifying thought that *he never did anything for me*, the old grief of having loved him so much when he never loved me—all this reduced me to a state of utter despair. I flung the proofs all over the table, threw on a light overcoat, put on my galoshes and hat and slipped out of the house.

Her daughter Masha had noticed her hasty departure and, like Leo the night before, took off after her. Sonya says she "stumbled" in the snow toward the Convent of the Virgin with the intention this time of freezing to death in a wooded portion of the Sparrow Hills across the river.

> I remember I had liked the idea that Vasily Andreyevich had frozen to death in the story and that I too would meet the same end. I didn't regret what I was doing. I had staked almost my whole life on one card—my love for my husband—and now that game was lost and I had nothing to live for.

Masha finally caught up with her and again, like Leo the night before, dragged her home. But two attempts on successive days to leave home and end it all did not suffice. Sonya tried again on the third day, this time simply stealing out of the house, hailing a cab, and telling the driver to take her to the Kursk railway station. What she planned to do when she got to the station she does not say. Presumably, with so many trains there arriving and departing, she would end it all just as Anna Karenina had done. But once again she was foiled. This time her son Sergei joined Masha in rescuing her. "How my children guessed that I had gone there," Sonya says, "I shall never know."

Each time she was brought back, Sonya goes on, she "felt foolish and ashamed of myself." It is clear from the rest of the lengthy diary entry—if it is not evident from what went on before—that the three-day nightmare left Sonya more irrational than ever. From now on her diary divulges a woman wounded, drifting toward insanity. Every year her condition, to the despair of her husband and children, grew a little worse.

"That night [February 7]," she says, "all the painful feelings inside me intensified to a point of unbearable anguish. I vaguely recall thinking that anybody Lyovochka touched was doomed to perish. . . . I still feel that my love for him will be the end of me, and will destroy my soul." If she can only get free of her love for him, she tells herself, she can be saved. "If not, one way or another, I am done for. He has killed my very soul—I'm already dead!"

Again, on the third night of the great blowup, Sonya says they made up. "After I had been sobbing for a long time, he came in, kneeled before me on the floor and begged me to forgive him. If he could just keep a fragment of that compassion for me alive, then I still might be happy with him." But she really cannot mean it. In the very next sentence she complains that, "having tortured my soul, he then called in the doctors to examine me."

The three days of terror and anguish had frightened Tolstoy. Skeptical as he was about physicians, he hastily called in three of them to examine his wife. She tells about that, too, sarcastically.

> It was comical the way each one prescribed medicine according to his own specialty. So the neurologist prescribed bromide and the specialist in internal diseases prescribed Vichy water and drops. Then the gynecologist was called in, referred cynically to my "critical time of life" and prescribed *his* particular medicine. I haven't taken any of it.

Not that she didn't feel ill.

> I've been running around the streets for three days and nights, with barely a stitch on, in 16 degrees of frost,* frozen to the marrow, and at my wit's end—naturally I'm ill. . . .

And in the end she blames the whole "episode" on her love of her husband. If she hadn't loved him so much, she wouldn't have become so wrought up when he failed to reciprocate. It was an argument she had often repeated in her diary. "We've made peace again," she writes for the hundredth time. But this does not cheer her up. She lapses once more into her grievances about her husband: "He is morbidly resentful of his family." And she goes on once more to justify herself: "Is it my fault that God has given me such a restless, passionate temperament?"

* Two degrees Fahrenheit.

Despite all her despair, her jealousy, and her resentments, Sonya ended this marathon diary entry on a note of triumph. "The story has been given to both me and the *Intermediary*. But at what a price!"

Many years later Sonya recalled her anguish at that time and offered a new explanation. "I realize," she wrote, "that the main cause of my despair was my premonition of Vanechka's imminent death."[29] For several months before her attempts that winter to leave home and kill herself, she kept noting in her diary the deteriorating health of her youngest child and favorite son, Ivan—Vanechka, as the family fondly called him. He was now seven years old. Both parents had a special feeling of love for this last child. He seemed so frail, gentle, generous, sensitive, intelligent, and loving. To Sonya, he was the one bright spot in her life. She adored him. Leo, who was disappointed in his older sons, thought that Vanechka might well follow him—as a writer and, as he put it, as one who could carry on his good work and God's work after he died.

The opening pages of Sonya's diary for 1895 are full of her growing worries about Vanechka. On January 5 she noted that Vanya, as she also called him, had been "ill all day" and it "terrified" her. "His life is so closely linked with mine. . . . He is such a weak, delicate little child—and so good!" Three days later she noted that Vanechka was still ill with a fever and a bad stomach. "It breaks my heart," she wrote, "to see him suddenly grow so thin and pale." She took the boy's temperature. It was 104 degrees Fahrenheit. There "was hardly a flicker of life in him." On January 9 she reported that her ailing little boy had been unable to eat his dinner and that she was "worn out with worry and anguish." On January 11 Vanya developed a "rasping cough," and when it did not get better Sonya called in the doctor, who, after examining the boy, assured her that there was nothing to worry about, that he found nothing wrong in the chest and throat, and that it was merely a bad case of flu. On January 20:

> Vanya is very ill, with a high temperature. . . . I went to see Dr. Filatov this evening and he prescribed large doses of quinine. Lyovochka is annoyed that I consulted him.

The sage of Yasnaya Polyana could be awfully inconsistent about doctors, whom he claimed to regard as useless, doing more harm than good. He had just called in *three* of them to treat his wife. But he objected to her consulting a physician about Vanya. At the beginning of February, Vanechka did seem on the mend. His temperature subsided. "I feel much happier about him now," Sonya, relieved, wrote in her diary on February 1.

She felt better about her husband, too. "Relations with Lyovochka are good and passionate," she noted. At this point her son Sergei, when he edited her diary, cut out twenty-five words. Perhaps they can be imagined. But then the great row over Tolstoy's sending his short story to the *Northern Herald* broke out and Sonya ceased writing about her son's illness to concentrate on telling the story of the blowup. Not until February 21 did she note anything more in her diary about Vanechka. He had a sore throat and the doctor informed her that the boy had contracted scarlet fever.

And then:

> February 23: My darling little Vanechka died this evening at 11 o'clock. . . . My God, and I am still alive!

She did not touch her diary again for twenty-eight months. On June 1, 1897, she took it up again.

> It was two years ago, on February 23, that my little Vanechka died. Since that time I closed the last page of my diary, as I closed my life, my heart, my feelings, my joy And I haven't yet recovered. . . .

She never did recover—fully. The death of Vanya devastated her. She could not be consoled. She could not be reconciled to it. The loss left her lifeless, unable more than before to cope rationally with her problems. "Mama is terrible in her grief," Masha Tolstoy wrote a friend. "Her whole life had been with him [Vanya]; she had given him all her love."[30] As her son Sergei later wrote: "With his [Vanya's] death my mother seemed to lose interest in life, and the hysteria latent in her character revealed itself with great force."[31] Her nervous system seemed permanently damaged, with dire consequences for herself and her family.

Leo Tolstoy did not mention the death of his son in his diary until February 26. His reaction was quite different from that of his wife. "We've buried Vanechka. A terrible—no, not a terrible, but a great spiritual event. I thank Thee, Father. I thank Thee."

He returned to the subject on March 12. Strangely, he began to think of what Vanechka's death did for him.

> The death of Vanechka was for me . . . a manifestation of God, drawing me towards Him. And so not only can I not say that it was a sad, painful event but I can say outright that it was a joyful one—not joyful, that's a bad word—but a merciful event, coming from God, disentangling the lies of life, and bringing me closer to Him.
>
> Sonya can't see it that way. For her the pain—almost physical—of separation conceals the spiritual importance of the event. But she astonished me. The pain of separation immediately released her from all that was darkening her soul. . . . She astonished me during the first days by her amazing power of love.

He is astonished but critical.

> She suffers particularly because the object of her love has gone from her, and she thinks that her happiness was in that object and not in the love itself. She can't separate the one from the other; she can't take a religious view of life in general or of her own. . . .
>
> I try to help her, but I can see that I haven't helped her so far. But I love her, and to be with her is both painful and good for me. . . .

To Alexandrine, whom he now affectionately called "Granny," and whom he addressed in a latter of March 31 as "my dear beloved old friend," he wrote of Vanya's death and its effect on him and his wife.

> Sonya's mental anguish is very serious. . . . Her grief is very great. She used to take refuge from everything in life that is painful, incomprehensible and vaguely worrying to her, in her love . . . for this boy who was truly exceptionally endowed, both

spiritually and emotionally. (He was one of those children who are prematurely sent by God into a world not yet ready for them, one of those ahead of their time, like swallows arriving too early and freezing to death.) And suddenly he was taken away from her . . . and . . . it was as though nothing was left to her in this worldly life.

As for himself:

The loss is painful to me, but I don't feel it nearly as much as Sonya, firstly because I had and have another life, a spiritual one, and secondly because Sonya's grief prevents me from seeing my own deprivation. . . . I feel sorry for her and am troubled by her condition. Generally speaking, I can say that I am well.

The death of Vanechka brought the Tolstoys closer together—again. As the funeral procession approached the Pokrovskoye cemetery outside Moscow, Sonya wrote later, "Lyovochka recalled how he used to drive along that road to our dacha in Pokrovskoe after he had first fallen in love with me. He wept and caressed me." As the coffin was being lowered into the grave, Sonya adds, he embraced her and held her to him. In a letter to her sister Tatanya a month later, Sonya wrote: "Lyovochka is being very kind to me. . . . I find his kindness and affection very comforting."

In the letter to Alexandrine four days after that, Tolstoy confided to his cousin how the death of Vanya had affected his relations with Sonya.

We have none of us ever felt so close to each other as we do now, and I have never felt either in Sonya or myself such a need for love. . . . I never loved Sonya as much as I do now. . . .

But once again—the old story! Three weeks after the death of Vanya, Tolstoy had written in his diary that the reason Sonya was suffering so much was that "she has invested all her spiritual energies in animal love for her little one."

Coming across those words in his diary, Sonya bristled. "Why *animal love?*" she asked. "My feelings for Vanechka, and our love for one another, was fundamentally spiritual in nature. We lived in a spiritual communion with one another . . . and despite the differ-

ence in our ages we always spoke on such a lofty, abstract plane."[32]
She appreciated Leo's renewed love for her after the tragedy, but
she did not like the put-down. "Why do all your references to me
in your diaries," she wrote him, "treat me as if I were evil? Why do
you want all future generations and our grandchildren to abuse my
name as a frivolous, evil wife who made you unhappy? I cannot ask
you to love me, but spare me my name."[33]

In a postscript to a letter to Strakhov on February 14, that
difficult year of 1895, nine days before the loss of Vanya, Tolstoy
told him to tear up and burn the sheet on which he was about to
write. He then confided to his friend the story of Sonya's jealousy
of the woman editor of the *Northern Herald*.

> Sofya Andreyevna was very upset that I gave my story
> [*Master and Man*] to the *Northern Herald* for nothing, and added to
> this she had almost a crazy fit of jealousy toward Guryevich
> (which has no semblance of a foundation). . . . She was near to
> suicide.*

Before the year was up she was very near to falling in love.
Perhaps she had. With another man! And Leo Tolstoy did not like
it. He, who had found Sonya's almost crazy fits of jealousy a bitter
cross to bear, now became almost insanely jealous himself.

---

* "If you write to me about this," Tolstoy concluded the letter, "write in such a
way that it won't be seen that I have written to you." This was the first sign of
deviousness that Tolstoy, in trying to cope with his wife's tantrums, employed. It
would not be the last.

## THIRTEEN

# Sonya's
# Strange Infatuation

$A$s she entered her fifties, Sonya Tolstoy began to look at her life in a new way. Despite her desolation over the death of Vanechka and her despair over the way her marriage had turned out, she realized that life had to go on and that she might find some happiness, some fulfillment, by liberating herself somewhat from the constraints of married life. She had lost, she felt, the love of her husband. Might she not perhaps find it elsewhere? Pure love, that is.

In her diary of July 29, 1891, Sonya had made a curious entry. She had been reading Bourget's novel *Un Coeur de femme* and it had fascinated her, she said, because she had read in it her own thoughts and feelings. The novel, Sonya noted, was about "a woman of the world loving two men at the same time."

> I know how possible it is to love two men, and it is described here very truthfully. Why must one love always exclude another? And why can one not love and remain honest at the same time?

Apparently the thought appealed to her. A few days later she wrote in her diary:

> I sometimes feel the need of a warm, gentle affection and a mutual friendship, and I keep thinking how good it would be and that it is never too late to try. . . .[1]

Four years later, in the summer of 1895, she began to think that she had found what she sought: a warm, gentle affection and pure friendship—in a most unlikely figure.

Music had led her to him. She had always loved music and was proficient enough at the piano to play duets with her husband: Beethoven, Chopin, Schumann, especially. After the death of Vanya she found solace in music. Indeed, without it, she said, she could not have survived. Wintering in Moscow, she had attended a good many concerts, and this had led her to the man who now began to figure in her life. Her love of music brought her also a love of the musician.

He was Sergei Ivanovich Taneyev, a distinguished pianist and composer, pupil and friend of Tchaikovsky, teacher of Scriabin and Rachmaninov, a director of the prestigious Moscow Music Conservatory.

Taneyev was a great musician but, to most Russians who knew and admired him, he was not a very attractive man personally. Leo Tolstoy had rather disliked him from the beginning. One April evening in 1889 Taneyev, a great admirer of the writer, had called on him in Moscow—"interrupted" him, Tolstoy grumbled in his diary.

> Read him my article on art. He's a completely ignorant man ... and imagines that he is in possession of the last word in human wisdom. ... Taneyev gets on my nerves.[2]

Tolstoy had no inkling then how much more Taneyev would get on his nerves six years hence when his wife began seeing the musician alone and prattling to her diary about her love for him.

Taneyev was hardly a man to intrigue a woman, even a woman of fifty-one. A thirty-nine-year-old bachelor, with a high-pitched voice and an effeminate manner, he apparently had never had a woman in his life except his old childhood nurse, who still lived with him and looked after him. He was a chubby little man with small, reddish eyes, a pug nose, and fat cheeks that somehow shone like a baby's. He seemed bashful in public and awkward, and his close-fitting suits made him look slightly ridiculous. But he was modest and simple in his ways, sensitive to others, and kind. His delicate touch at the piano seemed to transform his listeners, especially Sonya, who found herself being carried away (particularly when he played things like Mendelssohn's *Songs Without Words*) by the music and the man. As her son Sergei put it, "She transferred to Taneyev the effect of the music he played."

Sonya invited him to spend the summer at Yasnaya Polyana and he joyfully accepted—not because of Sonya, whose worship of him he seemed unmindful of, but because of the opportunity of seeing so much of Leo Tolstoy, whom he worshiped. He arrived with his nurse and his piano, and the summer passed serenely, Taneyev spending his days composing and practicing and his evenings dining with the family, playing chess with Leo and, usually—when the game was over and the family had gathered in the living room—the piano. Even the great writer, who could not like the musician personally, listened raptly as the pianist went through Bach, Beethoven, Chopin, Schumann, Tchaikovsky, and some of his own compositions. Neither Tolstoy nor his guest seemed to be aware of Sonya's growing infatuation as the summer of 1895 passed. Taneyev is not mentioned in Tolstoy's diary that summer and Sonya, it will be remembered, ceased writing in her diary that year after the death of Vanechka in February. Actually, relations between the Tolstoys seemed to improve that fall, after the departure of Taneyev.

On October 24, Tolstoy saw his wife off for Moscow and noted next day in his diary:

> As she sat in the coach I felt terribly sorry for her . . . sorry that she's depressed, sad and lonely. . . . At the bottom of her heart she's afraid I don't love her and that the reason for this is the difference in our views of life. And she thinks I don't love her because she hasn't come to me.

He then addressed her directly.

> Do not think that. I love you still more. I quite understand you, and know you couldn't come to me, so you are left alone. But you aren't alone. I am with you, just as you are, I love you, love you to the very end with a love that could not be greater.[3]

Not content to express his love in his diary, he wrote her directly later that day.

I wanted to write you, darling friend, on the very day of your departure, under the fresh impression of such a strong feeling I experienced. . . . The feeling I experienced was of a strange tenderness, pity and completely new love for you, such a love that I transferred myself entirely to you and felt the same that you were feeling. This is such a holy good feeling that one ought not to speak of it. This feeling of ours is strange, like an evening glow. Only now and then the little clouds of our differences diminish the brightness. I am always hoping they will disperse by night and that the sunset will be bright and clear.[4]

Sonya wrote back to him as soon as she received the letter.

Darling friend, Lyovochka! . . . These little clouds which, it seems to you, still sometimes darken our good relations are not entirely terrible. They are purely outward, the result of life, habit, the inertia to change, weakness; but they do not come at all from inner causes. Inwardly, the basis of our love remains serious, firm and harmonious . . . we both love one another. . . ."[5]

But when Sonya rather recklessly invited Taneyev back for a second summer, her husband rebelled. The prospect of the musician coming again greatly annoyed him. In this diary he spoke disdainfully of Taneyev:

. . . who disgusts me with his self-satisfied, moral and ridiculous, so to say, aesthetic (real not outward) obtuseness and his *coq du village* situation in our house. It's an examination for me. I'm trying not to fail.[6]

Apparently, during the winter Leo had begun to notice—and resent—his wife's growing attachment to the composer. Sonya rarely missed a Taneyev concert or a chance to meet him at some friend's house, and she had invited him continually to their Moscow home that winter to play.

Taneyev did not stay long when he returned to Yasnaya Polyana in the summer of 1896, departing the first of August much to Tolstoy's relief. That fall the Tolstoys exchanged endearing letters.

"Dearest darling Sonya," Leo wrote to her on November 13.

You ask whether I still love you. My feelings for you now are such that I think they can never change, because they contain everything that can possibly bind people together. . . . We are bound together by the past, and the children, and the awareness of our faults, and compassion, and an irresistible attraction. In a word, we are wrapped up and tied together well and truly. And I'm glad.

Actually, Tolstoy was still uneasy about Sonya's relations with Taneyev. For one thing, he decided to spend all the rest of the winter with his wife in Moscow, apparently feeling that his presence would discourage her from seeing so much of Taneyev. At the end of his last letter to Sonya, he had written: "Why are you still out of sorts and your letters dispirited?" The answer, though perhaps Sonya was unconscious of it, was her growing passion for the composer.

Tolstoy could not be blind to it after his arrival in Moscow. He worked fitfully on a big essay on art. But it did not go well. He turned to ideas for fiction.

A wife's betrayal of her passionate, jealous husband; his sufferings, struggle and the pleasure of forgiveness.[7]

All through December that year Tolstoy was deeply depressed. He could not make up his mind what to do about Sonya's obsession. He could not overcome his jealousy. But he did not want to admit that he had it. "Five days have passed and very painful ones," he noted in his diary in Moscow on December 2. "Everything is still the same." December 12: "I've suffered a lot during these days. . . . I'm not even trying to write." Three days later he records that Sonya made a "strange" request: that they visit Taneyev's nurse.

Christmas was approaching but he could not get into the spirit of it. On December 20: "I've done no work and I feel a depressing melancholy." The festivities on Christmas Day made him "feel better at heart." But the next day he fell into a state of dejection, complaining that he was still not writing. His "devil," he added, meaning his jealousy of Taneyev, wouldn't leave him.

The new year brought no relief. January 4, 1897: "Still nothing good to note about myself. . . . The devil won't go away." It bugged him on January 12: "I can't sleep from depression." He finds "revolting" Sonya's "senile *flirtation*" or "worse." He could stand Sonya's "senile flirtation" no longer. He stormed out of the house and, with his daughter Tanya, went to stay with friends who owned an estate not far from Moscow. The straw that broke the camel's back was Sonya's insistence on going to Petersburg in February to hear not only a concert of Taneyev but also his rehearsals. From his host's house on the first day of February, he wrote Sonya bitterly:

> . . . It's terrible and humiliatingly shameful that a complete outsider, an unnecessary and quite uninteresting man, rules our life and poisons the last years of our life; it's humiliating and painful that one has to ask when and where he is going and when he is playing at what rehearsals.
>
> This is terrible, terrible, shameful and repulsive. And it's happening just at the end of our life . . . a life spent well and purely—just at the time when we have been drawing closer and closer together in spite of everything that could divide us. . . . Suddenly, instead of a natural, good and joyful conclusion to 35 years together, there is this repulsive vileness which has left its terrible imprint on everything. I know you are miserable and you are suffering too, because you love me and want to be good, but so far you can't, and I'm terribly sorry for you because I love you. . . . Goodbye, and forgive me, dearest. I kiss you.

In a postscript he asked her to destroy the letter. And he added that he wanted to help her "escape from the terrible, hypnotized state in which you are living." He warns that there is only one possible solution to the problem: "that you should wake from your sleep-walking and return to a normal, natural life. May God help you."

But Sonya did not want to wake from her sleepwalking. Just the opposite. The more she saw of Taneyev, the more she liked him; the more she heard him playing the piano, the more she wanted to hear. And she, who had been so jealous of her husband, even of long-past affairs that she read about in his diaries, now began to resent *his* jealousy. He was full of "morbid jealousy," she wrote in her diary of June 2, 1897.

> I don't know if I am guilty. When I first grew close to Taneyev I thought how nice it would be to have such a friend in

my old age: calm, kind and clever. . . . Now look what has happened!

What had happened was that Sonya, without consulting her husband, had again asked Taneyev back to Yasnaya Polyana for the summer. This was too much for Tolstoy. More sleepless nights for him. More sobbing. "It was deeply painful to me," Sonya reported in her diary the next day, "to see the horror on Leo Nikolayevich's face when he heard of Taneyev's arrival. He is morbidly jealous."

Sonya might have felt less defiant had she received and pondered an anguished letter that Tolstoy wrote her on May 19 from Yasnaya Polyana, after five sleepless nights.

> My dear, darling Sonya:
> Your intimacy with Taneyev is not merely unpleasant to me, but dreadfully agonizing. . . . For a year now I haven't been able to work, and I'm not living but continually being tormented. You know this. I've said so to you in anger, and I've said so with entreaties. . . . I've tried everything and nothing has helped: the intimacy continues and even grows closer, and I can see that it will be like this to the end. I can't bear it any longer.

He had made up his mind to "go away" but he just couldn't do it—she would suffer too much, he went on. On the other hand, he said, he was *"almost* unable" to go on living as they had:

> You know this . . . and you are a good woman and you love me and yet you didn't want to save me and yourself from these terrible, unnecessary sufferings.
> What is it to be? Decide yourself. Think it over and decide yourself how to act.

Leo offered five ways out of their mess.

> The best way is to break off all relations . . . in such a way as to free yourself once and for all from this terrible nightmare which has been oppressing us now for a year. No meetings, no letters, no portraits, no mushroom picking . . . but complete freedom.

The second solution, he wrote, was for him to go abroad, parting from Sonya forever. This was the most difficult solution, he thought, but "a possible one, and 1,000 times easier for me than continuing the life we have been leading this year." The third way out, he suggested, was for them both to go abroad and remain "until the cause of all this has passed." The fourth, which was the "most terrible choice" and one he could not think about "without horror and despair," was to go on living as they had. There was a fifth solution: ". . . the one you suggested: for me to stop looking at it the way I do and wait for it—if it is anything—to pass, as you say."

He had tried the last but it hadn't worked. He simply couldn't endure what was going on between his wife and Taneyev.

> I've experienced this for a year and have tried with all my heart, but I can't. . . . On the contrary, the blows falling all the time on the same place have aggravated my pain. . . .
>
> Sonya, darling, you are a good, kind, fair-minded woman. Put yourself in my position and try to understand that I can't feel otherwise than . . . agonizing pain and shame, and try to think, darling, of the best way out. . . .

For some reason Tolstoy did not send this letter to his wife. Perhaps he thought she would soon end the affair with her composer friend on her own. If he did, he was mistaken. Taneyev, apparently oblivious to the storm he had caused in the life of the Tolstoys, arrived at Yasnaya Polyana on June 3. This time he must have begun to suspect what was happening, and he left on June 5. Sonya regretted it, but Leo was relieved.

Sonya wrote in her diary:

> Sergei Ivanovich [Taneyev] left today and Leo Niko-layevich immediately became calm and cheerful again, and I am calm too for I have seen him. It is only because Leo Nikolayevich is suffering that he makes these jealous demands that I have nothing more to do with Sergei Ivanovich. But to break off relations with him would make me suffer too. I feel so little guilt and so much calm joy in my pure, peaceful friendship with this man, that I could no more tear him out of my heart than I could

stop seeing, breathing or thinking. . . . I miss Sergei Ivanovich more than anything.[8]

Tolstoy may have felt relieved at the hasty departure of Taneyev but the tension between him and Sonya over the musician remained. The next day there was a terrible row. Sonya described it in her diary. Leo had mentioned to her that his life had been utterly transformed by religion. His inner life, maybe, Sonya retorted, but certainly not his external life. "It hadn't changed a bit."

> That made him furious, and he shouted that in the past he used to hunt, farm, teach and accumulate money, whereas now he didn't do any of these things. And a great pity too, I said. It had been much better for his family in the past . . . and it had been a great help to me when he made some money. . . . Now he bowls about on his bicycle, goes out on whichever of the horses he feels like riding, eats the large meals that are cooked for him and not only refuses to bother himself with his children but frequently forgets about their existence altogether.
> At this he exploded with rage, saying I ruined his life.[9]

Sonya says she was so taken aback that she ran out of the house "intending" to kill herself, to "go away, die, anything not to have to suffer like that again. What a joy it would be to live out the rest of one's days amicably with a good, quiet man, not to be tormented by any more insane, jealous scenes." That evening, she concludes, they "made it up"—it must have been for the thousandth time. But again!—not for long.

On July 8 Tolstoy wrote his wife that he was leaving for good. He made no mention of Taneyev or Sonya's infatuation with him. He was leaving, he said, just as the Hindus did as old age approached, to dedicate the last years to God.

> So please forgive me if my action causes you pain, and above all, Sonya, let me go freely and don't try to find me, don't complain of me, don't condemn me.
> The fact that I have left you doesn't mean that I am dissatisfied with you. . . . And I do not condemn you, but on the contrary I remember with love and gratitude the long 35 years of our life together, especially the first half of that time when,

with maternal self-sacrifice characteristic of your nature, you bore so steadfastly what you considered you had been called upon to bear. . . . You give much maternal love and sacrifice, and it's impossible not to appreciate you for it. But in the latter period of our life, in the last fifteen years, we have drifted apart.

He said he couldn't imagine that *he* was to blame.

Nor can I blame you . . . and I thank you and remember you with love, and always shall remember you for all you have given me. Goodbye, dear Sonya. . . .

Yours affectionately,
Leo Tolstoy

This letter Tolstoy did not send either. He still could not bring himself to the point of leaving a wife of thirty-five years. Despite all, despite the hatred and the jealousies, he still loved her. Nor did he want to desert the children, though by this time most of them had grown up and his two favorite daughters, Tanya and Masha, despite their father's fierce opposition, were in love and about to marry and start new lives in another place. Their son Leo, twenty-eight, who had caused his parents much concern by his wild life, got married that year to a Swede. He already had a small estate of his own. Only two children remained in the household—Misha, eighteen, and Alexandra, a fierce-tempered girl of thirteen. Still, all the children (and pretty soon the grandchildren) spent a good deal of time visiting their ancestral home, some taking sides in the war between their parents, others trying to make peace between them. They remained very much involved in their parents' lives. They let their father know, whether they sided with him or not, that they strongly opposed his leaving their mother.

But if he did not immediately give the letter to Sonya, he nevertheless intended her to read it—perhaps someday when he summoned the courage to flee Yasnaya Polyana. Also, the next day, according to Sonya, "relations with Leo Nikolayevich improved again." And that may have made Tolstoy hesitate to deliver the letter. So he hid it in the upholstery of a leather-bound chair in his study. (Four years later, when he became seriously ill, he told Masha of its existence, asking her to keep it and to see that it did not become public until fifty years after his death. But he neglected to give it to her, and when he recovered from his illness, he concluded that there was no urgency about turning it over. Ten years after he hid it, he learned that his wife was planning to reupholster the chairs in the study. He retrieved the letter and gave it, along with a second one, to Masha's husband, Prince Obolensky—Masha had died the year before—requesting him to give them to Sonya after his death. Obolensky handed them over to Countess Tolstoy soon after that event, and, according to him, she tore up one of them in his presence but kept the other and later deposited it in Leo's papers.)

Sonya continued to pine for her composer friend. She enticed him back to Yasnaya Polyana for a few days in July. "I haven't told Leo Nikolayevich, for fear that the news will distress him," she noted in her diary. "I just hope he won't be jealous again. If Sergei Ivanovich only knew, how shocked he would be! I cannot hide my joy at the thought of having . . . my dear, cheerful, honest friend here to talk to." Next day, Sonya reported in her diary, there were more "unpleasant scenes." When one of the children at dinner happened to mention Taneyev's visit, Leo flushed "crimson" and said that was the first he had heard of it. He demanded that Sonya either extinguish her special feelings for Taneyev or break off relations with him.

> Both suggestions are utterly preposterous [Sonya responded in her diary]. One cannot simply *extinguish* the feelings one has for a person. As for *actions,* which *are* under one's control, I have done nothing I could be reproached for. . . . To demand that I break off relations with this kind, honest, sensitive man would be needlessly to insult him and needlessly to compromise me.[10]

Tolstoy's rage could not be squelched, Sonya admitted the next day, despite her "tender caresses," her "loving care," her "patience in the face of Leo Nikolayevich's rude and unjustified accusations over Taneyev's visit." It was her own business, she said, and concerned no one but God and her own conscience.

Tolstoy did quiet down once Taneyev arrived. They played chess, went for walks, and in the evening Leo joined the family in listening to Taneyev at the piano. One evening Tolstoy and the children went for a walk and Sonya found herself alone with her beloved.

> We were alone in the drawing room, and it was wonderfully peaceful. He played two sonatas—what joy! . . . I have spent such a happy week with Sergei Ivanovich.[11]

They took walks together through the Zasyeka forest and to nearby villages. And she took photographs of him. "My heart aches," Sonya confided to her diary the day her friend departed, "for our walks, the music and the soothing presence of that dear man." She could not believe, she concluded, that such periods of bliss "would not return."

She could not get Taneyev out of her mind. She says she kept dreaming of him. And thinking of him.

> I thought a lot about Sergei Ivanovich today. . . . There is something about him that everyone loves. I can think calmly of him now; it's always that way after I've seen him. But my life feels constantly empty without him.[12]

She could not hide her feelings from the family, and now the children began to criticize her.

> Masha [her daughter] told me today that Ilya [her son] was mortified to discover that my intimacy with S.I. was the talk of Kiev. . . . Public opinion is so odd! Why should it be wrong to *love* someone? But I'm not at all troubled by this gossip. I am happy and proud to have my name associated with such a fine, moral, kind, gifted man. My conscience is clear. . . .[13]

Her eldest son, Sergei, kidded her about her infatuation, she noted in her diary. "Today Seryozha said: 'Mama is in her second childhood. I shall give her a doll and maybe a china set too.' " She did not find the remark funny, she said.[14] Next day she noticed that her children were again "attacking her over Taneyev."

> Well, let them! This man has brought such richness and joy to my life; he has opened the door to the world of music, and it was only through hearing him play that I found happiness and

consolation. His music brought me back to life after Vanechka's death, when life had deserted me. His gentle and happy presence has soothed my soul, and even now I feel so peaceful, so comfortable after I have seen him. . . .[15]

Finally, Sonya began to awaken from her fantasy, but only slowly. All through the winter of 1897–98 in Moscow, she continued to see Taneyev and, in her diaries, express her love for him. She had moved to Moscow early that fall and by September 13, 1897, she was again rhapsodizing about her musician friend. Taneyev had called on her twice that day. She was out to her dentist to get her first false teeth fitted and then had gone shopping.* To her joy, he tried a third time, arriving in the evening. The children had gone out.

> So the two of us [Sonya related in her diary] spent the evening alone together. We talked all evening about art, music, Leo Nikolayevich's writing—Taneyev is so fond of him—and of all the boundless hopes of one's youth. . . . Sergei Ivanovich played me his beautiful symphony, which affected me deeply. It is a marvelous work, such lofty, noble music.

She woke up, at least somewhat, and then she would slide back into her romantic worship of the man. A few weeks later, on October 23, she went off with an uncle to call on Taneyev and felt "bored and guilty." She also felt, she says, that "that *must* be the last time." She would not be seeing him again. By the middle of November she was reporting in her diary that she had seen nothing of Taneyev. He had injured his leg cycling, she said, but she would not visit him because she did not want to "hurt Lyovochka."[16]

Next day, though (November 16), she had "such a desperate, helpless desire to see that man play again." Would it ever happen? she asked despairingly.

---

* Sonya's false teeth gave her a great deal of trouble. On October 19, 1897, she confided to her diary: "My new teeth are all wrong. They will have to be done all over again. It's so annoying to have wasted a whole week at the dentist." On the twenty-fifth again: "I stayed for a long time at the dentist's. . . . He tortured me terribly and even now my false teeth are hurting me." She was very vain about it. "To think that I have reached the point of wearing false teeth—I used to shudder at the thought."

It would, of course. Over the Christmas and New Year's holidays Sonya and her husband again patched things up. On his arrival in Moscow on December 5—he had kept postponing the trip from Yasnaya because of his "suffering" from Sonya's flirtation—they fell into each other's arms and wept with joy. Sonya even promised, she says, not to see Taneyev again. "We had such a pleasant talk," she adds, "it was such a joy to promise him that I loved him so very deeply."[17]

Yet again! But the very next day they were at odds. Sonya discovered that her husband had noted in his diary that she had confessed to the crime of seeing Taneyev—"something she had never done before," he said—and it filled him with joy. Sonya read it and exploded!

> God help me to endure this! Once more he has to present himself to future generations as a *martyr* and me as a *criminal*. . . . God forgive him for his cruelty and injustice to me.[18]

So, taking her revenge, although it meant breaking her promise, she began to see Taneyev again. The very day after she had sworn in her diary that she would not visit him, she admitted: "I have such a desperate, helpless desire to see that man play again—will it never be granted me?" Two days after Christmas: "I yearn to hear him play—maybe I never shall," she wailed. And finally, on February 3, four weeks into the new year (1898), she met Taneyev at a concert and, to her joy, they sat together. All the old feelings returned. She loved his running comments about the music. After it was over, she gave him a lift home in her sleigh. She felt a little guilty about it:

> . . . as though I was concealing some shameful secret. But I felt sorry for Sergei Ivanovich wearing his thin coat in the wind and cold and it seemed only natural to give him a lift.

It seemed natural too when the composer resumed visiting Sonya at home, as he did three weeks later. "We saw little of each other," she recorded in her diary, "and spoke little. We shall have more conversations together during those long evenings when I am here on my own . . . without Lyovochka."[19]

Daughter Tanya, who was falling in love with a married man with six children, objected to her mother's seeing Taneyev and, according to Sonya, "said a great many spiteful things about Sergei Ivanovich's visit." What an indignity! "That's the way," Sonya snorted in her diary, "to stop a good sympathetic friendship between two people!"[20]

And now the composer began to wake up, briefly. As spring approached, he apparently began to ponder what he had done to Countess Tolstoy, wife of the man he worshiped as a great writer and artist. Sonya spotted him at a party but she thought he snubbed her. "There is no doubt," she says, "that he is avoiding me. I am sure of it. But why?" She noted it was not the first time. Recently at a concert he had suddenly left her side and gone to sit by himself in the gallery.[21]

The cooling off did not last very long. Three days after she thought he had snubbed her, he was back at the Moscow home, and though Leo was present, Sonya wrote that the musician's "presence had an immediate soothing effect on me. He is such a kind, even-tempered gifted man."

That might be, but Leo disagreed. He did not even care for the man's music. On this particular evening, Sonya records, he did not like Taneyev's symphony and "told him so."

All that spring of 1898 Sonya saw a good deal of Taneyev and her love for him seemed to deepen. One after another of her diary entries attest to her increasing infatuation with this man.

> April 25: Sergei Ivanovich came and it was all wonderfully calm and ordinary.

Toward the end of March, she had spent four days in St. Petersburg attending rehearsals and then the concert in which Taneyev's symphony was played under the conductorship of Glazunov, a fellow composer. At first, she says, Leo refused to let her go, finally agreeing to "release" her. It would be a bone of contention between them for months to come.

Sonya remained in Moscow much later that year. On May 9, she noted that Taneyev came over to play a Beethoven sonata and a Chopin nocturne. "What a delight it was," she exclaimed, "and how he played! . . . I knew he was playing for me, and I was grateful to him. But why stir up these terrible feelings which may have been asleep in my heart? It's too painful." At the end of May, with the lovely spring turning to summer, there were wonderful meetings, some of them, Sonya thought, almost like miracles.

> I was playing the piano in the corner room one evening, longing to see Sergei Ivanovich again and hear him play, when through the window I saw three figures approaching. . . .

Taneyev was one of them, and as usual, after the other two old friends of the Tolstoys' had left, he played for her. He came again on the evening of the twenty-ninth with Goldenweiser, another noted pianist.[22] And then on the thirtieth:

> I returned home, went out on the balcony and whom should I see but Sergei Ivanovich sitting on a bench in the garden reading a newspaper. I was terribly pleased. Dinner had been laid in the garden for Misha and me and we laid a third place for him. And what a nice, cheerful dinner we had. . . . Then Misha went off and left the two of us together. . . . Sergei Ivanovich played. . . . Then we sat and talked, as people talk when they trust each other completely—frankly, seriously, without shyness or stupid jokes. . . . There wasn't a dull or awkward moment.
>
> What an evening it was! It was my last in Moscow—and perhaps the last such evening in my life.[23]

When Sonya arrived at Yasnaya Polyana the next day there was no one to meet her. Leo had gone off with his daughter-in-law Sonya to stay with friends some distance away. Sonya was deeply annoyed. "He had promised to meet me at Yasnaya," she complained in her diary, "and instead he sets off with Sonya, his daughter-in-law, to gallivant around visiting neighbors. . . ."[24]

Sonya invited her sister to Yasnaya in July, and Tanya Kuzminsky did her best to bring peace between the quarreling spouses. Tolstoy had always adored her, and listened patiently while Tanya assured him that Sonya's friendship with Taneyev was quite innocent, however annoying, and was based on her sister's need for the solace of music after Vanya's death. To her sister, Tanya spoke quite harshly, scolding her for her behavior with the composer.

Tanya departed on July 28 and that night after they had gone to bed Sonya and Leo began discussing her relationship with Taneyev and the matter of Leo's intense jealousy. As usual the talk led to a quarrel, this time so bitter that Sonya in despair begged him to cut her throat and end it all. Tolstoy wrote up the account in the form of a dialogue to send to Tanya Kuzminsky. It is a lengthy piece, and it depicts Tolstoy's whole attitude to the Taneyev affair—along with giving Sonya's answers to his jealous questions about it. It gives the reader a revealing firsthand account of how Sonya and Leo talked to each other in the midst of their bickering. "Talked" is probably too gentle a word. According to both of them, they shouted and cursed.

> Some valve maintaining the equilibrium in my brain [Sonya admitted] flew open. I lost all control of myself. I was terrified, shaking, sobbing and raving.[25]

She took to bed for two days "in a darkened room, without food or light," she says, "without love, hate or emotions. . . . I just wanted to die."[26]

According to Tolstoy, the following dialogue took place.

### The Dialogue

Leo demanded that she "repent at heart" for her "feelings" toward Taneyev.

> SHE: I can't repent, and I don't understand what it means.
> I: It means discussing with yourself whether the feeling which you have for this man is good or bad.
> SHE: I don't have any feelings, good or bad.
> I: That's not true.
> SHE: The feeling is so unimportant, insignificant.
> I: You must decide whether this was a good feeling or a bad one.
> SHE: There's nothing to decide. This feeling is so unimportant that it can't be bad. . . .
> I: No, the exclusive feeling of an old, married woman for another man is a bad thing.
> SHE: I have no feeling for a man, only for a person.
> I: But this person is a man.

SHE: He isn't a man for me. . . . There isn't any special feeling for the person.

I: Why tell lies?

SHE: All right. There was once. . . . But it's over now. I'll do anything not to distress you.[27]

But Tolstoy would not accept this concession. He kept harping that it was her *feelings* toward Taneyev that was the terrible crime. He kept insisting that she acknowledge it.

SHE: Always the same old thing. . . . I've done nothing wrong. . . .

And so it went. So long as she would not admit her "crime," Tolstoy said, "there was no way out." He accused her of having no moral judgment. Having thus wounded her, he proposed they stop talking. "It's two o'clock," he said. But Sonya insisted on going on. He had asked her what her *feeling* was and what she really wished to do. Very well, she would tell him. She wished that Taneyev "should come once a month to stay a while and play, like any good acquaintance." Just when Leo thought she was on the verge of confessing and promising not to see Taneyev again—she said that! For him, it proved her guilt.

"If a visit once a month would be pleasant," he retorted, "then once a week or every day would be more pleasant still."

SHE: Oh, always the same old thing. It's torture. Other women are unfaithful to their husbands, but they aren't tormented as much as I am.

In her case, she said, "there were no actions." But Tolstoy would not accept that she had not slept with Taneyev. What about her trips to Petersburg, "and to this place and that? You've become a sort of lady of the conservatoire." These words, Tolstoy says, "for some reason angered her."

SHE: You want to torment me and deprive me of everything. It is cruel of you.

Whereupon, says Tolstoy, Sonya became hysterical. "Her anger reached its peak."

SHE: You have tormented me for two hours. . . . It's terrible. Goodness knows what your cruelty will lead to.

I: But I prayed and wanted to help you. . . .

SHE: It's all lies, deceit. You can deceive other people but I can see right through you!

I: What's the matter with you? I just wanted to do good.

SHE: There's no good in you. You're evil, you're a beast. *I will love good and decent people, but not you. You're a beast.*

After which, Tolstoy goes on, "there followed terrible and cruel words: threats, suicide, curses, on everyone, on me and our daughters."

"Look here," Sonya cried, "where the parting is, cut the vein in my neck, here it is." She pushed her neck up to him, baring her throat. "It was dreadful," Tolstoy says. Finally he held her in his arms to stop her shaking and kissed her on the forehead. "She couldn't get her breath for a long time, then she began to yawn and sigh and dropped off to sleep."

"I don't know how this madness can be resolved," he wrote in conclusion. "I don't see any way out."

But in the turmoil of the Tolstoys' life, there was always a way out—for the moment.

On August 22, Sonya celebrated her fifty-fourth birthday. There were presents from the children and a grand family reunion. Sonya reported in her diary that Leo "was such . . . lively, scintillating company." His seventieth birthday followed on the twenty-eighth and again there was a pleasant family reunion.

September 23 was the Tolstoys' thirty-sixth wedding anniversary. By that time, as usual, Sonya was back in Moscow and Leo remained at Yasnaya Polyana. Sonya did not like his absence but she was full of tender feelings for him.

September 23: My wedding anniversary. Today I have been married to Leo Nikolayevich for thirty-six years—and we are apart.

It saddens me that we are not closer. . . . I have made so

many attempts to achieve some sort of spiritual intimacy with him. There is a strong bond between us—I only wish it was based on something more congenial. But I am not complaining, it is good that he's concerned about me, guards me so jealously and is afraid of losing me. With no cause. Whomever else I might love, there is no one in the world I would *compare* with my husband. Throughout my life he has occupied far too great a place in my heart.

But she had not given up Taneyev—by any means.

Even before she left Yasnaya that summer, on August 30, she had been in raptures after receiving a letter from Taneyev and then at his sudden appearance in person.

> I received such a clever, charming letter from Sergei Ivanovich this morning, and I showed it to Leo Nikolayevich, who thought the same. . . . Then just an hour after I got this letter Sergei Ivanovich himself arrived. . . . This evening after he had taken a short nap, he played a game of chess with Leo Nikolayevich, then sat down at the piano. And oh, how marvelously he played! Such depth, such intelligence, such seriousness—it would be impossible to play better. Both L.N. and Mashenka were in ecstasies—and so, of course, was I. . . . Leo Nikolayevich said his performance was superb, quite the last word in music—no one else could match Sergei Ivanovich's playing, he said.

The very day Sonya returned to Moscow, on September 15, Taneyev dropped around with other friends and they had what Sonya describes as a "merry evening." He came the next evening, too, but there were so many visitors, Sonya says, that they had no opportunity to talk. "We simply exchanged a few words intelligible only to us." Yet that day, Sonya also wrote in her diary, she "suddenly" longed to be with her husband again, "to make him happy, not to waste one moment of my life away from him—yet when Sergei Ivanovich left, the thought that I wouldn't be seeing him again for some time made me quite wretched. . . ." Torn between these two emotions, she added, she longed to run off and take her life. For the first time Sonya seemed terribly upset that she was in love with two men. She began to feel guilty at seeing so much of Taneyev.

"I made a grave mistake," she wrote in her diary September 22, "by personally delivering some books to Sergei Ivanovich."

> I very much regret this now, but I have been quite beside myself recently, lying awake until four in the morning, haunted by the misery of loneliness and the vanity of life, and desperately searching for something to grasp hold of, something to save me from this depression.

But her spirits revived five days later when Taneyev called.

> He and I strolled about the garden together, and I asked his advice about various matters. What a dear friend he is! He responded so seriously and thoughtfully to all my doubts and questions . . . and comforted me. After lunch he played a Beethoven sonata and the andante from a Tchaikovsky concerto. He played formidably well. His visit, his advice, his sympathy and his music gave me strength to live, gave courage to my spirit and peace to my soul.[28]

On November 8 she ran into Taneyev "at a rather dull concert" and, with a friend, walked home with him, she says, "under the starry sky." In the garden they looked at the star-studded heavens through binoculars. Sonya was amazed at the beauty of the firmament. Afterward Taneyev played and, as usual, Sonya was carried away. "Someone with this sort of musical gift has enormous power!" she wrote in her diary.

> November 27: S. I. Taneyev arrived this afternoon. . . . I love him best when he comes like this, just to see me. He had composed the most beautiful impressive work . . . and had come to play and sing it through to me. . . . We sat chatting, and read an article of musical criticism. One always has such a peaceful, interesting time with him. We get on so well—it's a great shame that L.N.'s jealousy weighs so heavily on this simple friendship with Sergei Ivanovich.

But there were occasions that fall when they did not get along so well. Each of them appeared to be coming down to earth, especially Taneyev. Sonya may have had, as she says, a merry evening with him and others when she got back to Moscow on September 15. But she mentioned that something "astonished her about her friend that evening."

> He told me that when I was at the Maslovs' I had deeply offended him by laughing at his ugly white cycling socks, saying they made him look like a clown.

When they met "accidentally" at a concert October 31, their conversation, Sonya reported, was "brief." "We barely greeted one another, and he rather discourteously went on talking with some old man he was with."

Things did not improve over the holidays. On February 4 of the new year (1899), again at a concert, they had what Sonya describes in her diary as a most "unpleasant exchange." He mentioned to her that he had gone to see a woman friend and she had graciously driven him home. For the first time Sonya felt a streak of jealousy. His remark, she says, made her "seethe with rage." She adds that she was very haughty and disapproving of him and that he was very embarrassed and stalked off.

Unable to get along with the two men she loved, Sonya was again in a fit of depression. On the last day of the century, she wrote in her diary:

> Life is so hard! Where is the happiness? Or peace of mind? Or joy? . . . I live from day to day without any goal or serious purpose in life. If I cannot please those around me, I try not to poison their lives. . . .

So despairing was she that she did not touch her diary for nearly a year. On November 5, 1900, she took it up again to record, among other things, that "things have changed somewhat with Sergei Ivanovich. We seldom see one another. . . ." Still, she was ambivalent about him, adding that when they did meet it was as though they never parted.

He was growing cool toward her, but she could not stand giving him up completely and forever, as she had promised.

> November 15: It makes him [Leo] angry and anxious whenever I see Sergei Ivanovich but I miss both him and his music—I

don't want to hurt Leo Nikolayevich, but I can't help missing
him [Taneyev] dreadfully. It's all very sad and irreparable.

On December 23, Sonya went to a rehearsal of a program in
which Rachmaninov was playing and Chaliapin singing. As so
often, she ran into Taneyev but found him "in a strange, sardonic,
unfriendly mood." There is no mention of Taneyev in her diary
again until the next summer when she was to go to Moscow from
Yasnaya on business. There, she says, she saw Taneyev.

There has been a cooling off in our relations recently, and I
have neither the energy nor the inclination to maintain our
former friendship. Besides, he really isn't the kind of person one
can be friends with. Like all gifted people he is always seeking
new experiences and he looks for other people to provide them.[29]

New experiences? Other people? Did that mean new women?
Was Sonya Tolstoy at last being dumped by this "gifted" man? Her
son Sergei believes the end of the affair came in 1904.

That year, he says, Taneyev received a letter from Countess
Tolstoy which in his diary he called "absurd." The letter was not
found in his papers and probably he destroyed it. But an idea of its
contents can be garnered from two letters Taneyev wrote her at the
time. Sonya had complained—it was not the first time—that at a
concert he had rudely left her. On November 15, 1904, Taneyev
replied that he would not be calling on her that day because he was
not ready to give her the explanations which she "insistently demanded." One reason, he said, was that she had asked him not to
address his reply either to her address in Moscow or to Yasnaya
Polyana.

Two days later he wrote her again, saying it would have been
easy for him to explain why he left his seat beside her at the concert
"by merely pointing out that everybody present at a concert can
enjoy the unrestricted right of giving up his seat and leaving the
hall during the intermission." He went on:

However, the questions raised by you in your letter involve
such a number of facts, relationships and misunderstandings as
to make me incompetent to act as you wish. . . .[30]

Apparently, Sonya finally understood. Taneyev was embarrassed by her attention and wanted to cool it. But both he and the Countess had some time before come to the conclusion to do just that. Sergei Tolstoy quotes a letter Taneyev wrote to Sonya back in August 1898, in which he asks her to convey to Tolstoy his warmest greetings. Making no mention of Sonya herself, he tells her how grateful he is for all that he has received from the "Master's writings."

Sonya's diary tells of the ending of this strange chapter in her life. On December 27, 1902, she ran into Taneyev at a dinner. "Relations with him," she noted in her journal, "were cold, strained and formal."

On September 21, 1910, shortly before Tolstoy's flight and death, Sonya noted in her diary that she had called on Taneyev's nurse in Moscow to find out how he was. "He was still in the country," she wrote in her diary.

> I should love to see him and hear him play. This good calm man was such a help to me after Vanechka's death and gave me such spiritual consolation.
> But this is not possible now. I no longer love him as I did, we do not see each other any more for some reason, and I have done nothing at all for a very long time to bring this about.

Later, in her autobiography, Sonya tried to sum up her affair with Taneyev. Repeating what she had written so often—that after the death of Vanechka, she had found solace in music—she goes on:

> But it was Taneyev's music that affected me more powerfully than any other. Sometimes I had only to meet Sergei Ivanovich and hear his calm, soothing voice to feel comfort. . . . I was in a distressed state, and it also coincided with my critical period. In the mood I was in at that time . . . I didn't think much about it. To all appearances he was not very interesting . . . always equable, extremely reticent, and a complete stranger to me to the very end.

Granted, as seems most probable, that they never went to bed together, was Taneyev really, as Sonya wrote in the end, "a complete stranger" to her? Not if you believe her diary, so full of passionate declarations of love.

Her fling with Taneyev and her life with Tolstoy had made her ponder a great deal about love. On September 19, 1897, on a dull and windy Moscow day, she had written in her diary: "I am lonely and want love. But where is it?" On October 2, back in Yasnaya Polyana for a few days, she had reflected further:

> The best, strongest and yet most painful thing in the world is love and love alone. . . . Love gives inspiration, energy and happiness; it brings an ability to work to the artist, the scientist, the philosopher, to women and even to children. I don't mean sexual love—but any kind of love. . . . My affection for my husband and other people was also spiritual, mental and aesthetic rather than physical. No matter how repulsive my husband has been to me in his physical habits,* I have been able to love him throughout my life, thanks to the richness of his mind—as for the rest I have tried to shut my eyes. . . . My affection for Taneyev was also due not to his physical appearance but to his wonderful musical genius. The noble, earnest purity of his music must come from his soul.

All through her life Sonya had tried, not always successfully, to understand that to be married to a genius one had to accept certain things that one would not take from the rest of mankind. She kept thinking of this one day in November 1897, on her way up to Moscow on the train from Yasnaya Polyana. She was reading a biography of Beethoven.

> He was one of those geniuses whose world center was his own creative power . . . while all the rest of the world was merely an accessory to it. Beethoven gave me insight into Leo N.'s egoism and indifference to everything around him. The world to him is merely the environment of his genius and he takes from it only what can serve his work. He discards the rest. He takes from me, for instance, my copying, my care for his physical welfare, my body. My whole spiritual life is of no interest to

---

* A few months after their marriage, Sonya had confided to her diary: "The physical side of love means a great deal to him. That's dreadful—for it's exactly the other way around for me." (Sonya's diary, April 29, 1863.)

him—for he has never even taken the trouble to understand it. . . . And yet the whole world worships such men.[31]

On June 7, 1915, nearly five years after Tolstoy's death, Sonya Tolstoy scribbled in her notebook that Taneyev had died the day before. She was "deeply shaken," she wrote, by the "sad news."*

According to Sergei, his father never blamed Taneyev for his mother's "infatuation," and understood "the abnormality of the situation."[32] He understood it, but he did not like it. As the twentieth century arrived, he gave up writing Sonya about it or complaining in his diaries. He was seventy-two when the 1900s came, and he felt there was not much time left on earth for him—ten more years, as it turned out. He was writing well again, a big novel, some long stories, some articles, including a long and difficult one on art. He sought peace and quiet to get on with them and to get on with the last years of his life.

But peace and quiet were not to be granted such a stormy genius in such a tempestuous household. Other bones of contention arose or were resurrected. Sonya's hysteria grew worse, not always without provocation, and her tantrums more frequent and more violent, and Leo Tolstoy became a desperate old man engaged in a deadly war with an unbalanced wife he both loved and hated—and could not much longer abide.

* Aside from her regular diary, Sonya had begun keeping a notebook, jotting down briefly her daily doings. It ran from 1905 to 1907 and from 1909 to 1919, shortly before her death.

# FOURTEEN

# No Rest, No Peace
# for the Writer
# at Seventy

To MAKE MATTERS WORSE, after all the difficulties with his wife, Tolstoy saw his darling daughters Tanya and Masha fly the coop. Tanya, thirty-four, who had rejected many suitors in order to devote herself to her father, whom she worshiped, had fallen deeply in love with a man fifteen years her elder, who had a wife and six children. Masha, twenty-seven, who was even closer to her father, and who had also rejected more than one man, had fallen in love with a penniless, shiftless aristocrat, her distant cousin Prince Nikolai (Kolya) Obolensky, She, who was so serious about life, a most zealous Tolstoyan who, out of belief in her father's ideals, refused to accept her share of the inheritance when Tolstoy deeded his properties to his family, now wanted to marry a play-boy.

Tolstoy was shocked. How could his favorite daughter, who more than all the rest of the children had understood and accepted his precepts, desert him now? And for marriage, an institution he had long deplored. And since Obolensky though penniless refused to work for a living, how were they to live? He questioned her in a letter.

> Judging by your life recently—more idle and luxurious than before—and by Kolya's life and habits, you'll need a fair sum to live on. . . . How have you envisaged this? What does he think about it? How and where does he want to work and *does* he want to work . . . ? Do you intend to ask for your legacy?[1]

In another letter shortly afterward, he reminded her that "of all the family, you alone understand and appreciate me."[2]

And again, in a third letter:

> You must have guessed that your decision means failure to me; you know it full well; on the other hand I am glad to think that it will be easier for you to live after abandoning your ideal, or rather after mingling your ideal with baser assumptions, by which I mean having children.[3]

But this time his devoted daughter was adamant. On June 2, 1897, Masha married Prince Obolensky.

"I feel sorry for Masha," Sonya wrote in her diary the next day, though not mentioning the wedding the day before. Tolstoy expressed the same feeling in his diary a few days later. "Masha got married and I was sorry for her, as one is sorry for a thoroughbred horse that is made to carry water."[4]

And now there was Tanya to deal with—the gentle, sensitive, intelligent, fun-loving eldest daughter who, unlike the other children, had managed to balance her adoration of her father with an affection for, and an understanding of, her mother.

She had fallen "head over ears" in love, as she put it in a diary entry of November 1, 1896. "I don't think I ever fell in love like this before." The object of this madness, as she also put it, was a middle-aged man, Mikhail Sukhotin. For some time they had been meeting secretly and exchanging love letters that Tanya contrived to keep from the rest of the family. Her remorse at falling in love with a married man with children was immense, as was her feeling of guilt that she had not breathed a word of it to her revered father. She felt she was acting "shamefully."

"I have ruined my life—soiled it and ruined it irrevocably," she lamented in her diary five months later.[5]

> I am constantly trying to break off all relations with him, but he will not let me, and I must say that when I am with him I feel lighthearted, joyful and extraordinarily tranquil. . . . But for me, every time I see him without Papa's knowledge, is such a torment, such a trial, that I can hardly hold back from telling Papa.

She had held back, she says, because she was afraid he would "torture" her "with his suspicions and his attempts to look after me." Those attempts were not long in coming. On October 14, 1897, after a tearful Tanya had told her father of her love, he wrote back to express his displeasure and opposition.

> I have received your letter, dear Tanya, and I simply cannot give you the answer you would like. . . . Why a pure girl should want to get mixed up in such a business [as marriage] is beyond me. If I were a girl I would not marry for anything in the world. And as far as being in love is concerned—since I know what it means; that is, that it's an ignoble and unhealthy sentiment—I would not have opened my door to it.

If she wanted to go "dancing," which is the way he perceived rushing into marriage, then "go dance. I take comfort in the thought that when you have finished dancing, you will become as you were before, and ought always to be." What she was proposing to do, he went on, was "irresponsible"; she was acting with "the total unconsciousness of one possessed." The thing to do, he concluded, was "not to bind oneself to someone else but to lock oneself in a room and throw the key out the window."[6]

But Tanya, like Masha, could not heed her father despite her great love for him. She had mentioned in her diary how ashamed she felt before Sukhotin's wife and before his children, "even though he says that I take nothing away from them and though I know that his wife ceased loving him long ago and that living with her is for him a heroic effort."

Just when the situation seemed hopeless—Tanya had finally promised herself that she could not continue to carry on with a married man, love him wildly though she did—Sukhotin's wife died. They were now free to marry. And Tanya told her parents that was what she was going to do. The wedding took place in Moscow on November 14, 1899. According to Sonya, neither she nor her husband attended the ceremony. But as Tanya left their Moscow home to drive to the church, her father sobbed—"as though," Sonya says, "she was taking leave of the most precious thing on earth." As for Sonya, she admits that when she went to Tanya's empty room she also sobbed. "For us, her parents," she noted in her diary, "this marriage was a tragic blow. . . . Leo Ni-kolayevich grieved and wept terribly for Tanya, and November 24, he fell ill."[7]

Before taking to bed, he had noted in his diary:

> I am in Moscow. Tanya has gone away—God knows why—with Sukhotin. It is painful and humiliating.

The thought of her departure, so close upon that of Masha, leaving him alone with Sonya, except for their fifteen-year-old daughter Sasha, aroused his old disdain of women.

> For seventy years my opinion of women had done nothing but sink, and yet it must go lower still. The problem of women? One thing is sure! It is not solved by allowing women to run one's life, but by preventing them from destroying it![8]

Once again Tolstoy escaped from the turmoil and disappointments of family life. He had been involving himself in trying to prevent further Tsarist persecution of an obscure religious sect, the Dukhobors, who described their cult as "the World Brotherhood of Christians." In Russian, Dukhobors meant "spirit wrestlers." Egged on by the Orthodox Church, the Tsarist police were doing all they could to stamp out this heresy, conscripting the Dukhobor youth into the army, tearing the younger children away from their parents and placing them in Orthodox convents, and trying to forcefully convert the elders into the Orthodox faith.

Tolstoy became their champion. To the dismay of the church and the government, he exposed their plight to Russia and the outside world. Such was his prestige not only at home but abroad that his action aroused the conscience of the world—and the curses of the Orthodox Church and the government in Petersburg. The *Petersburg Gazette,* which published his account of the plight of the persecuted sectarians and his appeals for funds to help them, was warned by the authorities not to publish any more appeals from Tolstoy and forbidden to accept donations. The capital's chief of police then shut the newspaper down for two months.

As he had done before when the Tsarist government took a dim view of his helping out in famine relief, Tolstoy appealed for foreign aid. He had sent one of his closest followers, Pavel Biryukov, to the Caucasus (where the Dukhobors had been exiled by Alexander I) to investigate the persecution of the Dukhobors and to learn more about the sect itself. Biryukov returned and wrote a pamphlet for Tolstoy entitled *The Persecution of Christians in Russia in 1895.** Tolstoy sent the report, which could not be published in Russia, along with a letter of his own, to *The Times* of London, which published them on October 23, 1895.

"The censorship in Russia," Tolstoy wrote *The Times*, "will not pass my article and so I turn to you with the request to publish it in your paper."

Tolstoy's letter and article in *The Times* was bitterly resented by the authorities in Petersburg, who saw what they regarded as a local matter swollen into an international issue. Pobyedonostsev, Tolstoy's implacable enemy in the government, who had been wise enough to urge restraint in moving against Russia's greatest writer, now asked Tsar Nicholas II to arrest him. Nicholas, like his father, Alexander III, rejected his minister's advice. He, too, did not intend to make a martyr of Tolstoy. But, as often before, the government could get at the old man by taking action against his followers.

Learning that the persecution of the Dukhobors was growing worse, Tolstoy encouraged Biryukov and Chertkov to write a manifesto asking for help for the sect.

"A terrible cruelty," it began, "is now being perpetrated in the Caucasus. More than 4,000 people are suffering and dying from hunger, disease and exhaustion, blows, torture and other persecutions at the hands of the Russian authorities." Tolstoy wrote a postscript and all three signed the manifesto. At the beginning of 1897, it was secretly circulated around Russia. The government reacted swiftly. Biryukov and Chertkov were arrested and sent into exile, Chertkov for ten years in England.

Tolstoy was crushed. He hastened to Petersburg to see his

---

* Biryukov's report was somewhat flawed. He did not delve deeply enough into the real nature of the Dukhobors. He did not notice that the sect had been badly split, nearly half denying the leadership of Peter Verigin, a charismatic, autocratic figure who had been exiled by the Russian government. In his exile, Verigin had read Tolstoy's religious works, and peddled them to his flock as coming to him from God. He himself claimed to be the incarnation of God. But that the Dukhobors had been treated savagely by the Tsarist authorities there could be no doubt, as Tolstoy stressed in his letter to *The Times*.

disciples before they left. The loss of Chertkov was especially hard to take, for he had become the practical manager of the Tolstoyan movement, getting out its publications, spreading the word by hook or by crook, and organizing special campaigns such as the battle to save the Dukhobors. The Master was afraid that his chief disciple would not be able to accomplish much in England.

> I'm very much afraid [he wrote him] that you will be corrupted in England. I've just received the *Review of Reviews* and read it, and I caught such a breath of that astonishing self-satisfied English dullness, that I put myself in your place and tried to think how you could get on with them.[9]

He was depressed, too, that once again the Tsarist government had arrested and exiled his dearest disciples and not put a finger on him. He talked about it in a letter to a follower:

> You probably know that Chertkov and Biryukov have been sent into exile. . . . That is all very well and good. The sad thing is they won't lay a finger on me. . . . They [the people in authority] are defeating their own purpose, however, for by leaving me free to speak the truth they are compelling me to speak it. And much remains to be done.[10]

Far from content to speak out only for the Dukhobors, Tolstoy took up the persecution of other religious sects in Russia. The Molokhans, or "milk drinkers" (as the name in Russian suggests), who lived near his estate in Samara, were now, Tolstoy learned, being subjected to the same brutal treatment as the Dukhobors. Among other things, their children were also being snatched away from the parents and put in an Orthodox monastery. Tolstoy was so furious when he learned of this that he wrote a sharp letter to the Tsar, protesting. He was in no mood to be diplomatic, even with the Emperor of all the Russians.

> Majesty, for the love of God, make an effort and, instead of avoiding the matter and sending it to commissions and committees, decide, without asking anyone's advice, you yourself, acting on your own initiative, that these religious persecutions, which are causing the shame of Russia, must cease; the exiles must be sent back to their homes, the prisoners released, the children

returned to their parents, and above all the whole administrative
laws and regulations must be abolished.

He did not hear from Nicholas II. So he sent a second letter.
This, too, went unanswered. But the old warrior did not give up
easily. At the begining of 1898 he asked his daughter Tanya, who
had not yet married, to go to Petersburg and see what she could do
for the Molokhans. Tanya, who had often been accused by her
father of seeking the pleasures of life among the affluent, now
showed an intelligence and a toughness that surprised her parents.
She went straight to the man directly responsible for religious persecutions—Pobyedonostsev, procurator of the Holy Synod. Literally cornering him in his office, she made an eloquent appeal to the
minister, who, to her surprise, blamed the persecution of the
Molokhans on the bishop of Samara, whom he called "overzeal-
ous." He would ask the provincial government to release the children to their parents.

The old procurator—the real power in the Orthodox Church,
and very close to the Tsar—who had tilted with Tolstoy for years
and finally asked for his arrest, was most cordial on this occasion,
Tanya reported. But also coy. Though Tanya had identified herself
when she made the appointment to see the procurator, and again to
his aides before she was ushered into his presence, and had told him
frankly that her father had sent her to see him, Pobyedonostsev
pretended at the end of the interview not to know who his visitor
was. He accompanied her to the stairway and suddenly, she recounted in her diary, when she was at the bottom of the stairs,

> . . . he called down to me, "What is your name?" "Tati-
> ana," I said. "And your patronymic?" "Lvovna," I replied "So
> you're a daughter of Leo Tolstoy?" "Yes." "The famous Tati-
> ana?"

Tanya adds that all the way home she tried to imagine "why
he pretended not to know to whom he had been speaking."[11]

Pobyedonostsev had assured Tanya that he would ask the
governor of Samara to intervene for the Molokhans. He turned out
to be as good as his word.

But the persecution of the Dukhobors did not cease and Tolstoy became more determined than ever to save them. He increased

the pressure from abroad by writing letters to friends and followers, especially in England and America. Finally, in a long letter to "Foreign Newspapers," on March 19, 1898, he announced that thanks to the intervention of the Dowager Empress, Marya Fyodorovna, the Russian government had relented and agreed to let the Dukhobors emigrate abroad.

But there were, he told the foreign press, twelve thousand of the Dukhobors, they had very little money themselves except what they could get from the sale of their property, and it would take a lot of money—perhaps a million rubles—to pay for their resettlement. After negotiations by Chertkov and others, the Canadian government agreed to accept the emigrants and resettle them in Canada. Tolstoy, who said he despised money, now threw himself into the task of raising a small fortune. He asked rich Russian industrialists to contribute generously. He sent out new appeals to England and America begging for money to finance the emigration of the Dukhobors. He pledged himself to sell to the highest bidder in Russia and abroad two short stories he was working on and a long novel—the first since *Anna Karenina*—which he had almost finished. He realized that he was breaking a solemn vow not to take money for anything he wrote these last years but, in this instance, he told the doubting Chertkov, he must make an exception to help the Dukhobors.

"Since it is now apparent how much money is still needed to resettle the Dukhobors, I intend to do as follows," he wrote his disciple in England:

> I have three stories: *Irtenev,** *Resurrection,†* and *Father Sergei.* . . . . I would like to sell them on the most profitable terms to English and American newspapers (newspapers, it seems, are the most profitable) and use what they bring in for resettling the Dukhobors.[12]

About this time, Tolstoy heard that the newly founded Nobel Prize in literature, the very first one, might go to him. The prize was worth 100,000 rubles.‡ What a nice contribution that would make for transporting the Dukhobors to Canada! So he wrote the

---

* Later entitled *The Devil*.
† *Resurrection* was scarcely a "story." It was, in fact, a lengthy novel.
‡ $1,012,500 today.

*Stockholm Dagbladet* suggesting that the sum be given to the Dukho-bors. But, alas, the eminent Swedish Academy, which selected the Nobel Prize winners, apparently did not share the view of most of the rest of the world that Tolstoy was the greatest writer of the time. It selected instead a Frenchman, Sully Prudhomme. It never did choose Tolstoy.*

In the end the Nobel Prize money was not needed. Tolstoy got an advance on the Russian serial rights to the novel *Resurrection* of 100,000 rubles, an "exorbitant sum," Sonya thought. She had opposed her husband's getting involved with the Dukhobors in the first place, complaining that the "fortune" Tolstoy was giving them would mean reducing their own children and grandchildren to "eating black bread." (Actually, the children and grandchildren had already inherited over half a million rubles.)

Tolstoy's royalties from the sale of the novel as a book to Russian and foreign publishers also brought in a large sum. And there were sizable gifts from donors in America, England, and Russia.

The Tolstoys found the subject another cause for argument. When Tolstoy chided Sonya for opposing his work for the Dukho-bors, she replied:

> I simply can find no pity in my heart for people who refuse military service, force the poorest of peasants to enter the army in their place, and then demand millions to enable them to leave Russia. If one is going to help give money to anyone it should be to our own humble peasants, who are dying of hunger, not these arrogant revolutionary Dukhobors.

Contrasting Tolstoy's well-publicized renunciation of royalties to his decision to now get as much as possible from *Resurrection* and the short stories, she continued in her diary:

* To a group of Swedish writers who wrote to him of their great disappointment that he had not received the Nobel Prize, Tolstoy answered (in French): "I am very happy that the Nobel Prize has not been awarded to me. First, it saved me from great embarrassment, that of disposing of the money, which like all money, in my view, can only lead to evil. Second, it has given me the honor and great pleasure of receiving expressions of sympathy from so many highly esteemed, though unknown, persons." Tolstoy was not being very honest with the Swedish writers. "Embarrassment" or no, he made no secret of wanting the Nobel Prize money to help the Dukhobors. (Tolstoy's letter, January 22, 1902.)

I cannot accept, either in my heart or my mind, that after renouncing all authorial rights and publishing this in the newspapers, it should now be necessary for some reason to sell his story for a huge sum . . . and to give this money not to his grandsons, who don't even have white bread to eat, not to his impoverished children, but to the Dukhobors, complete strangers. . . .

And, again, Sonya accused her husband of seeking publicity and fame. "This means of course," she wrote, "that the whole world will now know about Tolstoy's part in helping the Dukhobors, and it will be in all the newspapers and history books. Meanwhile his children and grandchildren have to eat black bread!"[13]

Tolstoy's last great novel burst upon the world in 1899 like a clap of thunder from heaven. It outraged the Russian government and the Orthodox Church, as well as many conservative readers. In Paris, of all places, it was regarded as too scandalous for publication and several French publishers turned it down. In England, most of the lending libraries refused to stock it. In the puritan United States, the newspapers that ran it as a serial and the publisher who did the book censored it heavily. In the first printing of the book, Chapter 17 of Part 1 was eliminated entirely.

In Russia, of course, the censor was brutal. He made some 497 cuts. Only 25 of the 129 chapters escaped his knife.* Tolstoy put up with it only because he desperately needed the royalties to help resettle the Dukhobors.

In Russia not only the government and the church castigated the novel—even in its highly censored form. Most of the critics did too. It was inferior Tolstoy, they said. But the public loved it. The publisher could hardly print enough copies to keep up with the demand. To most Russians it was the best novel Tolstoy ever wrote. The reviewers conceded that it was a great piece of fiction. But, compared to *War and Peace* and *Anna Karenina,* they thought it was terribly flawed. There was too much preaching in it. Too much unadorned propaganda for Tolstoy's cranky opinions.

But, to some, that was part of its greatness. For, more than any other novel or tract or short story of Tolstoy, it summed up best all

---

* The unaltered text of *Resurrection* was not published in Russia until 1935, twenty-five years after the death of the author.

the thoughts, all the feelings that had been churning in him through his long life. The novel seemed to have a definite purpose: to indict Western civilization as a hollow thing and expose, as no one before him had dared to do, the evils stemming from the violence and mindlessness of the Russian government and the hypocrisy of the Russian Orthodox Church. His indictment shook Russia and shocked her, and it upset the rest of the world, where Tolstoy was read and revered. How could there be so much brutality and injustice, he asked, in a Christian country? How could this barbarism go on in a supposedly civilized society? Was not a revolution inevitable? He was sure it was, but that did not give him any relief. The tyranny of the revolutionaries, he predicted, would be just as bad as that of the Tsar and perhaps worse (as it indeed turned out to be).

The cast of characters in *Resurrection,* as in Tolstoy's two previous big novels, is large but two heroes occupy most of the reader's attention: Prince Nekhlyudov and Katyusha Maslova. Unlike in other novels, there are no subplots to complicate the story; only the tale of the two heroes. The reader can concentrate on them.

The novel, which derives from Tolstoy's old notes on the "Koni story," opens with a court scene—one of the greatest scenes Tolstoy ever wrote, full of wonderful descriptions of everyone in the courtroom: the judges, the jurors, the lawyers, the jailers, a tiresome Orthodox priest, and, of course, Katyusha, a prostitute on trial for stealing a hundred rubles from a client. That doesn't seem too interesting a start—a petty theft of only a hundred rubles. It strikes one as a rather commonplace story. But suddenly one of the jurors, Prince Nekhlyudov, recognizes the fallen woman. Some years before, when she was a young servant in his family's household, he had seduced her and she had borne a child. He feels that he is responsible for the young woman's fall, for the family had kicked the pregnant girl out of the house and she had been unable to earn a living except as a prostitute. The Prince, torn by guilt, resolves to atone for what he did.

When Katyusha is sentenced to imprisonment in Siberia, Nekhlyudov, a wealthy man brought up in an aristocratic household and engaged to marry a woman of his class, sets out with the prisoner and a sorry band of condemned political and criminal convicts for the frozen wastes of Siberia. Again, in the telling of that rough journey to purgatory, Tolstoy is wonderful in his descriptions. And he introduces some memorable characters: drunks, whores, thieves, murderers, police guards, and revolutionaries. An odd collection, quite different from his previous novels, where one met mostly people from his own upper class.

And in telling of their plight he denounces the institutions he believes help bring about their downfall, and which continue to brutalize them. The sordidness of the prisons they occupy, the farce the judges make of justice, the sadism of their jailers, the hypocrisy of the Orthodox priests who pretend to minister to them, the horrors of what the Siberian chain gangs go through, the very cruelty of the government that permits such things, indeed promulgates them, draw the author's wrath.

He cared little that some of the characters were often depicted in black and white. He cared little this time for style in his writing. There was little poetry in it. He was too concerned with getting his message across: that this was a hell of a world we were living in and something had to be done about it.

The hierarchy of the Orthodox Church in Petersburg was outraged at what Tolstoy had written of the church in *Resurrection*. To them, he was sacrilegious, blasphemous, heretical, and had been in his writings for a long time. As far back as 1876 the archbishop of Odessa had called him "this latter-day heretical master." The archpriest of Kharkov had branded him in 1891 as "an impious infidel." During Tolstoy's work in famine relief, as we have seen, the Orthodox priests had denounced him to the starving peasants as a devil in disguise, and forbade them to take bread from him.

And now, in *Resurrection*, this new onslaught against the church and against the procurator of the Holy Synod, Konstantin Pobyedonostsev, whom Tolstoy held up to ridicule in the character of Toporov. "In the depths of his soul," the author said of Toporov, "he did not believe in anything." Though he himself was the chief censor of the book, Pobyedonostsev allowed most of the passages about him to be published. What the procurator of the Holy Synod and the church fathers resented most in the book was Tolstoy's constantly ridiculing the church, its dogma, its rites, and its teachings.

There was, for instance, the scene in the chapel of the prison, where Katyusha was awaiting shipment to Siberia. Never had a divine service of the church been so savagely satirized.

The priest, having decked himself out in a special brocade costume, odd looking and highly uncomfortable, cut some bread into little pieces which he arranged on a plate, before dipping them into a goblet of wine as he uttered various names and prayers. The sacristan, meanwhile, read and sang . . . numerous orisons in Slavonic, which were hard enough to understand in themselves and were rendered totally unintelligible by the breakneck pace at which he recited them. The chief object of these prayers was to ask God's blessing upon the Emperor and his family.

Tolstoy grows even more satiric when he comes to the actual communion.

The priest lifted the napkin covering the plate, cut the central piece of bread into four parts, dipped it into the wine and then put it into his mouth. He was supposed to be eating a piece of the body of God and drinking a mouthful of blood.

Having given the bread and wine to the worshiping prisoners,

he carried the goblet behind the partition where he proceeded to eat up all the little pieces of God's body and drink the remaining blood; then he carefully sucked on his mustache, wiped his mouth, cleaned the cup and, feeling very chipper, the thin soles of his calfskin boots creaking smartly, strode resolutely forth.

Sonya was "revolted" by this scene. It was "intentionally cynical," she said. "It is nothing but a crude attack on those who have faith and it disgusts me."

The church fathers and Pobyedonostsev decided that they had had enough of Leo Tolstoy's blasphemy. What they had been reluctant to do ever since the famous author in *Confession* denied the divinity of Christ and maintained it was blasphemous to worship him as God, they now did.

On the morning of Sunday, February 24, 1901, Metropolitan Anthony of Petersburg, the head of the Russian Orthodox Church, climbed the stairs to the pulpit in the Cathedral of Our Lady in the capital and read an edict excommunicating Leo Tolstoy from the Orthodox Church. It had been written by Pobyedonostsev but it was signed by the three metropolitans, one archbishop, and three bishops.

God has permitted a new false prophet to appear in our midst today, Count Leo Tolstoy. A world-famous author, Russian by birth, Orthodox by baptism and education, Count Leo Tolstoy, led astray by pride, has boldly and insolently dared to oppose God, Christ and his holy heirs. Openly and in the sight of all, he has denied the mother who nurtured him and brought him up: the Orthodox Church; and he has devoted his effort and God-given talent to spreading doctrines which are contrary to Christ and the Church, and to undermining their fathers' faith in the minds and hearts of the people—the Orthodox faith, which upholds the universe, in which our ancestors lived and were saved and in which Holy Russia has remained strong until this day.

In his works and letters, circulated in great numbers throughout the world and especially within the frontiers of our beloved fatherland, he preaches the abolition of all dogma of the Orthodox Church and of the very essence of the Christian faith with fanatical frenzy; he denies the living and personal God glorified in the Holy Trinity, Creator of the universe; he refutes our Lord Jesus Christ, God and Man, Redeemer and Savior of the world, who suffered for us and our salvation . . . He refutes the immaculate conception of the human manifestation of Christ the Lord, and the virginity, before and after the Nativity, of Mary, Mother of God, most pure and eternally virgin; he does not believe in the life hereafter or in judgement after death; he refutes all the Mysteries of the Church and their beneficial effect; and, flouting the most sacred articles of faith of the Orthodox community, he has mocked the greatest of all the mysteries: the holy Eucharist. . . .

Therefore, the Church no longer recognizes him among her children and cannot do so until he has repented and restored himself to communion with her.[14]

The edict was ordered posted on the doors of every Orthodox church in Russia. The government forbade the mention in the press of Tolstoy in connection with the edict, and that included, the order read, publication of "any telegrams or other expressions of sympathy for Count L. Tolstoy, excommunicated by the church."

The excommunication of Russia's most revered writer aroused a storm of protest throughout the land—and, indeed, abroad. The government and the church had calculated that, given the hold of the church over the masses, Tolstoy would be discredited and his great influence with the people would be destroyed. But, as might have been predicted by more realistic authorities, just the opposite occurred.

A new painting of Tolstoy by Repin had recently been hung in an art exhibition at a Petersburg gallery. On Monday, February 25, the day after publication of the edict of excommunication, a large crowd gathered before the painting. Ironically, in light of the timing, the portrait was entitled "Tolstoy at Prayer," and it showed him kneeling barefoot, like Saint Francis, in prayer in the midst of a forest. At one juncture the crowd started applauding Repin's work and then all 398 of them signed a telegram of sympathy and support for the proscribed writer.

Tolstoy was in Moscow and out for a long walk that Sunday. As he turned into Lubyanka Square, he was surprised to see a crowd of several thousand—mostly students, workers and peasants, it seemed to him. Suddenly an ironic cry broke out: "There he is, the devil in human form!" The crowd surged around him, shouting, "Three cheers for Leo Nikolayevich! Hail to the great man! Hurrah!" The joyous press of the people against him became so severe that mounted police had to rescue him and escort him home in a sleigh. There he found a pile of telegrams of support. Fresh baskets of flowers lined the hall. Dozens of persons, friends and strangers, were crowding the entry to sign a guest book and jot down a word of sympathy.[15]

Sonya, who had not approved of the work for the Dukhobors and had not liked *Resurrection*\*—though she loyally wrote out a fair copy for the printer, as she had done for most of his writings— nevertheless was outraged by the excommunication. She, as his wife, could criticize the Master at will, and did, but she deeply resented what she thought was unfair criticism from others. An-

---

\* She was not only "disgusted" at some of the scenes that she thought were unfair to the church but because the early relationship of the book's two leading characters reminded her of a similar case in which, before their marriage, her husband seduced a young woman servant, who was kicked out of the house when she became pregnant.

grily, she sat down and wrote Metropolitan Anthony himself, he who had first read the edict in the cathedral in St. Petersburg.

> Having read in the newspapers yesterday of the cruel decree of the Holy Synod exiling my husband, Count Leo Nikolayevich Tolstoy, from the Church, I cannot remain silent. My indignation and my grief have no bounds. . . . If I put myself in the place of the Church, to which I belong and from which I shall never separate . . . the resolution of the Holy Synod is incomprehensible to me.

Whereupon Sonya took a crack at the church hierarchy that was as sharp as anything her husband had written:

> Those who are guilty of betraying the faith are not those who go astray in their search for truth, but those who stand haughtily at the head of the Church and, instead of practicing love, resignation and forgiveness, transform themselves into religious executioners. God will sooner pardon those who give up their earthly possessions to live a life of humility and charity outside the Church than those who wear glittering miters and decorations and who condemn and excommunicate.

Tolstoy was grateful for his wife's intervention, and yet the old misogynist could not quite accept a woman getting involved in his religious controversy. Perhaps he would answer the Holy Synod himself. On further reflection he responded, on April 4, 1901. After reiterating his criticism of church dogma, his belief that Christ was a man and not the son of God, his feeling that the sacraments were really "base, crude magic," he stated his own beliefs:

> I believe in God, whom I understand as Spirit, as love, as the Source of all. I believe that He is in me and I in Him.
> I believe that the will of God was never more clearly expressed than in the doctrine of the Christ-Man; but to regard Christ as God, to pray to him, are in my mind the greatest possible sacrilege. . . .
> I believe that the intention of our individual lives is to augment the sum of love for Him.

I believe that this added measure of love will secure daily increasing happiness for us in this life and in the other. . . .

I believe there is only one way of progressing in love: prayer. Not public prayer in temples, which is explicitly condemned by Christ (Matthew 6:5–13), but prayer as He himself has taught us, solitary prayer, which consists of restoring and strengthening, within oneself, an awareness of the meaning of our life, and a belief that we must be ruled by the will of God.[16]

This reply to the Holy Synod, in which Tolstoy summed up perhaps more clearly than ever before his religious beliefs, was not allowed to be published by the Russian press. But it was circulated throughout Russia in handwritten and typed copies and was published everywhere abroad, bringing a new wave of congratulatory letters and telegrams from all parts of Russia and the world.

Once again the authorities in Petersburg, government and ecclesiastical, pondered how to silence the irrepressible writer, with his cursed world following. Some wanted to imprison him; others opted for exiling him. But once again they did not dare.

"Let anyone lift a finger against Tolstoy," a Russian editor wrote in his diary—he did not dare to put it in his newspaper— "and the whole world will be up in arms and our government will turn tail and run."

The most that the authorities in Petersburg could hope for was that the seventy-three-year-old heretic would soon die. And when, in the summer of 1901, Tolstoy fell seriously ill with malaria, the government warned its provincial governors and police chiefs not to allow any demonstrations of sympathy should his death occur.

But it did not. The old man simply was not ready to depart this earth, however much he loathed all its injustices. The summer before, after noting again the splendors of nature at Yasnaya Polyana, "the meadows and woods, the wheat, the plowed fields, the meadowlands," he had written in his diary: "Nature moves and affects me. I think: will this be my last summer?" It had not been. And despite his illness, he thought this summer of 1901 would not be his last either.

But it was a close call. One doctor, summoned from Moscow, told Sonya that her husband had the "pulse of the death agony." The children were summoned to Yasnaya Polyana, but soon their father rallied. On July 23 Sonya wrote in her diary, "Leo Nikolayevich is on the mend. Thank God! Thank God for yet another reprieve."

The illness had brought them closer together—again! Sonya had told of it in her diary:

> Yesterday morning I was putting a hot compress on his stomach, when he suddenly gazed intently at me and began to weep, saying: "Thank you, Sonya. You mustn't imagine that I am not grateful to you or that I don't love you. . . ." And his voice broke with emotion, and I kissed his dear, familiar hands, telling him what a pleasure it gave me to look after him, and how guilty I felt when I could not make him completely happy, and begging him to forgive me for being unable to do so. . . . Then we both wept and embraced.
>
> For such a long time my soul has yearned for this—a deep and serious recognition of our closeness over the thirty-nine years we have lived together. . . . The things that occasionally have happened to destroy this were mere external delusions and never altered the powerful inner love that has bound us together all this time.[17]

At the worst moment of his illness, when the doctors and the family despaired, Tolstoy had talked to his wife about death, which all his life he had feared. "I am now at a crossroad," he had told Sonya. "I would just as soon go forward [to death] as backwards [to life]. If this passes now, it will be just a reprieve." Then he reflected a little and added: "But there is still so much I want to tell people!"[18]

Decency, Tolstoy told his wife jokingly when he was on the mend, demanded that he should die the next time he fell ill. To which Sonya says she replied that life was depressing when one was old. She hoped to die soon, she added.

"No, one must live!" he replied. "Life is beautiful!"

To give him another chance to live, the doctors urged the family to take Tolstoy south to the Crimea for the winter. And when an acquaintance, Countess S. V. Panina, a wealthy aristocrat from Petersburg, offered them her "dacha," as Sonya put it, at Gaspra, on the southern shore of the peninsula, they accepted. They set out for the south on September 5, 1901.

And despite the old patriarch's insistence on living like a

muzhik, they traveled in style! Paul Boulanger, a close friend and follower of Tolstoy, and an official of the railroad company, succeeded in getting the president of the line to lend Tolstoy his luxurious private sleeping car for the journey. It had a number of individual staterooms, each with a toilet—a wonder to the Tolstoys, who had not yet adapted to indoor plumbing—and a salon with a grand piano.

It was a triumphant journey for the great writer. In spite of the government warning against any public demonstrations for Tolstoy at station stops along the way, thousands of students turned out to acclaim their hero at the railway station at Kharkov. And there was a similar, if somewhat smaller, demonstration when they arrived at Sevastopol. There they stayed over a day so Tolstoy could rest. But the sight of the city excited him and he took Sonya and their party to see the famous Fourth Bastion where he had commanded an artillery battery in the Crimean War. The rail line stopped at Sevastopol. Next day they set out by coach over a mountainous, rocky, winding coastal road past the old Tatar villages to Gaspra on the sea.

Countess Panina's "dacha" turned out to be a large place designed by an English architect in the English Gothic style. Luxury was everywhere and Tolstoy frowned when he saw the marble stairways, the frescoed ceilings, the elegant furniture, enough paintings on the walls to fill a museum, and, outside, great parks of cypresses, flowers of all kinds, arbors of grapes, and a splashing fountain. And greatest of all—a spectacular view of the Black Sea.

The fresh sea air and the hot sun soon revived Tolstoy. Even as December came, when Moscow and Yasnaya Polyana were deep in snow with subzero temperatures, it was tropically warm. On December 4, for instance, Sonya could write in her diary: "Another hot day, brighter and lovelier than yesterday. The sun is as hot as summer." They had arrived on September 8, and by late October, Leo was well enough to resume taking long walks and visiting and receiving friends.

Two of those friends were Anton Chekhov and Maxim Gorky, who had come to the Crimea to try to cure their tuberculosis and who were living nearby at Yalta. In fact, Chekhov was consumed by it—and had only three more years to live. Tolstoy was soon seeing them day after day.

He had first met Chekhov in 1895 and taken an immediate liking to him, invited him to Yasnaya Polyana and become an admirer of his writing—not all, but some of it. Chekhov had originally been a Tolstoyan but gradually repented of it. It was all right to speak of brotherly love, as the old sage did, but what Russia needed most, Chekhov thought, were decent public schools, better universities, sanitary hospitals with good doctors (he was a doctor himself), and freedom for Russians to write and think what they pleased.

"Logic and a sense of justice tell me," he wrote a friend, "that there is more love in electricity and steam than there is in chastity and abstention from eating meat."

Still, Chekhov revered Tolstoy as a writer, as a critic of the Tsarist regime, and as a friend. Tolstoy loved the younger writer so much that he was tempted to say the most outrageous things to him.

One day, as they sat on the terrace overlooking the sea discussing literature, Tolstoy suddenly turned to Chekhov. "Shakespeare's plays are bad enough," he said. "But yours are even worse."[19] And he went on, "My dear friend, I beg of you to stop writing plays." To others he had confided that he could not stomach even the best of Chekhov's plays—*The Three Sisters* and *The Sea Gull* in particular.

Chekhov took it all good-naturedly. He would let the old Master talk on, a wan smile crossing his face. Tolstoy was so great a writer and a person that he could excuse him for these outbursts.

Gorky could too. Though their ideas, like their backgrounds, were far apart, Gorky, the proletarian writer who had fought his way up from the lower depths, educated himself, and become a Marxist and a major writer, greatly admired Tolstoy as an author and an idealist, though he could be critical enough of his philosophy and some of his attitudes.

"He is like a God!" Gorky exclaimed after they had become acquainted. But not a perfect God. Gorky, who had grown up with the poor and oppressed, the peasants and the workers, did not like the Master's vulgarity when he spoke of women.

"He is very fond of talking about women," Gorky remembered from that winter in the Crimea, "but always with that coarseness of the Russian muzhik, which used to grate on my ears." And Gorky describes a conversation while he, Chekhov, and Tolstoy were strolling through the gardens of Countess Panina's villa. Tolstoy suddenly turned to Chekhov.

"Did you fuck a lot of whores in your youth?" he asked.

Chekhov smiled sheepishly, Gorky says, and mumbled a few inaudible words. Tolstoy went on, boastfully: "I was an indefatigable fucker."[20]

"A man goes through earthquakes," Tolstoy said to Gorky one day at Gaspra, "epidemics, the horror of disease, and all sorts of spiritual torments, but the most agonizing tragedy he ever knows always has been, and always will be, the tragedy of the bedroom."

"His attitude toward women," Gorky wrote later, "is one of obstinate hostility. There is nothing he likes so much as to punish them. . . . Is it the revenge of a man who has not obtained as much happiness as he was capable of, or an enmity toward the humiliating impulses of the flesh? Whatever it is, it is hostility and very bitter."[21]

Tolstoy did not like Gorky's plays any more than those of Chekhov. One afternoon, when Gorky had come over to read Tolstoy some scenes from his great play *The Lower Depths*, the old Master listened a few minutes and then interrupted:

> "What made you write this?"
> I explained as well as I could.
> "You rush at things like a cockerel. You are always trying to smooth over seams and cracks with your own coloring. . . . Better not daub, it'll be worse for you afterwards . . . you must write more simply."

Whereupon Tolstoy made a detailed critique of all the characters in the play.

> "Your old man is unlovable, one doesn't believe in his goodness. Your prostitute is good . . . have you met that sort?"
> "Oh yes."
> "One can see that. . . . Your heroes are not like real characters, they are all too much alike. You probably don't understand women; all your young women are failures. One doesn't remember them."[22]

They never did quite hit it off, Sergei Tolstoy wrote in his recollections of Gorky at Gaspra. And Gorky admitted that for all his admiration for the great writer, he was hard to take personally.

"Sometimes he is self-satisfied and intolerable," Gorky wrote later. "One never stops marvelling at him, but one would not care to see him too often, and I could never live in the same house with him—not to mention the same room."

When Tolstoy died, Gorky remembered him differently.

As the new year (1902) began, Tolstoy felt well enough to take on the Emperor of all the Russians. Isolated as he might be in Yasnaya Polyana, and now on the shores of the Black Sea, he had for some time been mulling over the state of Russia, feeling that the forces of reaction, intent on carrying out an oppression of the Russian people, were driving the country toward revolution. In a long and brutally frank letter, which Sonya feared could get them into trouble, he now wrote to Nicholas II about his fear that dire things might happen to Russia unless the Tsar reversed his policies and restored freedom for all the population. Probably never before in the long history of the Romanovs had a Russian emperor heard such frank words from a subject.

"Dear Brother," Tolstoy began his letter, explaining that he felt this form of address was appropriate

> because I address you not so much as a Tsar but as a man-brother and furthermore because I am writing to you as if it were from the next world, since I expect to die very soon.
>
> I did not want to die without telling you what I think of your present activity, of what it could be, of what great good it could bring to millions of people and to yourself, and of what great evil it can bring to those people and yourself if it continues.

Tolstoy summed up how he saw the situation.

> A third of Russia is in a state of emergency, i.e., is outside the law. The army of police—open and secret—is constantly growing . . . the prisons, places of exile, and labor camps are overflowing with political prisoners, to which workers are now being added. The censorship has descended to nonsensical pro-

hibitions. . . . Religious persecutions were never so frequent and cruel as they are now. . . . Armed forces are set out against the people, with live cartridges. In many places there has been bloodshed between brothers and more cruel bloodshed will inevitably follow.

Tolstoy told the monarch he was getting bad advice from those around him.

It is amazing that you, a free man, a reasonable and good man, can follow their terrible advice to do, or to allow to be done, so much evil.

The Tsar, on ascending the throne, had told the people that they must forget the idea of having a constitutional democratic government. The Romanov autocracy, he had proclaimed, was the only form of government suitable to the Russian people, whom he advised to abandon their "foolish daydreams" of a parliamentary democracy.

"Autocracy," Tolstoy now told the Tsar,

is an obsolete form of government that may suit the needs of a people somewhere in central Africa but not the needs of the Russian people.

Tolstoy then ticked off a number of mistakes the Tsar had made from the very onset of his reign. "The people," he wrote, "can be oppressed by violent measures, but they cannot be governed by them."

The author proposed a solution for Russia's problems that he must have known would fall on deaf ears in St. Petersburg. First, get rid of the oppressive laws that kept the Russian workers down. But most important of all, the government must abolish the right to private ownership of the land. For years Tolstoy, inspired by the ideas of the American economist Henry George, had been advocating this. The peasants, the great majority of the people, he said, demanded it. They had always believed, even in the days of serfdom, that the land belonged to those who tilled it. The idea had become a burning passion with Tolstoy, as he now made clear to the Tsar.

> I personally think that in our time the private ownership of
> the land is just as obvious and as crying an injustice as serfdom
> was 50 years ago. I think that its abolition will place the Russian
> people on a high level of independence, well-being and content-
> ment.

And Tolstoy inserted a few lines that he must have felt would please the Tsar and show that he was not as great a threat and danger to the regime as the Emperor probably thought.

> I also think that this measure will undoubtedly get rid of all
> the socialist and revolutionary irritation which is now flaring up
> among the workers and which threatens the greatest danger to
> the people and the government.

Tolstoy had long opposed the socialists and the peasant revolutionaries because they sought change by violence.

"Dear brother," he concluded, "you have only one life in this world," and the writer hoped he would get back on the right track before it was too late. "Think about this," he admonished the Tsar.[23]

No answer came from Nicholas II, blind to the necessity of drastic reforms which might save his throne and make life more bearable for the Russian people. Tolstoy knew he had received the letter because he had entrusted it to the Grand Duke Nikolai Mikhailovich, the Tsar's uncle, who owned a large estate near Gaspra and came over to pay his personal respects to the author. The Grand Duke promised to deliver it, did so, and so informed Tolstoy. The letter was not published in Russia until years after the Tsar had been deposed by the Kerensky government and later murdered by the Bolsheviks—apparently on the instructions of Lenin.

Sonya intensely disliked her husband's letter, which she had dutifully copied from his final draft. She described it as

> an angry, insulting letter, abusing everything on earth and giv-
> ing him [the Tsar] the most absurd advice on how to run the

country. I do hope the Grand Duke does not give it to the Tsar, for if he does, it will infuriate him and he may take some action against us.[24]

Indeed, some action was taken. The police surveillance of the Tolstoys was increased. No member of the family could venture out without being followed by a detective. Visitors to the Tolstoys were carefully checked by the police.

Tolstoy's health at Gaspra had its ups and downs. Sonya's diary chronicled its daily course—she was nursing him day and night. By December 23, 1901, Sonya was writing in her diary that "Leo N. is fully recovered," and two days later that they had a "festive Christmas." Early in January he fell ill again, suffering, Sonya wrote, "from infiltration of the liver, a weakness of heart and a disorder of the intestines." But by January 8 he had recovered enough to exhibit his old stubbornness about taking his medicine. He refused to take it.

"I'm tired," Sonya confided to her diary that day, "of this forty year struggle. I'm tired of having to employ tricks and stratagems to get him to take his medicine."

> January 26, 1902: My Lyovochka is dying. . . . My life cannot go on without him. . . . It's all over now. Help me, Lord.
>
> January 29: I am suffocated by tears and crushed by the weight of my grief. . . . Yesterday Dr. Shchurovsky suggested Lyovochka inhale some oxygen, and he said: "Wait a bit, first it's camphor, then it's oxygen, next it'll be the coffin and the grave. . . ."

Tolstoy had fought all his life against his fear of death and it was evident that he had still not conquered it. "Yesterday," Sonya noted down, "he said to Seryozha: 'I thought it was easy to die, but it isn't, it's terribly hard.' "

The children had all been summoned to Gaspra and their father repeated his feeling about death to Tanya. "It's very hard," he told her, "to cast off this familiar skin."

Sonya's diary:

> January 29: My Lyovochka had a terrible night. . . . I sat up with him until four in the morning.

On top of all his other ills, pneumonia had set in.

> February 3: Last night I was again plunged into despair. His temperature went up to 104 [Fahrenheit]. It was a terrible night.
> February 7: The situation is almost, one might say, totally hopeless. His pulse was inaudible all morning.
> February 15: The doctors say there is still hope.

But Sonya noticed that for the past three days he had been getting weaker and refusing to eat.

The old warrior, however, could not be beaten. Gradually he recovered and was his old irritable self, able to get about and argue with his wife, children, Gorky, and Chekhov. For a moment Gorky became disillusioned and his affection for the Master cooled.

"Count Leo Tolstoy is an artist of genius," Gorky wrote a friend, "but although I admire him, I do not like him. He is exaggeratedly self-preoccupied, he sees nothing and knows nothing but himself."

In the spring, just when the Tolstoys believed that they could leave the Crimea, Leo fell ill again—this time with typhoid fever. But he soon conquered it, to the amazement of his doctors, some of whom had rushed down from Moscow and Petersburg to attend to him.

Sonya's diary, June 26: "Yesterday we finally left Gaspra."

They took a steamer to Sevastopol—the first time Sonya had ever boarded a ship.

> June 27: "(Yasnaya Polyana) Today we returned home from the Crimea."

Despite Sonya's despair when it looked as if her husband might die, despite her loving care of him month after month during his long illness at Gaspra, and his occasional expression of gratitude, the gulf between them had not narrowed. Sonya was bitter about it in her diary.

"Now that physical infirmity has forced Leo Nikolayevich to abandon amorous relations with his wife (this was not so long ago)," she wrote on December 2, 1901, at Gaspra, "instead of that peaceful affectionate friendship which I have longed for in vain all my life, there remains nothing but complete emptiness."

> Morning and evening he greets me with a cold, formal kiss. He calmly accepts my anxieties about him as his due; he frequently loses his temper. . . . I think more and more of death.

On December 8, as Tolstoy was getting ready to take off for nearby Yalta to visit his daughter Masha, Sonya had tried to help him pack. But he had "snapped" at her, she says, "so peevishly" she almost burst into tears.

> December 8: Gaspra. It grieves my heart that my husband and I should be living here like two strangers!

As the new year began, she complained in her diary of her husband's obstinacy, "his tyrannical behavior." In mid-February, when it seemed the end was near and that Tolstoy would not recover, she mused in her diary how she would like to forget all the heartaches he caused her. "But instead I cried bitterly today for the way he persistently scorns all my love and concern for him."

If, during Tolstoy's illness at Gaspra, which almost cost him his life—an illness during which Sonya devotedly nursed him day and night for nine months, alternately despairing and rejoicing when his condition turned worse or better—they could no longer get along, what prospects were there for a bearable future once they returned to Yasnaya Polyana, where their life together had begun with such hope forty years before and then, amidst all the fame that came to him, and all the children, deteriorated into one of the worst marriages that ever was?

Sonya gave her answer to the question four months after their return to Yasnaya. On November 4, she wrote in her diary: "It is sad here on the ruins of our vanished happiness."

# FIFTEEN

# War and Revolution, Illness and Death

*I*N THE LATE SUMMER of 1906, while Tolstoy was lamenting to his daughter Masha that the only reason he had not left home was the certainty that Sonya would come after him "and everything would begin all over again," Sonya fell desperately ill. Her husband felt relieved. Her time had come, he told his children, who hurried from their various homes to be with their mother in her final hours. That was God's will, he said, and they should do nothing to thwart it.

But whether the children loved her or not, they did not wish her to go if the doctors could save her life. They summoned physicians from Tula and Moscow, who quickly diagnosed a uterine tumor and advised immediate surgery if she was to survive.

Tolstoy balked. He detested doctors and thought they did more harm than good. Why not let Sonya die graciously, according to God's will?

Her condition grew worse. Peritonitis set in. A priest was called and Sonya confessed and took Communion. The surgeon asked Tolstoy's permission to operate immediately. Since Sonya was too weak to be transported the eight miles to the hospital in Tula, the surgeon had brought an operating table, surgical instruments, and an assistant and a nurse with him. He could do it in the house.

Tolstoy refused.

"But if we don't operate, she will die," the surgeon warned.

Tolstoy glared at him as if the doctor were his mortal enemy. "Do as you please," he finally said.[1]

Then Tolstoy fled the house and strode out into the woods, telling the children that if the operation was a success to ring the bell twice and if not . . .

"No, don't ring the bell at all. I'll come back when I'm ready."

An hour later the surgeon broke out of the room and announced that the operation was a success. Countess Tolstoy would live. A large tumor had been removed from her uterus but it was a benign fibroma.

Sasha raced to the woods to tell the good news to her father. Espying him, she yelled out, "Papa, it's a success!"

"What a blessing!" Tolstoy responded. Did he really mean it? Sasha, who worshiped her father and hated her mother, noticed that "what showed on his face was not joy but great pain."[2]

Some time later, when Sonya had come out of the anesthetic, Tolstoy tiptoed into the sickroom. According to his son Ilya, he came out choking with "indignation."

"Good heavens!" he exclaimed. "What a horrible thing! A human being can't even be left to die in peace!"[3]

Retiring to his study, he picked up his diary and wrote: "Sonya operated on today. They say it was a success. But it was very hard on her. How death assuages one! During the operation I went to the woods. I was nervously exhausted. Then I wrote a bit about Henry George."

It took him several days, Ilya reported, "until he calmed down and ceased from abusing the doctors for what they had done."[4]

Recently, some of the Tolstoys *had* died. In December 1903, Tolstoy had got word that his beloved cousin, his "Granny" Alexandrine Tolstoy, had fallen seriously ill. He promptly wrote her a most tender letter. For some years, after a quarrel in Petersburg in 1896 over religion, they had been estranged. But both had forgiving natures—at least with each other—and they had renewed the great love and friendship that had existed between them for over half a century.

Alexandrine, my dear kind old friend: Tanya Kuzminskaya wrote to tell me about your illness. I am writing this letter only to tell you how often in my relations with you I have felt this love and goodness of yours, and feeling it have become better myself. . . . Goodbye, for now, my dear; be assured of my sincere love for you and my gratitude for all the good you have given me during the half century of our friendship.[5]

Alexandrine promptly replied:

Dear Leo, whom I have loved so long, your tender friendly letter was all the more gratifying to me because I felt in it the very, very sincere note which always rang out between us during the days of our youth. . . .

On March 21, 1904, Alexandrine, eighty-six, died in her apartment in the Winter Palace in Petersburg. It was a loss for Tolstoy of one who had connected him with the golden past. She had been his most faithful friend and confidante. Now there was no one in whom he could confide, as he had for so long with "Granny."

Another link to the past, and one closer to home, was lost before the year was up.

On August 23, 1904, Leo's older brother Sergei died at his estate at Pirogovo. He was seventy-eight, and had been struggling for years with an excruciatingly painful cancer of the tongue. He had been Leo's favorite brother, although relations between them had cooled in recent years after the younger brother, having achieved world fame, began to preach his Gospel message. The taciturn, misanthropic Sergei, though he admired Leo tremendously for his writing, was put off by his inability to practice what he preached. It was all right for him to preach the glories of poverty and abstinence but it was hypocritical to continue to live in luxury and make his wife bear one child after another. Sergei himself had three daughters with his Gypsy wife; he had been stern with his peasants and had lived in as much comfort as he could afford. Where Leo had been a lover of mankind (if it followed his precepts), Sergei had been a misanthrope.

Leo hurried to Pirogovo as soon as he heard of his brother's death and, in spite of his age and his infirmities, insisted on being one of the pallbearers. In his diary on August 26, he noted:

Seryozha has died. Quietly, without the awareness that he was dying. . . . A real religious feeling was denied him. . . . But all is well just the same.

Sergei, he told Sonya, had been his "incomprehensible and beloved brother" and, he wrote later, "remained utterly unique, utterly himself, very handsome, aristocratic, proud and above all, a more upright and honest man than I have ever known."

Leo was now the last of the four Tolstoy brothers—the last surviving link with the family's past.* In a household where there was so much turmoil, it made him feel lonelier than ever.

There was another blow the autumn after Sonya's illness. On a cold, wet, windy day in late November 1906, Masha, Tolstoy's favorite daughter, and the only one in the household close to him, came back from a long walk at Yasnaya Polyana shivering and shaking. She and her husband, Nikolai Obolensky, were spending the winter at Yasnaya. She had caught cold. Doctors, called in from Tula and Moscow, found it had turned into pneumonia. Her health had always been delicate—now the pneumonia threatened her life.

"Masha's state," Tolstoy wrote in his diary on November 23, "greatly alarms me. I love her very, very much."

She was the only one in the family, he believed, who understood him and what he preached. She was a true Tolstoyan. More than that. She had devoted much of her life to helping the poor in the village. She was the one, with Tanya, who tried to smooth over the difficult relations of her parents. More than anyone else at Yasnaya Polyana, her brother Ilya said, she kept the family together. Even Sonya, who was sometimes put off by her daughter's complete devotion to her father, and who often said in her diary that she found it difficult to love the child, recognized Masha's goodness.

On the twenty-sixth the doctors abandoned all hope of saving her life. Again, as with Sonya when it seemed she might die, Tolstoy declined to shed tears at the prospect of his daughter's imminent death. Writing Chertkov that day about Masha's illness, he told of his feelings—or lack of them:

> She has had pneumonia for eight days now and is very, very ill. For me, selfishly, her death is neither terrible or pitiful, although she is my best friend of all who are near me. . . . Contrary to reason it does hurt me and I pity her—at her age she must have wanted to live†—and I just pity her sufferings and

* Except for his sister Marya, who had tucked herself away in a convent and whom he rarely saw.
† She was thirty-five.

those of her near ones. These vain endeavors to prolong her life by medical treatment are pitiful and evil itself.

Masha died early the next morning and Tolstoy added a line to his letter. "I wrote this letter in the morning and now at 1:00 A.M. Masha has died. I haven't yet been able to appreciate the full loss."

Masha died in his arms and he went immediately to his study to record his feelings. They were strange.

> November 27, Yasnaya Polyana: Just now, one o'clock in the morning, Masha died. A strange thing. I didn't feel the horror or fear or awareness of anything exceptional taking place, not even pity or grief. I seemed to consider it necessary to arouse in myself a special feeling of emotion, grief, and I did so, but at the bottom of my heart I was more composed than I would have been in the case of another person's bad or improper behavior— not to mention my own. . . . Yet this event belongs to the realm of the body and is irrelevant. I watched her all the time she was dying: wonderfully calmly. For me she was a creature experiencing revelation. I watched her revelation and it made me glad.

And then the old man's mind wandered off.

> In serious moments when, as now, the body of a loved one still lies unburied, one sees clearly the immortality and wrongfulness and depressing nature of the life of the rich. . . . But they have no essential work, only amusement. . . . The best remedy against grief is work. . . .

He contrasts "the falsely sympathetic letters" he has received and the simple-minded village idiot, Kunya, who loved his daughter.

> I said: "Have you heard about our grief?" "Yes, I've heard," and then she said, "Give me a kopek."
>
> How much better and easier that is.
>
> November 29, Yasnaya Polyana: They have just taken her away to be buried. Thank God, I am still in good spirits.

He had walked in the funeral procession to the little Kochaky cemetery, where his parents and two of his children, who had died shortly after birth, lay buried. Along the way the peasants emerged from their huts to give the sign of the cross before the coffin, some of them also handing the priest a few kopecks to hold a requiem for the Tolstoy daughter, who had done so much for them. Tolstoy declined to follow the procession to the grave site, turning back at the entrance to the cemetery and setting off for home. His son Ilya saw him take off.

> I watched him walk away across the wet, thawing snow with his short, quick old-man's steps, turning his toes out at a sharp angle and never once looking back.

Later, Ilya would offer an explanation for his father's peculiar reaction of joy to the death of his most beloved daughter. Tolstoy, he said, had always found it impossible to express tenderness—even for those he loved. Ilya thought this might have been because he never had a mother—she had died when he was two years old. "During his lifetime," Ilya says, "I never received any mark of tenderness from him whatever."[6]

This was written long afterward. At the moment, Ilya seems to have been in the doghouse. He had been ill. And broke. "Poor, pitiful Ilya," his father had addressed him in a letter of December 21 that year:

> Illness, as a condition that keeps us away from temptations and brings us nearer to death, is a very useful condition. I advise you to make the best possible use of it.
>
> I am very sad that with you, as with all my sons, I cannot communicate sincerely.
>
> Goodbye, I wish you a longer and productive illness.[7]

Tolstoy had been depressed too by what was happening to his country: the Russo-Japanese War, which broke out on January 27, 1904, and the government's oppression, which reached its climax with "Bloody Sunday" in St. Petersburg on January 9, 1905; this, in turn, provoked the revolutionary outbreaks that followed.

From the very outset the war was a disaster for Russia. On the first day of hostilities, without a declaration of war or any warning, Japanese torpedo boats sank a good part of the Russian Pacific fleet at Port Arthur. The harbor and the city itself, attacked by land and sea, surrendered just before Christmas, on December 20, 1904.

Tolstoy at first castigated both his own country and Japan for going to war. When asked by an American newspaper to explain his position, he wrote: "I am neither for Russia nor Japan. I am for the workers of both countries who are being deceived by their governments and forced to take part in a war that is harmful to their well-being and in conflict with their conscience and religion."

Nevertheless, with the news of each defeat the old veteran of the wars in the Caucasus and of the famous Fourth Bastion at Sevastopol in the Crimean War was pained and depressed. When the news of the disaster at Port Arthur reached him, Tolstoy was deeply affected. "Ah, that's not how they fought in my day! Surrendering a fortress when you have ammunition and an army of forty thousand men! It's a shame!" And in his diary of December 31, 1904, he wrote: "The surrender of Port Arthur has made me miserable. I suffer from it. Patriotism."

The surrender of Mukden in Manchuria in February 1905, and especially the destruction of the Russian Baltic fleet on May 14, 1905, in the Straits of Tsushima after a seven-month voyage from its home bases were the final blows to Russian pride. Tolstoy shared the humiliation of the Russian people. But he now developed a curious explanation for the Russian disasters. His diary:

> May 19, 1905: News was received yesterday of the destruction of the Russian Fleet. The news struck me with particular force for some reason. It became clear to me that it could not have been otherwise: it's impossible to hide the incompatibility between the Christian faith and war. . . . And therefore in a war with a non-Christian people for whom the highest ideal is the Fatherland and the heroism of war, Christian people are bound to be defeated. . . . I am not saying this to console myself for the fact that we have been beaten by the Japanese. The shame and humiliation are as sharp as ever.

And then Tolstoy, in seeking scapegoats, blamed not only the Japanese but the Jews!

June 18: The debacle is not only that of the Russian army, the Russian Fleet and the Russian State, but that of pseudo-Christian civilizations as well. . . . The tradition began long ago with the struggle for money and success in so-called scientific and artistic pursuits, where the Jews got the edge on the Christians of every country and already earned the envy and hatred of them all. Today the Japanese have done the same thing in the military field, proving conclusively, by brute force, that there is a goal which Christians must not pursue, for in seeking it they will always fail, vanquished by non-Christians.

He came back to this theme in his diary of August 30, 1905. It seemed to him now that most of mankind's troubles were first caused by what he claimed were the radical differences between Christ and Paul. "I should like to write something to prove how the teachings of Christ, who is not a Jew, were replaced by the very different teachings of Paul, who was a Jew."

The revolution which Tolstoy had warned the Tsar in his letter from the Crimea was inevitable unless he halted his repression now began to break out. For one thing, the debacles of the war with Japan had alerted the people to the woeful incompetence of the Tsarist army and navy. But most of all, the workers were aroused by the oppression of the government, by the lack of freedoms enjoyed in the West—the freedom even to organize a union, to answer with a violence of their own. Strikes not only shut down vital industries but, more important, shut down the railways, the post and telegraph offices, paralyzing the nation. In the countryside peasants began burning the homes of the landowners and sometimes killing them.* The Tsar's only answer was more repression.

It reached its climax on Sunday, January 9, 1905, when Father Gapon, an Orthodox priest, led a peaceful procession of several thousand workers to deliver a petition to the Tsar at the Winter Palace in St. Petersburg. It demanded the legal right to an eight-hour day. As the procession approached the palace, troops opened fire, killing in cold blood several hundred and wounding many more. The massacre became known as Bloody Sunday and it aroused the bitter indignation of the Russian workers, of the liberal middle class, and

* One of Sonya's brothers was among the murdered.

of the civilized world abroad. Historians would later see it as the turning point in the Russian revolutionary movement, which led to violent strikes and brutal oppression throughout the rest of 1905, and in twelve years to the revolution that overthrew the Tsar, and a second revolution the same year that brought the Bolsheviks to power and seventy years of oppression as savage as that of the Romanovs, if not more so.

To the dismay of the workers, whom Tolstoy had told the American press he was for, the Master's reaction to the massacre of Bloody Sunday was to condemn those who had organized the workers' procession!

> Those who arouse the workers imagine they will influence the government. . . . This is a mistake. . . . The Tsar is not free. He talks now to one, now to another. He is a pitiful, insignificant, even an unkind person.[8]

Later, in the fall of 1905, there were revolutionary outbreaks in Moscow. The workers took to the streets and erected barricades, and were savagely put down by imperial troops, with losses of hundreds more lives. "The revolution," Tolstoy wrote in his diary on October 23 at Yasnaya Polyana, "is in full swing. People are being killed on both sides. . . . The frivolity of the people who are making the revolution is astonishing and disgusting. . . ."

He advised the populace not to take part in it. But that was only possible, he admitted, "for a person who takes a religious attitude."

He also blamed the intelligentsia—and women—for the strife. "The intelligentsia," he wrote in his diary of June 20, "has contributed a hundred times more evil than good to the people." He saw another evil in the growing influence of women in Russian public life. "For the existence of a reasonable, moral society," he wrote, "it is necessary for women to be under the influence of men. But in our society it is the reverse: men are under the influence of women." Most women—and men—in Russia must have been surprised to hear it.

On October 17 the Tsar, giving in to the revolutionary pressure, issued a manifesto promising various freedoms: of the press, of speech, of assembly, of the right to form associations such as political parties. He also granted a parliament—the Duma—some power in the making of law.

This was not quite the constitutional parliamentary monarchy demanded by the liberals, but most of them welcomed it as a first step. Not the old sage of Yasnaya Polyana. "There is nothing in it for the people," he said. He quarreled with his son Sergei, a mild liberal, over the subject.

> You want a constitution, they want monarchy, the revolutionaries want socialism, and you believe you can fix things for the people. I can guarantee you that the lives of men in general will not improve until every single man strives to live well himself and not interfere in the lives of others.[9]

If everyone followed God's precepts, he kept telling the public, then Russia's problems would be solved. But never by revolution or by liberal parliamentary government.

The stream of history was passing the old prophet by. Russia was sliding into a state of permanent revolution. Tolstoy knew it, but he did not know what to do about it other than appeal to both parties as good Christians. The workers in the streets, mowed down by the bullets of the cossacks, could not believe that their salvation lay in the worship of God. The Russian socialists, the Socialist Revolutionaries, even the liberals, turned away from Tolstoy. He was not going to help, despite all his talk of being for the workers. But the Tolstoyans worldwide, those who believed in his teachings of nonviolence, remained loyal to him, though some questioned his political views. Even the fanatical disciple Chertkov in England balked at publishing an article of the Master cursing both sides for the upheavals in Russia.

Chertkov would shortly reenter the Tolstoys' lives. In 1908 he was allowed to return home for good from England and he promptly bought from Alexandra, the Tolstoys' youngest child and the only one still in the household, a small estate at Telyatinki, near Yasnaya Polyana, where he proceeded to build a large, ugly villa and recruit a staff of loyal Tolstoyans to help him in his endeavors on behalf of the great prophet, of whom he considered himself the chief disciple.

After his long exile abroad he wanted to be near Tolstoy night and day. He returned determined to take him over lock, stock, and barrel: the great writer and prophet himself, all his literary works, even the letters and diaries. Only he—and not the quarrelsome, neurotic wife—was qualified, he believed, because of his closeness to the Master's thoughts and wishes, to see that every scrap of the Master's writings, the unpublished stories, essays, plays, the letters and diaries, along with all that had been published, saw the light of day. Thus, due to him, Leo Tolstoy would be recognized all over the world as the greatest writer and thinker of his time. Thanks to him, Chertkov, all of the author's *oeuvre* would be made available to mankind.

Sonya, alarmed by his return and especially by his settling down so near to Yasnaya Polyana, was just as determined to frustrate Chertkov's designs. Despite the ever more frequent and violent clashes, which were making life increasingly miserable for them both, Sonya wanted her husband of forty-six years to herself. She would not share him with this intruder. She wanted to retain the rights to go on publishing his works prior to 1881, as he had promised her. She wanted the letters and diaries, not only to keep them out of Chertkov's hands but so that eventually she could publish them and give her family some income—contrary, of course, to her husband's wishes that no profit should any longer be made from the sales of all he had written. She would take care of Leo Tolstoy's posterity. It was her task, not that of the overbearing outsider, Chertkov.

For the next two, and last, years of Tolstoy's life, the bitter strife between Sonya and Chertkov, and between her and her husband, would dominate life at Yasnaya Polyana and make it an inferno. The stately old Tolstoy house became a battlefield.

Sonya found herself confronted by two formidable adversaries, both of whom, she began to suspect with some reason, were conspiring to rob her and her children of their rightful inheritance. To make matters worse, one of the children—Alexandra, the only one still at home—joined in the conspiracy against her.

Sonya herself, exhausted by the burden of bearing so many children (thirteen in all), and of raising those that survived, of running the estate and looking after her husband, and worn out too by the long war "to the end" between them, was beginning to lose her mind, and she knew it.

In a diary entry of January 14, 1905, she had noted: "I asked him [her husband] to forgive me for my unstable frame of mind." Years before, she had begun to worry about it. Back in 1897, on October 23, she had scribbled in her diary: "I feel unbalanced, unhinged. Today I felt so melancholy I could have killed myself."

# SIXTEEN

# *The Return of Chertkov*

*T*HERE WAS a brief armistice between the antagonists because of the celebration of Tolstoy's eightieth birthday on August 28, 1908.

It had not been a good year for the great writer. He had suffered several light strokes and occasional losses of memory. And his quarrels with Sonya had become more frequent, bitter, draining. There were more antagonists in the household too. They, in league with Alexandra, were backing not only the master of Yasnaya Polyana but Chertkov in their battle against Countess Tolstoy. Sonya felt more and more alone, outnumbered by the enemy, and this added to her feeling of desperation and helplessness.

The first of Alexandra's new allies was a strange character, Dr. Dushan Makovitsky, a Slovak physician and ardent Tolstoyan who, after visiting his idol several times, finally came, toward the end of 1907, to stay for good at Yasnaya Polyana, where he acted as family doctor and as physician to the peasants in the village. He was an anemic little man, bald-headed and with a goatee and waxen skin, selfless, modest, and fanatically devoted to Tolstoy and his teachings.

Saintly though he was, working long hours to minister to the poor peasants, tireless in his caring for Tolstoy and his family, he had one weakness: he hated Jews. Tolstoy, who loved him, once said: "Dushan is a saint. But since there are no real saints, God gave him a fault too: his hatred of Jews."* The little doctor grew angry whenever Jews were discussed in the household, urged the family never to buy from the Jews, and avidly read the anti-Semitic journals from Moscow and Petersburg.

Alexandra remembered his rebuking her when she returned one day from Tula with some goods she had bought from a Jewish shop.

"Oh Alexandra!" he called out. "Shame on you! Why should you buy from Jews? Why not support your own people? You know that the Jews hate you. They will sit on your neck some day."[1]†

Aside from his rabid anti-Semitism, Tolstoy said, Dr. Makovitsky had a heart of gold. Sonya was not so sure. For she came to think that this kindly man had joined the conspiracy, siding not only with Leo but with Chertkov and Alexandra against her.

Ironically, another "conspirator" who had joined the household—he lived nearby, but came to the house every day—was a Jew with whom the doctor had the best of relations. This was Alexander Goldenweiser, a distinguished pianist and professor of music at the Moscow Conservatory.

There was a third ally, Nikolai Gusev, the young secretary of Tolstoy and a devout Tolstoyan, but he would soon be arrested and exiled for having participated in "revolutionary propaganda and circulation of forbidden books"—that is, Tolstoy's books. It was a blow to the old man, but for Sonya it meant one less enemy in the house.

Alexandra—or Sasha, as the family called her—who played a crucial role in the last two years of her father's life, was now, in 1908, a boyish, heavyset, broad-faced, hot-tempered young lady of twenty-four, fond of horses and dogs, making friends with women, and uninterested in men outside the household. She was no great

---

* Tolstoy, as we have seen, was not without his prejudices against the Jews. Every once in a while in his diaries he pauses to find fault with them. Typical is an entry in his diary for January 4, 1906, at Yasnaya Polyana. It was right after New Year's and he was feeling—and thinking—"bad things." "The Jewish faith," he wrote, "is the most irreligious. A faith in which the denominator is infinite. A proud faith that they are God's only chosen people. . . ."

† In *The Tragedy of Tolstoy,* Alexandra notes that Dushan was no great shakes as a physician. Whenever anyone in the family was seriously ill, she says, they sent to Moscow, 128 miles away, for a doctor.

beauty. In fact, some found her rather homely. One day, when she entered her father's study, he exclaimed: "My Lord, how homely you are!" Sasha told the story herself and said she replied: "It doesn't bother me. I don't intend to marry anyway." Sasha was also overweight. "You're too fat!" her father told her one day. "You must work—do some physical work."[2]

She loved and worshiped her father and hated her mother, who in turn had little liking for her. There was a poisonous chemistry between them that made them uncomfortable in each other's presence.

And Sasha had resented her mother's favoring her little brother, Vanechka, over her. Gossips told her that when the young boy died, the grieving mother had cried out, "Why him? Why not Sasha?" Also, Sasha could not forgive her mother for her "affair" with Taneyev. Feeling that Sonya was completely and always wrong in her quarrels with Tolstoy, she had sought not only to replace her as her father's helper in his work but to replace her in his life.

So, gladly and passionately she joined her father and Chertkov and the others in the war against Sonya. Sasha's brother-in-law, Obolensky, noted that she had begun to do everything she could to aggravate the hostility between her parents. Worse than that. She began to betray her mother, ardently helping Chertkov to further his schemes to rob Sonya and the other children of the family inheritance and gain possession for himself of all Tolstoy's writings. She began to conspire with him to shut her mother out in the cold.

Now that, after his long exile, Chertkov had settled near Yasnaya Polyana, he came over every day to confer with Tolstoy, advise him on various problems of the Intermediary, the Tolstoyan publishing house, snatch whatever the Master had written the day before—pages of a short story or an essay, a letter, an entry in a diary—and dwell on Sonya's impossible demands on her husband.

Ten years of exile in England had not softened Chertkov's authoritarian, despotic ways or broadened his narrow mind. He was determined to carry out his self-appointed role as chief priest of the Tolstoyan movement—flattering and praising the old man but not hesitating to criticize him when he felt that the Master was straying from his teachings. But above all else, he warned Tolstoy against what he considered his shrewish, crazy wife. Sonya was the chief obstacle to his taking over the Master and all his works. Chertkov was determined to destroy her if she insisted on standing in his way. And Sonya, instinctively, knew it. She tried her best to make her husband see that Chertkov was an unscrupulous, conniving, deceitful man who was poisoning their already difficult relations and conspiring to take him over, along with all his works, to the detriment of the family.

But Tolstoy could not, or would not, see it. He replied: "That man has sacrificed everything for me. Not only did he give up his wealth and position in society, but he has devoted all his energies to the publication of my works." Obviously unaware of Chertkov's sinister hold on him, the old man felt an obligation to do for his disciple whatever he asked.

Two old friends who were still close to Tolstoy despaired of the great man's coming so much under the influence of a person they found deceitful and conniving.

Biryukov, Tolstoy's former secretary, and later biographer, and probably closer to the writer than anyone save Chertkov, wrote: "It was very painful to me to see how Chertkov tyrannized Tolstoy and sometimes forced him to do things that were completely at odds with his ideas."

Aylmer Maude, Tolstoy's English translator and biographer, and close friend, was more outspoken about Chertkov. "I never knew anyone," he once said, "with such a capacity for enforcing his will on others. Everybody connected with him either became his instrument, quarrelled with him or had to escape."

But the old patriarch, like all of us, had a blind spot. To the very end he could not see Chertkov as he was.

Just before his birthday, Tolstoy fell ill again. He thought it might be the end and hastily drew up in his diary a list of his last wishes—a sort of informal will. He had already made such a list back in 1895, when he wrote in his diary a page he asked to be considered his will.*

---

* Earlier, in 1882, he had given his wife power of attorney to manage his estates, and in 1892 he deeded all his property to his wife and children, each to have an equal share.

My Will will be roughly as follows. Until I write another one it will be entirely as follows:

1. Bury me in the place where I die, in the cheapest cemetery . . . and in the cheapest grave . . . as paupers are buried. Lay no flowers or wreaths, and make no speeches. If possible, bury me without a priest or a burial service. . . .

2. Do not announce my death in the newspapers and do not write any obituaries.

3. Give all my papers to my wife and Chertkov, Strakhov.[3]

He added his daughters Tanya and Masha and then crossed out their names and wrote: "My daughters need not bother about this." His sons were a different matter.

My sons I exclude from this commission, not because I have not loved them (I have loved them . . .) but they are not fully aware of my thoughts, have not followed their course, and might have their own particular views of things, as a result of which they might keep what ought not to be kept and throw out what ought to be kept.

He asked that his diaries from his former bachelor life and of his married life be destroyed except, in the first case, what might be worthwhile and, in the second case, "anything that might not be unpleasant for anybody." He added that Chertkov, out of his great love for him, had promised to do that. Before he ended, he had second thoughts about destroying the diaries of his wild youth.

But no, let my diaries stand as they are. At least they will show that despite all the triviality and worthlessness of my life, I was still not abandoned by God. . . .

Despite his promises to Sonya that she could publish all his works written before 1881, he asked his heirs to renounce the copyright on them and make all his writings available to the public for free. Having written that, he proceeded to tell his heirs that he was only "asking" them to do this, not "willing" it.

If you do it, it will be good. . . . If you don't do it that's your own affair. . . . The fact that my works have been sold these last two years has been the most depressing thing in my life.[4]

The fact that Sonya's publication of his earlier and most important works (especially *War and Peace* and *Anna Karenina*) had brought a fortune that enabled the Tolstoy family to live in luxury apparently escaped the writer's notice. Later, the disposal of his copyrights—the subject of his subsequent wills—would become the chief cause of the bitter quarrels between Sonya and Chertkov and between her and her husband.

The last miserable year of Leo's life, his son Sergei has written, "can only be correctly understood in connection with his Will"—the last ones.[5] But even the first one aroused Sonya's ire, because she didn't learn of it for years—until 1902—and because her husband's request for all his works to be made available free to the public threatened to deprive the family of its chief source of income.

By making his works public property, Sonya wrote in her diary when she belatedly learned of his will, "we only line the pockets of the rich publishers. I told L.N.," she added, "that if he died before me I would *not* carry out his wishes and would not renounce the copyrights of his works."[6]

Now in 1908 as he lay ill, the aged writer—about to become eighty years old, and fearing that he might be dying—again took to his diary to express what he wanted done with his body and his works in case that happened. "I must be dying," he began.

> . . . I would like to say a few things, trivial though they are, about what I would like done after my death. First, I would be glad if my heirs would make all my writings public property; if not, then certainly all my writings for the people, for example the *Primers* and *Readers*. Secondly, though this is the most trivial of all, I do not wish any rites to be performed at my burial. A simple wooden coffin and anyone who wishes can carry it or convey it to the Zakaz wood opposite the gully to the place where the green stick is.[7]

The green stick! Tolstoy had not forgotten it after all these years. When he was five, and his eldest brother Nikolai ten, the latter had called in all four brothers and told them he knew a secret that, when it became universally known, would ensure that there would be nothing but love between people, who would be happy forevermore and belong to a great Ant Brotherhood! The secret, said Nikolai, was carved on a green stick which lay buried on the edge of a ravine in the Zakaz forest.

The idea of the Ant Brotherhood bringing universal happiness and health and love played a powerful part in Tolstoy's young imagination. Years later he testified to that.

> I used to believe that there was a green stick on which words were carved that would destroy all evil in the hearts of men and bring them good, and I still believe today that there is such a truth, and that it will be revealed to men and will fulfill its promise.

He wanted to be buried, he added, beside that green stick on the edge of the ravine in the Zakaz forest—in memory of his brother Nikolai.

Though on August 11 that year he felt so ill that, as he wrote in his diary, he "must be dying," he recovered enough a week later to jot down ideas for seven works of fiction.* As his birthday on August 28 approached he began to wish people wouldn't make such a fuss about it.

"I fear the nearness of the 28th by the increased number of letters," he wrote in his diary on the twenty-first. "I'll be glad when it is over."

It seemed that year that the whole world, and especially the whole of Russia, with the exception of the Tsarist reactionary government and the reactionary Orthodox Church, wanted to celebrate Tolstoy's eightieth birthday. Committees were set up in Petersburg and Moscow to organize the celebration and to solicit money in Russia and abroad for a Tolstoy birthday fund. The old philosopher took a dim view of it.

"All my life," he said, "I have hated all kinds of jubilees. It seems like a mockery that in my old age, when I must think of death, people want to do such an unpleasant thing to me!"

The government and the church also took a dim view of so

---

* Idea number two: "The gentle, sincere son of a priest does well at school and theological college, and is married and ordained. The daughter of a neighbor in his parish gives his mother, a vain and intellectual woman, a book to read. He reads Tolstoy and questions begin to arise."

many Russians of all classes, high and low, celebrating the birthday of a revolutionary and an infidel. Secret telegrams went out from Petersburg to the provincial governments ordering that any public birthday celebrations for the writer be suppressed.

The Orthodox fathers regarded a birthday commemoration for such a heretic as insulting to the church and to religion. They launched fresh attacks on the "Russian Judas," as the bishop of Saratov called him in a searing outburst. Tolstoy, he proclaimed, was "an infidel and revolutionary anti-Christ . . . a corrupter of youth, an intellectual murderer, morally rotten to the core, the Russian Judas reviled and accursed."

Even friends who remained loyal also to the church urged him to call off the celebration because it would offend the faithful. To one of them, Princess Dondukova-Korsakova, he wrote that any celebration of his birthday would be "highly tormenting and diffi-cult to bear."

To one correspondent and ardent Tolstoyan, who had written him that it would be more appropriate for him to spend his birth-day in prison, the old man replied: "Really, nothing would satisfy me so much and give me so much joy as actually being put in prison, a really good prison, stinking, cold and short of food." Finally, he wrote the head of the committee in Moscow to desist and to get all the other committees to cancel their commemoration plans. "I urgently request you to stop the preparations for the jubilee, which will cause me nothing but suffering. . . . Cancel this jubilee and set me free."

Though the committees dissolved themselves, a cancellation proved difficult to carry out. As the birthday approached, Yasnaya Polyana was besieged by journalists and photographers from all over the world. Even an operator of a new-fangled motion-picture camera showed up.

The birthday "commotion," as Alexandra called it, began early on the day of August 28. The journalists and photographers insisted that Tolstoy come out and pose and talk to them. Scores of visitors began driving up to the house, many of them having come by train from Moscow and even further. Employees of the small local post office groaned under the burden of delivering letters, telegrams, and packages—some two thousand of them, according to Sonya's account. Trying not to notice all the fuss, Tolstoy spent the morning in his study working on his *Cycle of Reading*, a selection from what he thought were great gems of world literature (including some of his own writings) to be published by Chertkov and sold for a few kopecks so that peasants and workers could be inspired by the writers and philosophers of the world.

At noon the old man was wheeled out into the living room to be shown some of the hundreds of birthday presents. He was still suffering from a thrombosis of the nerves in one leg and was confined to a wheelchair. There were dozens of boxes of candy, scores of books, an album of drawings and watercolors from Repin, Pasternak, and other Russian painters. Admirers from France sent twenty bottles of San Rafael wine with an inscription "the best friend of the stomach." From a group of seventy-two waiters in Petersburg came a beautiful nickel-plated samovar with engraved inscriptions of some of the titles of the author's books. The Ottoman Tobacco Company of Petersburg sent a case of cigarettes, on each package of which was a portrait of Tolstoy. Having given up smoking long before as an evil habit, he returned the cigarettes, writing the company that he had stopped smoking twenty years ago and had always "warned people of this bad habit."

There was one grizzly "present." A Moscow woman, who gave her name as "O. A. Markov," enclosed in her birthday package a rope, along with a note in answer to Tolstoy's manifesto against the death penalty—he had been crushed by the growing number of executions carried out by the Tsarist government. The note read: "Count, here is the reply to your message: you can do it yourself, no need to bother the government with it, it isn't so difficult. And you will be doing a favor to your nation and the young." It was signed: "A Russian mother."

Tolstoy was hurt. Though he had received hundreds of letters from unknown persons for whom he had no time to reply, he insisted on writing to Mrs. Markov, saying: "You would make me very happy if you would explain to me the reasons for your ill feelings." Later Tolstoy's secretary, Gusev, established that there was no such woman living at the address she had given. Most probably the "gift" came from a crank.

Tolstoy was pleased by the seventeen hundred telegrams and letters he received from people in all walks of life and from many countries. At a gala family birthday dinner for thirty people that evening around a large horseshoe table—the patriarch sat in his wheelchair at a separate table wedged into the big one—his sons read the contents of some of them.

From the faculty of the Polytechnical Institute of Petersburg: "We wish you many more years of life in your struggle against the powers of darkness." From the Moscow Art Theater: "The Art makes its bow today, great teacher." It was signed "Stanislavsky and Company."

"Do not be silenced, old man, inspired by God. A peasant."

"God grant that your life may last long, great sower of love and justice. Peasant Wheelwrights."

"To a seeker of God, a Catholic priest sends his greetings."

A group of teachers wrote: "Receive our respectful homage to the genius, the knower of Russia's heart."

A group of English writers—George Bernard Shaw, George Meredith, H. G. Wells, and Thomas Hardy among them—sent a message of congratulations, as did Gerhart Hauptmann, the playwright, from Germany, and George Kennan, an engineer who had traveled extensively in, and written books about, Siberia, from America. Sonya, seeing how fatigued Leo was becoming, called a halt to the readings and ordered champagne to be passed around. Outside the house hundreds of well-wishers sat down to an open-air buffet. As the evening progressed, they started chanting that they wanted to see their idol. Tolstoy, a very tired man by now, was wheeled out to thank them but he was too fatigued to say more than a few words.

Finally, he was taken back to the house, where he played a round of chess with his son-in-law Sukhotin, Tanya's husband, and then, in the big living room, he called on Goldenweiser to play some Chopin études. Exhausted, he finally went to bed. When Sonya tucked him in for the night, he seemed very happy despite his fatigue. She sensed that he felt close to her, their lifelong strife, for the moment at least, forgotten.

"Ah, how good that was, how good!" Sonya says he cried out to her. She also wrote in her diary: "What an enormous amount of love and respect people have for him." She must have thought that night that their last years together might be more serene and loving after all.[8]

But it was not to be. Some curse seemed to hang over them and they resumed their quarreling. It seemed to some of the children that Chertkov was largely responsible. Since his return he had persistently tried in his devious way to turn Tolstoy against his wife so that he alone could inherit all the works of the Master, edit them as he pleased, and give them to a grateful world.

Chertkov's endeavor to make Tolstoy see what a monster he had married went back at least twenty years. Early in 1887, Chertkov had written Tolstoy a nasty letter pitying him for having such a wife. He himself had just married Anna Dietrich, a thin, young student lost in the contemplation of philosophy and in the worship of her husband. Chertkov was boastful of her, and—since the Master and the disciple often exchanged intimate glimpses of their private lives—even by 1887, he knew a great deal about the great writer's difficulties with his wife. Instead of helping them to solve their problem, he set out to inflame it so that he could replace Countess Tolstoy in her husband's life.

In a letter to Tolstoy about what a wonderful woman he had married, one who understood him and was of immense help to him in his work, Chertkov slyly commiserated with his idol for not having the good fortune with a spouse that he himself had. Sonya came across the letter while snooping around in her husband's study and was furious.

> I read Chertkov's letter [she wrote in her diary] describing in woeful tones his deep spiritual communion with his wife, and commiserating with L.N. for being deprived of this joy; what a sad thing it was, he wrote, that L.N., of all people, should be denied this sort of communion. . . . To think that this sly, stupid, devious man has fooled L.N. with his flattery and now wants (like a "good Christian," I dare say) to destroy all the things that have kept us together for nearly 25 years. . . .
>
> He [Tolstoy] must end this relationship with Chertkov, for it involves nothing but lies and evil: we must get as far away as possible.[9]

Fortunately for Sonya, it was Chertkov in the end who got away as far as possible, when ten years later he was exiled to England for a whole decade. Tolstoy and his disciple kept in intimate touch by post, but Sonya felt that Chertkov in England was less of a menace than Chertkov in Russia.

But now he was back, living right next door, seeing her husband every day and poisoning their relationship, which, over the years had been poisonous enough. Chertkov himself, not without glee, described a quarrel between the Tolstoys that he himself witnessed on December 4, 1908, three months after the birthday party. The tiff was over the subject that had now become the most common cause of conflict between Tolstoy and his wife: the disposal of his papers—the diaries and letters and, above all, his literary works, published and unpublished.

> Sonya, turning to Leo, irately asserts that the property rights to all his writing belong to the family. Leo objects. She runs to her room and fetches a pocket diary written in her hand and reads her own record to the effect that Leo had given as public property only those writings which had appeared in print during his lifetime (and after 1881). Leo begins to object. She shouts him down. Finally . . . he obliges her to hear him. (She had just said that she was not concerned about herself, but that her children would assert their claims.)
>
> Leo: "You imagine that our children are like rogues who want me to do something opposed to what is most dear to me."

Sonya attempted to interrupt him.

> Leo: "No, let me finish. . . . You know the principles for which I've renounced these rights. . . . I gave you my fortune, I gave you my early writings, and now it seems that I ought to give my own life. . . . It is astonishing how you torment yourself without any need." And he left the room, firmly closing the door behind him.[10]

Tolstoy could not see that it was Chertkov who was poisoning life with his wife. "If she [Sonya] only knew and understood," he wrote in his diary on July 12, 1909, "how she alone is poisoning the last hours, days, months of my life!" They had quarreled over Sonya's wanting to prosecute a Petersburg publisher who had brought out, without her permission, two of Tolstoy's earlier writings for which he had given her the rights. Leo became so angry that he threatened to take back all of her rights to his works if she prosecuted. He wanted to tell her, he says, how she was ruining his last years on earth. "But I can't say so," he adds, "and I don't expect any words to have any effect on her."

A couple of years before, back in 1907, during the revolutionary outbreaks when peasants had burned down the barns and sometimes the houses of the landlords and even shot at them, Yasnaya Polyana was spared except for a few cases of peasants felling the Tolstoys' trees for firewood and lumber or an occasional raid on their vegetable garden. But even when these minor things happened, and once when the night watchman was fired on by garden thieves, Sonya became panicky and asked for police protection. This, the governor of Tula was only too happy to provide. He thought it would take Tolstoy down a notch when the public learned that the great apostle of nonviolent resistance to evil was now protected by armed guards of the State, whose police powers he said he always despised. The governor sent half a dozen police to Yasnaya Polyana, two of whom were posted inside the house.

Their arrival infuriated Tolstoy. When Sonya tried to defend her action, Tolstoy cried: "Enough, enough! If you cannot understand that life with police guards who seize peasants and throw them into prison is intolerable to me, there is no use talking!"

"Then what do you want?" Sonya replied angrily. "To have all of us here shot to death? Yesterday they shot at the gardener, tomorrow they will shoot at us. They will carry everything away. We cannot stand aside and be robbed, can we?"

"Such conversations," as Sasha called them, occurred, she says, every day. She quotes her parents' notebooks.

> Sonya: "A disagreeable conversation with Leo over the guards. . . . I am morally imprisoned, and then I get the blows too—Leo has been disagreeable to the guards."

> Tolstoy: "It would be better perhaps to go away, to disappear. . . . Life here at Yasnaya Polyana has become entirely poisoned for me."

The quarrel over the guards, Sasha says, went on for two years—until they finally left. Then Sonya, adamant, hired a mounted Circassian guard, who kept molesting the peasants and providing the Tolstoys with new fuel for discord.[11]

Abruptly, on July 2, 1908, Tolstoy started a secret diary. "I'm starting a diary for myself," he began, "a secret diary." He felt that the reading of his diaries by others—especially Chertkov (to whom he was now giving them) and Sonya (who snooped around until she found them)—kept him from being frank about himself and his eternal strife with his wife. The secret diary lasted only sixteen days, but in it he poured out all his sorrows at the life he felt he was being forced to live.

He went on that first day:

> My soul is sorely depressed.
> At times I ask myself what I should do— Go away from everyone? Where to? To God, to die? . . . I wish for death.
> After writing this there was an incomprehensible boorish and cruel scene over the fact that Chertkov had been taking photographs.* Doubts occur to me . . . whether it wouldn't be better to go away and hide like Boulanger† . . . to escape from this life which is poisoning me.
> Help, Lord, help!
> Death is the only place one can really go to.

Next day:

> I'm still struggling just as agonizingly. . . . Life here at Yasnaya Polyana is completely poisoned. Oh, help, help me, God within me.
> July 6: Chertkov has just told me of a conversation he had with her [Sonya]. "He [Tolstoy] lives and enjoys every luxury and says: 'it's all pharisaism, etc.' I am the one who is sacrificing herself . . . !"
> Help me, Lord. Again, I want to go away. And I can't make up my mind.

* It wasn't Chertkov who had been taking photographs but an English photographer whom Chertkov brought along to the house to photograph the great writer. Sonya resented it.

† Paul Boulanger, a close friend who lived nearby but worked for the State railway at Tula, had squandered a large amount of his company's money at cards and disappeared, leaving a note that he was going to kill himself. Actually, he fled to the Caucasus and then abroad but returned to the vicinity of Yasnaya Polyana a year later and resumed his relationship with Tolstoy.

July 7: It was agonizing yesterday. I counted up my money and thought about how to go away. I can't see her without unkind feelings. . . .

How clearly one can see in her all the horrors of the love of body, love of self carried to the extent of loss of all spiritual sense of obligation. It's terrible for both others and herself.

July 14: It's still very depressing to bear with and endure. Sonya's character. Egoism, that exudes everything that is not herself and which goes to comic lengths, vanity, self-satisfaction, cockiness, condemnation of everybody, irritability. I had to write it down. I'm sorry for her.

As abruptly as it began, the secret diary ended sixteen days later, on July 18. The old man simply could not deny Chertkov's insistence that he must see all the diaries, open or secret. Tolstoy dutifully handed the secret diary over to Chertkov in August, asking him to copy out what he thought worth preserving and destroy the rest. Chertkov, of course, copied it all. He was glad for his own purposes to have the Master's ill feelings toward his wife in writing. It made him more determined than ever to destroy her.

And then suddenly, at the end of March 1909, Chertkov was expelled from Tula province for "subversive activities" (i.e., propagating the works of Tolstoy) and had to settle on the estate of a relative near Moscow. Sonya was greatly relieved, though to please her husband, she wrote a letter to the press protesting the expulsion. Tolstoy this time could hardly bear not having his disciple near him. He took his resentment out on his wife.

On the morning of May 13, at breakfast, there was a row over a short story of his, *The Devil,* which Tolstoy wanted to give to Chertkov; Sonya insisted it belonged to her. Their wrangling became so intense that he retreated to the garden to cool off. There he wrote to her a "posthumous" letter describing what had been boiling up within him, but which he had not had the heart to say directly to her.

This letter will be given to you when I am no longer here. I write to you from beyond the grave in order to tell you what I wanted to tell you so many times and for so many years for your own good, but was unable to tell you when I was alive. I know that if I had been better and kinder I would have been able to tell you during my lifetime in such a way that you would have listened to me, but I was unable to do so. Forgive me for this and forgive me for everything in which I was to blame throughout the whole time of our life together and especially the early time. I have nothing to forgive you for, you were what your mother made you: a kind and faithful wife and mother.

And then he let Sonya have it:

But just because you were what your mother made you and stayed like that and didn't want to change, didn't want to work on yourself, to progress towards goodness and truth, but on the contrary clung with such obstinacy to all that was most evil and the opposite of all that was dear to me, you did a lot of evil to other people and sank lower and lower yourself and reached the pathetic condition you are in now.

The irate husband, having got this off his chest, put the letter away to be discovered after his death. Sonya did not see it until then.

Early in June that year, Tolstoy decided to visit his daughter Tanya at Sukhotin's estate in Kochety. The prospect made him feel so good that he invited Sonya to come along. His spirits improved, as they usually did while visiting his eldest daughter. He and Sonya had even become reconciled to her husband, Mikhail Sukhotin. But there were depressing moments, too. Touring the neighborhood, Tolstoy was appalled by the wretched poverty of the peasants.

I feel keenly the insane morality of the luxuries of the rulers and the rich, and the poverty of the downtrodden state of the poor. I suffer almost physically from the awareness of being party to this madness and evil. . . .

The main thing is the tormenting feeling of poverty—not the poverty but the humiliation of the oppressed state of the people . . . French talk [at dinner] and tennis, and side-by-side hungry, ill-clad slaves, oppressed by work.

I can't stand it.[12]

But he did, basking for the rest of the month in the hated luxury of the great estate. He enjoyed it so much that he let Sonya leave for Yasnaya Polyana before his own departure. He did not tell her there was another reason he stayed on. Tanya had told him that the banished Chertkov was looking for a place to live in the village of Suvorovo near them in the Orel province. As soon as he heard Chertkov had arrived, he galloped over on horseback to see him. It was a joyous reunion. "Radiant meeting," the older man called it in his diary. When Sonya wrote asking when he was coming home, Tolstoy answered: "My plans are indefinite." When she persisted a few days later, he replied that he was "putting off" his departure.

When he finally got back to Yasnaya Polyana on July 3, it was a stormy meeting. Sonya scolded him for seeing Chertkov and asked what they had been up to. She also told him she did not want him to attend the Eighteenth International Peace Conference in Stockholm later that summer, which he had been invited to address. Sonya thought the trip would be too fatiguing for a man of his age in precarious health. He insisted that he would go, and his diaries show that he was already working on his speech.

"I have to go," Sasha heard him saying to her mother, "and say the things that perhaps no one else will undertake to say." He wanted especially to talk about how military conscription was un-Christian. But Sonya was insistent. According to Sasha, she threatened to poison herself if he went to Stockholm. She had become increasingly nervous the last few months, says Sasha. One day she overheard them arguing.[13]

> "Promise me that you won't go to Stockholm! What does it cost you to promise?"
> "I consider it my duty to go."
> "You want to kill me! You have no pity!"
> "Enough! Enough!"
> Tolstoy left the room in tears.*

The conflict was solved when the Peace Congress called off its session that year as a result of crippling strikes in Stockholm. There were some, however, including Tolstoy himself, who believed the meeting was canceled because the organizers feared what Tolstoy

---

* Sonya told her daughter Tanya, who had been summoned to Yasnaya Polyana because of the fierce quarrels over the Stockholm meeting: "I thought they wanted to poison me. Dushan made me take some sweet powder or other. Well, he's not a nice person, and he loves your father. I thought he wanted to get rid of me." (Tatiana Tolstoy, *Tolstoy Remembered,* p. 225.)

might say. Still, he was asked to address the Congress the following year, in 1910. He declined.

Sonya was not content that this particular argument had been settled. She jumped on her husband for one thing after another. Tolstoy's diary that late summer of 1909 is full of complaints that he couldn't sleep. The Countess couldn't either. His diary, July 21:

> In the evening Sonya Andreyevna was weak and irritable. I couldn't get to sleep till 2 or later. I woke up feeling weak. Sonya hadn't slept all night. I went to see her. It was something quite mad. She said Dushan [Dr. Makovitsky] had poisoned her, etc.[14] I am tired, and I can't take it anymore. I feel the impossibility, the absolute impossibility, of a reasonable and loving relationship. *C'est le moment ou jamais.* ["It's now or never."] I terribly want to go away. . . . Help me, God. Teach me.

Five days later there was what Tolstoy described in his diary as a "terrible burst of anger on the part of Sonya." They had been quarreling over two things: Tolstoy's insistence on going to Stockholm (the meeting had not yet been canceled), and Sonya's demand that he give her all rights to publish not only his works written before 1881, as agreed, but all those written after that date. Tolstoy told her he could not accommodate her on either subject.

Sonya was beside herself with rage. She rushed to her room and returned flaunting a bottle of morphine and yelling that she had poisoned herself.

"I snatched it from out of her hands," Tolstoy wrote in his diary that night, "and threw it downstairs. I struggled." He retired to his bedroom to calm down. "She is pitiful and I'm truly sorry for her," he added.

In reality he was becoming desperate. Chatting with Dr. Makovitsky one day, he suddenly said: "I should like to leave home and go somewhere abroad. How can I manage a passport? No one must know about it, at least for a month." If he applied for a passport in the normal way, he would have had little difficulty. But then Sonya would learn of it and keep him from leaving. "I do not want to depend upon a hysterical creature," he said. "Her illness is mental, not physical. . . ."[15]

But Tolstoy still could not bear to think of the harm he would do to his wife if he left her. To a follower, E. I. Popov, who had urged him to get away from his wife, he responded that he agreed with him, but that he could not do it because he could not, he said, "cause grief and unhappiness to a woman who in her own mind fulfills everything that falls to her lot as a wife. . . ."

Still, the urge to leave would not die. It would creep up again, each time more urgently, as the last months of his life ticked away. And it became more intense as Leo and Sonya plunged into the greatest struggle of their life: the final battle over the rights to publish his works upon his death, a death which he kept telling his diary—and friends—could not be far off. For Sonya it was a matter of survival for her children and their offspring and, though she denied it, for herself. The royalties would be virtually the family's only source of income. For the aging writer it was a matter of principle: he did not want his works to be sold for profit after his death (though, as Sonya told him, the publishers themselves, without royalties to pay, would make a handsome profit). And he felt there was only one person who could faithfully carry out his wishes and that was Chertkov, his beloved disciple. There was no one, of course, who agreed with him more fully than the crafty ex–guards officer. In fact, earlier that summer he had suggested it.

To facilitate the matter, a legal will* would be necessary and on September 3, 1909, Tolstoy set off with Sasha for Chertkov's temporary quarters near Moscow, to discuss it secretly with his disciple. Sonya, suspecting something, insisted, to her husband's and daughter's annoyance, a few days later, on following them. If the conspirators were up to something, and she suspected what it was, she wanted to be on hand to thwart them and save her family, as she said, from "starvation."

Behind her back, a few days after her arrival, the old man, helped by Chertkov and Alexandra, drew up a will and signed it. The testament left all his writings after 1881 to the public. This was only confirming the agreement with Sonya to give her all his works written before that date. But the conspirators added a paragraph— namely, that Chertkov would become Tolstoy's literary executor. Thus, he alone would decide which of the Master's writings to publish and how and where to publish them.

On their way back home, the Tolstoys stopped off for a couple of days in Moscow, staying in their old home, now occupied by

---

* The "wills" that Tolstoy had written in earlier diary entries were not legal.

Sergei and his family. There Sasha lost no time in stealing away to check with a lawyer, A. K. Murayev, about the legality of the will they had just drawn up. The lawyer found it quite illegal, telling Sasha, she says, that it was impossible to will literary property to the public—one had to specify an individual person or persons to bequeath it to. He promised to draw up a new document that would satisfy the law.

As the Tolstoy ménage arrived at the Kursk station in Moscow to entrain for home, the great writer was mobbed by a crowd of several thousand admirers. The family made its way to the station platform only after much friendly shoving. Tolstoy could hardly climb into the railway coach, he was so exhausted. On the way he suffered a mild stroke and became unconscious. Dr. Makovitsky and Sonya and Sasha feared for his life. At Yasenki, the railroad station nearest to Yasnaya Polyana, Tolstoy had to be carried to a waiting coach. Back home, Sonya and Sasha undressed him. He was still unconscious.

Sonya looked at him and panicked. What if he died? she thought. Chertkov and her scheming youngest daughter, Sasha, would get hold of his papers, especially his diaries—they already had most of the recent ones—and publish them, exposing her to the world as a shrew, a second Xanthippe. She must prevent that, and at any cost. Dashing around the bedroom, she started yelling at the still-unconscious Tolstoy.

"Lyovochka! Lyovochka! Where are the keys?"

The old man apparently regained some consciousness for he muttered: "I don't understand . . . what for?"

"The keys, the keys to the drawer with the manuscripts!"

Alexandra intervened. "Mother," she says she begged, "leave him alone. Don't try to make him remember things. Please!"

"But I have to have the keys! He will die and the manuscripts will be stolen!"

"No one will steal them. Let him be, I implore you!"[16]

Two new figures joined the conspiracy to induce Tolstoy to make a proper will: Goldenweiser, the musician and Tolstoyan, and F. A. Strakhov, a young follower of Chertkov.* After Tolstoy's

---

* Not to be mistaken for Nikolai Strakhov, historian, author, critic, and close friend of Tolstoy, by this time deceased.

return to Yasnaya, all three had lost no time in working out with the lawyer Murayev several drafts of the proposed will. Chertkov decided to send the one he liked best to his idol, asking him to read it over and consider signing it. He picked Strakhov as messenger, and the conspirators fixed a date for his departure from Moscow: October 26, when, they were told, Sonya would be in the city. But she turned up on the train to Yasnaya Polyana with Strakhov, much to his embarrassment; he continued on anyway in the hope that he could catch Tolstoy alone for a few minutes to discuss the will.

One day while Sonya was out, Strakhov showed Tolstoy the draft of the will, explaining that, to make it legal, the writer would have to deed his literary property to a definite person or persons—not just to the public. The old man read it, seemed to approve it, but then turned to the younger man. "The whole affair," he said, "is very painful to me. And it is all unnecessary—in order to secure that my ideas are spread by such measures. Take the example of Christ," he said.

> Now Christ—although it is strange that I should compare myself to him—did not trouble that someone might appropriate his ideas as his personal property, nor did he record his ideas in writing, but expressed them courageously and went to the cross for them. His ideas have not been lost. Indeed no word can become completely lost if it expresses the truth and if the person uttering it profoundly believes it is the truth. But these external measures for security come only from our nonbelief in what we are uttering.

He left the room but soon returned. His young caller thought he had a counterargument that might impress his host. The case of Christ, he said, was different: He did not write down his ideas and, of course, received no payment for them. But Tolstoy did. If he did nothing to see that all his works became public property, as he said he wished, then he would be furthering the rights of private property, which he said he detested. The argument hit home to the old sage, who had been preaching for years against the right of private property, which he considered a sin. Again he left the room, saying he would think it over. He was gone for what Strakhov considered an extremely long time. Indeed, the old man had a ride on his favorite horse, Délire, returned to take a nap, and only after dinner called Strakhov and Alexandra to his study.

He had decided, he told them, to leave to Sasha all his literary works, including those published before 1881, even though that meant breaking a promise to his wife. Sasha replied that it would be too much for her and that it would bring attacks on her from the rest of the family, especially from her mother. But Tolstoy insisted. He told Strakhov to work out the details with Chertkov and his lawyer. From Sasha he extracted a promise that she would give up her rights so that all his works could be published "for the people" by anyone, without payment of royalty. Chertkov, though, would be the sole editor and alone would decide what would be published, and he could also publish the works himself. Strakhov left as quickly as he could and rushed to Tula to telegraph Chertkov that his mission had been successful.

Tolstoy made one more request of his daughter: after his death to take the money from the early sale of his works and buy back Yasnaya Polyana from her mother, brothers, and sisters and give it to the peasants. This, says Sasha, she ultimately did.[17]

On November 1 Strakhov, accompanied by Goldenweiser, returned to Yasnaya Polyana with the finished document for Tolstoy to sign. He and Goldenweiser would witness it. They arrived late at night. The Countess had gone to bed. Tolstoy received Chertkov's emissaries in his study, and after they entered, he quickly locked both doors. He seemed to fear that Sonya would burst in upon them at any moment and make them call off the whole thing. Strakhov later admitted that he had certain pangs of conscience because they were acting behind Countess Tolstoy's back. But he considered himself to be a mere messenger, and his conscience was not pricked deeply enough to make him hesitate. After getting up several times to check the locked doors and to listen for any signs of his poor wife approaching, Leo Tolstoy looked over the will and signed it. His two visitors attested to it as witnesses.[18]

To Chertkov it would seem that at last he had triumphed over Countess Tolstoy. He, not she, would get everything Tolstoy had ever written and, since he would have possession of this literary treasure, he alone would be able to edit and publish it. He had achieved his lifelong ambition. This would give him the place in the world he sought. Countess Tolstoy and her children and grand-children might be deprived of their chief source of income, but surely they had enough from their estates to live on. If not, let the five idle sons go to work to earn a living.

Sonya knew nothing of what had gone on that evening while she was asleep. At breakfast the next morning she was most cordial to the two visiting conspirators. She knew nothing, but she was suspicious. She had a gut feeling about what her enemies, including her beloved husband, were up to. And she was enraged at the thought that her husband of forty-seven years might have made a last will and testament without consulting his long-suffering wife, the mother of his thirteen children. Under the sinister influence of the despicable Chertkov, had he disinherited the family?

She strongly suspected he had. At any rate, she had to find out. At once! Leo, with his infirmities and old age, might go any day now. From the autumn on, she kept frantically searching his study and bedroom for the document. Her snooping drove her husband to the brink. And her failure to find the will drove Sonya to the brink and then over. She could no longer cope with what she thought was going on around her—a gigantic conspiracy to deprive her and the children of their rightful inheritance. But she could fight it, desperately, to her last breath.

As the final year of Tolstoy's life (1910) approached, he and Sonya became locked in deadly conflict. In the wings, Chertkov, also fearing that his idol might die any day, did his best to inflame it. The children, as we have seen, took sides and joined in the war: Sasha, for her father and Chertkov; the four youngest sons for their mother; the two eldest children, Sergei and Tanya, attempting to remain neutral and striving to prevent a final catastrophe.

In the end, as it turned out, they could do little. Their parents were, by now, beyond saving. Try as they might, Sergei and Tanya could not prevent the last year of the life of Russia's most famous writer and spirit from being the worst, the most desperate and miserable, in his life. It would be the same for his wife. In her mind, worse—for she would lose everything.

• BOOK THREE •

*The*

*Last*

*Year*

*1910*

# SEVENTEEN

# The Beginning
# of the End

*T*HE YEAR STARTED well enough.

"In the first part of 1910," Sergei Tolstoy recalled in his memoirs, "things went better and there was a certain degree of peace at Yasnaya."[1] Sonya did not bother to jot down anything in her regular diary until the year was half over—until June 26, when she resumed it. She did keep, in addition to the regular diary, a daily notebook in which she briefly and rather perfunctorily noted the humdrum events of her day.* These notebooks covered the years between 1905 and 1907 and from 1909 until 1919.

The first mention she makes in her notebooks of her problems with Leo is an entry for May 29, 1910, in which she alludes to a "painful discussion with Leo Nikolayevich."

> Reproaches flung at me for our privileged life, after I complained about the difficulties of running the estate. He wants to drive me out of Yasnaya. . . . I went out [of the house], terrific heat, aching leg, wild pulse, lying down in a ditch, and stayed there. They sent a horse for me. Stayed in bed all day, wept, did not eat. . . .

The preceding Christmas had been observed with the usual warmth at Yasnaya Polyana. There was a big Christmas tree. Most of the children and grandchildren arrived to celebrate. Sonya, as

---

* Typical was an entry for January 22 about her husband's health. "He is always constipated. In the evening I administered an enema with oil."

usual, bustled about superintending the holiday festivities. Outwardly the bearded old patriarch joined the others in exuding the
Christmas spirit. Inwardly the holiday depressed him. "Very sad,"
he wrote in his diary on January 4, 1910. "Those around me are
very alien to me." And on January 7, he scribbled in his notebook:
"I suffer not so much helpless anguish as unceasing shame before
people. Is it possible that I shall finish my life so, in this shameful
condition? Lord help me."

All through the rest of the winter and into spring he kept
recording in his diary how depressed about life he had become. Not
because of strife with his wife—at least for the moment. What he
hated most of all was the life he felt forced to live—a family life of
luxury and frivolity while all around them the peasants, in their
wretched huts, were half starving.

> April 12: Tormenting pangs caused by consciousness of the
> vileness of my life surrounded as I am by working people hardly
> able to keep themselves and their families from starvation. In
> our dining-room fifteen people are gorging themselves on pan-
> cakes while five or six servants who have families, are running
> about hardly able to prepare and serve up what we devour. I am
> tormented and terribly ashamed.
>
> April 13: Awoke at 5 and kept wondering how to get away,
> or what to do, and I do not know. I thought of writing, but to
> write while remaining in this kind of life seems repellant. Talk to
> her about it? Change things gradually?

He decided to talk to her. He and his wife had gone to visit
their daughter Tanya at Kochety. "To Sonya for the first time," he
noted in his diary on May 9, "I expressed part of what weighs on
me." He described to her the "insanity" of their lives. But still he
did not feel up to provoking a break. "To soften what I said," he
added, "I kissed her silently. She quite understands that language."
He who all his life had been so sensuous—so like an animal, he had
admitted—was still trying to convince himself that it was Sonya
who was the lusty one.

But for five months they had managed to avoid the savage
battles that had nearly wrecked their lives the last years. Both
seemed to hope that this would continue and that, after all, they
would achieve peace and understanding in their old age. And then

in June, the loveliest month of the year in the country, Leo and Sonya were at it again, joined by Chertkov, who had been permitted by the authorities to return to his place at Telyatinki, a couple of miles from Yasnaya Polyana. Each day from now on the ugly strife became more poisonous. As Tolstoy had predicted, it was to be literally a battle to the death.

The first serious quarrel that year—at least the first recorded in their diaries—came on June 7. As we have seen, Sonya had insisted on replacing the police guard at Yasnaya, which her husband so detested, with an armed Circassian, whom Tolstoy hated even more. The new guard, Tolstoy felt, was harder on the peasants than the police had been. Just the day before, he had received a complaint that the Circassian was beating the peasants. It made him, Tolstoy said, "very depressed."

Next morning, Sonya recorded in her daybook, there was "more unpleasantness with Leo Nikolayevich as to why I keep a Circassian forester." It *looked* bad, she claimed her husband said, to keep a Circassian at Tolstoy's home.

> I said that with him the trees are not stolen and so all is peaceful; there are no police and no criminal proceedings. It turned into another painful conversation, with yet more recriminations. I was in tears almost all day. Leo Nikolayevich is in a terrible state: he torments both himself and me.

The same day Tolstoy jotted down in his diary:

> Slept badly, very little. Spoke to Sonya about the Circassian and there was the usual emotion and irritation. I am very depressed. I keep wanting to cry.

His daughter Tanya, too. She had recently spent a few days at Yasnaya Polyana and was sickened by the renewal of the squabbles between her parents. More than any of the other children, she had tried to be fair to each of them and had done her best to keep their union from falling apart. But now, after returning to Kochety and thinking over the situation at Yasnaya, she wrote her mother that she agreed with her that she had taken on too many duties at home, especially that of administering to her husband's material needs, and it was time in her old age to take matters easier. What her father wanted and needed, Tanya wrote on June 14, was for his wife to understand and respect his inner life.

> You suffer when he eats badly; you try to save him from boring visitors; you surround his material life with every possible care, but that which is dearer to him you somehow lose sight of. How touched he would be and how much he would return a hundredfold your efforts if you had as much concern for his inner life.

But Tanya could no longer reach her mother, who replied:

> I am not capable of arranging a new life. Papa's so-called inner life has been hidden from me for a long time and in reality taken away from me by that hateful Chertkov.[2]

That hateful Chertkov! Frustrated at being prevented by the authorities from living in the vicinity of Yasnaya Polyana, and fearing that Sonya, in his absence, was reestablishing her influence on Tolstoy and the disposal of his works, Chertkov now urged the Master to visit him at his new place at Meshcherskoye, near Moscow.

"I've decided to go to the Chertkovs," Tolstoy wrote in his diary on June 12. Apparently he had made his decision a day or two before, because, accompanied by his daughter Alexandra, Dr. Makovitsky, and his new secretary, Valentin Bulgakov, he set off for Meshcherskoye early on the twelfth. Too many summer visitors and passing pilgrims had sapped his strength. The trip offered a chance to get away for a few days from them—and from the torments of his wife.

Once in the company of Chertkov, he regained his good spirits. All was quiet and relaxing in the household. There was an insane asylum nearby and Tolstoy took to visiting it, fascinated by his talks with the inmates. When he asked one if he feared death, the man replied: "Why die? Live!" As he was leaving he said he hoped they would meet again in this world. "Why this world? There is only one world." Tolstoy was happy, though surprised, to hear such agreement with his own ideas from such a source.

He seemed happy and surprised too that he had found so much peace and quiet. All the pressures, all the strife that made his life at Yasnaya Polyana so difficult had, for the moment, vanished.

"In general, since he has been staying with the Chertkovs," Bulgakov wrote in his diary only four days after their arrival, "Leo Nikolayevich appears to feel very well. He is always very animated and eager to talk. I think this is a rest for him after the constant bustle of his own house."[3]

In the quiet of his new environment, Tolstoy started to write again. He wrote two articles and, for the first time in years, turned back to fiction, dashing off two stories: *Unexpectedly* and *Grateful Soul*.

"Apparently," wrote Bulgakov, "he is in the grip of a very successful creative impulse, which I am sure is the result of the quiet, peaceful life at Meshcherskoye."[4]

In this mode, Tolstoy noted in his diary: "I must try to fight Sonya, consciously, with kindness and love."[5] And he wrote her friendly, warm, newsy letters. Only two days after arriving at the Chertkovs', he wrote assuring her that "however good it may be to visit, it is better to be home. And I shall return, as I intended, certainly no later than the 24th, if all goes well with you and me." And then affectionately:

> How are you and your affairs?—both the editing and the household? Don't they worry you too much? To have a tranquil mind is the main thing. . . . Goodbye, my dear old wife. I kiss you.[6]

On the nineteenth, he got off another and more chatty letter telling Sonya what he had been up to.

> I am expecting your letter, dear Sonya, but meanwhile I write to let you know about myself and to talk to you. All goes well here. . . . How time flies! I have not had time to look around, and a week has already gone by—only five days more. We have decided to leave on the 25th. How are things with you? What have you been up to? . . . Au revoir, dear Sonya. I kiss you.

He was breaking off, he added, to go to lunch. The whistle had blown. After lunch he added a postscript. It was to prove a fateful one, though obviously he did not realize it. "I have just received the welcome news that Chertkov is permitted to be at Telyatinki during his mother's stay there. They are going there on the 27th. . . . How extraordinary such permission—for the period of his mother's stay. I kiss you again."

The news sent Sonya into a rage. She lost all control of herself. *Welcome* news, indeed! That evil man was coming back to haunt her! And her husband welcomed it! Sonya summoned her secretary, Varya Feokritova, a close friend of Alexandra's. She told her to get off an urgent telegram to her husband: "Sofya Andreyevna's nerves are in bad shape. Insomnia. Weeping. Pulse: one hundred." To protect herself and perhaps to indicate that Sonya was exaggerating, Varya added, "Asked me to telegraph." And, at Sonya's behest, Varya signed her own name, too, to the telegram.

Back at Meshcherskoye, Alexandra received the wire at 5:00 P.M. on June 22. Her father was napping. When he awoke she showed it to him, pointing out that Varya's words "Asked me to telegraph" were really a way of saying that Sonya was most probably not in as bad a way as she claimed. At Sasha's urging, her father wired back: "More convenient to come on the 24th. But if indispensable will come tonight."

"More convenient!" That snapped another nerve of Sonya's. As soon as she read those words, her secretary noted, "she began to sob, flung herself on the bed, and cried: 'Don't you see this is Chertkov's expression? He won't let him go! They want to kill me, but I have some opium myself. Here it is!' " Whereupon, Varya says,[7] "Sonya ran into a cupboard and showed me a phial containing opium and another of ammonia, and yelled that she would poison herself if her husband did not return at once."

"Send an urgent telegram," she cried, and ran over to a table and hastily scribbled it out: "I think it necessary to return. Varya."

"Why have you signed my name?" Varya says she asked. "It's your telegram, not mine."

"Let me use it," Sonya responded, "or they will say that I am summoning them and will not come."

"Well, as you please," Varya says she answered and hurried off to the telegraph office to send the message.*

Before retiring that frantic evening, Sonya wrote in her diary:

---

* Alexandra tells of her mother sending another telegram on June 22 saying, "I implore you to come on the 23rd. Quickly." She signed her own name, but the formal one, "Tolstaya." (Alexandra Tolstoy, *The Tragedy of Tolstoy*, p. 229.)

Tolstoy confirms receiving it. His diary of June 23 began: "Had just lain down but had not yet fallen asleep when the telegram arrived: 'Implore you to come the 23rd.' I will go and do what I have to do. May God help me!"

Of course he has not come. . . . A telegram: 'More convenient to come tomorrow morning.' It is Chertkov's heartless
style. For two days I have not taken anything into my mouth.
Have prepared two poisons: opium and spirits of ammonia. Still
lack the courage. Is it possible that I am a coward? Is it not
worse to live? . . .

The next day, she added: "They arrived in the evening. A
painful explanation. Everything by which I have lived my long life
is lost. Love is lost and broken."

"Found things worse than I expected," Tolstoy wrote in his
diary. "Hysteria and exasperation beyond description. Restrained
myself pretty well, but was not gentle enough."

Tolstoy and his party had arrived at Yasnaya Polyana at
eleven that evening of the twenty-third. Sonya was in bed and,
according to Alexandra, "moaning loudly." Her daughter thought
she was faking it a bit. When Tolstoy entered the room, she says,

. . . the moan became an uninterrupted wail. "You have no
pity," Mother screamed at him. "You have [a] heart of stone.
You love nobody but Chertkov. I shall kill myself, you will see.
I shall take poison!" In a tender, trembling voice Father begged
her to calm herself, but the more he pleaded the more she wailed.

Her ravings, Sasha says, went on until 4:00 A.M. when, out of
exhaustion, she fell asleep.[8]

In truth she had raved to her diary the whole day, or most of
it, while awaiting her husband's return. What she wrote in it reveals a rapidly deteriorating mind, plummeting toward madness.
She wonders herself whether it is "the beginning of insanity." She
calls the entry "A Sick Woman's Ravings—*Memorandum Before
Death.*" Perhaps she meant it for the press—she headed it "YET
ANOTHER SUICIDE." She says she wrote it in a severe fit of hysteria.

I was waiting for Leo Nikolayevich, and feared that he
would not come. . . . Had he not come I should probably have
poisoned myself. I have never been in a worse state in my life.

"I am sitting alone," she begins, "and thinking only of Leo
Nikolayevich's return from the Chertkovs . . . for three days I have

not eaten or drunk anything. I have spasm in my throat and pain in my heart. . . . Today my head aches terribly."

> What is the matter with me? Hysteria, a nervous stroke again, the beginning of insanity? I do not know. . . . Where do so many tears come from? . . . Let me confess the truth. I was wretched because of the long separation from Leo Niko-layevich. . . . He has a repulsive, senile love for Chertkov (in his youth he used to fall in love with men) and is completely subject to his will. . . .*
>
> Chertkov is our *divider*, a cunning, despotic and heartless man, who has made himself the person nearest to Tolstoy. . . .
>
> I am immensely jealous of Leo's intimacy with Chertkov, I feel that he has taken from me all I have lived by for forty-eight years. . . . Now I am completely thrown aside. . . .
>
> Yesterday when I was in a terrible state of physical and mental suffering and not responsible for my actions, I became frightened of myself and what I might do. So I appealed to the man I love to save me from myself, and sent him a telegram saying: "I implore you to come." Instead of coming he sent a reply saying that it would be *more convenient* to come on the 24th— that is, two days after Varya's first telegram telling him that I had fallen ill with a *severe nervous breakdown*. In the words "more convenient" I recognized Chertkov's cold style, and all my sufferings were accentuated by that reply. I was enraged and wept again.
>
> And yesterday when I was quite beside myself, I might easily have done something desperate. All the methods of suicide passed through my mind, and the best way of all seemed to be to sink beneath the waves of the sea.

The end that Anna Karenina took in the novel had always been in Sonya's mind, and her thoughts returned to it now. "I did not like the idea of throwing myself on the rails," she continued, "though I thought of going to Stolbovo and lying down under the train in which Leo Nikolayevich would be traveling *more conveniently.*

---

* After these words Sonya wrote, and then half erased, something in the margin that her son Sergei says "does not admit of publication." (Sergei Tolstoy, *The Final Struggle*, footnote to p. 193.) Simmons (*Leo Tolstoy* p. 737) noted this too, and added that in Sonya's diary this last year unprintable words, usually referring to Chertkov, were "fairly frequent."

I thought of going to Tula to ask the governor's permission to buy
a pistol . . . and then shooting myself in the temple. In my cupboard there is a large phial of opium, and I have prepared both
opium and spirits of ammonia."

She looked up in a medical book, she says, the results of opium
poisoning. "First excitement, then sleepiness—and then the end.
There is no antidote for it."

> I must write my husband, who recently went with Chertkov
> to visit a hospital for insane women, and ask him if he studied it
> well, as Chertkov would probably find it *more convenient* to place
> me in it. But no! I will not allow that. I have the opium.

Her troubled mind wandered. She called on her son Andrei,*
who had recently visited Yasnaya Polyana, to "avenge your
mother's death! You loved me and understood." She recalled her
husband's loving letters from Meshcherskoye and now branded
them "falsely affectionate." They were written to fool her, she now
saw, at the very time her husband was "continuing to enjoy and
revel in his pitiful, senile love for his handsome idol." She was now
afraid of her husband, she wrote, and saw his eyes staring at her in
anger "for infringing his enjoyment—those eyes which always look
on me with hostility, but once doted on me so passionately." As she
tossed on her bed in self-inflicted anguish, she saw a vivid picture

> of a rounded coffin-lid covered with rose-covered or white bro-
> cade, and under it—myself. How enormous my nose will seem if
> it sticks up. My husband will go away. He will be annoyed that
> his customary way of life is temporarily disturbed. . . . And the
> children? Away, away with all thought of them. There is pain
> enough already in my heart. I loved them very, very much. . . .
> But all the same we are now living apart.†

---

* Andrei, Tolstoy's ninth child, had been in the doghouse with his father since
beginning an affair with the wife of the governor of Tula province. Tolstoy had
written the governor apologizing for his son's deportment and expressing his
sympathies. He promised to do whatever he could to bring his son to reason.
Tolstoy also wrote the governor's wayward wife, imploring her to give up his son
and not leave her husband. But she did. Andrei divorced his first wife, and he and
the governor's wife were eventually married.
† Actually, Alexandra was still living at Yasnaya Polyana.

Oh, what anguish! May there be more and more of it so that it will be easier to poison myself! . . . What a turmoil there will be. . . . What will the whole world say? What nonsense! What does it matter? An interesting occurrence. No one in the whole world will know that I perished from the cruelty of my husband's lost love, and from jealousy of a *man*. . . .

Another hour has passed. It will be over soon! I shall take poison a few minutes before his arrival. I shall watch his fright and angry joy—revenge on him for deserting me for a *man*—and I shall fall asleep forever.

It is late. They have lit the lamp. The rain has passed. My husband will come directly. . . . The phial is in my hand. . . . Shall I put it off? No, with his arrival fresh torment will begin. . . . I hear the wheels of the carriage. . . . It is coming up the driveway.

Quicker! Quicker! It will be too late. . . . I have drunk the opium. . . . He is coming.

All who witnessed that frantic homecoming have agreed that from that moment on, Countess Tolstoy began to fall apart and that the last descent into insanity finally had begun, though subsequent diary entries will show that there would be lucid moments indeed and that, at times, she would react to what was going on around her sanely enough—an aging, sick woman, pining for her lost love and surrounded, she believed, by enemies—not only Chertkov and his followers but her own dear husband and daughter, conspiring to destroy her and her family. She was facing a situation she could no longer cope with. She was striking back wildly and insanely to defend herself.

"From that time on," Sergei Tolstoy recalled, "Sofya Andreyevna's hysterical condition became much more acute."

As for Tolstoy, his visit to Chertkov, Alexandra says, was "the last pleasant period of my father's life. Days of misery followed. Father knew no rest, day or night." Bulgakov, Tolstoy's devoted young secretary, wrote in his diary that his idol's "calvary, which took him to his grave, began with these two telegrams received at Meshcherskoye." Once Tolstoy had returned to Yasnaya, he says, "one misunderstanding was compounded by another until they formed a tangle that could not be unraveled."[9]

The night of their arrival back at Yasnaya Polyana, Bulgakov had stood by, an unwilling witness to the ghastly scene that Countess Tolstoy had made. "I shall try to get some sleep," Tolstoy had said to Bulgakov as dawn was breaking over Yasnaya Polyana. And he bid the man good night.

"My heart is wrung," Bulgakov closed his diary that night, "for this great and dear old man."[10]

Next day things went a little better, Bulgakov noted. Sonya herself wrote in her diary that they had "made peace. We decided that we would make a fresh start . . . and would spare one another. But will that last long?"

Tolstoy, in *his* diary, did not see that peace had even begun.

> Sonya came to me during the night, still unable to sleep. She came again in the morning. She is still agitated and does not calm down. Went for a walk after a tormenting conversation with her.

On June 25 there was another ugly scene. "Sofya," wrote Dr. Makovitsky in *his* diary, "continued yesterday's torture of Leo Nikolayevich and of herself." He, Sasha, and Goldenweiser described what happened. When Tolstoy met her in the living room she suddenly fell down, complaining that she had injured her leg. When he attempted to console her she dashed away, running from one room to another, her husband, Sasha, and Makovitsky in pursuit. They finally found her hiding behind a bookcase in the library, brandishing a vial of opium and shouting, "One more gulp! Just one." Sasha and her father tried to snatch the poison from her. The little doctor was skeptical. "In my opinion," he wrote in his diary, "she did not drink any at all." But her gasps left her husband limp and drained. "Sonya was excited," he wrote in his diary, "and there was the same suffering again for both of us."

But more was to follow. That day, Sonya raised a question that had been haunting her for a long time, driving her to distraction. Where were his diaries of the last ten years? she asked her husband. Were they with Chertkov? And what had he written about her? Chertkov would surely use it to destroy her. Tolstoy tried to evade the question. One of the few times in his life with her, he dissimulated. He told Sonya he did not know where his diaries were. "You are lying to me!" she screamed. Then he said he had them.

But when she demanded to see them, he hesitated, finally admitting that they were at Chertkov's.

"There may be a police search there," Sonya said, "and then all will be lost! I need them for my own memoirs."

"He has taken precautions," Tolstoy said. "They are in some bank."

> "Where? What bank?"
> "Why do you want to know that?"
> "Because I'm the person nearest to you—your wife."
> "Chertkov is the nearest to me, and I don't know where the diaries are."

She asked him to at least show her the diary entries he had written during his visit to Chertkov. "Let me see what you've written about me!"

To quiet her, Tolstoy went to his study, searched through his papers, and found his diary. Sonya glanced rapidly over it. She stopped at an entry he had made at Meshcherskoye the week before: "I must try to fight Sonya . . . with kindness and love."

"Why must you fight me?" she asked him. "What have I done? What is there in me that you want to fight?"

"The fact that we disagree about everything," he replied. "About the land and religion."

"The land is not mine," Sonya argued. "I consider it family property."

> "You could give away your own land."
> "But why are you not offended by Chertkov's landed property and his fortune of a million?"
> "Ah! I will be silent! Leave me alone!"

Sonya swears there was "at first a cry and then silence."[11]

Furious, she went to her bedroom, snatched thirty rubles from the cupboard, and dashed out of the house. It was very hot and it was raining hard and she realized she could not get to the railway station. Circling the house, she lay down on the wet grass of the lawn. When she returned, her clothes were dripping and Tolstoy urged her to change them lest she catch cold.

"No, I'll stay like this," she said. "I'll catch cold and die." She rushed away and Tolstoy found her lying on the balcony outside his bedroom. He begged her to go to her room and put on dry clothes and take a nap. But she remained on the balcony, moaning so loudly that Tolstoy could not sleep when he finally fell on his bed exhausted.

"Sonya is agitated again, and again causes us both to suffer," Tolstoy jotted down in his diary. "Lord help me!"

The news that Sonya had been fearing reached her on the evening of the twenty-seventh. Bulgakov reported that Chertkov had arrived with his mother at Telyatinki, a couple of miles away. The news sent Sonya into another tailspin.

"Chertkov has arrived!" she screamed at Varya Feokritova. "I can't stay here!" To Goldenweiser she sobbed: "I admit that I am perhaps out of my mind. But I can't control myself. If I see *him* [Chertkov] God knows what will happen to me. I had better go away . . . and then come back when I am quieter."

"Last night she spoke of going away somewhere," Tolstoy wrote in his diary that evening. "I did not sleep all night and I am very tired."

He had told Goldenweiser that his wife "was unquestionably mentally deranged." In his diary that night he added: "Insanity is always the result of an irrational and therefore immoral life. . . . Insane people always attain their end more successfully than healthy people because they have no moral values: neither shame, nor truthfulness, nor conscience, nor even fear."

That day he had also told Goldenweiser that he was thinking of calling a psychiatrist to examine Sonya. Perhaps it would help her and also relieve the terrible tension in the house. "Everyone here," he added, "is in such a depressing and unnatural condition—unable to speak naturally about anything. We have to conceal things from her and she finds out and screams that everybody is lying." One little matter that Tolstoy had concealed from his wife was that he had run into Chertkov the day after his arrival while taking a walk. They had discussed Sonya's state and the poisonous atmosphere at Yasnaya Polyana.

Bulgakov, who reported this to his diary, noted sadly: "Yasnaya Polyana has turned into a sort of fortress, with secret meetings, parleys, and so forth."

The next day, June 28, Chertkov arrived at Yasnaya to try to make peace with Countess Tolstoy. He brought with him what he thought was a letter of conciliation. He hoped Countess Tolstoy would soon meet his mother, he wrote, "a good and worthy woman," and that good relations between them would help establish a new bond between him and Sonya. Then he got to the point.

> In this connection, I feel it necessary to tell you that I have heard that you have lately expressed an inimical feeling toward me. I cannot believe that such a feeling can be other than temporary irritation evoked by some misunderstanding which a personal meeting would very quickly dispense as an extraneous, superficial obsession.

He reminded her that at Tolstoy's eightieth birthday party she had "cordially" told him that he was the family's best friend. "No secret calumnies by my enemies, though they may temporarily provoke you against me, can alter that fact." He was confident that at their "first personal encounter," all that seemed to come between them would be easily removed.

> It is a long time since we've met, and conceptions of me have evidently formed in your mind which will crumble away at the first renewal of our personal relations. I am so convinced of this that I most zealously ask you to allow me to kiss your hand and attest my unimpaired and sincere devotion.[12]

Sonya did not fall for the flattery or the evasions. Her resentment of this disciple was too deep. Replying on July 1, she told Chertkov bluntly that her first hostility toward him had come only a few days before when she felt he had kept her husband at Meshcherskoye after she had fallen ill and begged him to return.

Then Sonya got down to the main reason for turning on him— the diaries of Leo Tolstoy over the last ten years.

"Give me back the diaries!" It had been wrong, she said, for him to take them in the first place. He had simply stolen them. But she would forgive him now if he returned the diaries. Until then, she went on, "it is painful for me to even see you after I have been so deceived by you." She explained that she herself was writing her memoirs and needed the diaries so she could continue.

If you put any value on your relations with me and on Leo Nikolayevich's tranquility (which will be fully restored if you and I are friends during the last years of his life), then I ask you with a suffering heart and with readiness to love and value you even more than of old: Give me back Leo Nikolayevich's diaries! . . .

If you fulfill my request we shall be more friends than ever. If not, our relations will be painful to Leo Nikolayevich to witness, but it is beyond my power to force myself to act otherwise.

Chertkov did not take kindly to this blunt response. Despite his confidence, as he wrote in his letter, that a meeting between them would "crumble away" their differences, it turned out otherwise. Shortly after Sonya had posted her letter to him on July 1, Chertkov arrived for their first personal encounter in some time. His visit turned out disastrously for everyone.

"Chertkov has been rude to me," Sonya scribbled in her diary. First, after a brief, rather formal meeting with her, Chertkov had withdrawn with Sasha and Tolstoy to Leo's study. Their concerting behind closed doors aroused Sonya's easily aroused suspicions. She hovered outside the study, put her ear to the keyhole, desperately trying to find out what they were saying. Finally, she could stand it no longer and burst through the door.

"Another plot against me!" she shouted. Tolstoy was so taken aback that Sasha took him away to another room, leaving Sonya and Chertkov alone in the study. The real Chertkov quickly emerged. When Sonya stormed at him about the diaries, repeating what she had just written to him, Sonya says he flew into a rage.

"You're afraid," he shouted, "that I shall use the diaries to unmask you! If I really want to, I could drag you and your family through the mud"—a fine expression, Sonya noted, "for a supposedly decent man."

"I have enough connections," Chertkov continued angrily, "to do so. The only thing that has stopped me is my affection for Leo Nikolayevich." According to Sonya, he reminded her of the case of Thomas Carlyle, whose friend Froude, he said, had unmasked his wife, Jane, and showed her in the worst possible light.

Finally, Sonya says, Chertkov "shouted" at her "that if he had such a wife as I, he would have shot himself or run away to America."

Angrily, Sonya followed Chertkov out of the study, where they ran into Tolstoy and Alexandra. In their presence she turned to Chertkov and asked him to promise to return the diaries. "I will return them," Chertkov said coldly, "but to your husband and not to you."

Whereupon he sat down and, according to Alexandra, scribbled out a note to Tolstoy saying he would return them to him as soon as he had finished making the deletions that the author had asked him to make.

"And now," said Sonya, "let Leo Nikolayevich give me a written promise that he will give them to me."

Her husband was angered by the very idea.

"This is all we needed," he huffed, "that a husband should give a written promise to his wife."

To quiet her, however, he gave her an oral promise, saying, "I promised you I would give you the diaries and I will."

Sonya was pleased but skeptical. "I know that there is only one purpose behind all these notes and promises: to hoodwink me. Chertkov will drag out his imaginary work on the diaries and won't ever give them to anyone."[13]

Nothing, it seemed, could keep her from being miserable and sorry for herself. Her diary the next few days is one long lament.

> July 5: I have no life. Leo Nikolayevich's heart has become as cold as ice, and Chertkov has got him in his clutches.

She was vexed and jealous, she said, at the sight of the two of them sitting on a low divan together when Chertkov came over that evening. She felt they looked awfully happy sitting so close to one another. Again, in her desperation, she used several words that her son Sergei says were "unprintable." She was further displeased when she heard them discussing sanity and suicide, thinking they were talking about her.

"Can't you change the subject!" she cried. "Always madness, insanity, suicide. I won't hear any more of it."

That night, after everyone else had gone to bed, Sonya took up her diary again. "Something hangs over this house, some heavy oppression which crushes and kills me. . . . There is still the same iciness in Leo Nikolayevich."

Sonya's obsession with the diaries did not let up. In her journal of July 7, in the morning, she complained that Leo's diaries were now being written especially for Chertkov; her husband never "dared say a loving word in them about" her.

Actually that day turned out to be, relatively, one of the happiest Sonya had had in a long time. For one thing, she noted, her husband had quarreled with Chertkov. Chertkov, she learned from Goldenweiser, had told the Master that if he listened to all the stories about him (Chertkov), he risked making a fool of himself.

The old man did not like the expression. "You're a fool yourself," Tolstoy replied angrily. "Everybody knows you are an idiot!"

Late that night Sonya rejoiced in her diary that her icy husband was truly melting. She had not yet lost him, after all! "Nothing can disrupt the union of our hearts! . . . We are joined by a life-long and endearing love!"

She had gone into his room as he was going to bed and asked him to promise her that he would never leave her. "I promise. I will never go away from you. I love you!"

> His voice trembled [Sonya went on in her diary]. I burst out crying, embraced him, and said that I was afraid of losing him, and despite the stupid but innocent passions I have had in my life I had never for a moment ceased to love him more than anyone on earth. Leo said it was the same with him, and that I have nothing to fear; that the bond between us is too great for anyone to be able to infringe. I became happy and went into my room, but returned and thanked him for taking a load off my heart. Then I said good-night to him and went back to my room but after a little the door opened and he came in.
> "Don't say anything," he said to me. "I just want to tell you that our talk this evening has been a joy to me—a great joy!" And he wept and embraced me and kissed me again.

He was hers, hers again, she rejoiced, and she promised "to be kinder to everyone"—even to Chertkov. Next day she was still exulting about the happy turn of affairs. "My husband's caress has completely calmed me," she wrote in her diary, "and this is the first day I have passed in a normal mood." She went out to the fields and picked a bouquet of wildflowers for him.

Tolstoy was not so sanguine. That evening, he noted in his

diary, Sonya had again shown resentment of his seeing Chertkov and he had been unable to calm her. They had a long talk, he says, but "not a quieting one." Dr. Makovitsky noted in *his* diary that there had been quite a scene and that later Tolstoy had told Alexandra: "She is finishing me off!"

He felt differently after their late-night encounter. "Late in the evening," he wrote in his diary, "we had a very good talk."

Despite Sonya's hopes, the truce did not last very long. The rift was too deep.

The very next day, July 8, Sonya began her diary: "Oh, God! When will all this distressing and mean scandal and tale-bearing end! . . . They pull me all to pieces, discussing me and accusing me of something or other." Later, when Leo came in soaked from a horseback ride in the rain, he "angrily rejected," she says, her offers to give him a rubdown with spirits. Sonya was even more unhappy when, later in the day, Chertkov came over and shortly set off on horseback with Tolstoy for a ride in the woods, leaving Bulgakov, for whom a horse had been saddled, behind. This aroused Sonya's suspicions. "What talks and acts will there be in their tête-à-tête?" she wondered. Why couldn't her husband get his own diaries back from Chertkov?

"He will publish them and will try to inform the whole world, as he said, that it would be much better to shoot oneself or to run away to America than to live with such a wife as I."

On the night of July 10, as everyone in the household was going to bed, a terrible row broke out between Sonya and her husband—again over Chertkov and the diaries. Sonya grew hysterical and rushed to the balcony outside Tolstoy's bedroom and lay down on the bare boards of the floor. She began to groan. Her husband asked her to desist so he could get some much needed sleep. He was very tired.

"So you drive me away!" Sonya cried. "I will kill Chertkov!" And she bounded off the balcony, rushed out to the lawn, and lay down in the wet grass. It was uncommonly cool for July and she shivered. Alarmed when she did not return, Tolstoy woke up his forty-year-old son, Leo, who was at Yasnaya Polyana on a visit, and Dushan Makovitsky.

"She has gone again!" he told them. "She is probably out there somewhere on the lawn. Please try to bring her back."

It was dark, but with the help of Sonya's dog, Dushan and Leo junior finally found her. When they started to lift her up to take her back to the house, she pushed them away—like a "half-demented woman," her son says, crying, "No! I will not go back! He put me out of the house—put me out like a dog!" And she fell back on the grass. She would not return, she said, unless her husband himself came and fetched her.

Leo rushed back to his father. They had not been on good terms for years. The son could not accept Tolstoyism and blamed his father for most of the quarrels between his parents.

"Well, did you find her?" the older man asked. "Is she coming back?"

The son looked at his father angrily. "No, she will not come back unless you go to her. She says you put her out of the house!"

"No! No! Go back to her. Don't leave her!"

"I don't want to leave her but you are her husband, and it is your duty to go to her."

Tolstoy rather reluctantly gave in, went out to the lawn, and brought his moaning wife back to the house. It was 2:00 A.M.[14]

"Barely alive," he wrote in his diary. "A terrible night till 4 o'clock. And worst of all was Leo. He scolded me as though I were a child and ordered me to go out to the lawn and fetch Sofya Andreyevna."

# EIGHTEEN

# The Last Month

*I*N DESPERATION, Tolstoy summoned his eldest daughter, Tanya, and her husband to come to Yasnaya Polyana. Tanya seemed to have more influence on her mother than anyone else in the family. She had always tried to be fair to both.

Tanya arrived on July 12 and was appalled at what she found. The situation, bad as it had been when she was last there a few weeks before, had further deteriorated. Her mother was in a pitiable condition, rustling around the place and staring at everyone as if she were mad. Her father seemed bent and broken. He seemed to be unable to fully comprehend what was happening or how to cope with it. The eldest son, Sergei, who like Tanya was welcomed as a peacemaker, had arrived the day before. He joined his sister and her husband and Sasha in a parley to try to find some solution.

Sonya, as often when her two eldest children visited, and especially when Leo junior came, calmed down a little. On the very day Tanya and her husband arrived, she set off for Telyatinki to visit Chertkov's mother. Since young Bulgakov was also going to Telyatinki, Sonya kindly offered her husband's secretary a ride. But once they were en route, her spirits sagged and her crazed mind turned to the diaries. Bulgakov says she wept all the way. Suddenly, she begged him to tell Chertkov, who had been his mentor, to return the original copies of her husband's diaries.

"Let him copy them," she said, "if he will just return the originals! Tell him that if he returns them to me I shall be in peace. I shall be well disposed [toward] him again. He can visit us as before, and we shall work together for Leo Nikolayevich. Will you tell him this? Tell him, for God's sake!" Weeping and trembling, he says, Countess Tolstoy gazed at him imploringly. Her tears, he felt, were absolutely sincere.

"I could not look at this weeping and unfortunate woman," he wrote in his diary that night, "without feeling a deep compassion." It was in this mood that he accosted Chertkov, hoping that if his old mentor only returned the diaries there would be peace at Yasnaya Polyana and his beloved Tolstoy would be rescued from the hell he was living in.

But when he told Chertkov of his conversation with Countess Tolstoy, the disciple-in-chief became terribly agitated.

"Do you mean to say," he broke in, "that you came straight out and told her where the diaries were?"

To Bulgakov's utter amazement, he says, his aristocratic host made a hideous grimace and stuck out his tongue at him.

"No, I did not tell her anything," Bulgakov said, "because I do not know where the diaries are."

Chertkov curtly dismissed him.[1] From that day on, Bulgakov, who owed his job with Tolstoy to Chertkov's recommendation, began to have doubts about his old backer and to see that his struggle with the Countess was not a black and white matter, and that Sonya sometimes had reasons for acting the way she did, and deserved not only compassion but understanding.

In the meantime, Sonya was taking tea with Chertkov's aged mother. In her diary of July 12, she reported their conversation.

> She had invited me in order to learn why I had begun to hate her son. I explained it to her, spoke of the diaries and of how her son had taken my beloved husband from me. To which she said:
>
> "And I have always been grieved that your husband has taken my son away from me." Which was also true.

July 13 was another bad day—and night—for Sonya, at least in her imagination. When Chertkov arrived that day, Tolstoy handed him a brief letter he had written expressing regret that there had been a misunderstanding about their failure to meet the day before. It was innocent enough, but the suspicious Sonya did not like it. She seized it on the pretext of wanting to read it and then, she says, she burned it.

Her diary on the thirteenth is full of recriminations and exclamations of self-pity.

> I did not go to the bath today because I'm afraid of drowning myself. Only *one moment* of decision is needed, but I have not yet found it. . . . I searched for his last diary but did not find it. He knows that I have devised a way of getting it, and has hidden it somewhere. But I shall find it. . . . Where can he have hidden it?
>
> We are like two silent and cunning enemies, spying on and suspecting one another! . . . Lord, have pity on me!

That was written during the day. That night, in her diary, she was even more in despair—and disarray. And she was surprisingly frank about herself.

> Let it be granted that I am demented, and that I have an *idée fixe* that Leo Nikolayevich should get back his diaries from Chertkov. . . . What is necessary for everyone to be happy and to do away with all my sufferings?

Simple. Get back the diaries. If not, she imagines how sorry her husband and the rest of the family will be to have let her die because of the diaries.

> Looking back they will all understand that it was not worth it . . . to torment me to death by refusing to fulfill my desire. They will explain my death by everything on earth except the real reason . . . and no one *will dare* when looking at the corpse, killed by my husband, to say that I could have been *saved* in so simple a way, by returning to my husband's writing table four or five leather-bound notebooks.

She begins to rave madly.

> These two obstinate men—my husband and Chertkov—stand firm, hand to hand, to crush and kill me. And I fear them! Their iron hands have squeezed my heart. . . . I give them the

opportunity of *saving* me by returning their diaries. If they don't wish to avail themselves of it, the diaries will remain by *right* with Chertkov, but the right of life and death will be mine. . . . What a terrible wind outside. . . .

I am madly agitated, frightened, and I torment myself. . . . Oh, what a mockery, what pain, what hell!!

The diaries, she says at the end, must be returned!

In the middle of that sleepless night her husband came to her and she told him that he must retrieve the diaries or she would kill herself.

Tolstoy had begun to think that he could well afford to take back his diaries if it pacified his raving wife. He was even prepared to go further. On the morning of July 14 he wrote her a long letter saying he would retrieve his diaries—and, though reluctantly, give up seeing Chertkov. For the first time in years, he wrote in agonizing detail what he had not dared to say. Eloquently and sadly, not only with his mind but with his heart, he analyzed their lamentable situation, as he saw it. It is one of the most moving letters he ever wrote.

1. I shall not give my present diary to anyone: I'll keep it to myself.

2. I'll take back the old diaries from Chertkov and will keep them myself, probably in the bank.

3. If you are troubled by the thought that my diaries, or the passages which I wrote, under the impression of the moment, about our disagreements and conflicts—that these passages might be used by future biographers, ill-disposed towards you, then. . . . I am glad of the opportunity, if you are afraid of this, to express in my diary, or in this letter, my attitude towards you and my appreciation of your life.

Just as I loved you when you were young, so I have never ceased to love you and still love you despite the various causes of coolness between us. The causes of this coolness were (I don't mention the cessation of conjugal relations) . . . my greater and greater alienation from the interests of worldly life and my revulsion towards them, whereas you didn't wish to, and were not able to part with them, not having in your soul those principles that led me to my convictions, which was very natural and for which I do not reproach you. That's the first thing.

Secondly (forgive me if what I shall say is disagreeable to you, but what is now happening between us is so important that we shouldn't be afraid to express and to hear the whole truth)—secondly, your character over these last years has become more and more irritable, despotic and uncontrollable. The manifestation of these traits of character couldn't help but cool, not my feeling itself, but the expression of it. That's the second thing.

Thirdly, the chief cause was that hateful one for which neither you or I are to blame—namely our completely contrary understanding of the meaning and purpose of life: . . . our way of life, our attitude towards people and our means of livelihood—property—which I considered a sin and you a necessary condition of life.

So as not to part with her, he went on, he had submitted to a life that was painful to him, but which she had taken as a concession to her views. That was one reason their misunderstandings "grew greater and greater." Nevertheless, he repeated, he had never ceased to love and appreciate her. Passionately, he now expressed that appreciation.

I, a dissolute and profoundly depraved man sexually, and no longer in the prime of youth, married you, a pure, good and intelligent girl of 18, and despite my filthy and depraved past, you have lived with me and loved me for nearly 50 years, living a difficult and laborious life, rearing children, nursing them, bringing them up, looking after them and me. . . . I have nothing to reproach you for. As for the fact that you didn't follow me in my emotional, spiritual journey, I cannot and do not reproach you, because the spiritual life of every man is a secret between man and God, and other people shouldn't demand anything of him. And if I did demand anything of you, I was wrong and I was to blame for it.

This was a true description, he continued, of his attitude to and appreciation of her, regardless of what he may have written in his diaries.

Fourthly, he informed Sonya that if his relations with Chertkov were painful to her he was prepared not to see him again, though it would be painful both to him and his friend. "But if you wish, I'll do so." Then he laid down a condition.

If you don't accept these conditions of mine for a good and peaceful life, I shall take back my promise not to leave you. I shall go away. . . . Because it is impossible to go on living as we are doing now. I could continue to live like this, if I could endure your sufferings, but I can't.

Try to think calmly, dearest, try to listen to your heart . . . and you will decide everything in the right way. . . . Stop tormenting yourself, darling—not others but yourself—because you are suffering a hundred times worse than anyone.

But to decide anything in the right way was now beyond the capacity of Sonya Tolstoy. Leo, finally, desperately, had made all the concessions. He was offering to do everything that she herself had said was necessary to restore peace and love to Yasnaya Polyana. He was ready to take back the diaries. Though it pained him, he was willing to give up seeing Chertkov That was all she had asked. But he had gone further. He had reassured her of his love—it was not lost for her after all, as she had feared. But by now, even understanding was denied her. She did not seem to realize that her frantic wishes, the denial of which had driven her toward suicide, had now been granted. She did not grasp the meaning of the letter. Instead, she made caustic comments about it in the margins.

"Leo's letter to me today," she wrote in her diary, "is a scrap of our former happiness, but a small worn-out scrap! What an ending to my long and formerly happy married life!" Still, in the end, she admitted that this, July 14, was "a happy day." The diaries were back! Tolstoy had lost no time in retrieving them from Chertkov. After writing his letter to Sonya, he had dispatched a note to Chertkov saying Alexandra would come over to get the diaries during the day.

According to Bulgakov, that set off a flurry of activity in the Chertkov household. Everyone was mobilized and set to work hurriedly copying diary extracts that compromised Sonya, and which she might suppress if she got her hands on them.

That she could not do, because her husband, after showing them to her, sent them over to Tula to be deposited in a bank in his name. It had been "painful," Bulgakov wrote in his diary, for Chertkov to part with the diaries.

Still Sonya was not satisfied, even though the diaries had been taken back from her mortal enemy and were now in safekeeping.

"If only I am not cheated again!" she exclaimed in her diary. "If only that Jesuit Chertkov does not wheedle those diaries out of Leo secretly!" She could not sleep for fear he would. "Did not sleep all night," she recorded on the fifteenth. She now convinced herself that Leo had deceived her. "He promised in Chertkov's presence to give the diaries back to *me* and he has deceived me by putting them in the bank." She must make her husband give her the keys to the strongbox where the diaries now were, and—to make sure—the receipt the bank had given on deposit of the diaries. When he refused, Sonya erupted again.

Leo tried to calm her down but he could not. He emerged from her room crying: "I can't. I can't. This is my last sacrifice!" According to Varya Feokritova, Sonya fell on her knees before him in the corridor and seized hold of his legs, screaming, "This is my last request! Give me the keys, and give me authorization to take the diaries. I don't believe that you won't return them to Chertkov!"

"Get up! Please get up! For God's sake, stop this and leave me alone!" Varya says he was trembling.

Sonya jumped up and ran to her room. An instant later she yelled that she had drunk a whole vial of opium. "I have poisoned myself!" Her husband, still out of breath, rushed upstairs to her.

"I said that on purpose to deceive you," she told him. "I didn't drink it." Tolstoy, Varya says, "pale and with a violently beating heart, went out into the garden."[2] When Sasha came out to console him, he told her: "Go see Mama and tell her that her behavior is forcing me to leave. I shall immediately go if she continues."

His threats to leave angered and frightened Sonya, and she sat down to write him a letter to tell him so.

> I write to you because it is difficult for me to speak after a sleepless night. I am too agitated. During the night I thought it all over: how you caressed me with one hand and held a knife in the other. Even yesterday I felt dimly that the knife had already entered my heart. That knife is your threat to leave me secretly if I remain what I am now, that is, a woman who is certainly ill. This means that I shall be listening every night to hear whether you are going away, and that I shall be tormented by any long absence. How can I get well? I am now trembling all over. . . . What a life! I shall certainly die soon. I shall certainly break to pieces.

By Chertkov's letter (over which for some reason you cried) it is evident that he hopes you will return the diaries to him for some . . . work or other he is doing;* and again I experience a day and night of torment lest you should *secretly* give them all back to him. Or will you perhaps have pity on me and give me the key and the papers to keep? Let me have them, my dear one! . . . It would relieve me of those two oppressive suspicions: (1) that you will go away from me *secretly* and (2) you will secretly give the diaries back to Chertkov. You know I am quite ill and have to admit—as I must—that I am insane. Forgive me and help me!

But the old patriarch could no longer help. He had kept trying but failed. Nor could his daughters, sons, and friends aid her. Sonya seemed unreachable. What about calling in a psychiatrist? Another doctor? Tolstoy, who loathed doctors and was absolutely sure they did more harm than good, would not think of it. Sonya resented the very idea. Apparently it was Sergei, Tanya, and Sasha, among the children, who now insisted upon it. On July 19, Dr. D. V. Nikitin, the family physician in Moscow, arrived at Yasnaya Polyana accompanied by a well-known psychiatrist, Dr. G. I. Rossolino, a professor at the University of Moscow Medical School. After a day spent examining the reluctant but courteous Countess, they diagnosed her illness as a "degenerative dual constitution: paranoid and hysterical, with a predominance of the former." Later, in a letter to Alexandra, Dr. Rossolino explained in more detail.

She has a combination of two degenerative characteristics: hysteria and paranoia. The first shows itself in the specially vivid coloring of all her experiences and a concentration of all her interests on her own personality, even to the extent of sacrificing truth and her own best feelings, and becoming unconscious as to the means she employs to attain her ends. The second is indicated by excessive suspiciousness and by forming incorrect conclusions based thereon as to Leo Nikolayevich, his teachings, his relationship with Chertkov, etc.[3]

He recommended that the couple separate until Sonya recovered. She was indignant. She would not separate from her husband

* In giving back the diaries, Chertkov had written a note to Tolstoy suggesting that they be kept at Yasnaya Polyana so that they would be quickly available if needed "for work."

of forty-eight years for anything in the world! That would only mean turning him over to Chertkov.

> They have broken my heart, exhausted me by torture [she wrote in her diary] and have now called in doctors: Nikitin and Rossolino. Poor things! They do not know how to cure someone who has been mortally wounded from all sides. At first the doctors advised that Leo should go away in one direction and I in another—they did not know where. Then when I did consent but burst into sobs at seeing the whole aim of those around me was to part me from Leo Nikolayevich, the doctors seeing their powerlessness, began to consult. . . .[4]

They advised her to take baths, walk more, and try not to get agitated. "Simply laughable," she characterized their advice. Next day she began to become suspicious as to why the doctors had been summoned. "Were they called in," she asked herself in her diary, "to certify me as insane?" At any rate, she thought their visit was useless. Tolstoy too. He was glad to see the doctors depart the next morning. "Rossolino," he wrote in his diary, "is amazingly stupid in a learned way—just hopeless."

The old man, though, had something else to think about and it bothered his conscience. Two days before, on July 17, he had stolen away to Telyatinki on an errand that he dared not mention to his wife. Chertkov had concluded that Tolstoy's will, which had been drawn up at Chertkov's urging at his place at Krekshino the year before, was not foolproof. It had deeded all of Tolstoy's literary property to his daughter Alexandra, who had agreed to turn it over to Chertkov. But Sasha had been in poor health recently and Chertkov was afraid that if she died before her father, the old man might make his wife the literary heir. Sonya, of course, did not know the contents of the will, though she had begun to suspect its existence. Chertkov wanted the will changed to stipulate that if Alexandra died before her father, the copyrights, after her father was gone, would go to Tanya, the Tolstoys' eldest daughter. That had been done and now Tolstoy rode over to Telyatinki to sign the new will.

"Went to Chertkov's," he noted in his diary on July 17. "Things went well enough."

But Sonya was suspicious. If her husband, she wrote in her diary the next day, July 18, had concealed his diaries from her, then there was something in them that he found necessary to hide. When Tolstoy returned from Chertkov's, Sonya questioned him. Had he been unfaithful to her in one way or another? True, the diaries for the last ten years had been deposited in a Tula bank. But Leo was continuing to write his diary every day and not, as he once had done, showing it to her. What secrets was he recording in it? Her husband, she says, assured her that he had never been unfaithful.

Did Tolstoy, perhaps, have a look of guilt on his face as he reassured his wife? He had hardly returned home before Chertkov was after him to sign still another will because the one of July 17 had been found faulty by his lawyer. It had omitted, he advised the Master, the legally necessary expression that Tolstoy had been of sound mind and in full possession of his memory when he affixed his signature to it.

So another meeting had to be arranged for Tolstoy to sign the revised will. He was afraid to go again to Chertkov's lest his wife follow him. When he set off for his daily ride on his favorite mount, Délire, Sonya was not particularly suspicious. She did not know that he had arranged to meet secretly in the Zasyeka forest with three emissaries from Chertkov. They were bringing him the revised will for him to copy in his own handwriting and sign. The three were Goldenweiser, the pianist; Sergeyenko, an intimate of Chertkov; and Chertkov's secretary, a young man by the name of Radinsky. Tolstoy arrived first, posted himself on a hillock, and, rather impatiently, awaited the conspirators, who were late. They finally arrived and Goldenweiser espied the old patriarch, wearing, he says, a "white blouse . . . his long beard fluttering in the breeze." Looking for a place where they would not be observed, they rode over a field of rye stubble and entered the woods. Soon Goldenweiser noted, he says, a fallen stump of an old tree and he suggested that it would be a convenient place for Tolstoy to write. Under Russian law, a person making a last testament had to write it out himself. Seated on the log, Tolstoy began to write, copying out what the lawyers had drawn up. But his eyesight was poor in the gloom of the forest light and he asked Goldenweiser to dictate the text to him.

"We look like conspirators," he paused once to say, and then

finished the document. The others checked it and found one spell-
ing mistake, but when Tolstoy started to correct it, Goldenweiser
held him off. He was afraid any mark of correction might make the
document invalid. So Tolstoy signed it as it was and the three
witnesses affixed their signatures. In a society where it was important to note the identity of each witness, Goldenweiser signed himself "artist," Sergeyenko "citizen" and young Radinsky "son of a
lieutenant-colonel."

As they started to mount their horses Tolstoy said: "What a
trial this all has been." He seemed to feel guilty that he was making
his last will and testament behind ' is wife's back and the backs of
the children—except Sasha, who k ie v about it—and also because
he, who hated the authority of the State, was now conforming to its
tenets by writing a formal, legal will which would be subject to
probate by the State courts once he was gone.

Tolstoy must have felt guilty also because in the will he had
again reneged on his solemn promise to give Sonya rights to everything he had written before 1881. In this final draft, he deeded
to Alexandra everything he had ever written and might still write,
including "dramatic works, translations, revisions, diaries, private
letters, rough drafts, jottings and notes—in a word, everything
without exception."

Sonya and the children were completely cut off, for though he
was leaving all his works to his daughter Alexandra, she had agreed
to turn everything over to Chertkov. In case there was any doubt
about that, Chertkov came to Yasnaya Polyana the next day and
induced his mentor to sign a supplement to the will stating that all
of Tolstoy's works, without exception, were to be placed on his
death at the disposal of Chertkov to edit and publish as he pleased.

Sonya smelled a rat. The impressionable young Bulgakov noticed it. "I was amazed," he later wrote, "at Sofya Andreyevna's
intuition. She seemed to feel that something awful and irreparable
happened."[5] In his diary that evening he wrote: "Sofya Andreyevna
seems to foresee trouble. Again she is displeased about something
and keeps the whole house in a state of tension—as if she expected
something to explode in some painful and unexpected way. . . . She
was in a dreadful state, nervous and upset, she was rude and an-
tagonistic to everyone."

Everyone was strained and dejected, Bulgakov went on.

"Chertkov looked as if he had swallowed a poker: he drew himself up and his face turned to stone." It was a terrible evening. At the dinner table, Sonya says, her husband got angry with her, "raised his voice and began to say unpleasant things."

Years later Sonya returned to her diary of July 22 and added in the margins: "Leo N. wrote his Will that day. . . . After writing it he could no longer look me calmly in the eye. He was irritable with me and suspected that I was rummaging in his papers and looking for something. . . . He was upset at having written the Will in secret from his family."*

In her new agony, Sonya decided to leave. "I have decided to leave, if only for a short time," she wrote in her diary on July 25. The day before, she had overheard Tolstoy and Chertkov talking in low tones in the writer's study.

"Do you agree with what I wrote to you?" Tolstoy had asked. "Certainly, I agree," Chertkov answered.

"Another conspiracy!" Sonya confided to her diary. "Lord have mercy on us!!"

When, with tears in her eyes, she says, she asked Leo to tell her what "agreement" they were talking of, "he made a sullen, spiteful face and stubbornly refused to tell me anything."

Tolstoy confirmed what happened in his diary of the twenty-fourth:

> She did not leave Chertkov and me alone. . . . But I got up and asked him if he agreed with what I had written him. She overheard me and asked me what I had said. I told her that I did not choose to answer, and she left, upset and agitated.

From that day on, her son Sergei later wrote, she began to suspect that her husband had written a secret will. "She began," he added, "in all sorts of ways to discover it." That search, carried out by constant spying on him and snooping in his papers—and Tolstoy's growing resentment of it—led inexorably to the final chapter in the great writer's life.

Now, on the morning of July 25, Sonya began to pack her bags. She still had not decided where to go—perhaps just to a hotel in

---

* In his diary that night (July 22, 1910), Tolstoy did not dare to put down what he had been up to. "I wrote in the woods," he wrote enigmatically. "It is well."

Tula or their home in Moscow, which they had not used for years. She collected from her drawer her passport, a revolver, a vial of opium, a few rubles, and "some writing work," she says, and prepared to depart. But first, she must write her husband a letter explaining why she was leaving. And then, of course, a press release. She wanted the newspapers to know the truth about why she was leaving her husband of forty-eight years. Sasha, to whom the reporters would come, would not tell the truth. Just the other evening Sasha had spat at her. Nor would her husband tell her side of the story—only his.

To Leo she wrote:

> Goodbye, Lyovochka!
> Thank you for my former happiness. You have exchanged me for Chertkov. You both secretly agreed about something. . . . The doctors advised me to go away and now I have done so, and you are quite free to have any secrets and meetings with Chertkov. But I cannot bear to see all that any longer. I cannot. . . . I have exhausted myself with jealousy, suspicions and grief because you have been taken away from me forever. . . .
> Spat at by my daughter, and rejected by my husband, I abandon my home for as long as my place is occupied by Chertkov, and I will not return until he goes away. . . . Be well and happy in your *Christian* love of Chertkov and of all humanity—your unhappy *wife,* for some reason, alone excepted.

For the press notice she wrote her own headline: "The Facts Can Be Verified on the Spot."

And it must be said that she wrote lively, journalistic, but hardly objective, copy and her naïveté was touching.

> In peaceful Yasnaya Polyana an extraordinary event has occurred. The Countess Sofya Andreyevna has abandoned her home, the home where for forty-eight years she has lovingly cared for her husband, giving him her whole life. The cause of this is that Leo Nikolayevich, enfeebled by age, having fallen completely under the influence of Mr. Chertkov, has lost any will of his own, has allowed Mr. Chertkov to utter rude remarks to Sofya Andreyevna, and constantly consults him secretly.
> Having suffered for a month with a nervous illness on ac-

count of which two doctors were summoned from Moscow, the Countess could no longer endure the presence of Chertkov, and abandoned her home with despair in her soul.*

Early in the afternoon Sonya set off in a carriage for Tula, saying good-bye to the family. Tolstoy thought she was only going off to meet their son Andrei and his family, who were arriving for a visit, at the railway station at Tula. He obviously had not yet seen her letter. To Andrei, as they met on the station platform, Sonya confided that she had left home. He would not hear of it. He would not leave her until she agreed to return with him to Yasnaya Polyana. Reluctantly she agreed.

Back at the estate, Tolstoy greeted her amiably. After her departure he had found her letter. According to Sonya's diary, her husband was amazingly adorable. "I'm grateful to you for coming back, dear one. Thank you," she quotes him as saying. He realized, she says he told her, that he could not live without her. Thank God she had returned. And, she adds, he embraced and kissed her, and she cried for joy.

But not for long. She could not refrain from taking advantage of his good spirits to bring up again the question that had been burning in her for a week. Would he please tell her what the "agreement" was with Chertkov? "He at once became silent," she went on in her diary, "made an angry face and refused to say anything, though he did not deny that they had a secret." Still, she could not get over the warmth with which he had first greeted her. "God be thanked that I have felt his heart and his love once more!" she exclaimed in her notebook.

Tolstoy's entry in *his* diary that night was laconic. "Sonya did not sleep all night, and then decided to leave home, and drove to Tula. There she met Andrei and returned home, quite good but strangely exhausted."

He had promised Sonya that he would cease seeing Chertkov, at least for the time being. So that there would be no misunderstanding with his beloved disciple he wrote to him on July 26.

> I think I need not tell you how pained I am both on your
> account and on my own, at the cessation of our personal inter-

* Sonya pasted her letter to her husband and her press release in her diary of July 26, 1910.

course, but it is necessary. I console myself with the thought that this sickly position will pass away and that the cessation is only temporary. Meanwhile, we will write to one another, and I will not hide either my or your letters if she wishes to see them.

Chertkov could hardly stand the prospect of not seeing his idol in person, but he agreed reluctantly. He was unable, however, to refrain from stirring up, as he had for so long, the Master's misgivings about his wife. He was not going to surrender to her. Regardless of his personal feelings, he wrote back the next day, he was

fully prepared, if necessary for your tranquility or simply because you think it would be well, not to see you for a day, for a whole period or until death takes one of us.

But, he went on, he would not hide his fear

lest from a wish to pacify Sofya Andreyevna you may go too far and abandon that freedom that is essential to anyone seeking to obey, not his own will but the will of God. And that is why I am prepared without murmur never to see you again if you are sure you are obeying the voice of God. It seems to me that a promise to act this way or that should never be given to anyone. Nor should one place himself in a position which makes one's actions dependent upon another person's decision.

The disciple was giving the Master a lesson in ethics. But the latter stuck grimly to his promise. For the moment he was deeply disturbed by something else: the animosity of two of his sons, Andrei and Leo. They were placing themselves strictly on their mother's side. Like her, they wanted to know if he had made a will disinheriting his wife and children. Visiting Yasnaya, they first tried Alexandra, the only one among the children who knew about the will.

Andrei, who had become sort of a ne'er-do-well, conservative in his political and social attitudes and sharply opposed to his father's philosophy, accosted Alexandra. He spat on the opinions of "the old man grown foolish," he said to his sister. He wanted to know if there was a will. Alexandra refused to answer. The next day, July 27, both brothers confronted her.

"Tell us," Leo asked, "has Father made any kind of will?"

Again the sister refused to answer.

"But just tell us—is there a will or not?"

Sasha would not answer. Frustrated, Andrei determined to ask his father. Bursting into his study, he said, "Father, I must talk to you."

"What is it? Speak."

"There is much turmoil in the family," Andrei said, "and Mother is upset, and we wanted to ask you if you have any sort of will."

"I do not consider myself obliged to answer you."

"Ah, ah, ah? So you don't want to answer?"

"I do not."

Andrei turned and left the room, Sasha says, "slamming the door." Later he insisted to his sister that their father was "crazy."[6]

After her sons' efforts, Sonya again tried to pin her daughter down.

"Sasha," she asked, "do you ever tell a lie?"

"I try not to," Sasha answered.

"Then tell me: has Father a will or not?"

But Sasha would not answer. "I cannot and will not," she said evasively, "during Father's lifetime, speak of his death."

Tolstoy himself now began to have growing doubts about having signed a will behind his family's back and disinheriting them all. Had he not violated his own teachings in acting in such a way? His old friend and biographer Biryukov, who was visiting briefly at Yasnaya Polyana, told him frankly that he ought not to have made a will in secret, that he should have called in all the members of the family and told them frankly what he intended to do. His friend also chided him for having drawn up a formal will, since it was contrary to his position that he did not recognize the authority of the government or the legality of its acts. Such an admonishment from an old and trusted friend deeply disturbed Tolstoy. "I see my mistakes very clearly," he wrote in his diary on August 2. "I should have called together all my heirs and told them of my decision instead of drafting it in secret. I am writing to Chertkov to the same effect."

> I talked yesterday [he wrote to Chertkov] with Posha [Biryukov] and he very correctly told me that I was at fault in having made my Will secretly. I should have done it openly,

informing those whom it concerned, or I should have left things as they were and not done anything. He is quite right that I acted badly, and now I regret it. It was bad to do it secretly. Above all, it was certainly wrong to avail myself of an institution of the government that I reject by drawing up a Will in secret form. . . .

Chertkov panicked. He hastily got off a letter to the Master.

The painful truth . . . is that all these scenes that have occurred recently—the arrival of Leo Lvovich and Andrei Lvovich [Tolstoy's sons] has had one definite practical aim: . . . (after separating you from me and if possible also from Sasha) to extort from you by means of persistent pressure, or to learn from your diaries and papers, if you have written any Will depriving your family of their literary inheritance.

Moreover, Chertkov warned, Tolstoy's two sons were contriving to have him certified as feebleminded in order to deprive the will of its validity. For once, the old man stood up to his disciple. He replied that things were not as bad as Chertkov imagined. "Things are quite quiet now," he wrote back, "and it is well with me." To his diary he confided: "Chertkov has drawn me into a conflict that is painful and repulsive for me."

On July 29 he had started a new diary—"A Diary for Myself Alone," he called it. Since everyone in the household—not to mention Chertkov and his entourage—was reading his journal, he decided that he could only express his innermost feelings at this difficult time in a secret diary, which he hid in all sorts of places in his study and bedroom. "I am beginning a new diary," he wrote, "a real one for myself alone." Often when finishing it late at night he would insert at the beginning of the next day's entry: "IIA—meaning "If I am alive." He was growing that desperate. His wife, too.

Though he was keeping his promise not to see Chertkov, a steady stream of letters arrived from Telyatinki. Once more Sonya was suspicious—since Chertkov's letters were always promptly returned to him so that she would not see them. On August 2, after Bulgakov had arrived with some mail from Telyatinki, Sonya asked her husband: "Is there a letter from Chertkov?" Her husband, she says, grew furious, saying, "I think I have a right to correspond with whomever I please." He tried to explain to her that he and Chertkov had, as he said, a "vast amount of business" connected with the printing of his works. But she would not listen. "If it was only *that* sort of business," she hit back, "then there wouldn't be any secret correspondence." From suspicion grew anger. And in her fury she made a new charge against her eminent husband: that he was a homosexual and that Chertkov was his lover and they were exchanging love letters.

Tolstoy was so taken aback that he could hardly speak. Sonya said she could prove her accusations, whereupon she displayed a page of his diary that he had written on November 20, 1851—fifty-nine years ago, when he was twenty-three. He was soldiering in the Caucasus then and sowing his oats in the bordellos and Gypsy cafés. Sonya read the accusing words to him

> I have so often fallen in love with men. . . . There was the case of Dyakov [a youthful friend]. I shall never forget that night when we were leaving Petersburg by sleigh, and wrapped under the sledge-rug I wanted to kiss him and weep. There was a feeling of voluptuousness in it.

Everyone at the dinner table listened with shock as Sonya read out the words. It would have been bad enough, they thought, if the Countess had hurled her charges and read from the diary in a private meeting between the two of them. But before the whole household! The ubiquitous Bulgakov described the scene in his diary.

> Another painful nightmarish scene this evening. Sofya Andreyevna overstepped all bounds, and said some insane and dreadful things to Leo Nikolayevich in justification of her hatred of Chertkov.

Tolstoy, Bulgakov says, arose and rushed out of the dining room toward his bedroom, "his hands stuck in his belt and his face as though indignation and horror at what he had heard had frozen it."

There was a click. Leo Nikolayevich had locked his bedroom door behind him. Then he went from his bedroom to his study and locked the door leading into the dining room, thus shutting himself in his two rooms as if in a fortress.

His unfortunate wife ran from door to door, beseeching him to forgive her, saying "Lyovochka, I won't do it again!" But he did not answer.

God knows what feelings of outraged dignity he was suffering behind those doors!

Behind those closed doors that night Tolstoy described briefly the scene in both his regular and secret diaries. In his regular one he wrote: "A painful scene in the evening. I was greatly agitated. I felt such a rush of blood to my heart." In his secret book he wrote: "In the evening an insane letter from Sonya Andreyevna, and a demand that I should read it. She came and began to talk. I shut myself in my room and afterward escaped to Dushan." The doctor found his heartbeat irregular. His pulse was over a hundred.

"Tell her," Tolstoy said in a broken voice, "that if she's trying to kill me, she will soon succeed."

Next day Sonya wrote: "I fear I am going out of my mind."

# NINETEEN

# The Last Weeks

S ONYA'S CHARGES that her husband was having a homosexual affair with Chertkov shocked and angered the disciple's aged, devoted, proud, aristocratic mother, who was about to leave Telyatinki for one of her other estates. She got off a sharp letter to Countess Tolstoy.

> I cannot leave this place without expressing my astonishment and indignation at the odious accusations you are spreading about my son. . . . All who know my son know the nobility of his character, his sincerity, truthfulness, his irreproachable morals and his decency in all matters.
>
> I do not understand your motives or your aims, Countess. I cannot believe that these hostile feelings are evoked by an unworthy jealousy of the longstanding friendship and devotion of my son for Leo Nikolayevich, a friendship you yourself for so many years regarded approvingly . . .
>
> In any case, whatever your motives may be, your conduct in regard to my son is so unfair, cruel and ill-natured that I, as his mother, cannot refrain from appealing to your heart and conscience and begging you to bethink yourself. Tear out of your soul, Countess, the evil and insanely monstrous feeling, which causes so much suffering not only to my son and your husband but to all those around you. . . .
>
> In the Lord's name I beseech you: do not let your conscience be completely stifled. . . .

"I received a letter today," Sonya wrote in her diary on August 3, "from E. I. Chertkova, filled with reproaches. I quite understand her feelings as a mother: she idealizes her son and does not know him. I replied to her in restrained, courteous and somewhat proud terms." Sonya denied that she had spread any "odious accusations" against her son but she wanted to repeat

> what I said to you when we met: your son's despotic influence on my husband (who is enfeebled by age) has so increased that he has gradually separated him from me and set him against me. . . . He has come between us after 48 years of married life, and I am definitely unable to endure his presence.
>
> Yes, I am insanely jealous of Leo Nikolayevich and will not yield him up though the struggle should kill me. . . .

Try as she might, she could not get Chertkov off her mind. Though the next day passed peacefully, as both Tolstoy and Sonya attested in their notebooks—"Nothing depressing happened today," he wrote—Sonya ranted in her diary about Chertkov. First, she wrote, she was wondering whether she could possibly make peace with him. Perhaps she could forgive him and cease to hate him.

> But when I think of *seeing* that figure again I want to cry and cry out. I cannot bear any more of these acute, tormenting sufferings. . . . There is an evil spirit in Chertkov. That is why he frightens and torments me so.

The relative tranquillity at Yasnaya Polyana lasted just a day. Next day, August 5, Sonya began her diary: "Passed a terrible night. . . . How offensive I find it that my husband does not even take my part when Chertkov is rude to me. How he fears him! How completely he is under his thumb. Shame and pity!" She prayed a long time on her knees, she wrote, "asking God to turn my husband's heart from Chertkov to me and to soften his coldness toward me. . . ."

Tolstoy was finding it increasingly difficult to bear living without seeing his devoted follower. "My letting myself be cut off from Chertkov," he confided to his diary the same day, "is ridiculous, humiliating, shameful and sad." He searched for some excuse to resume seeing him. And for an excuse to get away from it all.

Sonya's renewed spying on him was getting more and more on his nerves. Sasha had told him that whenever he went out for his daily walk or ride, her mother followed him to see if he was secretly meeting Chertkov. He had been full of pity for her, but with Sasha's report, he says, he began to pity her less. Sonya's malice and her snooping, he wrote, were becoming more than he could bear.

> I think of going away [he wrote in his diary on August 6] and leaving a letter, but am afraid to do so, though I think it is the best for her. . . . The constant secrecy, and fear for her, oppressive.

He no longer had, he said, the desire or the strength to continue his writing. This added to his despair. "Help me, Father," he wrote, "help me, in these last days and hours of my life." Some days he felt contrite.

> August 7: A state of despondency. Tried to write. . . . I've seldom met a person more endowed with all the vices than I am: lasciviousness, self-interest, malice, vanity and above all self-love.

He ended the diary that evening with a strange sentence. He wrote that the fact that he admitted his loathsome shortcomings "explains the success of my writings."

Tanya, the beloved daughter and peacemaker, arrived back at Yasnaya Polyana to find things worse than she expected. Her father quickly told her of his will. Since her mother and younger brothers had mentioned their suspicions, Tanya was not surprised. She approved it in general, she told him, but regretted that he had broken his promise to his wife to allow her to publish all he had written before 1881.* Her doubts about the will were nothing compared to her certainty that her father must get away for a while from the worm's nest at Yasnaya Polyana. She urged him to come to stay with her at Kochety, where she lived happily with her husband,

---

* On August 12 Tolstoy wrote Chertkov that he did not consider himself bound by the promise—"before her or his conscience." "I am bound," he said, "simply by compassion and sympathy." A rather lame explanation.

Mikhail Sukhotin. He must come alone, she insisted. A brief separation from Sonya was absolutely necessary.

Sonya was terrified at the very idea. She says Leo sprang it to her on August 8, saying: "The best thing of all would be for me to go to Tanya's for a week. The separation would calm us."

At first, she says, she did not think it was a bad idea. Going to Kochety would distance her husband from Chertkov. They could not possibly meet, even in secret, as she suspected they might be doing at Yasnaya. "I think it will be a good thing," she wrote in her diary on the eighth. "Let us both have a rest from tearing at the heart." But soon she was having second thoughts.

> August 10: Yet another separation from him seems unbearable. We have already been separated a great deal this summer, and how long have we to live? But apparently Leo is weary of life at Yasnaya Polyana. . . .

That evening she added:

> On Saturday, Lyovochka goes to Kochety with Tanya. And what will happen to me? . . . How am I to get well here? They will all abandon me.
>
> August 12: Leo Nikolayevich is obstinately set on going to Kochety. . . . If he goes it will be acting in a way that is painful for me. His going is a new wish to be free of me, but I do not wish to be separated from him and cannot live so, and after about three days I will go there myself.

Tanya says that her mother used every weapon in her arsenal to make sure she could go along to Kochety with her husband. Sometimes she used her illness as an argument; at other times she became indignant at the notion that anybody would want to take her husband away from her so that he could have a rest. "Have a rest from what?" she demanded of Tanya. "A rest from my love, is that what you want? . . . What would you say if I took your husband away so that he could have a rest away from you?" "In the end," Tanya wrote, her mother resorted to "the ultimate persuasion."

> One day when I was with my father in his study she came in, burst into floods of tears, and begged us to take her with us.

She was afraid of being left alone. She gave her solemn promise
that she would leave him in peace.

That evening, Tanya noted, he wrote in his secret diary:

> Things are going from bad to worse. She didn't sleep all
> night. Toward morning . . . she came in with a spate of horrors!
> . . . I will not bear it. May God come to my aid! She has reduced
> everyone to exhaustion, herself most of all. She is coming with
> us.

On the fifteenth of August they set out early for Kochety—
Tolstoy, Sonya, Tanya, Alexandra, Dr. Makovitsky, and Bulgakov.

The first three days at Kochety went fairly well. Sonya doted
on her granddaughter, Tanechka, Tanya's only child. "What a
dear, charming, affectionate, little girl!" Sonya exclaimed in her
diary. "How she caressed me and kissed me! There is at least
someone who is pleased to see me."

"We arrived peacefully," Tolstoy wrote in his diary, as if
thankful to the Lord. Yet on the journey, he wrote, he reflected
"that if those alarms and demands are renewed, I will go away with
Sasha." Already, on the evening of their arrival, there had been
more words between them about the infernal diaries. Sonya touched
on it too in her notebook. She reported that when she went to say
good night to Leo she caught him asking Sasha for his diary. "What
is it you want?" Sonya asked him.

"I asked Sasha for my notebook," he said. "I give it to her to
put away; she copies out my thoughts."

Even earlier that day, shortly after they arrived, the old subject
had come up again.

"Does Sasha read your diaries?" she asked.

"I don't know. She copies out my thoughts."

"But if she 'copies out,' what does 'don't know' mean? Another
lie!"

"You are agitated about everything," Leo said. "That's why I
hide things from you."[1]

But Sonya's peevishness those first few days was nothing compared to her explosion on August 18 when she happened to read in
an old newspaper something the family had been hiding from her

for four days. It was an announcement from the government in Petersburg that Chertkov would be allowed to remain at Telyatinki.

The news sent Countess Tolstoy shrieking through the house. "Here is my death sentence!" she screamed. "I shall kill Chertkov! I shall pay someone to poison him!"[2]

To make matters worse, Sonya wrote in her notebook, the news cheered up her husband. "His step became light and brisk, and he seemed younger."

In *his* diary that evening Tolstoy wrote: "Sofya Andreyevna fell ill on learning that Chertkov had received permission to live at Telyatinki. . . . 'I will kill him!' she exclaimed. I asked her not to talk that way. . . . Something will happen, help me God!"

August 22 was Sonya's sixty-sixth birthday—"the day of my unfortunate birth," she wrote in her daybook. She was more expansive in her diary. "My birthday. I am 66 and still as energetic, acutely impressionable, passionate and, people say, youthful as ever." It was true. Despite her age and her nervous breakdowns and her sorrows, real and imagined, she had survived well, her hair not yet turned gray, her figure heavier but not by much, her energy and passion undiminished. The family, including her husband, congratulated her on her anniversary. "One must congratulate a wife on her birthday," she wrote sarcastically in her diary, "if only for the sake of propriety." She added that she looked into his eyes to see if she could catch "even a momentary glimpse of his former love." But in vain. Tolstoy, in *his* diary, did not mention her birthday. "I am behaving pretty well," he boasted.

Six days later, on the twenty-eighth, came Leo's birthday. He was eighty-two, white-haired, white-bearded, bent, prone to one little illness after another, but his mind was still vigorous and his genius as a writer undiminished, though in recent years he had done little more than pamphleteering. Sonya did not neglect to notice the anniversary both in her daybook and her longer diary. Tolstoy must have hoped for a peaceful day to mark the occasion. But it was not to be. In fact, his birthday turned out to be one long, dreadful ordeal for both. Sonya admits it began early in the morning when she went to him to offer birthday congratulations. She wished him a long life but could not refrain from adding that she meant a long life "without any deceptions, secrets or obsessions—

and chiefly that he might toward the end of a long life become truly enlightened." Her husband did not appreciate such good wishes. But this incident was only a curtain raiser for the main birthday event.

In the evening they fell into an argument over Leo's insistence that chastity was the Christian ideal and ought to be practiced by everyone. That would all be very well, Sonya retorted, if her husband were a monk, an ascetic, and lived a celibate life.

> But at his wish I have become pregnant 16 times: thirteen children and three miscarriages. In those days he suggested to me, a young woman, that he could not work or write well if I refused to sleep with him. I said if chastity was fully attained there would be no children and without children there would be no Kingdom of God on earth.

"For some reason," Sonya records, these remarks made him very angry and he began to shout at her.

"What is the use of talking to you! You don't even want to understand anything! You don't even listen!"

Sonya says her "sick soul" could not bear his "angry tone." She burst into tears and went to her room.

But the day's ordeal was still not over. When he went to bid her good night, asking her why she had become upset, they fell easily into the third quarrel of the birthday. All the old reproaches of both sides, Sonya says, were revived. When, finally, she asked him what she could do to help restore peace, he replied: "Abandon the copyrights, give the land away, and live in a cottage." "All right," Sonya said, "I agree to our going to live together in a cottage."

> As soon as I agreed, Leo Nikolayevich rushed to the door and cried out desperately: "For God's sake, leave me alone! I will go away! It is impossible to be happy if, like you, one hates one half of the human race. . . ." "But whom do I hate?" I asked. "You hate *Chertkov and me*. . . ." "Yes, I hate Chertkov but I won't connect you with him." And so my heart was once more pierced by his irrational love for that idol of his from whom he cannot tear himself apart.

She became more determined than ever, she says, to keep the two men apart. "And if I do not succeed, I will kill Chertkov! Then let come what may! As it is now, life is hell!"

The night of his eighty-second birthday, Tolstoy, weary from the long day of turmoil, wrote in his diary "for himself alone":

> Continually harder and harder with Sofya Andreyevna. Not love, but a demand for love that resembles hate and changes into hate. Yes, such egotism is insanity. What saved her before was having children. It was animal love, but self-sacrificing all the same. When that was past there remained terrible egotism, egotism of a most abnormal character—insanity. Neither Dushan [Dr. Makovitsky] nor Sasha admit that she is ill, but they are wrong.

Next evening Sonya suddenly decided to leave Kochety alone to return to Yasnaya Polyana, though Tolstoy, alarmed at her condition, insisted on sending Sasha along with her. Her pretext was that she wanted to see her son Leo before he left on the thirty-first to stand trial in Petersburg for disseminating his father's works. The main reason seems to have been that she felt everyone in the house was coming to hate her. "Foolish people," she said, were referring to her as Xanthippe, the shrewish wife of Socrates. On that last evening, though, the pendulum had swung the other way. Tolstoy was most loving in seeing her off. That afternoon he had assured her again, as she wrote in her diary, "(1) not to see Chertkov, (2) not to give him the diaries, and (3) not to let him photograph him." Sonya had been much annoyed that Chertkov was constantly photographing the Master. As she departed Kochety, she noted later in her diary, "Lyovochka and I wept in each other's arms, kissing and weeping."

Tolstoy confirmed in *his* diary the fond parting that evening, though the morning, he wrote, had been "terrible," with Sonya repeating one of her old tricks of hiding in the garden to the alarm of the household. Nevertheless, "she was very touching as she said goodbye. She asked everyone's forgiveness. The pity I feel for her makes me love her so much. I wrote her a little letter."

He expressed a warmth he had not shown toward her for a long time—though not without also admonishing her.

You touched me so deeply, dear Sonya, as you were leaving, with your good, sincere words. If you could manage to overcome in yourself that—how can I put it?—that in yourself [which is] the cause of your self-torture, how good that would be for you and me. I was sad all evening, depressed. I can't stop thinking of you. . . . Write me, I beg you.

Your husband, who loves you,
L.T.

Her husband's letter at first gladdened her heart, but after reading it over several times, she found his suggestion that she master herself most objectionable. He wanted her to master herself, she concluded, so she could agree to his resuming relations with Chertkov. "But that is unthinkable," she told her diary. In a note to her daughter Tanya, in which she told of her reaction to the letter, she explained her feelings. She offered her husband

the same choice as before: either I, his wife, or Chertkov. There can never be room for us both. Never! I shall be at peace only when I understand that your father *firmly* and *truly* confirms my rights and my place with him as his loving wife, and that he not exchange me for the man he now loves so insanely.

The first thing Sonya did when she got back to Yasnaya Polyana was to tear down from the walls of Tolstoy's study pictures of Chertkov and Sasha, and replace them with a portrait of her husband's father and one of herself. On September 2 she called in a priest to exorcise Chertkov's evil spirit from Tolstoy's rooms. To Varya Feokritova she explained: "I want to have a service performed and Leo Nikolayevich's rooms sprinkled with holy water. Chertkov's spirit reigns here. It must be smoked out (with incense)." According to Goldenweiser, she also told the priest all about her troubles with her husband.

When Sasha returned to Kochety on the following day she lost no time in tattling to her father everything that had happened at home. He was not surprised but he was disheartened. "Sasha came back," he wrote in his diary. "It is as painfully depressing as ever at home. Bear up, Leo Nikolayevich! I'm trying . . ." Next day: "Sasha has brought bad news. . . . She [Sonya] burns portraits and has a service performed in the house. When I am alone I prepare myself to be firm with her . . . but when she comes in I weaken. I shall try to remember that she is an invalid." He had not been surprised because, the day before, he had received a letter from his wife: "The same suspicions, the same spitefulness and the same (were it not so terrible and so tormenting) comical demands for love." His spirits did not improve when he learned that she would be coming up to Kochety shortly, bringing, he feared, those suspicions and spitefulness.

She arrived back on September 5 and got a cool reception, she says, from her husband and daughter Sasha. Soon she and Leo were at it again. Chertkov, more determined than ever to destroy the Countess to make sure that all of Tolstoy's literary works would come to him as the will stipulated, wrote the Master about a discovery Goldenweiser had made in Varya Feokritova's diary. Varya, as a close friend of Sasha, had become very much a creature of Chertkov's, sending him her diaries and also confidential reports of what Countess Tolstoy (whose secretary she was supposed to be) was up to. Now her diary revealed that Sonya was plotting not only to inherit the Tolstoy copyrights before 1881, which she had always had, but to get hold of the Master's writings *after* 1881.

"Everybody will believe me," she said to Varya, "if I say they were written before 1881." If that didn't work, Sonya went on, she and her sons would break the will—if there was one, as she strongly suspected—on the grounds that the great writer had been feeble-minded when he signed it, and that if he had been of sound mind he never would have disinherited his family.

Tolstoy was horrified by this piece of intelligence. Strangely, he reacted to it hypocritically. "It is painful," he wrote in his diary, "that in her bewildered mind there is a thought of representing me as having become weak in the head, thereby making my will, if there is one, invalid."[3]

If there is one? A strange remark, after all that had happened, to make in his own diary. If Sonya was obsessed by her suspicion that there was a will disinheriting her, Tolstoy was uncharacteristically deceptive about it, even to himself.

While Chertkov was trying to turn his mentor even more against his wife, he was at the same time writing Sonya, urging that they make up. It was an oily letter. And a long one—some

twenty-five hundred words. And somehow Chertkov contrived to
be both obsequious and reproachful. Her enmity to him, he began,
was surely based on a misunderstanding, which he wished to clear
up.

> With regard to the misunderstandings between us ... I
> shall at any time be glad to give you a completely frank expla-
> nation of all my actions in connection with Leo Nikolayevich's
> writings, to which you attribute improper motives. ...

He apologized for sometimes losing his temper and saying
unkind things to her, such as when he had said that if he had a wife
like her he would shoot himself. He asked her forgiveness. As for
her jealousy of him, there was no reason for it. "A feeling of some
kind of jealousy toward her husband's close friend," he wrote
smugly, "is unfortunately characteristic of wives."

> If certain feelings of jealous enmity of your husband's
> friends is natural to you, that should have shown itself in you in
> the very beginning. And in fact it did. ... Now, since this
> summer your attitude toward that jealous disposition which
> you always had has suddenly and completely changed so much
> that instead of trying to restrain it as before, you suddenly de-
> cided to give way to it without the least restraint, openly and
> publicly announcing that you were jealous of Leo Nikolayevich
> and me.

There was "another fundamental reason" for her hatred of
him, he went on.

> I think the fundamental reason for your fundamental hatred
> of me lies in nothing else than your fear lest I should obtain
> control of Leo Nikolayevich's writings and dispose of them in my
> own way. ... What would be more natural than for such a man
> (as your husband) to entrust some one of his nearest friends who
> shared his views, the task of attending to the publication and
> dissemination of his new writings? ... This, and only this, has
> always been my role in my relations with Leo Nikolayevich as a
> writer. ... You see, such activity ... does not afford me person-
> ally the least advantage. On the contrary, it is accompanied by

great and incessant cares (not to mention very great expense)
and lately and most distressingly, by reproaches and hostility on
the part of Leo Nikolayevich's children, in which, to my still
greater regret, you yourself have joined.

He finally wound up:

I beseech you, Sofya Andreyevna . . . to reestablish the good
relations that existed between you and me for so many years.
You would not only relieve your own suffering . . . but also afford
Leo Nikolayevich, who is suffering incomparably more than you
appear to imagine, the relief and the joy he needs.

In God's name, I ask you to throw off that burden of hostility and hatred of me, which oppresses you and torments others. . . .

> With respect and despite everything,
> sincere devotion to you.
> V. Chertkov

Though he had promised to give her a "completely frank explanation" of all his "actions in connection with Tolstoy's writings," he did not mention the secret will. And he lied to her when
he said he was only concerned with the Master's new writings—
that is, after 1881.

Sonya was not taken in. Her reply was even longer than Chertkov's letter and it was sharp and biting. It also showed the tormented state of her mind.

In your letter you evade all the chief questions that I put
clearly, and you always speak of *misunderstandings*. That is a phar-
isaical method. Misunderstandings should be honestly explained. You write that you are always ready to do so. But how
many times have I asked you to tell me what disposal you are
making of Leo Nikolayevich's papers and manuscripts in the
event of his death, and you have always angrily refused to tell
me? You do not love the truth. . . .

She hated him, she said, for many good reasons. For insulting
her, for taking her husband away from her, for grabbing her husband's diaries and manuscripts and not returning them, and for

thus making her suffer more in the last two years than she had all the previous years of her life. For each charge she went into detail. His insults:

> When I asked you to return his papers you attributed to me the dishonorable motive that I was afraid lest you should show up me and my children by means of the diaries, and you venomously said: "If I wish, I could besmirch you as much as I please. . . ."
>
> To misunderstand those words is impossible. I am really not so stupid. . . . Finally you said that if you had such a wife you would have shot yourself or gone to America. And afterwards you said to my son Leo: "I don't understand a woman like that who spends *all her life* killing her husband."
>
> Why should you now want to have relations with a murderess?

As to the diaries he took and kept:

> His diaries are the holy of holies of his life, and consequently of mine with him. They are the reflection of his soul, which I have become accustomed to and to love, and they should not be in the hands of an outsider. . . .
>
> You will say that he gives them to you himself. But in that I perceive your ever-increasing influence over the ever-weakening will of an old man. . . . You have enslaved him by your despotic character (as to which your mother agreed with me). In the taking from me of Leo Nikolayevich's love and the intrusion of an outsider in our loving marital life I feel a will of the evil one. . . . There never was and there never will be anyone between us. . . . I have given Leo Nikolayevich a categorical choice: either you or me. He has chosen the latter. . . . But if he does not keep his promise, I will leave him.[4]

She saw through his false pleas to her, she said. His aim "was very naive and only too clear: you want to renew your personal relations with Leo Nikolayevich." As for reconciliation between Chertkov and her—that was out of the question. "I consider everything between us finally ended, and that you are quite superfluous in our life." She squeezed in near the end one final barb: "I have seldom met anyone who—apart from interested motives—has liked you."

Sonya showed Chertkov's letter to her husband—they were still at Kochety—and he hastily got off a few lines of his own to Chertkov.

> Sofya Andreyevna has shown me your letter and she is sending you an answer. I fear, with you, that no good results will follow. She is very irritated, not irritated, *ce n'est pas le mot*, but unhealthily agitated. She suffers and cannot master herself. I have just talked to her. She came here thinking that I should go back with her to Yasnaya, but I refused, not fixing a time for my departure. This distressed her very much.

One wonders why Tolstoy felt it necessary to relate to Chertkov how he refused to give in to his wife about returning to Yasnaya Polyana. It reinforces Sonya's charge that her husband, the world-renowned writer, teacher, and moralist, had truly come under the thumb of his despotic disciple and sought now only to please him. It seems rather pitiful and sad that Tolstoy felt obliged to show a friend who despised his wife that he was now, as Chertkov had urged, standing up to her. His note to Chertkov seems rather disloyal to her and unnecessary.

It showed the ascendancy that Chertkov had now gained over the aged writer. Other letters at this time seem to confirm it. On August 11, Tolstoy had received a long letter from his disciple warning him again that his wife and sons were plotting to get legal rights to *all* his writings. This, he wrote, would be "a scandal unprecedented in literary history." Therefore, he argued, the will must remain unknown to Sofya Andreyevna and her sons, for if they knew of it they "might still hope, by insistent pressure in every possible way, to succeed in getting you, were it but at some moment of your most helpless physical weakness or even on your death bed, to renounce what is expressed in that testament." Arrogantly, the disciple wrote that in his opinion the will ought not, as Tolstoy had written him, conflict with the demands of his conscience.[5]

Meekly, the Master wrote back that he regretted the pain he had caused his friend by having written him that he regretted drawing up the secret will.

> The conclusion I have come to from your letter is that Biryukov was wrong,* and that I was wrong in agreeing with him . . . and that I fully approve of your conduct. . . . I do not now regret what has been done (i.e., that I wrote the Will) and I can only be grateful to you for your participation in the matter.

All summer long Chertkov had kept peppering the Master with advice. Tolstoy's diary, August 9: "A good letter from Chertkov. He writes correctly about the methods of dealing with mentally unbalanced people."

In early September the Tolstoys were still with their daughter Tanya at Kochety but, as we have seen, Leo was not getting the peace and rest he had come for, nor was Sonya, who was scarcely keeping her promise to leave him in peace. On August 17, only two days after they arrived at Kochety, Sonya had noted in her diary: "I have thought of Yasnaya Polyana lately and feel as if I did not want to live there again. I want a *new* life, new people, new surroundings. How tired one is of everything there!" In her misery she recalled how, back at Yasnaya, she had asked Leo "whether he would pass the 22nd and 28th (our two birthdays) at Kochety, or return to Yasnaya, and he replied: 'Why, what days are these? . . . but you stay at Yasnaya, and come on the 28th for my birthday.' "

> I went crimson with grief and annoyance. Much I need to celebrate his birthday if he wishes to separate himself from me so carefully! . . . And to think that this malignant strife has risen between two people who love each other so much! Is it old age? . . . Sometimes I look at him and it seems to me that he is dead, that all that was active, good, sagacious, sympathetic, truthful and loving, has perished and been killed by the hand of a heartless sectarian—Chertkov.

Sonya went on in her diary of August 20: "There will be no more happiness in my life at home. I must reconcile myself to that or seek happiness in another and in others!" Her husband's diary of the same day: "Today, remembering my wedding, I thought it

---

* See page 291. Biryukov, one of Tolstoy's most intimate friends, had frankly told him that he had been wrong in drawing up a secret will disinheriting his family. So Tolstoy had written to Chertkov that Biryukov was "quite right."

was just a fatality. I was never in love. But I could not avoid marriage."*

Perhaps at this late stage in his life, what he resented most in Sonya was that she was preventing him from writing. There is a plaintive note about that in his diary of August 21.

> Sofya Andreyevna still the same. Tanya tells me that she had not slept during the night because she had seen a portrait of Chertkov. The position is perilous. I want so much . . . to write.

That urge, which had made him so towering as a writer, would boil up in him until the very end. He returned to the subject a few weeks later, on October 2. He had been reading Maupassant's story *En Famille,* and it inspired him to thinking of writing another novel.

> Yesterday reading Maupassant's story made me want to portray the vulgarity of life as I know it. And during the night the idea came to me of placing a spiritually alive person in the midst of vulgarity. . . . It could either be a man or a woman. Oh how good it could be, and how it attracts me! What a great work it might be! . . . Maybe I shall do it.

This was in his regular diary.

But that evening, for himself alone, he revealed that his zeal to return to writing fiction had cooled. With Sonya getting worse and worse, how could he write?

> Today I felt very strongly the need for creative writing, but I saw the impossibility of devoting myself to it because of her, of my persistent feelings about her, and of my inner struggle. Of course this struggle and the possibility of victory in it are more important than any conceivable work of art.

Sonya left Kochety, alone, on September 12, but not before the usually gentle Mikhail Sukhotin, Tanya's husband, had dressed

---

* He forgot what he wrote in his diary of September 12, 1862: "I'm in love as I never thought possible to be in love," and that he had written Sonya that if she did not agree to marry him, he would shoot himself.

her down for the way she was destroying her illustrious husband. He said that unless she relented, Tolstoy would leave her.

"Your glory as Tolstoy's wife will collapse! Tolstoy is running away from his wife who had poisoned his existence!"
"I shall write to the papers! I shall justify myself!"
"No, there won't be any justification then. He'll be gone. A man in his 82nd year does not leave his wife just like that for nothing at all."

Sukhotin suggested she was faking her mental illness.

"No. I'm really ill."
"If you are, then follow the doctor's advice. Part with Leo Nikolayevich. Otherwise he will be forced to leave you, you'll see."
"If he does, I'll print a death letter in the papers about all he did, and then I'll poison myself and disgrace him all over Russia."
"But nobody will believe you! Nobody!"[6]

Tolstoy, in his diary that evening: "Sofya Andreyevna has left after some terrible scenes."

# TWENTY

# The Last Days

TOLSTOY LEFT KOCHETY for home on September 22 so that he could be with his wife on their forty-eighth wedding anniversary the next day. Her diary had been full of bitter reproaches of him for not returning sooner. He had written on the fourteenth lovingly enough, inquiring about how she got home and saying, "Please let me know, my dear Sonya. I kiss you. *Au revoir*." He promised to do his part to improve their relations and suggested that if she helped him he was quite sure they would succeed.

But in her present troubled state, Sonya chose to misread the thrust of the letter. "Had a letter from Leo Nikolayevich," she jotted down in her diary. "It was like a douche of cold water."

In her absence, which he cherished, he had thought about her a good deal. September 15: "I cannot accustom myself to regard her words as raving. All my troubles come from that. It is impossible to talk to her, for she is not bound either by logic or conscience or truth, or by what she herself has said. That is terrible. Not to speak of any love for me—of which there is not a trace—she does not even need my love. She only needs one thing—that people should think I love her. That is what is so terrible."

September 17 was a special day for the lonely Sonya. It was her name day (very important to Europeans) and also, she noted in her diary, the anniversary of the day forty-eight years ago when Leo Tolstoy had proposed marriage to her. She did not forget the anniversary, but he did. "He has not even written me," she sighed in her diary. Her mind went back to that exciting day when they became engaged. "And what has he made of that eighteen-year-old Sonechka Behrs, who gave her *whole* life to him with such love and truthfulness? He has simply tortured me of late by his cold cruelty and extreme egotism."

And she kept weeping and complaining because he was lingering on at Kochety.

> September 18: Wept all morning. . . . My heart is breaking from the malicious revenge my husband is taking for Chertkov, and his indifferences to me. Sometimes I hate that evil man, who so assiduously tortures me.

On the twenty-first she had gone to Moscow on business for a couple of days—concerning the estate and her publishing ventures. But her trip did not make her forget that her husband was not returning to her. "Leo Nikolayevich has obeyed Chertkov," she insisted to her diary, "and has *run away* from his wife—not to America but to his daughter at Kochety."

While she was whining about her husband's lack of love for her, she was thinking in Moscow of an old love she herself had had.

> Went to see Taneyev's old nurse and to hear something of him. He is still in the country. I would like to see him, and hear him play. At one time, after Vanechka's death, that kindly and calm man helped me much toward spiritual tranquility. Now that is no longer possible. I no longer love him so much and for some reason we do not see each other. I have made no effort at all in that direction.[1]
>
> September 22: There is a kind of hell in my heart. Such distant relations with my husband never existed before. Chertkov evidently had a great deal of influence. Neither letters nor news.

Her husband arrived home late that evening. Before leaving Kochety that morning, though he was returning for a forty-eighth wedding anniversary, he was filled with foreboding. "I am travelling to Yasnaya," he noted in his diary, "and terror seized me at the thought of what awaits me there."[2]

What he expected, he got. "Found Sofya Andreyevna exasperated when I reached home," he wrote in his diary late that night.

"Reproaches and tears." For once Sonya's version did not differ much from his: "Last night Leo, Sasha and the doctor arrived, and instead of being glad, I reproached him, burst into tears and went to my room to let him rest after his journey."

As they awaited his arrival—he did not appear until midnight—Sonya chatted with Bulgakov. He was struck by her hostility toward her husband. "She said outright that she no longer loves him," he wrote in his diary. "From what she says, she has been awaiting his return without her customary feeling of joy."

"And that's all because of Chertkov," she told him. "He meddles in our domestic life. You know, before he appeared, such a thing never happened."

The naive young secretary tried to suggest a reconciliation, saying that if only the Countess realized that the Count could never forget Chertkov, there might be a basis for compromise. But he soon saw that such an idea was "inconceivable" to her.

> The dissension between them has gone so far that it is evidently too late to mend matters. It now becomes clear to me that the tragedy of Yasnaya Polyana will be of long duration, or it will end quite suddenly, but in a way that nobody has foreseen.[3]

The last part of his prediction was not far off the mark.

Late as it was when Tolstoy arrived home, he went to Sonya's room to have a talk with her. Apparently it did not go very well. "There was a terrible scene," Tolstoy told his secretary. "She is so pitiful! I was truly sorry for her." He had himself remained mostly silent, he said, but at one juncture he said something that upset her. "She asked me why I had not returned sooner, and I said: 'because I didn't want to.' And that provoked her and brought forth goodness knows what."

He intended, he said, when the moment was right, to talk to his wife about seeing Chertkov again. "It's really ridiculous—to live practically next door to each other and never meet. For me this is a great loss!"

"My wedding day," Sonya began in her daybook on September 23. "Having wept all morning over my 48 years of marriage! What have I for all my love and my life of self-sacrifice?" In her diary (she now kept both a daybook and a diary) she began, "Well, this is our wedding day. . . . I wanted to go to my husband, but on opening his door I heard him dictating something to Bulgakov so I went out to wander about in Yasnaya Polyana, recalling the happy times (not very many) of my 48 years of married life."

The one thing she wanted most that day, besides an expression of his love, was to have a photograph taken of her husband and herself together. For one thing, Sonya thought a picture showing them standing lovingly together on their forty-eighth wedding anniversary, when it appeared in the newspapers, would put an end to the gossip that was beginning to spread all over Russia of their long marriage having broken down. She persuaded Bulgakov to snap the picture, put on a white dress and fixed a screen in the living room to improve the light. The old man was reluctant to be photographed, even on this occasion, but when Sonya reminded him of all the photographs he had let Chertkov take of him, he could hardly refuse his wife.

"It was an extremely painful procedure," Bulgakov reported in his diary. Sonya was flurried and nervous and her husband was obviously irritated, especially when she asked him to turn and look at her, which he silently refused to do. "I felt embarrassed to look at them," Bulgakov says, as he squeezed the camera bulb. He snapped four pictures but when Sonya developed them it was found they were underexposed. There had not been enough light indoors.

Next day Sonya persuaded Leo to go outside, where the light was better, for a new attempt. It was a raw, chilly day and Sasha resented her mother's making her father risk a chill. But Sonya insisted and Bulgakov obligingly snapped them again.

It is a poignant portrait. Sonya had asked her husband to turn toward her as she gazed into his eyes. But he stubbornly refused. So the photograph shows him, unmindful of her, glaring sternly at the camera, trying to hide his annoyance, his left hand thrust into his pocket.*

It is a sad picture of two great persons who, after nearly half a century of marriage, no longer could be compatible. It is the last photograph of Tolstoy and his wife together and the last, ever, of him alive.

* Tolstoy summed up his feelings in his diary that evening: "Again a request for a photograph as a loving couple. I consented, but felt ashamed all the time."

Sasha was furious with her father not only for letting himself be photographed with her mother but because he had done nothing to restore the pictures in his study of herself and Chertkov which Sonya had torn down and replaced with portraits of herself and Tolstoy's father. She reproached him so bitterly that he cried out she was as bad as her mother. The rest of the day Alexandra sulked and refused to do any letters for him. Finally, in the evening, he rang for her and asked her to take some dictation. He started to dictate a letter and then stopped. "I don't need your stenography," he said, "but your love!" Taken aback, Sasha, who worshiped her father, begged his forgiveness. They clasped each other and wept.[4]

Next morning, when Sasha went into his study, she found that the old portraits of herself and Chertkov had been restored. But not for long. Sonya says she just "happened" later that morning to go into her husband's study. When she saw that he had restored the portrait of Chertkov, she went wild. "I tore his hateful face to bits," she noted in her diary. Tolstoy was out riding with Dushan. Sonya burst into the room where young Bulgakov was conversing with Marya Alexandrovna Schmidt, an aged family friend of many years' standing and a devoted Tolstoyan, who lived in a small farmhouse nearby.

"I have burned Chertkov's portrait," Sonya yelled. "The old man wants to kill me. He has purposefully re-hung Chertkov's picture!"

She disappeared for a moment and then came back, brandishing torn shreds of the Chertkov portrait. She then went to her room. Suddenly from within it a shot rang out. Marya Alexandrovna rushed to Sonya's room to find her firing away with a toy pistol. She was "practicing," she said.

A little later, when Tolstoy returned from his ride and lay down for a nap, another pistol shot was heard. But he refused to go to his wife. If she was firing the pistol to attract his attention, it was a futile gesture as far as he was concerned.

Tolstoy commented on it in his secret diary that evening (September 26):

> Another scene because I had re-hung the portraits in their old places. I began to tell her that it is impossible to live like this. . . .

Dushan says that she fired a toy gun in order to frighten me.
I was not frightened however and did not go to her—which was
really the best thing to do. But it is very hard. Lord help me!

Sasha and her friend Varya Feokritova had gone off to visit a
sister-in-law of Sasha's at an estate just beyond Tula. But old
Marya Schmidt was so alarmed by Sonya's behavior that she sent
a message imploring the two young women to return at once. They
arrived back at midnight to be greeted with angry reproaches from
Sonya. And, as so often happened, the longer she raved, the worse
she became. Finally, in a burst of hysteria, she ordered Varya to
leave the premises the next day, and turning to her daughter, she
shouted: "I shall throw you out of the house, as I did Chertkov."*

Though it was late, Sasha found her father still sitting in his
study. She told him of her mother's threats and said she had decided to move with Varya to her small house at Telyatinki. Sasha
says she thought her father would follow her and leave home but,
to her surprise, he approved of her going. She could still come over
daily to help him with his correspondence. Tolstoy, bidding her
good night, told her: "It brings the solution nearer! This cannot go
on!" The harassed old man seemed to be thinking of a final solution. What they were all going through at Yasnaya Polyana could
not go on.[5]

In the midst of all this Chertkov was not being very helpful. "A
letter from Chertkov," Tolstoy noted in his secret diary for September 24, "full of reproaches and accusations. They are tearing
me to pieces." Chertkov had written him accusing him of letting his
demented wife interfere with their lives. "You have allowed yourself to be forced into a false position."

The Master was not pleased. "You have produced a painful
impression on me," he replied. Chertkov really, he said, had no
idea how difficult it was to solve his problem, which he alone must
do. "Your letter pained me. I felt that I was being torn in two. I
depicted a personal note in what you wrote. If you want to do me
good, please let us talk no more about that letter of yours."[6] Chertkov replied meekly, asking the Master's forgiveness.

---

* "During the morning," Bulgakov noted wryly in his diary, "the atmosphere in
the house was quite alarming, and by late evening it had resolved into a perfect
tempest between Sofya Andreyevna and Alexandra."

But he persisted, with his usual lack of tact and his insensitivity toward others, even to Tolstoy—and with a vicious malice toward Countess Tolstoy. He seems to have reached the height of this when he responded to a letter from a Bulgarian Tolstoyan, Christo Dosev. The Bulgarian had asked whether it was true that the great Tolstoy had become enslaved by his wife. "I know of no worse slavery in the world," Dosev wrote, "than being enslaved by a stupid, coarse woman." Chertkov answered this man, unknown to him personally, denying that the great author was enslaved by his wife and then, pulling out the dagger, revealing the most intimate details of the struggle between Tolstoy and his wife, even going so far as to quote Tolstoy's private diary.

If the great writer had not yet left his wife, Chertkov explained, it was only because of his sense of duty toward his family and because God had not yet willed that he should go. And then the poison:

> A free and peaceful life (away from Yasnaya Polyana) in comparison with the hell in which he now has to live, would indeed be a real paradise. . . . It is very painful to me that the crazy will of a woman who does not love him but hates his soul, and whom egotism, malice and avarice have driven insane, should have control over personal communications between Tolstoy and ourselves—his nearest and most devoted friends. As for that, it was a cruel fate that he should have an implacably cruel jailer, such as his whole life has been bound up with, in the person of Sofya Andreyevna.

Chertkov's wife, with the full concurrence of her husband, sent on to Tolstoy copies of Dosev's letter and Chertkov's reply. The correspondence was "painful and awkward" for Tolstoy, he let the couple know. And it was "unpleasant" that the privacy of his diaries had been infringed. Still, Tolstoy's reaction made it clear that he was not so much under Sonya's heel as Chertkov's. He wrote his disciple meekly, praising his letter to Dosev. It was very "salutary" for him, he said, and in his diary he wrote that the letter "is chiefly a program for me, which I am far from carrying out."[7]

On September 24 Tolstoy made a note in his diary: "I have lost my small diary." It was the one for himself alone. He mentioned it to Bulgakov when the secretary arrived for work the next morning. "I can't remember just where I put it," he said.

> You know, in one notebook, I jot down the thoughts that will go into my diary. The diary is read by Chertkov and Sasha, but the little notebook is absolutely private, and I never let anyone read it. I've searched everywhere and can't find it. It is possible that Sonya has found it.

It was more than possible. While he was out riding, Sonya, snooping in his study, had found it hidden in a tall boot of his. She had read it and hidden it in her bedroom. The disappearance of the diary was alarming news at Yasnaya Polyana and Telyatinki—if Tolstoy's suspicion was correct. For if she read it she would know about the secret will—not its contents but that it existed. And, from her struggle with Chertkov over the diaries and the current manuscripts, she could pretty well guess what was in it.

Countess Tolstoy does not mention this little theft in her diary, but both their journals agree that the twenty-fourth was another miserable day for them. "Once again," Sonya began, "Leo shouted at me because I wanted to read his unpublished manuscript *The Wisdom of Children,* of which *not a single copy* could be found in the house. Chertkov had already seized the manuscript, and I spoke of him as a *collector.* Leo got terribly angry and shouted at me."

Tolstoy's diary:

> The day began quietly. But at lunch there was talk of *The Wisdom of Children,* assertions that Chertkov is a collector and has kept things. What would he do with the manuscripts after my death? I asked her rather heatedly to leave me in peace. . . . But after dinner she began to reproach me for shouting at her. . . .

She now began to follow him when he went out for his daily walk or ride, hoping to catch him if he was having a secret rendezvous with Chertkov. She describes how it went one day in her diary of September 27.

> Leo Nikolayevich went for a ride alone along the highway, and I followed him in the cabriolet. Looking behind him every so

often he kept riding farther and farther ahead, evidently assuming that I would soon feel the cold (for I was thinly dressed) and turn back for home. But I did not, even though I was chilled through and later caught a bad cold. I returned with him, by which time we had covered 15 miles.

Tolstoy noted it in his diary for himself: "Today she rode out after me on my ride, probably spying on me. Pathetic but difficult. Lord help me!"

Next day she did not go out spying but later wished that she had. "Every chance is against me," she lamented in her diary. And she recounted how her husband set out to visit Marya Schmidt and ran into Chertkov, who was on his way to visit a neighbor. What lousy luck! "My heart ached," she wrote in her diary, "to think of their joy in seeing one another."

There were days, miraculous days, few and far between, when peace and quiet descended on Yasnaya Polyana and even Sonya forgot her sorrows and her hates and rejoiced in life with her illustrious husband. According to her journal, there was one such day that otherwise terrible autumn. Sonya described it in her diary on September 29.

> Relations with Leo Nikolayevich are calm and friendly, and I am happy! I sat with him after he had had his lunch today, and I ate something too—pancakes with curd cheese. It was wonderful to see the joy on his face. . . . "Ah, how glad I am that you are eating again at last," he said. Then he brought me a pear and tenderly begged me to eat it. When other people are not here he is generally kind and affectionate to me, much as he used to be, and I feel he is *mine* again.

In the beginning, Tolstoy saw that day somewhat differently. "I am in a bad mood," he wrote in his regular diary. "Everything is bad, everything torments me, everything is contrary to my wishes." He resented that "the new edition will be sold for hundreds of thousands." He was thinking, also resentfully, of an offer a Russian publisher had made to Sonya—a million rubles for the rights to his complete works after his death. Tolstoy thought this was terribly sinful. He wanted all his works to be made available to the general public for free. Later that evening, when he came to write in his secret diary, he felt better about the day. Sonya was better, he wrote. "Today for the first time I saw the possibility of winning her over with kindness and love. Oh, if only . . . " He did not finish the sentence.

On the evening of October 3 Tolstoy suddenly fell ill and this time it seemed so serious that his family feared for his life. He had seemed all right in the morning when he took a long walk. But in the afternoon he had insisted on going for a ride with Dr. Makovitsky. It was raw and chilly outside and, after a six-mile canter, he had returned stiff from the cold. His legs were numb and he felt so weak that he collapsed on the bed and fell asleep without removing his boots. Sonya was concerned but felt assured when he went to sleep. When he did not come down for dinner, however, she became alarmed and, after serving the soup, left the table to see how he was.

She found him unconscious, muttering strange words, and rushed back to the dining room to fetch the doctor. Everyone at the table raced to his bedroom—Dr. Makovitsky, Bulgakov, Biryukov, and son Sergei and daughter Tanya, who had just arrived at Yasnaya Polyana for a visit. Sasha, and even Chertkov, were summoned from Telyatinki. Soon after the doctor and the others arrived in his room, Tolstoy went into convulsions, his jaws twisting and his legs thrashing so wildly that three men—the doctor, Bulgakov, and Biryukov—could scarcely hold him down. At first Sonya kept remarkably cool, considering her emotions—fetching hot water bottles for his feet, making a compress for his forehead, and a solution for an enema. But soon she could no longer control her feelings. Grabbing his feet and kissing them, she prayed aloud: "Not this time, O Lord! Not this time! Please God, spare him."

Sonya was not aware that Chertkov had arrived. He remained downstairs in the doctor's room and did not risk seeing the Countess and her family. But he wanted to be on the scene, in case the Master died, to claim what the old man had offered him in his secret will. Despite her despair and the terrible feeling that she should be deemed responsible if her husband died, Sonya was composed enough to slip quietly into her husband's study and make off with a portfolio of his papers. Tanya caught her in the act, stopped her, and asked what she had taken. "The diary," Sonya replied. "They surely would have stolen it if Father had died."

The great writer suffered five convulsions that evening, each one lasting two or three minutes. But by midnight they were over and he went to sleep. Early in the morning, when he awoke, he seemed surprised to see so many people hovering about his bedroom. He could not believe it when they told him what had happened. Within a couple of days he seemed almost his old self, though he was still weak and the doctor advised him to remain in bed.[8]*

"The joy of his recovery," wrote Bulgakov the next day, "is as great as was the fear of death last night." There was another cause for joy that day, he noted. Sonya Tolstoy and her daughter Alexandra made up, promising to end their long feud and unite to make Tolstoy's last days peaceful. There were kisses and much weeping, each asked for forgiveness from the other, and, in the end, Sonya pleaded with her daughter to return to Yasnaya Polyana along with her friend Varya, from whom she also asked pardon.

It seemed, as Tanya believed, that her mother had learned some lessons from the crisis. Sonya not only achieved reconciliation with the strong-willed Alexandra but she invited Chertkov to come over to Yasnaya and pay a visit to her husband. She was lifting her ban on him.

But it pained her, and she was not sure she could endure it. "My God!" she exclaimed in her diary, "how difficult it will be for me if it is necessary to renew relations with Chertkov. Such a thing seems to me terribly hard and even impossible! But I shall have to do it."

Chertkov lost no time in accepting her invitation. He showed up at Yasnaya Polyana on the evening of October 7. Sonya says she "ached all over." She had arranged it so the visit would not be long; she had asked the doctor to give Tolstoy a bath that evening, in order, she admits, "to shorten Chertkov's visit." She also asked Leo not to kiss his friend, which caused Tolstoy, in his secret diary later that evening, to exclaim: "How repulsive!"

---

* Tanya believed that her father's illness at last opened her mother's eyes to the truth, but this was not to be. "She realized," Tanya says of her mother, "how far she herself was to blame for her husband's illness." If so, the realization did not last very long. (Tatiana Tolstoy, *Tolstoy Remembered*, p. 235.)

Chertkov was due to arrive at 8:00 P.M.

> When I heard the sound of the spring carriage through the ventilation window [Sonya reported in her diary] I thought I would die. I ran to the glass door to see what happened at their meeting but L.N. had just drawn back the curtain. I rushed into his room, drew back the curtain and took out the binoculars, straining to catch any expression of joy. But L.N., realizing that I was watching, merely took Chertkov's hand with a blank expression. Then they had a long talk. . . . Meanwhile I started his bath water and sent Ilya [a servant] to tell him that the water was ready and would get cold if he didn't hurry. Chertkov then stood up, said good-bye and left.
>
> I felt terribly shaken all evening. . . . I felt I was about to die. Leo kept taunting and tormenting me, saying that Chertkov was "the person closest to him" until I put my hands up and shrieked, "I can't listen anymore. That's enough."
>
> What an effort it cost me to let that idiot in the house, and how I struggled to control my feelings! I simply cannot endure him. He is the devil incarnate! . . .
>
> The best thing would be if Chertkov went away. The next best thing would be either his death or mine. The worst thing would be L.N.'s death.[9]

Tolstoy's diary for that day: "Chertkov was here. Very simple and lucid. We talked a great deal about everything except about the difficult position we are in. It is better so. He left soon after 9 o'clock. Sonya had another hysterical seizure, which was disgusting."[10]

His illness had not really reconciled them. On October 5, two days after his seizures, he had turned to his secret diary and written: "I struggle with any unkindly feelings for her [Sonya]. I cannot forget those three months during which she tormented me and all who were near to me. But I will master it."

On the eighth, the day after Chertkov's visit, he went to Sonya's room determined to have it out with her. According to Sonya he was agitated and "evidently displeased" with her. He asked her to hear him out in silence, but this was now beyond Sonya's capacity, and she interrupted him, she says, "a couple of times." He tried to talk to her about her insane jealousies and unwarranted animosity toward Chertkov. "Agitatedly and even angrily," Sonya reported in her diary, "he suggested that I had deliberately adopted a caprice. I ought to try to get rid of it, that he had no exclusive affection for Chertkov, but that there were other people nearer to him. . . ."

But Sonya was incorrigible.

> This of course is not true, but he has to try somehow to hoodwink me about his exclusive partiality for Chertkov. But there was no deceiving me. I know my husband too well. His throaty voice, his agitation, and his passionate speech, made me understand only too well that his whole interest and aim was to induce me to regard a renewal of relations calmly. But this is impossible.

Every time now that Leo took a ride or set off on foot for a little exercise, Sonya died a thousand deaths, suspecting that he was secretly meeting with Chertkov. Even when there was a quiet day— "Thank God!" as she noted in her diary on October 9—she was terrified that when Tolstoy left with the doctor for a ride that they were really going to visit Chertkov. She was in agony, she said, just thinking of it.

She now began to agonize over something else. While he was writing his diary on the evening of the eighth, she gazed through the window from the balcony at him in his study and was seized by a fear that he was going to leave her, "as he often threatened lately to do." Sonya was now obsessed by her fears: fear of her husband leaving her after a marriage of forty-eight years; fear of his seeing Chertkov; fear of Chertkov's receiving all rights to publish all of Tolstoy's works, including his diaries; fear, as she wrote in her diary on October 9, that this "repulsive, spiteful, loathsome man, in publishing Leo's letters and diaries, especially," would reveal "the most intimate details of our life" and thus brand her for all time as a shrew who killed her husband.

Every day that autumn her hatred of Chertkov grew a bit higher. On October 12 she began in her diary: "I keep discovering more and more vile things that Chertkov has done." She had by now—after reading Leo's secret diaries and probably a letter of the day before in which his disciple wrote the Master a reminder of

what the will contained and warned him again that his "mercenary" family might try to break it—a good idea herself of her
husband's last testament.

> He [Chertkov] has now persuaded Leo N. to give instruc-
> tions that the copyrights should not go to his children after his
> death, but should be made common property, as are his last
> works. And when Leo N. said that he would talk to his family
> about it Chertkov . . . would not let him! Scoundrel and despot!
> He has taken this poor old man in his dirty hands and forced him
> into these despicable deeds. But if I live, I shall have my re-
> venge, and he won't be able to do any such thing. He has stolen
> my husband's heart from me and stolen the bread from my
> children's and grandchildren's mouths.

She says she told Leo that day that she knew about his "instructions," noting that he looked sad and guilty but said nothing.
"I said it was a mean trick, that he was planting strife and discord
and that his children would not give up their rights without a
struggle."

Sonya's snooping into Leo's papers rendered her another discovery, she says: how much her husband disliked her. "He has
forgotten everything," she exclaims, "forgotten what he wrote me
in his diary: 'If she refuses me, I shall shoot myself.' " That evening
she showed Tolstoy a copy of his diary during the time he had fallen
in love with her and proposed. He seemed "astonished," she says,
and reported: "How painful!" He now cast her, she thought, "in
the role of Xanthippe."

Tolstoy recorded his reaction to these scenes in his diary for
October 12 and 13. It was rather astonishing.

> October 12: Another conversation this morning and a scene.
> Someone had said something to her about some bequeathing of
> the diaries to Chertkov. . . .
> October 13: It appears that she has found my little diary
> and carried it off. She knows about some bequeathing of some-
> thing to someone, evidently related to my works. What she suf-
> fers on account of their monetary value! And she is afraid lest I
> should interfere with her edition. She is afraid of everything.

Strange indeed that this great moralist should write so hypo-critically in his own diary for himself alone. As for his accusing Sonya of wanting control of his works for "monetary" and "mercenary" reasons, an idea that Chertkov had cunningly cultivated in him, Sonya was quick to show him that he (and Chertkov) were wrong.

"If it has been suggested to you," she wrote Tolstoy the next day, October 14, "that I am guided by mercenary motives, then I am personally ready, like my daughter Tanya, to renounce officially the right to inherit my husband's property."*

October 13 had been a desperate day for Countess Tolstoy. She again thought of suicide. She had just read in the newspapers of a little girl of fifteen taking an overdose of opium and dying "quite easily—she just fell asleep." Sonya says she looked at her "big" vial of opium but realized she "lacked the courage." She then rehearsed in her diary the whole history of how the great Leo Tolstoy had become "enslaved" by despotic Chertkov.

> Eventually he persuaded and helped Leo N. to draft official renunciation of the copyrights after his death probably (I don't know in exactly what form it was written), thereby stealing the last crust of bread from the mouths of the children and grand-children who survive him. But the children and I, if I live, will defend our rights.
>
> Monster! What business has he to interfere in our family affairs?

She must put an end to her agony, she says.

> Otherwise Mr. Chertkov will next order *me*, not the manu-scripts, to be taken away and put in an insane asylum. . . . Or else, enraged with me for *unmasking* him, Chertkov will persuade my husband to go away with him somewhere. . . .

When Sonya suggested to Leo that "it was wicked and unkind of him to give instructions for his copyrights to be given after his death to the world rather than to his own family, he merely kept an

---

* Tanya had renounced the right to inherit her husband, Sukhotin's, property. So he had deeded it to his six children by his late wife.

obstinate silence and his general attitude was: 'You are sick, I must endure this in silence, but in my heart I shall hate you.' "

Thus rebuffed, she put her complaints in the letter she wrote to her husband the next day, the fourteenth. It was at once bitter, sarcastic, and poignant, a cry from a very troubled woman and a desperate appeal for understanding. Unbalanced as she had become, she wrote lucidly, sharply, and even eloquently.

> You ask me every day with apparent sympathy how I am and how I've slept; but every day there are also fresh blows that scorch my heart, shorten my life, and torment me unendurably. . . .
>
> It has pleased fate to reveal to me this new blow by which you are depriving your numerous offspring of your copyrights, though your accomplice in this affair ordered you not to inform your family. . . .

She chided her husband for his hypocrisy—and Chertkov's—in rejecting the government and then conniving to draw up a testament whose enforcement depended on the government's action.

> The government which both of you have abused and rejected in all your writings will, *according to law*, deprive your heirs of their last bit of bread and transfer it . . . to wealthy publishers and adventurers, while Tolstoy's grandchildren will be dying of hunger in consequence of his evil and vainglorious will. . . .
>
> Listen, Lyovochka, you pray when you go for walks! Pray then and consider well what you are doing under pressure from that wretch. Extinguish the evil, open your heart, evoke love and kindness, not anger and evil deeds and vainglorious pride (concerning your rights as an author) and hatred of me. . . .
>
> I am seized by horror at the thought that I may survive you and see the evil that will spring up around your grave in the memory of your children and grandchildren! Extinguish that evil while you are still alive, Lyovochka! Arouse and soften your heart! Arouse God and love in it—about which you preach to men so loudly.

When she took the letter to Tolstoy in his study, Sonya says, he cried: "Can't you leave me in peace!"

Tolstoy gives his version in entries in his regular and secret diaries. The regular diary: ". . . On the table there is a letter from Sofya Andreyevna accusing me, and inviting me to renounce something or other. When she came in I asked her to leave me in peace, and she went away. . . . Before going out I wrote Sofya Andreyevna and advised her to leave me in peace and not interfere in my affairs."

In his diary for himself alone he wrote: "A reproachful letter on account of some paper about rights, as if the question of money was the most important thing. This is better and more definite. But when she speaks exaggeratedly of her love for me and goes on her hands and knees and kisses my hand, I find it very hard. I am still unable to announce resolutely that I am going to ride over to Chertkov's."[11]

Strange evasions! Is this great and good man still kidding himself? Why write in his own diary that Sonya's letter invited him to renounce "something or other"? Or that Sonya had written him reproachfully "on account of some paper on rights." She had talked to him and written him begging him not to disinherit the family. Since that was what he intended to do—the secret will called for it—why could he not talk about it frankly with his wife and children? Or at least admit it to himself?

On the sixteenth of October, Sonya staged another terrible scene, one that convinced Tolstoy there was no hope, that life with his wife could not go on. It was destroying him. It all began when he announced to her that he was going off to visit Chertkov. She pleaded with him not to go.

"If you can, Lyovochka, don't go to Chertkov's for yet awhile! It is terribly hard for me."

But he told her he could not promise anything. The response sent Sonya into another tailspin. She set off wildly on foot to Telyatinki. Arriving at the entrance to Chertkov's house she threw herself down in a ditch, watching spitefully for her husband's arrival.

"I don't know what I would have done," she wrote in her diary, "had he ridden up. I imagined all sorts of things—how I would lie on the bridge over the ditch and be trampled on by Leo Nikolayevich's horse. . . ." Fortunately he did not come.

By the time she got home on foot it was dark and she was shivering from the cold. But she did not enter the house. She wanted to prolong Leo's anxieties. She was sure he had sent out a search party for her, once it turned dark. She stopped in the garden and sat down on a bench, under a fir tree by the lower pond. Her thoughts, she says, turned toward the pond, "and the cold water in which I could immediately, this very moment, find full and eternal forgetfulness of everything, and deliverance from my tortures of jealousness and despair. . . . But again cowardice prevented me from killing myself."

She got off the bench and lay on the frigid ground. Through the darkness, she says, she could see a light in Leo's windows, which meant that her husband was still awake. How he must be suffering! The thought apparently pleased her, because she "dozed off a little." It was in that condition that a search party, carrying lanterns, found her and dragged her back to the house. "I was," she says, "quite crazy with the cold, fatigue and agitations I had lived through."

She joined the family at the dinner table but she was so numbed with cold that she did not take off her coat, hat and gloves, sitting there, in her words, like a mummy, "not eating my dinner." She apparently thawed out, because later in the evening she went after her husband again. Why, she asked, could he not promise not to see Chertkov?

"Because I want my freedom! I don't want to be exposed to your whims! I don't want to be a boy or a rag under my wife's slippers at 82!" He said much more, Sonya says, "that was hard and offensive."

Sonya's lack of understanding of him came out in her diary that night. "He has some *idée fixe* that he wants to be *free*. Is he not free now, except as regards intercourse with Chertkov and his irrational wish to visit him?"

As their quarrel was subsiding, Tolstoy rather angrily repeated to her something that he had told her earlier in the day. "I take back all my promises I have given you," he said. "I promise nothing. What I want to do, I will do!"[12] What he meant—and surely Sonya understood—was that he took back his promises not to leave.* By now, the middle of October 1910, the idea of leaving

---

* Sonya's diary of July 7, 1910, had noted the promise. "I went to his room as he was going to bed and said: 'Promise me you won't ever leave on the sly, without telling me.' And he replied: 'I wouldn't ever do such a thing. I shall never leave you. I love you.' "

occupied Tolstoy's mind more and more. That night of Sonya's escapade, after describing her hysterics and asking God to help him in his tribulations, he confided to his diary that he had decided to leave, and go to his daughter Tanya. But having written that, he hesitated. "I told her that I do not and will not make any promises. . . . I shall hardly carry out my intentions of going away [to Tanya's] tomorrow. But I ought to do so. God help me!"

He began to discuss with Sasha, Dushan, old Marya Schmidt, and even more acquaintances his plans to get away. One of the latter was a peasant writer, M. P. Novikov, author of the book *The Concept of God as the Absolute Principle of Life*, a work very much influenced by Tolstoy. Novikov, who now came to Yasnaya Polyana for a brief visit, was an ardent Tolstoyan but blessed with a salty sense of humor, which Tolstoy liked. After he had confided his marital woes to his visitor, Novikov assured him that the peasants solved such problems quite easily. He cited the example of a peasant acquaintance whose wife was alcoholic and constantly drunk.

> At first the man was stupid. He ordered prayers from the priest, bought icons from the church and went on a pilgrimage to Sergey-Troitsa. But last summer he could no longer restrain himself. He took a whip and flogged the drunken woman a couple of times, and it acted better than saints!

Tolstoy laughed but then grew serious.

> I have suffered more than your acquaintance. For thirty years I have borne that cross, and still bear it. . . . I am roasted as if I were in Hell. . . . I wanted to get away. . . . [But] I could not run away secretly without causing an uproar, and my wife would on no account agree to my going to you or to anyone else. If I had insisted on it, we should have had at once the scenes customary to our circle: tears, hysteria and fainting fits which I could not have endured. . . . I will go away. I will certainly go away! We shall soon see each other again.[13]

The badgered old man meant it. On October 24, he wrote Novikov.

> In connection with what I said to you before you left, I'm turning to you again with the following request: if it should

actually happen that I were to come to you, would you be able to find me a little hut in your village, even a very small one, as long as it is warm. . . . I am also letting you know that if I should have to telegraph you, I shall do so not in my own name, but in that of T. Nikolayev.

Don't forget that all this must be known to nobody but yourself.

He was still desperately afraid that Sonya might find out. His planning was now becoming more specific. To Sasha, the day after he got his letter off to Novikov, he confided the details of the getaway. He would buy a ticket to Moscow but would get off the train at Laptevo, from which he could drive to Novikov's. If he was discovered, he told her, he would go elsewhere. That "elsewhere" he explained to Dr. Makovitsky. He would go to Tanya's, and from there to the Optina monastery. There, monks would surely take him in, he joked to Dushan, with the hope of converting him. He also intended to visit his eighty-year-old sister, Marya, who, after a somewhat Bohemian life, had become a nun at the Shamardino convent, eight miles from the monastery.

Not everyone Tolstoy told of his intention to leave approved. When he went over to tell the aged Marya Schmidt, she tried to dissuade him. "Dearest Leo Nikolayevich," she told him, "this is only a momentary weakness. It will pass." He replied weakly that he hoped so. But did he? "It is hard for me in this madhouse," he wrote that evening. And in his secret diary he added: "I feel more and more depressed by the life we are leading. Marya Schmidt tells me not to go away, and my conscience also restrains me to bear with her [Sonya], to endure. . . . God help me!" Before going to bed he added: "Nothing special has happened. Only a feeling of shame and the necessity of undertaking something." He wrote to Chertkov: "If I undertake anything, I will, of course, let you know. I may even ask your help."

The weather was terrible for a man of eighty-two with a heart condition and a tendency to catch pneumonia to be setting off on such a trip. The third-class cars he insisted on using when traveling by rail were usually unheated and full of tobacco smoke. And as the Russian fall turned to winter, it grew cold and the snows began to come. Sonya's diary recorded the arrival of winter. On October 16, she reported a light snowfall and, toward evening, "thirteen degrees [Centigrade] of frost and everything is frozen over."

October 21: The weather is terrible, 4 degrees of frost, a whirlwind of snow and frozen hail beating against the windows.
October 23: In the night there was a snow storm.
October 27: It snowed.*

October 27 is a fateful date in this story.

Sonya's spying on him was now getting quite unbearable for Tolstoy. In his secret diary on the twenty-third he noted that "Sofya Andreyevna followed me on foot to see whether I had gone to Chertkov's." He was now convinced that it was Sonya who had taken his diary for herself and hidden it. And now she began checking on his mail to see whether any letters were coming from Chertkov. Or even from Chertkov's wife. On October 23, he had written Anna, Chertkov's wife, a brief note about Dostoyevsky and his novel *The Brothers Karamazov*, which he was rereading and about which he grew hot and cold, liking it in one mood, and sharply criticizing it in another. Sonya, who also hated Mrs. Chertkov, holding her to be a fellow conspirator with her husband, asked Tolstoy what their "correspondence" was about. Spying on his outgoing mail, she had noted the letter to Anna, and then her reply. Tolstoy responded that he didn't remember exactly what he had written Anna, which Sonya told her diary was "a new subterfuge." She demanded to see the letters and, again, he answered that he didn't know where they were, which, "again," Sonya says, "was untrue." When she continued to nag him about it, he finally turned on her angrily and shouted: "I don't want to show them to you!"

"There was something ominous in his eyes," Sonya noted. It struck her so hard that she somehow felt an era was coming to an end. She decided to shut down her diary, which had chronicled so much of that time.

I have given up. I finish and seal up for a long time, this terrible diary, the story of my heavy sufferings. Curses on Chertkov!—the man who has made me suffer! Forgive me, O Lord!

In his secret diary for that night Tolstoy wrote:

* It must be remembered that the Russian calendar was thirteen days behind that used in the West. So the last days of October, Old Style, were nearly into the middle of November, New Style—a time when the severe Russian winter had set in.

Always the same oppression. Suspicion and spying, and on my side, a sinful wish that she should give me an occasion to go away. How weak I am! I think about going away. Then I think of her position and am sorry for her and cannot. She asked me for a letter from Anna Chertkov. All night I was aware of my painful struggle with her. . . . I woke up, fell asleep, and it was the same over again. . . . Yes, it is indeed unbearable—horrible.

Next day, October 26, Sonya picked a quarrel over another letter from Telyatinki, this time from Chertkov. He had given it to Bulgakov to take over to Yasnaya Polyana, remarking that it was not of a personal or confidential nature. Through her eavesdropping, Sonya learned that the young secretary had brought over a note from Chertkov that morning, and she demanded of her husband that he disclose the contents. "He told her," says Bulgakov, "that it was of a business nature and that on principle he would not let her read it." The predictable explosion occurred, and Sonya nagged Leo to the point where he fled to the safety of his room. Bulgakov feared he might have another stroke.

Unfortunately [wrote Bulgakov], even the threat of another attack does not persuade Sofya Andreyevna to keep her promise not to disturb his peace of mind. Again her jealousy of Chertkov, again scenes with Leo Nikolayevich and clashes with her daughter! And what is even worse she persistently questions him as to whether he has made a Will and demands a special memorandum assigning the rights to his literary works to her personally. What with her suspicions, spying and eavesdropping, the atmosphere of the house is troubled and uneasy.

It would grow worse the next day. Countess Tolstoy, Bulgakov felt, was driving her husband out of the house. "Among those close to Leo Nikolayevich, talk of the possibility of his leaving Yasnaya Polyana in the near future grows more and more insistent."

As the day of October 27 wore on, everyone at Yasnaya Polyana was filled with foreboding. Tolstoy had not slept well. "Had bad dreams all night," he began his diary. "The burden of our relations is getting worse." Sonya says she did not sleep at all and got up that morning feeling very nervous. She was still resentful, she says, at Leo's refusal to show her Chertkov's letter. What vexed her most was that he had defended his refusal by "standing on principle." She also had a foreboding. "My mind is troubled," she wrote in her diary. "Something is going to happen."

Alexandra remembered that, on the evening of the twenty-seventh, the atmosphere in the house was "depressing and strained." At evening tea Sonya was absent as Tolstoy sat down with Sasha, her friend Varya, and Dr. Makovitsky. She had sent word that she was working on some proofs. The atmosphere at the table was gloomy. No one spoke. After a while Sonya arrived. Sasha took her cup and left the room. Then Tolstoy followed and went off to his room, carrying his glass of tea.

It was the last evening Leo Tolstoy would ever spend at his beloved ancestral home at Yasnaya Polyana.

# TWENTY-ONE

# *Flight!*

**A**T THREE O'CLOCK on the chilly morning of October 28, 1910, Leo Tolstoy was suddenly awakened by the sound of footsteps in his study, adjacent to his bedroom. Through a crack in the door he could see a bright light and hear the rustling of papers. He knew at once that it was Sonya again searching through his desk. Again he heard footsteps, and he felt her passing him in the dark toward her own bedroom. Something cracked inside him. He had been enduring this snooping for years and it had become worse the last months. But this time it was once too often. "It was the final push," he confided to his diary, "that compelled me to take some action. I don't know why this aroused in me an aversion and indignation that I could not restrain." But it did.

He tried to go back to sleep, tossed from side to side in bed, but it was no use. He was too aroused. Finally, he had had enough of her years of spying on him, as he put it, "day and night." He sat up and lit a candle. The light attracted Sonya, who came into his room and asked him why he had lit a candle and if he was feeling bad.

At the sight of her, Tolstoy says, his aversion and indignation increased. "I choked and counted my pulse." It was ninety-seven. "I could lie there no longer," he says, "and suddenly I took the final decision to go away."

As soon as he felt certain she had gone to sleep, he put on his dressing gown and slippers and, carrying a candle, tiptoed downstairs to wake Dr. Makovitsky.

"I have decided to go away," he whispered to him. "You must

come with me." Dushan thought Tolstoy looked awfully nervous. He took his pulse. It had risen to one hundred. Tolstoy asked the doctor to join him upstairs as soon as he was dressed, warning him to be careful not to awaken Sonya. "We won't take much with us," he explained to Dushan—"only what is essential. Sasha will follow us in a few days and bring what is necessary."[1]

He went back upstairs and wakened Sasha. Like her father, she had had little sleep that night. She heard a gentle tap at the door. "Sasha, I am going away—definitely. Come help me pack," he said.

"Are you going alone?" Sasha asked. Though she had been waiting impatiently for this moment for years, she was now apprehensive. He told her he was taking Dushan. "I shall never forget," Sasha wrote later, "his figure as he stood in the door, a candle in his hands, his face lighting up, beautiful, full of resolve."[2]

Alexandra woke Varya Feokritova; they dressed and hurried to help Tolstoy pack. Alexandra says she was so nervous she kept dropping things. While the two young women packed his clothes, Tolstoy himself, outwardly composed, was carefully placing his papers in a small suitcase. They were mostly his diaries. He asked Sasha to keep his manuscripts. At every moment Tolstoy and his helpers were afraid Sonya would waken, hear them, and come running. "Hush, hush, make no noise," they kept whispering to each other.

Tolstoy took his daughter aside. "You will stay behind, Sasha," he told her. "I shall call you in a few days when I decide definitely where I'm going." He said he would probably go to visit his sister at the Shamardino convent. After that, he had no idea. The main thing was to get away from his wife's clutches.

The packing seemed endless, though there were only a few suitcases, and Tolstoy became nervous at the delay. The young women were having trouble—the straps of the bags would not pull together, the suitcases would not close. Finally, Tolstoy said he could wait no longer and, putting on an undercoat, a knitted cap, and mittens, hurried toward the stable to have the horses harnessed. In the pitch-dark, this proved more difficult than he expected. He missed the path to the stable, as he told it in his diary, "stumbled into a thicket, pricking myself, ran into the trees, fell, lost my cap and could not find it, made my way out with difficulty and went back to the house." There Sasha found him a new cap and a flashlight, and by its light he found the stable, aroused the coachman, and asked him to harness two horses for the droshky. Dushan, Varya, and Sasha dragged his suitcases to the stable. They found the old man restless and nervous. He was trying to help the coachman harness the horses and muttering that if they didn't get off at once, all would be lost—Sonya would find them. "I trembled," he admitted in his diary, "expecting to be pursued." And to Sasha he cried: "I feel we'll be overtaken any minute, and then everything will be lost."

Finally, toward six o'clock, the horses were harnessed and the bags stowed in the carriage and they were off. It was still pitch-dark and they had to ask a groom to ride slowly on horseback in front of them with a lantern, adding to Tolstoy's worries. They arrived at the Shchekino village rail station at six. But they had to wait an hour and a half for the first train out. The waiting seemed to Tolstoy an age, and as the minutes ticked by, he was in agony. "I expected her," he says, "to appear at any moment."

Finally the train arrived, they took their seats in one of the cars, and then, as the train started moving, Tolstoy breathed a sigh of relief. "My fears passed away," he says, "and pity for her rose in my heart—but no doubt that I had done what I had to do."

He had found time to pen Sonya a farewell note, which he asked the coachman to take back to Sasha, with whom he had arranged for her to show it to her mother when she got up.

Sonya slept late that morning and did not appear in the dining room until eleven o'clock. She rushed in frightened.

"Where is Papa?" she asked Alexandra.

"Father has gone!"

"Where?"

"I do not know."

"You don't know? Has he left for good?"

"He has left a letter for you. Here it is." And Sasha handed her mother the letter.

Yasnaya Polyana,
4 o'clock in the morning,
October 28, 1910

My departure will distress you. I am sorry about this, but do understand and believe that I couldn't do otherwise. My position in this house is becoming, or had become, unbearable. Apart from everything else, I can't live any longer in the conditions of luxury [in] which I have been living, and I'm doing what old men of my age commonly do: leaving this worldly life in order to live the last days of my life in peace and solitude.

Please understand, and don't come after me, even if you find out where I am. Your coming would only make your position and mine worse and wouldn't alter my decision. I thank you for your honorable 48 years of life with me, and I beg you to forgive me for everything for which I am to blame towards you, just as I forgive you with all my soul for everything for which you may have been to blame towards me. If you want to know anything, tell Sasha. She will know where I am and will send on what is necessary; but she can't tell you where I am because I have made her promise not to tell anyone.

Leo Tolstoy

Sonya did not finish reading the letter.

"He has left! Left for good!" she screamed at her daughter. "Farewell! I cannot live without him. I shall drown myself." She tossed the letter on the floor and ran out of the house just as she was, without overshoes, a coat, or mittens against the freezing weather. She headed for the pond, running down the path as fast as she could. Fortunately, Bulgakov had just arrived from Telyatinki and took after her, followed by Sasha.

They reached the pond just as Sonya was scampering along the plank to the jetty next to the bathhouse, where the laundry was done. The surface was slippery from soapsuds and Sonya slipped and fell, landing on her back. She clutched at the plank, Bulgakov says, turned over and crawled to the edge of the jetty and rolled off into the water. Bulgakov and Sasha jumped in after her.

"From the jetty," Bulgakov says, "I had seen Sofya Andreyevna's body lying face-up and open mouthed in the water, her arms spread helplessly as she sank." Suddenly she was completely submerged. Fortunately, she had not been able to get to the end of the jetty where the water was quite deep. The two rescuers found they could touch bottom—the water was only five feet deep—and they were able to pull her out. With the help of Semyon, the cook, and

Vanya, the footman, who had arrived at the scene, they were able to carry her, soaking wet and shivering, back to the house.

By that time she had recovered enough to order Vanya to go to the railway station and find out which train Tolstoy had taken and what his destination was. Before the servant could leave, she called him back and dictated a telegram to her husband: "Return at once. Sasha." The servant, puzzled as to whether he should obey, showed the telegram to Sasha, who told him to send it but also another that read: "Don't worry. Only telegrams signed Alexandra are genuine." One telegram requested by her mother was not sent by Sasha. "Telegraph Father at once," Sonya had asked her daughter, "that I am going to drown myself."

She tried a second time. She had hardly put on dry clothes before she was telling Sasha and Bulgakov that she would try other ways to do away with herself. "We had to take from her by force," Bulgakov says, "a penknife, some opium and several heavy objects with which she had begun to beat herself on the breast." Sasha noted that a hammer and a paperweight were among the "heavy objects" they took from her. Her second attempt at drowning did not get very far. Bulgakov says he caught up with her in the park and "almost forcibly led her back to the house."

For several hours she paced nervously about the house, sobbing hysterically. Once, Sasha says, she tried to throw herself out the window and later to jump down a well.[3] By the next morning, though she could not sleep, she seems to have recovered enough to sit down and write to her departed husband. It was a highly emotional appeal. Later, pinning it to a page of her diary, she called it "full of love and despair."

> October 29, 1910.
>
> Lyovochka, my dear one, my darling, return home! Save me from a second suicide, Lyovochka, my life long friend. I will do everything, everything that you wish! I will cast aside all luxury, your friends will be mine, I will undergo a cure, and will be mild, tender and kind. You must *save* me, you know it is said in the gospels that a man must never *for any reason* abandon his wife. My dear, my darling, friend of my soul, save me! Return if only to say farewell to me before our inevitable separation.
>
> Where are you? Where? Are you well? Do not torment me, Lyovochka. I will serve you lovingly with my whole body and

soul. Return to me. Return, for God's sake, for the sake of the love of God of which you speak to everyone, and I will give you the same submissive and self-sacrificing love! I promise it, dear one, modestly and firmly. We will simplify everything amiably, we will go away whenever you like and live as you like. And now goodbye! Goodbye perhaps forever.

Your Sonya.

Tolstoy and his faithful Dr. Makovitsky reached Kozelsk at five o'clock in the afternoon. It had taken them nine hours to cover some seventy miles on slow, jerky, smoky local trains. They had to change at Gorbachevo and the third-class car from there to Kozelsk was drafty, and filled with passengers and tobacco smoke. Tolstoy at first took refuge on the open platform at the end of the coach, where he could get a little fresh air at the intervals when smoke from the locomotive was not blowing by. But he soon returned to the middle of the coach. The passengers, mostly peasants and workmen, recognized him at once and gathered around. Blotting out for the moment what he had just been through, the old man was soon eagerly talking with them, inquiring about their lives but mainly doing what his audience wanted most—lecturing them about everything under the sun: Henry George's single tax, Darwin's theory of evolution, science and the state of education in Russia. This was a happy diversion from his worries.

Getting off the slow train at Kozelsk, they hired a cab to take them to the Optina monastery, some ten miles distant over a rough, badly paved road. The evening was crisp and chilly and Dushan worried about Tolstoy catching cold. The great author, excommunicated by the church, wondered whether the monks would take him in. But the friar at the hostelry was affable and gave the travelers a large, well-heated room. Tolstoy soon fell into a "restless" sleep. The next morning he intended to visit his sister Marya at the Shamardino convent nine miles away.

While waiting at Kozelsk for a cab, Tolstoy had got off two telegrams, one to Sasha and the second to Chertkov to tell them where he was. The zealous disciple had greeted the Master's flight with unfeigned delight. When he had broken the news to Bulgakov that morning at Telyatinki, the young secretary noted that his face lit up "and expressed joy and excitement." Chertkov had lost no time in getting off a letter to his mentor.

> I cannot express in words the joy I feel in hearing that you
> have gone away. . . . It was right of you to do so, and it would
> have been wrong of you to continue to live at Yasnaya Polyana
> under the conditions that had risen. . . . It is impossible to live
> without some spiritual respite. . . .

To make sure that the Master got his disciple's congratulation
and also, more important, to try to find out where he was heading,
Chertkov, as soon as he received Tolstoy's wire, dispatched his
secretary and confidant A. P. Sergeyenko with the letter and with
instructions to tell Tolstoy of Sonya's initial reaction to what had
happened.

To Sasha, Tolstoy had wired asking her to tell Chertkov that
he considered it best to refrain from seeing him for the time being.
The next day, October 29, he wrote to his daughter from the Optina monastery. A day's absence from Yasnaya had given him time
to reflect on what he had done and intended to do. He was bitter
about Sonya. After telling Sasha of his appreciation for what she
had done, "beyond your strength and youth," he added that he was
relying very much on his two eldest children, Sergei and Tanya.

> The main thing is for them to understand and to make her
> understand that life with all this spying and eavesdropping, these
> everlasting reproaches, this ordering me about at her own sweet
> will, this everlasting checking up on me, this simulated hatred of
> the man who is closest to me, this obvious hatred of me, but
> pretense of love—that such a life is not only disagreeable to me
> but utterly impossible. I want only one thing—to be free of her,
> and of this falsehood, pretense and malice which permeates her
> whole being. Of course they can't make her understand this, but
> they can make her understand that her whole behavior towards
> me not only does not express love, but seems to have the obvious
> object of killing it.

Sergei and Tanya, like all the other children except Leo, who
was in Paris, had been summoned by Sasha and now, the morning
after their father's departure, they held a family council: Sergei,
Tanya, Ilya, Andrei, Mikhail, and, of course, Alexandra. It was not
a harmonious meeting. All three younger brothers took their
mother's side, expressing understanding for what their father had

done but condemning him nevertheless and saying he should return. Tanya, as usual, declined to take sides. Disagreeing with her younger brothers, she said she would not condemn her father. Only Sergei approved his father's actions. Each agreed to send their father a note expressing his or her opinion—all except Mikhail, thirty-one, the youngest son, whom Bulgakov describes as sitting at the piano playing "bravura waltzes" and saying he didn't like to write. His conduct disgusted Bulgakov, who wrote of it in his diary: "His father had fled from his home, perhaps endangering his life, and his son could not spare the time to write him."

Ilya and Andrei were almost spiteful in their letters. "I know how painful life was for you here," Ilya wrote, "but then you regarded that life as your cross and I am sorry you did not endure that cross to the end." Andrei wrote more bluntly: "I have to warn you that by taking this final decision, you are killing our mother." He added that, though he realized how oppressive life had become for his father at Yasnaya Polyana, he should not forget that his wife suffered too. As for his complaints that he could not stand any longer living a life of luxury, Andrei wrote sarcastically: "Since you have endured it till now, you might sacrifice these last years of your life for the family and put up with these external surroundings." Tanya was brief and understanding. "Dear precious Papa," she began.

> You have always suffered from a good deal of advice, so I won't give you any. . . . I shall never condemn you. Of Mama, I will only say that she is pitiable and touching. She is unable to live otherwise than she does, and probably she will never change fundamentally. For her either fear or power is necessary. We all try to calm her.
>
> I am tired and stupid. Forgive me. Goodbye, my friend. . . .

Sergei wrote:

> I think Mama is nervously ill and in many respects irresponsible, and that it was necessary for you to separate (perhaps you should have done so long ago) however painful it is for you both. I also think that even if anything should happen to Mama—which I do not anticipate—you should not reproach

yourself. The position was desperate, and I think you chose the right way out.

Meanwhile, Leo was not getting much sleep, but otherwise, he told Dr. Makovitsky, he felt well and strong. As if to prove it, he had walked the nine miles to the Shamardino convent to visit with his eighty-year-old sister Marya. They had an emotional reunion. They embraced and wept, and the brother explained what had happened at Yasnaya Polyana. Marya, always devoted to him, did not disapprove and she expressed her sympathy. Tolstoy was relieved. Marya was the last link to the family past. He very much wanted her sympathy and understanding for having to break up the Tolstoy family he had built up over forty-eight years.

Strolling the gardens of the convent and into the village, Tolstoy liked the surroundings so much that he moved his things from the Optina monastery to the Shamardino convent inn. And he asked his sister to help him find a simple log hut in the village. This was a place where he could find peace and solitude. Never mind that the church had thrown him out. As he told Dushan, it might tolerate him in the hope of bringing him back to the faith.

Next morning Alexandra, accompanied by Varya Feokritova, arrived at Shamardino, though Tolstoy had not yet sent for her and was surprised to see her. She brought with her the letters the children had written, Sonya's anguished letter, and the latest news of the situation at home. The news upset him, especially the vivid description of Sonya's attempts to drown herself, and Sasha suddenly feared that her father might be weakening in his resolve not to return. So she told him of his wife's bitter words against him in the midst of all the hysteria. "He's a brute! He could not have acted with any greater cruelty! He wanted to kill me!" And she told of how Sonya had sworn that if he ever came back she would never let him out of her sight again. "I'll never let him escape again! I'll watch him day and night! I'll sleep at his door."

Sasha tried to assure him that things were now pretty much under control at Yasnaya Polyana. She had hired from Moscow a doctor, an old family friend who knew of Sonya's condition; a psychiatrist; and a trained nurse to look after her mother, try to quiet her nerves, and squelch any more attempts at suicide.

But she warned him that her mother apparently had figured

out that he had gone to Shamardino to see his sister and that if he lingered there she might come after him at any moment.

This news worried him and he called a council for that evening (October 30) of Sasha, Varya, Dushan and himself to decide what to do next. His dreams of settling down in a peasant hut amidst the tranquillity of the convent faded quickly. But before deciding where to flee next, he asked the others to leave him alone. He wanted to write Sergei and Tanya to thank them for their sympathy. And he needed to answer his wife's hysterical letter begging him to return. Sasha hoped that in it he would not begin to give in.

Tolstoy had been touched by the letters from his two eldest children. To Sergei and Tanya, he replied:

> Thank you very much, kind friends, true friends, Sergei and Tanya, for your sympathy in my grief and for your letters. Your letter, Sergei, gave me special pleasure. . . . I cannot help being afraid of everything and cannot free myself from a sense of responsibility but I had not the strength to act otherwise.
>
> Goodbye, and thank you, dear children. Forgive me for causing you to suffer—especially you, my darling Tanya. . . . I am hurrying away to avoid, what I fear, Mama overtaking me. A meeting with her now would be terrible.

He added that he did not yet know where they were going. He dated the letter: 4 A.M. Shamardino, October 31, 1910.

To Sonya he wrote:

> Shamardino,
> October 30–31, 1910
>
> A meeting between us, and still more my return *now*, is completely impossible. For you it would be harmful in the highest degree, so everyone says, and for me it would be terrible, since my present position, as the result of your emotional state, irritability and morbid condition, is even worse than before, if that is possible. I advise you to reconcile yourself to what has happened, to adjust yourself to what is temporarily a new position, and above all to have treatment.
>
> If you—I won't say love, but don't hate me—you must put yourself in my position a little bit. And if you were to do so, you

would not only not condemn me, but would try to help me find tranquility and the possibility of some human life, help me by making an effort to control yourself, and you would not wish for my return just now. But your mood now, your wish for, and your attempts at suicide which show more than anything else your loss of self-control, make my return just now unthinkable for me. No one except yourself can save all those near to you, myself and especially yourself, from the sufferings we are experiencing. Try to direct all your energy, not towards getting what you desire—my return now—but towards pacifying yourself and your soul, and then you will obtain what you desire.

I have spent two days at Shamardino and Optina, and am now leaving. I'll post this letter on the way. I'm not saying where I'm going because I consider separation to be essential for both you and me. Don't think I left you because I don't love you. I love you and pity you with all my soul, but I can't do otherwise than I am doing. Your letter, I know, was written sincerely, but it isn't in your power to do as you would wish. And it isn't a matter of fulfilling wishes and demands of mine, but only of your mental stability and calm, reasonable attitude to life. As long as that is lacking, life with you is unthinkable for me. To return to you when you are in this state would mean to renounce life, and I don't consider myself entitled to do so. Goodbye, Sonya dear; may God help you. Life is not a joke, and we have no right to throw it away at will, and to measure it by length of time is also unreasonable. Perhaps the months that are left to us to live are more important than all the years we have lived already, and we must live them well.

He signed it "L.T."

He did not show the letter to Sasha, and probably this was wise. For the letter, the last he would ever write his wife, held out hope for her that he might return. Not "just now," but when she had really calmed down, then, as he put it, she would obtain what she desired. The present position was "temporary." He also made this clear to Chertkov in a letter written that same night or early morning. "I am writing to Sofya Andreyevna," he informed his friend, "that I am not refusing to return, but making it a first condition that she should work on herself and calm down."

Chertkov, in such euphoria over the Master's leaving home, must have winced at all this, but as he read on he was more assured. For the unhappy man, so towering and sure of himself as a novelist and a moralist, was obviously still torn about the future with his wife. He could not quite make up his mind, and this contributed to his agony. At the end he wrote his disciple—the letter was dated Shamardino, October 31, 4:00 A.M.:

> We're afraid of everything and have decided to leave at once, at 4 A.M. Where we're going we don't yet know. . . . Keep a watch on what is happening at Yasnaya, and let me know if she finds out where I am and inform me by telegraph so that I can leave. A meeting with her would be terrible for me.

To his sister, the old nun, his "darling Mashenka," he got off a note, also at 4:00 A.M., asking her to forgive him for leaving without saying good-bye. "We're leaving unexpectedly, because I'm afraid Sofya Andreyevna will find me here. And there's only one train before 8:00."

As he prepared at four o'clock on the morning of October 31 to flee once again, he knew not where, from a wife he could not face, he had become, in the memorable phrase of Isaiah Berlin, "a desperate old man, beyond human aid, wandering self-blinded at Colonus."[4]

While Tolstoy was writing his letters, Sasha, Varya, and Dushan pored over railroad timetables and maps, trying to figure out where they should go. They finally decided to travel south to Novocherkassk, a town north of Rostov-on-Don, where a niece of Tolstoy, Marya Denisenko, and her husband lived. They would stay with them a few days and then decide to go either to Bulgaria, if they could obtain passports, or, if not, to the Caucasus, where Tolstoy would find many Tolstoyans. To throw Sonya off the track, they would buy tickets to a succession of small stations along the way, forgetting that Tolstoy, the most famous man in Russia, would be recognized wherever they went.

The old sage, who hated to plan ahead, was slightly annoyed when they presented their decision to him before going to bed. "It is not necessary to make plans," he told them. "We'll see tomorrow." But he could not sleep that night, and as he tossed in his bed, he realized that they could not wait until tomorrow to discuss their next step. Sonya might turn up at any moment.

Shortly after four o'clock in the morning of October 31, Alexandra again heard a knock on her door, as she had three nights before at Yasnaya. It was again her father and he was again telling her that they were leaving in a hurry. "Dress quickly," he told Sasha, "we're going right away." He had already sent for two coaches and horses. Tolstoy and Dr. Makovitsky set off in one, but the second one broke down and Sasha and Varya arrived in a makeshift buggy at Kozelsk just in time to see their train pulling into the station. Dushan had purchased the tickets while Tolstoy waited and, at 8:00 A.M., they were off on a train headed south.

Tolstoy was tired and lay down on the bench in their compartment, but he was too agitated to sleep. He asked Sasha to buy some morning newspapers at the next stop. To his horror he found, on glancing at them, the story of his flight plastered all over the front pages. He was taken aback. It had not occurred to him that what he had done would come out in the newspapers.

"Everything is known!" he exclaimed to Sasha. "The papers are full of it." The discovery depressed him and he lay back, trying to grasp the idea that his flight from his wife was now being made known through the newspapers to all of Russia and perhaps to the whole world. He felt a draft in the compartment, and asked Sasha to cover him with a blanket. When it looked as if he had dozed off, Sasha went out to the open section of the car. Everyone was eagerly reading the newspapers.

Two young men on a bench in front of her, "dressed with commonplace elegance," she says, cigarettes dangling from their lips, were discussing the news.

"A neat trick the old man played," one of them remarked. "I bet Countess Tolstoy didn't like it too well." And he chuckled "stupidly," in Sasha's opinion. "Packed up in the night, and ran away."

"And after she had taken care of him all her life," the other said. "Maybe her care wasn't so sweet to him."

Word that the great writer was on the train spread through the coaches, and soon a crowd was gathering around Tolstoy's compartment. Alexandra pleaded with the conductors to drive them away so that her father could get some rest. And her uneasiness was not helped when she realized that two plainclothesmen had got on at one station and were planting themselves outside the door of her father's compartment. Obviously the government had decided to keep a close watch on this dangerous author. The authorities in St. Petersburg were wondering uneasily what this heretic-anarchist was up to.

Tolstoy awoke about 4:00 P.M., apparently none the worse after eight hours on the slow, jolting, smoky train. But he did feel chilly and asked for more covers. It was cold in the car, Sasha says, and Dushan covered him with a steamer rug and his woolen cloak. But that was not enough, and as the train chugged along, he kept shivering from the cold. Dr. Makovitsky took his temperature. It was 100.6. Alexandra was suddenly alarmed. She sat down next to her father and prayed, "Father in heaven. Help us. Save us." Unconsciously, she mumbled the words so loudly that her father heard them and turned to her and said: "Don't lose heart, Sasha. All is well." But she had begun to think that all was not well. His chills did not cease and his fever kept slowly rising each time they took his temperature. They brewed tea and gave him that, and some red wine. But nothing helped.

Sasha panicked. "For the first time," she later wrote, describing the scene, "I realized that we had no shelter, no home. A second-class coach filled with tobacco smoke, strange people around us—and not one spot on earth where we could take refuge with a sick, aged man."

But, sooner than she imagined, they were forced to take refuge. Nothing could stop the rise of Tolstoy's temperature, and by six P.M., his condition had become so worrisome that Dr. Makovitsky decided they would have to get off at the next station. They had just left Dankovo and the next stop, they noted on their timetable, was a place they had never heard of, Astapovo. They would get off there.

A half hour later the train chugged into Astapovo. It was only a hamlet but it had a fairly large railway station—apparently it was a place where the crews changed. The train was to stop for fifteen minutes. As it came to a jolting halt, Dr. Makovitsky hurried down the platform and returned shortly with the stationmaster, who, because there was no inn in the village, offered to take in the great writer in his modest, four-room, red-walled cottage across the tracks from the station. Dushan and the stationmaster helped Tolstoy down the platform and placed him in the station's ladies' room while the stationmaster hurried to the cottage to ready a room. He and his wife trundled an old iron bed into the living room, to which Tolstoy was brought on the arms of Sasha and Varya as soon as it was made up. A large crowd lined the way across the tracks, the men lifting their caps as Tolstoy passed by, his legs unsteady, his breath short, clutching the arms of the two women. By the time they reached the house and got him into bed, the old man was somewhat delirious. He thought he was back at Yasnaya Polyana and gave directions for the night table and chair to be placed, as usual, within reach of the bed. He asked for a candle, matches, a notebook, a small lantern, to be placed on the table.

He finally went to sleep, and after fifteen minutes Sasha saw that his left arm and left leg began to twitch convulsively, as did the left side of his face. Alarmed, she sent for the district doctor, who happened to be at Astapovo, but it turned out he was not of much help. Toward nine o'clock Tolstoy awoke. He felt better. His temperature was down, his breathing more regular.

He turned to Sasha. "Well, how is it going?"

"Not very well," she replied.

"Come on, Sasha, don't lose heart," he said.

He fell asleep, and when he woke up around midnight he called to Sasha. "What do you think?" he asked. "Can we go tomorrow?" She replied that that was out of the question, they must wait another day. He sighed. He was ready to go. Later, in his sleep, Sasha heard him hashing over his flight. "To run away . . . run away . . . they'll overtake us."

Next morning, November 1, they took his temperature as soon as he awakened. It was normal. He asked again when they could press on. He was afraid that too many people had seen him get off the train at Astapovo to keep his whereabouts secret any longer. Sonya would learn and come after him. He called Sasha and dictated a telegram to Chertkov: "Yesterday fell ill, passengers saw me leaving train in weak condition, afraid publicity; now better, going on, take measures, advise."

But they were not going on. Despite the old man's improvement, Sasha wondered whether it was not her duty to honor a promise she had made to her mother—to notify the family if Tolstoy became ill. When she brought it up with him that morning, he would hear none of it. He begged his daughter not to reveal to the family where he was and that he was ill. But, he said, he would very much like to see Chertkov. Sasha promptly wired this message to him, and a reply came back shortly saying he would arrive at Astapovo the next morning. As the day progressed, Alexandra wondered if it was necessary. Her father's spirits rose so high that he called her in to take some dictation. He wanted to express some thoughts about God. Despite feeling better, did he have a presentiment that he soon might be confronting God? At any rate, he now set down to Sasha some of his ideas.

God is the unlimited all, of which man understands himself to be a limited part. God alone exists truly. Man is his expression in matter, time and space. . . . God is not love, but the more we love, the more man expresses God, and the more he truly exists.

After a nap he again called Sasha in and asked her to take a letter to Tanya and Sergei. He was upset, Sasha noted, by the thought that he had asked Chertkov to join him but not his two dearest children. "Several times he had to stop dictating," Sasha says, because of the sobs that rose in his throat.

Astapovo,
November 1, 1910

My dear children, Seryozha and Tanya:
I hope and trust that you will not reproach me for not having asked you to come. To have asked you, and not Mama, would have caused her great distress, as well as all your brothers. You will both understand that Chertkov, whom I did ask to come, occupies a special position in relation to me. He has devoted his whole life to the service of the cause which I have also served the last 40 years of my life. . . .
I thank you for your goodness to me. I don't know whether I am saying good-bye or not, but I felt the need to express to you what I have just said.
I also wanted to give some advice to you, Seryozha, that you should think about your life, who you are, what you are, what is the meaning of a man's life, and how every man should live it. The view you have acquired about Darwinism, evolution and the struggle for existence won't explain to you the meaning of

your life and won't give you guidance for your actions, and a life without explanation of its meaning and importance, and without the unfailing guidance that stems from it is a painful existence. Think about it. I say it, probably, on the eve of my death, because I love you.

Goodbye; try to calm your mother, for whom I have the most genuine feelings of compassion and love.

Your loving father,
L. Tolstoy

That evening, when Dr. Makovitsky and the district physician examined their patient, they were alarmed to find that his lungs were wheezing and that he was coughing up rusty-colored, bloody matter. The two doctors conferred outside the sickroom and agreed: Leo Tolstoy had pneumonia. It was decided to call Dr. Nikitin—the old family doctor and eminent physician—from Moscow at once. Since Sergei was in Moscow, Sasha wired him: "Situation serious. Bring Nikitin immediately. He wants you and sister to be informed. Fears arrival of the others." Some expert medical attention was needed. Usually Tolstoy's fever went down in the morning, but when he woke on the morning of November 2, his temperature was 102.5 Adding to his pains was a heartburn. His heartbeat seemed weaker, his pulse was uneven, and his respiration was thirty-eight to forty. All morning, Sasha says, he moaned loudly. But there was a break.

Chertkov, accompanied by Sergeyenko, arrived at nine and there was a joyful, tearful reunion. But it did not last very long. Tolstoy's condition grew more critical as the morning slipped by. By 11:00 A.M. his temperature had risen to 103.3, and it remained high for the next several hours.

At about three that afternoon, the stationmaster, Ivan Ozolin—"a most loveable man," Sasha called him—came into the cottage with some alarming news. He had just received a telegram saying that a special train carrying the Tolstoy family—the Countess, her sons, and a daughter—would be arriving at Astapovo at nine that evening.[5]

Back at Yasnaya Polyana, Sonya, according to her diary, had not eaten and had taken only a few sips of water since she woke up on the morning of October 28 to find that her husband had fled during the night. She had made no more attempts to kill herself since the special doctor, psychiatrist, and trained nurse arrived to look after her. Desperately, she had implored young Bulgakov to set out with her to find her husband, but he had gently refused, reminding her that in his farewell letter Tolstoy had asked that no one should come after him. She had sent for a priest and taken Communion. And at 4:00 A.M. on October 30 she had written Leo a second letter, begging him to return and trying to explain why she innocently happened to be poking around his study the night of his departure.

> Still no news from you, my dear Lyovochka, and my heart is torn to pieces. Is it possible that you do not feel an echo of them in yourself, my darling? You told Sasha to say that my having rummaged suspiciously among your papers was the last straw that caused you to leave home. That night when I was taking my letters downstairs . . . I really don't know what made me go into your study and touch your diary to convince myself that it was in place. . . .
>
> It was not suspicion that sometimes made me look at you: It was often that I simply wanted to look lovingly at you. My stupid jealousy of Chertkov that sometimes made me want to discover how much you loved him, is confirmation of that.
>
> Lyovochka, my friend, you know that you wrote all your artistic and spiritual work living with me. If my nervous disorder has lately hindered your working, forgive me, my dear one! Yesterday I began a strenuous cure.

She told him of her attempts to drown herself after learning of his flight. "You will be angry at hearing this, of course, but I was then, as now, out of my mind with despair."

> Lyovochka, my dear one, is it possible that you have left me forever? You know you used to love me. . . . Come back to me, my dear, my precious husband! Come back, Lyovochka darling. Don't be cruel. Let me at least visit you when I have recovered a little. . . . Forgive me, Lyovochka, return to me, *save me!* And let us live the last days of ours *together* in holiness and love.
>
> Read *this* letter attentively. . . . For the last time, my husband, my friend, my dear beloved Lyovochka—forgive me, save me, and *return* to me.
>
> Your Sonya

To get him back, she was even willing to make up with Chertkov. She asked Bulgakov to tell him she would like to see him.
"Once again," Bulgakov says, "as on that memorable day, the
twelfth of June, when she had appealed to him through me to
return the manuscripts and consent to reconciliation, I went to him
with the secret hope that this time the reconciliation would take
place."

But alas, Bulgakov says, his hopes were in vain.

> Chertkov was true to his nature: shrewd and alien to sen-
> timent. . . .
> "Why should I go?" he asked. "So that she should ask my
> forgiveness. It's a ruse to get me to send a telegram for her to
> Tolstoy."
> I confess that such a reply both surprised and pained
> me. . . . It was indeed a feeble excuse for not going.

Bulgakov did not have the heart to tell her. He asked Dr.
Grigory Berkenheim, who had attended the Tolstoys for some ten
years, to go to Telyatinki to try to persuade Chertkov to at least
come over for a talk with the Countess. But the doctor's effort, too,
was in vain and he told Sonya so. Nevertheless, she composed a
telegram to her husband and asked Bulgakov to send it. "Have
taken communion. Reconciled with Chertkov. Forgive me and farewell!" The high-principled young secretary declined to send it
since, he says, it was not true.

In the meantime, Sonya had received her husband's letter
from Shamardino, written on the night of October 30 and telling
her that a meeting between them—and still more, his return—was
"completely impossible." She quickly replied, on November 1, and
this time her tone had changed.

> I have received your letter. Don't be afraid that I shall come
> at present to look for you. I am so weak that I can hardly move.
> Nor do I wish to use any compulsion. Do what seems best to
> you. . . . Somehow it seems to me that we shall never see one
> another again, Lyovochka, dear one. . . . Yesterday I made
> peace with Chertkov. . . . Your words that a meeting with me
> would be *terrible* for you convinced me that it is impossible. . . .
> I kiss you, my dear old friend, who once loved me. . . . God be
> with you—take care of your health.

Next morning at 5:30 she got off another letter, this time attempting to explain further that she had never meant to spy on him.

> Before we part—perhaps forever—I want not to justify my conduct, about which you accuse me in your letter to Sasha, but simply to explain it. If I looked at you through the balcony door when you were playing patience, if I met you on your walks, or saw you off when you went riding and met you on your return—all that was not from suspicion, but from an irrational and passionate love I had for you. Probably I had a premonition of what has now happened. . . .
>
> Every day I made up my mind to say to you that I wanted you to see Chertkov, but somehow I always felt ashamed to *allow* you anything. . . . As regards the diary, I had formed a stupid habit of feeling whether it was there on the table when passing, and that night, when taking my letters downstairs, I looked into your study, and touched your portfolio merely by stupid habit. I did not *rummage* at all, did not search for anything or read anything, and I felt even at the time that I had been foolish and made a mistake.
>
> But you would have gone away anyway. I had the presentiment all the time.

She asked whether she couldn't see him for just "a few hours," promising that she "would go away afterwards."

> I shall not come without your permission—so don't fear—don't be afraid of me. I would rather die than see *horror* on your face when I appear.

In the meantime, newspaper reporters had begun to arrive at Yasnaya Polyana to interview Sonya and the children about what had happened, but Andrei had managed to send them away, saying the family could give out no information. But as reports in the newspapers came in blaming Countess Tolstoy for driving the great writer to such desperation that he had to leave his own home, Sonya felt determined to tell her side of the story. When the assistant editor of the newspaper *Russian Word,* an elderly gentleman with mild, courtly manners, called, Sonya agreed to see him. According to Bulgakov, who sat in on the interview, Sonya cursed her husband for having left her. "He's a brute!" she cried. "He could not have acted with any greater cruelty! He wanted to kill me!"

She gave the editor, says Bulgakov, "a very ugly picture of what had happened. She made a hideous scene in the editor's presence, flying about the room in her lilac-colored morning dress with her hair in disorder and denouncing both Leo Nikolayevich and Chertkov. It was very difficult to calm her."

But these antics gave the editor a colorful story and, in what he apparently thought was a gesture of gratitude, he had his paper send a telegram to Countess Tolstoy the next day, November 2.

"Tolstoy ill at Astapovo," it said. "Temperature 104."

Sonya hurriedly leafed through a railway timetable. She had never heard of Astapovo and hadn't the faintest idea where it was. When she located it—it was some 140 miles southeast of Tula on the Dankovo-Smolensk line—she found, on inquiry at the Tula rail station, that the last train that would get her there that day had left. A hasty family council with the children was called: Tanya and her brothers Ilya, Andrei, and Mikhail. They agreed they could not wait until the morrow. An old man of eighty-two with a temperature of 104 might not survive until then. So they ordered a special train from Tula that would get them to their destination the same evening.

When Sergei Tolstoy received Sasha's message telling him to hurry to Astapovo and bring Dr. Nikitin, he was on the train carrying him from Moscow to his estate at Nikolskoye. After querying a conductor as to where Astapovo was and how to get there, he got off the train at Gorbachevo and caught one directly to Astapovo, arriving there, he says, at eight o'clock on the evening of November 2.

He wanted to see his father at once but Sasha and Dr. Makovitsky held him back. They were afraid the visit might upset the sick man because it would signify that at least one member of the family had learned of his hideout. But, finally, the doctor relented. Sergei found his father half-conscious. But when the old man opened his eyes, he recognized his son and seemed surprised and rather uneasy.

"Sergei! How did you find me here? How did you know?"

Sergei says he had to lie—at least partly. So he said that a conductor had told him while he was on the train to his estate. But how would the conductor know? his father asked. And the son had to tell him another fib. His father closed his eyes and dozed off, and Sergei says his first impression was that the old man's condition was "not too bad."

Countess Tolstoy and her children arrived on their special train around midnight, and she, too, wanted to go immediately to see her husband. Good old Dushan dissuaded her for the moment and prevailed upon her to go to bed and get some rest after the arduous journey. In the meantime, the special Pullman car had been shunted to a side track. Since there was no place else to put up, they had decided to live in the car.

After Sonya retired to her compartment the children held another family council. They faced a difficult decision. What were they to do with their mother? If they allowed her to see her husband it might be fatal. On the other hand, didn't a wife, their mother, married to a man for forty-eight years and bearer of his thirteen children, have a right to see him on his deathbed?

Sasha was adamant. "I resolved," she says, "that I would not let Mother in unless Father himself expressed his wish for it, even if the doctors and the family should find it possible to admit her. No one had the right to violate his will." The others agreed.

"We decided," says Sergei, "to use every means to prevent our mother from going in to see our father before he himself asked for her—the chief reason being a fear lest the meeting might be injurious to him. Our mother, with pangs of heart, agreed with us, saying that she did not wish to cause our father's death. We did not quite trust her, however, and feared that she would go to him all the same and we decided to keep her under observation."

It was decided also that the three younger brothers—Ilya, Andrei, and Mikhail, who had sided with their mother—would not go in to see him.[6]

"They do not allow me to see him," Sonya complained to her diary the next morning.

November 3 was a busy and trying day for Tolstoy. Dr. Nikitin arrived that morning and, after examining him, confirmed that the sick man was suffering from an inflammation of a lobe of the left lung and that there were signs that it was spreading to the other lung. When Sasha questioned him uneasily, he told her that her father's condition was grave but not hopeless. Actually, during most of the day Tolstoy felt better. His temperature was normal, his breathing easier. He joked about his health with the doctor.

Alexandra went over to the Pullman car and reported the good news to her mother. But Sonya was not in a "repentant mood," Sasha found. On the contrary, she was cursing her husband for having left her. She did not seem to realize, Sasha thought, how gravely ill her husband was. When he got better, Sonya said, she would certainly not allow him to escape, but would watch his every step. "Wherever he goes, I will go," she kept repeating. And at any cost. Catching up with him this time cost her plenty—five hundred rubles, she said, to hire a special train. Sasha says her mother continued to speak "so ill" of her father that she "interrupted her sharply and left."

"It was difficult to understand my mother," Tanya Tolstoy recalled later of the nightmare week at Astapovo. "She lamented the fact that she wasn't being allowed to look after him. 'To think that I've lived with him for 48 years and that it's not me looking after him when he's about to die.' "

Sonya had remembered to bring along a little pillow she had embroidered for Tolstoy's bed, which he had become very fond of. When Dr. Makovitsky took it over to him, he asked immediately who had brought it. Dushan—the "holy Dushan," as Tanya called him—could not tell a whole fib, and answered that Tanya had brought it from Yasnaya Polyana. By this time, after Sergei's appearance, the old man had begun to realize that at least some of his children had come to Astapovo. He sighed at the news, but told the doctor he would like to see his daughter at once.

When Tanya went in, he greeted her warmly—he had always had a special love for the gentle Tanya—and then began to ask her about her mother. How was she holding up?

> That was what I was most afraid of [Tanya wrote]. I was afraid he would ask me questions about my mother. I wouldn't have known what to answer. I had never lied to him, and I knew that at this solemn moment I would be incapable of answering him with an untruth. But fortunately he put his questions in such form that a direct lie was unnecessary.

He asked her who was taking care of Sonya, and she was able to answer truthfully that her brothers were. But soon her father was again sharpening his questions. How did Sonya pass the days? How did she occupy herself? He wanted to know everything there was to know about how his wife had held up after his flight. Tanya tried to change the subject. "Are you sure talking about this does not upset you?" she asked.

"No! Go on, go on! What could be more important for me?"[7]

Tanya says that her "keenest desire" was that he would ask for her mother to come to him. "I longed ardently for a reconciliation between them before he died." But she did not dare bring it up at this first encounter. "It was clear," Tanya says, "that he was alarmed at the thought of seeing his wife."

Wearily, his strength fast ebbing, the old patriarch called for some writing paper and his diary. He wanted to jot down some things and get off a letter to Aylmer Maude, his English biographer and translator: "Astapovo, November 3, 1910. On my way to a place where I wished to be alone," he wrote, "I was taken ill . . ." He could get no further. He was too weak to go on.*

He called to Chertkov to help him with an entry he wanted to make in his diary. He would have to dictate.

> November 3, at Astapovo: Had a bad night. Lay for two days with a fever. Chertkov came on the 2nd. They say that Sofya Andreyevna has too. Seryozha came during the night. I was very moved. Today the 3rd, Nikitin and Tanya came, then Goldenweiser. . . . So much for my plan. *Fais ce que dois, adv . . .†*

He broke off in the middle of the French word and, gathering his last breath, continued: "And it's all for the good of the others, and above all for me," and then he fell back on his pillow exhausted.

He was, of course, unaware of the increasing hullabaloo outside the cottage. An army of journalists and press photographers had descended on the village to report about his illness. Even Pathé himself had dispatched a film crew to Astapovo to shoot motion pictures of whatever of interest they could find. The pioneer of this

---

* This note to Maude was the last letter he ever wrote.
† This is the last entry in a diary he had kept for sixty-three years. The French proverb was an old favorite of his and it appears early on in the diary: *Fais ce que dois, advienne que pourra.* "Do what you must, come what may." Tolstoy got halfway through the word "come" before giving up.

new-fangled contraption as an organ of news reporting gave specific instructions: shoot pictures of the railway station (which was prohibited in Russia) and Tolstoy's cottage, of Countess Tolstoy and her children, and of old Tolstoy himself, if possible.

In such a hamlet as Astapovo, the facilities for so many journalists were quite inadequate. The small telegraph office at the railway station was swamped by reporters filing their copy; extra telegraphers had to be brought from Tula and Moscow. The only place for the newsmen to eat was the small station restaurant. Many reporters had to sleep in the waiting room, but since the station was not large enough to accommodate them all, the railway authorities put them up in empty railway coaches hastily brought in from Tula.

Reporters were then, as now, a rapacious, hard-drinking, irreverent group. They were all over the place and they were loud and demanding. Sasha and Sergei refused to allow them entrance to the cottage. Young, athletic Sergeyenko, Chertkov's secretary, guarded the door. The children, besieged by the reporters, refused to speak to them. But Sonya received one after another of the correspondents in her private car and talked freely to them. Again, as in Yasnaya Polyana, she was anxious to contradict the widespread stories in the Russian press blaming her for her husband's flight. She complained bitterly to the reporters that her own children would not allow her to see her husband, even though he might be dying. She insisted that her illustrious husband had done it all as a publicity stunt. "He did it," she explained, "as a sort of self-advertisement to attract attention to himself."

After the flood of reporters from all over Russia, came substantial reinforcements for the police. Fearing riots if the troublesome author died, the minister of the interior sent out coded telegrams to the district and provincial authorities ordering them to mobilize for the worst and assuring them that police reinforcements were on the way. The governor of the province arrived on November 4, accompanied by the deputy director of the national police, who had come from St. Petersburg, and who disguised his presence by wearing civilian clothes. He ordered live ammunition to be issued to the gendarmes.

The church, too, became interested in what was happening at Astapovo. It wanted very much for Tolstoy to formally repent so that it could be said that he returned to the bosom of the church before he died. The metropolitan of St. Petersburg telegraphed Tolstoy imploring him to repent "before appearing for judgement at the throne of God." Chertkov, fiercely protecting the Master to the end, refused to show him the message. When the Holy Synod in Petersburg received no answer, it dispatched Father Varsonofy from the Optina monastery, where Tolstoy had stayed the first night of his flight. He must see Tolstoy at once. But the children refused him entrance to the cottage. It was not only because his presence might upset their father but because they remembered the trickery of the church when their father was ill in the Crimea and the doctors feared for his life. Then, according to Sergei, "the Holy Synod issued secret instructions that a priest should obtain access to Tolstoy, and in the event of his death should immediately announce that Tolstoy had repented, returned to the bosom of Mother Church, confessed and received the Eucharist before his death."

Now, adds Sergei, there were priests at Astapovo, led by Father Varsonofy, who had been sent on a similar errand. When they failed to get into Tolstoy's sickroom they did all they could to obtain from one or another of the family a statement that would have enabled the synod to announce that the famous author had repented on his death and returned to the church. That was one reason, Sergei says, why the children had agreed to keep their mother out of the cottage. They feared that if she had access to her husband she might, as a devout Orthodox, have been cajoled into making a statement that would have served the synod's purpose.[8]

Poor Father Varsonofy would not take no for an answer. He insisted on remaining in Astapovo, in the hopes that the family eventually would relent and allow him to talk to the dying man. His staying on presented a problem for the authorities. All the space in the station waiting room and in the railway coaches was taken by the members of the press and the police. They finally found the good father a corner in the ladies' waiting room.

How ironic for Tolstoy it had become! He who had fled from his home to seek peace and quiet was now the center of worldwide attention, surrounded, though he did not know it, by a horde of noisy reporters and photographers and police milling around the place he had come to. There was a certain irony too that the church, which had kicked him out, had now sent emissaries to this lonely place to beg him to come back. When the same thing happened as he lay deathly ill in the Crimea, he had said to his oldest son: "How is it, Sergei, that these gentlemen do not understand, even in the face of death, that two and two still make four."[9]

"Leo Nikolayevich gets steadily worse," Sonya began her daybook on Thursday, November 4. He had had a bad night. He slept little. The evening of the third he had had a painful attack of hiccups—something that would torment him day and night from now on. Dr. Makovitsky and Dr. Nikitin gave him a solution of sugared milk in soda water, but it did not help. Try as they might, the doctors could not stop the hiccups. Around 11:00 P.M. Tolstoy had lapsed into delirium. He kept asking Sasha, who was attending him, to take some dictation, but his words were so slurred she could not understand him. She suddenly realized, she says, that the great thinker and writer had reached a critical stage: he could no longer put down his thoughts in words. But by the morning of the fourth he seemed better and was quite able to make himself understood. To Chertkov he mumbled: "Perhaps I'm dying, but perhaps not." And to Sasha he dictated a telegram to his sons—who he believed were still at Yasnaya Polyana with their mother—saying he felt better but that his heart was so weak they must prevent their mother from coming to see him. "A meeting would be fatal," he said. Sergei took the "telegram" around to his mother, hoping that though it would offend her it would make her see the folly of wanting to see her husband now.

Folly or not, she did want to see him and, during the day, she slipped out of the Pullman car and strode stealthily over to the cottage. She had agreed not to try to break into the sickroom, but she felt she had the right to have a glimpse of her husband, if only through the window of his room. An alert photographer caught the sadness of the scene. His picture shows Sonya dressed in a long fur coat with a white peasant's scarf over her head, standing on tiptoe in the light snow at the window trying desperately to peer through it and catch sight of the man she had lived with for forty-eight years and who, in all probability, if the doctors were right, would now be leaving her forever. Behind her, at the bottom of the steps leading to the door, stands a basket of what looks like soiled laundry.

Someone inside spotted her and hastily pulled a curtain so that she could not see in. (It turned out to be her daughter Sasha.) Sonya turned, frustrated once again, and went back to her carriage.

She did, once, almost get inside the house. Sasha had answered her knock on the door and had stepped out to give her mother the latest news on her husband's condition. Sonya asked if she could come into the anteroom for a minute, promising not to try to enter the sickroom. Sasha says she was about to accommodate her when she heard the grinding of two movie cameras. She called to the men to cease. She was sure her mother had asked the cameramen to film her entering and leaving the house. Sasha turned her back. "You're keeping me from him," Sonya complained. "So why can't you at least let people believe that I have been with him!"

"There seems to be little hope," Sonya began her notebook on Friday, November 5. "I am torn to pieces," she added, "by my conscience, the expectation of a bad end, and the impossibility of seeing my beloved husband."

Her anguish came partly from the opinion of Dr. Berkenheim, who had arrived from Moscow earlier in the day in answer to an urgent request from the family. He brought with him a bed to replace the one Tolstoy was using; its springs were breaking down. He also brought a supply of oxygen, medicines, and some bottles of fermented milk. After examining the patient he was less optimistic than the other physicians. Tolstoy, he found, was a very ill man. The children were so alarmed by his diagnosis that they wired urgently to Moscow for two celebrated physicians who had also treated Tolstoy in the past: Dr. Vladimir Shchurovsky and Dr. Pavel Usov.

Even Dr. Makovitsky, usually so optimistic, admitted that Tolstoy had had a very bad night. He had been delirious for long spells. When he regained consciousness his speech was incoherent, he had difficulty breathing, his pulse was very weak, and his heartbeat uneven. His hiccups continued to torment him, coming back every twenty minutes and lasting at least five minutes. For the first time since taking to bed he seemed depressed. By evening, though, Dr. Makovitsky thought Tolstoy had improved. His temperature was only 99.3. He was coughing up mucus easily. There was not much blood in it. In spite of the opinion of Dr. Berkenheim, the other doctors were more optimistic. "We did not want to believe," says Dushan, "that this dear man was going to die."

Tolstoy himself was not so sure. To Tanya, who spent most of the day at his bedside, he turned in one of his lucid moments and murmured: "Here is the end and . . . it is nothing! *Nichevo!*" Earlier in the day his thoughts had turned to his wife. Raising himself up from his pillow, he said to Tanya: "So many things are falling on Sonya. We managed things badly." Tanya, who for years had tried to bring her parents together, said to him eagerly: "Do you want to see her? Do you want to see Sonya?" He did not reply. A little later in his delirium he muttered: "Escape . . . escape . . . after me . . . after me . . ."

Sometimes he chafed at receiving so much attention—from Tanya and Sasha and Sergei, Chertkov and Sergeyenko, Goldenweiser and Boulanger, not to mention a growing team of doctors. One instant, says Tanya, he raised himself desperately into a sitting position and said: "I advise you to remember one thing: There are a great many people in the world besides Leo Tolstoy, and you are all concerning yourself with Leo Tolstoy."[10]

Toward evening, when Sergei visited him, he found that his father's hiccuping had become almost constant. "He began slowly to move his hands over his breast, plucking at the blanket, and in a word, doing what the peasants call 'getting ready.' "

The eminent physicians, Shchurovsky and Usov, arrived at Astapovo from Moscow early on the morning of November 6. After examining the patient and conferring with the other doctors, they held out little hope that Tolstoy's life could be saved. The pneumonia had gone too far; the heart was too weak. After the meeting, Dr. Makovitsky says, their spirits sank. The first half of the night, he says, had not been bad—Tolstoy slept quite peacefully. But the second half did not go well. Tolstoy began moaning from the torment of the hiccups and a heartburn. His breathing was much more difficult than the night before. And he was choking. At noon the doctors began giving him oxygen. It did not help and Tolstoy asked them to turn it off.

Sergei took his turn in the sickroom at one o'clock that afternoon. He found his father in a bad state.

His face was bluish, his nose had sharpened, his respiration was very rapid. This was a heart attack involving severe spasms. Oxygen and the injection of camphor at last produced an effect, and little by little his heart resumed beating. In the evening he became much worse and his pulse was very alarming.

By ten o'clock Sergei became so apprehensive he ran to the railway carriage and told Tanya that things were very bad.

> My mother saw me, and asked about my father's condition. With a stab of the heart I replied: "Still the same" and went back to Ozolin's house. My father was tossing about and trying with loud and deep groans to rise from the bed. "I'm afraid I'm dying. . . . It's hard." A little later: "I will go somewhere where no one can interfere with me." Then he said in a loud voice: "To escape. . . . It is necessary to escape!"
>
> Soon afterward he saw me standing there in the semidarkness (only one candle in the room) and called: "Seryozha." I rushed to the bed and knelt down so as to better hear what he would say. He spoke a whole phrase, but I could make nothing of it. Later Dushan told me he had caught the words and noted them down. "Truth . . . I love very much . . . they all . . ."

Those were his last words. Sergei kissed his father's hand and went away, he says, confused.

Toward midnight, Tolstoy's condition deteriorated still more. His breathing was rapid and loud, says Sergei, his voice became husky, and his hiccups increased. Dr. Usov proposed a morphine injection and, though Tolstoy protested, it was given to him and it calmed him down, and soon he dozed off.

It was now the early morning of Sunday, November 7. The doctors took turns tiptoeing into the sickroom to take the patient's pulse and temperature and check his breathing. They worked by the light of one candle on his bed table, which left the room in semidarkness. Chertkov sat at his bedside, full of thoughts, perhaps, about his rights should his great mentor die. Alexandra and Tanya and Sergei, dog-tired from lack of sleep, came in and out. Everyone spoke in hushed voices.

By 3:00 A.M. there were few signs of life in the old man. Dr. Makovitsky took his pulse but could feel nothing. His breathing had almost stopped. His heartbeat was feeble. He was unconscious. Dr. Usov suggested to the children that they call their mother. He thought there was no chance of Tolstoy's regaining consciousness and thus no danger that he would awaken and recognize his wife and be terrified.

Chertkov left the room, and a few moments later Sonya walked through the darkness to the cottage. She moved slowly through the house and paused at the doorway to Tolstoy's room, peering into the semidarkness. Then, determinedly, as if to defy all the others standing about who she thought were probably blaming her for this tragedy, she walked to the bedside, bent over and kissed her husband's forehead, knelt and began to whisper: "Forgive me. Please forgive me," and a few other words that the others could not hear. Then she prayed, but her husband could not hear.

Fearing that Sonya might awaken him after all as her voice rose in prayer, Dr. Usov, at the children's urging, asked her to leave the bedside and go into the adjoining room. At first she hesitated and then slowly withdrew. The physicians, though they had abandoned all hope, gave the patient two more injections to ease the pain. Tolstoy did not regain consciousness. At five o'clock it became evident that the end was near. The doctors could do no more. The last moments of Leo Tolstoy's life were ebbing away. At 6:03, Dushan noted, his breathing stopped and Dr. Usov announced to all in the room, "The first cessation!" Then a faint sigh of breath. Then its cessation. Then again a slight sign of it, and finally a rattle. Then silence. "6:05!" one of the doctors, holding his watch, sang out.

Leo Tolstoy had died at 6:05 on the morning of Sunday, November 7, 1910.

Sonya, who ten minutes before the end had returned to kneel at the bedside and recite prayers, stepped back. Dr. Makovitsky— "good old Dushan," as the great writer had called him affectionately—stepped up to the body, bent over, and closed Tolstoy's eyes—those piercing eyes that had seen so much, and seen through so much.

Sonya, weeping, stumbled back to the railway car, took out her daybook, and wrote: "Leo Nikolayevich died at six o'clock this morning. They only let me in in time for his last gasps. These cruel people did not let me take farewell of my husband."

Then she returned to the cottage and kept vigil over her husband's body for the rest of the day, oblivious in her sorrow to the thousands of persons, mostly peasants from the surrounding villages, who filed by in final tribute to the man who, above all others in Russia, had championed the cause of the poor and the oppressed. Though the local priest had been forbidden by his superiors to

conduct any kind of religious service, the peasants broke out singing the wonderful old funeral hymn "Eternal Memory." The police
ordered them to cease, but they went on. A group of railway workers came with a primitive wreath of fir branches with the inscription "To the Apostle of Love." The painter Leonid Pasternak, who
had illustrated *Resurrection,* arrived from Moscow with his young
son Boris, the future Nobel Prize poet-novelist, to sketch a portrait
of the dead man. The sculptor Sergei Merkurov came with him to
do a death mask. Across the tracks at the railway station, weary
telegraphers took down hundreds of telegrams of sympathy pouring
in from all over the world.

Maxim Gorky received the news in Capri, where he was trying
to recover from tuberculosis. "Leo Tolstoy is dead," he wrote a
friend. "It was a blow to the heart. I wept from pain and grief, and
now, in a kind of half-crazed state, I picture him as I knew him. . . .
I remember his keen eyes—that saw through everything—and his
fingers, which always seemed to be modeling something in the air,
his talk, his jests, his beloved peasant words, and that strangely
indefinite voice of his. And I see how much of life that man embraced, how superhumanly wise he was. . . ."

The funeral train arrived at the little station of Zasyeka, near
Yasnaya Polyana, at seven o'clock on the morning of November 9.
It was a chilly, misty day—the thermometer had fallen below freezing and there were patches of snow on the ground. To the surprise
of the family, a crowd of three or four thousand, mostly peasants
from Yasnaya Polyana and surrounding villages, and workers from
the armament factories in Tula, had crowded onto the small station
platform. There would have been many more, the railroad officials
told Sergei, if the government in Petersburg had not forbidden the
railways to provide special trains from Moscow, 130 miles away.

The four sons of Tolstoy—Sergei, Ilya, Andrei, and Mikhail—
hoisted the coffin from the baggage car and, alternating with a
group of Yasnaya peasants, carried it the two miles to the great
house. Sonya, despite her exhaustion—she had been unable to sleep
for several nights—walked proudly behind the coffin. Chertkov had
tried to arrange that it be brought only to the entrance to the house
but not inside, and that it be opened only briefly for the mourners
to pass by. But the brothers overruled him, and when the cortege

arrived, they carried the coffin into the library. For several hours, until two o'clock, the peasants and workers filed by. The peasants had brought a wreath with the inscription: "Dear Leo Niko-layevich, the memory of your goodness will not die among the orphaned peasants of Yasnaya Polyana."

Around three o'clock in the afternoon, after the last mourner had passed by, Sonya bent over and kissed the forehead of her husband for the last time, the lid of the coffin was closed and sealed, and the procession set out for the burial place. Tolstoy had picked it himself—a spot in the woods a half mile or so from the house by the side of the ravine where, as we have seen, when he was five years old his elder brother Nikolai told him the green stick lay buried: someday it would be found and the lettering on the stick would reveal the secret of how everyone in the world could achieve happiness and universal love. It was now toward that sacred spot in Tolstoy's memory that the funeral procession moved, the sons again sharing with the peasants in carrying the coffin. The crowd followed along, singing "Eternal Memory." As the coffin was being lowered into the grave, everyone knelt down and the men removed their caps—all but one policeman, of several who had been as-signed to see that there were no demonstrations but who, except for this one, had discreetly withdrawn some distance from the clearing, behind the trees.

There were suddenly angry shouts from the crowd. "Police-man, on your knees! Take off your cap!" Slowly he sank to his knees. Again there was a chanting of "Eternal Memory," and gravediggers began to shovel dirt over the coffin. The family had asked that there be no speeches, but an old peasant stepped up to the grave and insisted on saying a few words about the goodness of the master of Yasnaya Polyana, and an ardent Tolstoyan spoke up to explain why the great writer had wished to be buried in this place. Sonya held up bravely. Her sons feared that she would weep hysterically at the grave site as her husband was being lowered to his last resting place. "My mother," says Sergei, "was silent and controlled. She did not shed a tear." Chertkov was not present. It was, as Sergei noted, the first public burial in Russia without a church service, just as Tolstoy, ardent Christian though he was but an implacable enemy of the church, wanted.

Slowly, sadly, Sonya and her children and their friends made their way back to the house, which seemed to them unbearably empty now that Leo Tolstoy was gone. Every hour brought a messenger with hundreds of telegrams of sympathy from all over the world—some three thousand in all by Sergei's count. Among them was one from the Social Democratic party in the Duma, the Russian parliament:

"The Social-Democratic fraction of the Duma, in the name of the proletariat, expresses its grief at the loss of the great artistic genius, the unconquerable and implacable fighter against officialdom. The enemy of all servitude, who raised his voice against capital punishment and was the friend of all the downtrodden."

All over the country the students demonstrated, shutting down the universities and issuing declarations of sympathy for the great author. In some places, at Petersburg and Odessa, the police, aided by the cossacks, had to be called out to quell these young men and women for whom Tolstoy represented the hope of the future, freedom from a mindless autocracy. The government in Petersburg feared that the student demonstrations might get out of hand and took measures to mobilize the police nationwide. Surely Tolstoy would have considered this a great tribute. But surely, too, the Tsar must have breathed a sigh of relief that this gifted, implacable enemy of his regime and his church was no more. The monarch was too stupid to see that, as Tolstoy had predicted, his days were numbered. In seven years he would be swept from the throne.

# Epilogue

SONYA OUTLIVED her husband by nine years. The first months were the hardest. What she jotted down in her day-book reveals how she felt. November 29, 1910: "Unendurable anguish, gnawing of conscience and pity for my late husband that amounts to suffering. How he suffered during this last period!" And on December 31: "Oh, these terrible sleepless nights alone with my thoughts and the darkness of my soul!"

Goldenweiser, the pianist and close friend of Tolstoy (and of Chertkov), visited Yasnaya that December.

> When I came out from Tolstoy's bedroom Sofya Andreyevna stopped me. I shall never forget her face and her whole figure. In a mumbling and broken voice she began: "What happened to me? What came over me? How could I have done it? I myself don't know what it was. . . . If you only knew what I am enduring! These terrible nights! How could I have been so blind? You know I killed him."

Gradually, as she became reconciled to what had happened and as her strength returned, she resumed her duties as the mistress of Yasnaya Polyana. She continued to manage the estate, began to write her memoirs, took up her correspondence again, received visitors and eagerly showed them through Tolstoy's study and bedroom and library. Daily she walked to the grave site and scattered flowers on it and prayed, no matter what the weather, even if it was raining hard or snowing heavily. Her nervous system improved. She no longer had hysterical outbursts.

Sonya became reconciled with Alexandra, who had betrayed her so shabbily. Each begged the other's forgiveness for what she had done, though this would not prevent Sasha from writing harshly of her mother in her two books about her father—which, in her old age, she came to regret.

Sonya never forgave Chertkov. They fought in the courts over the papers of Tolstoy which Sonya had earlier deposited in the Museum of History in Moscow. In the end, Sonya had her revenge. By decrees of December 6, 1914, after a four-year battle between the two, the Russian Senate decided to give her sole possession of these papers. Chertkov had told the courts that Countess Tolstoy would destroy the papers that she thought might put her in a bad light. But she did not. At the end of January 1915, she retrieved them from the Museum of History and deposited them "for perpetual custody" in the Rumyantsev Museum (later the Lenin Library, and perhaps soon to have another name).

By that time, the Great War had started and Alexandra had gone off to the front as an army nurse. At Yasnaya, food was scarce. The army confiscated most of the horses, making it difficult to sow and harvest the crops. And then, in 1917, the Kerensky revolution in March, which overthrew the Tsar, and after that the Bolshevik revolution in October. Bands of aroused peasants roamed the countryside burning the houses of the great estates, taking over the land for themselves. Yasnaya Polyana escaped. When a horde of revolutionaries approached it, they were turned back by the Yasnaya peasants, who fought with pitchforks and scythes to defend the place where their beloved Tolstoy had lived and tried to better their miserable lives.

The Bolsheviks ultimately took over and made Yasnaya Polyana a state farm, but allowed Sonya—they no longer recognized a "Countess"—to reside on the grounds until her death. Lenin himself, a great but critical admirer of Tolstoy, had seen to this.

The end for Sonya Tolstoy came in the late fall of 1919, almost on the same day of the month as her husband's. She fell ill with pneumonia, as Tolstoy had, and died on November 4. Sergei glanced at her face as she lay dead on her bed and found it "beautiful, calm, but the face of a stranger." She was seventy-five.

Just as her children had denied Sonya access to her husband

in the last days of his life at Astapovo, they now excluded her from what she wanted most of all on her death: to be buried by the side of her husband, Leo Tolstoy, in the little clearing in the woods. The children knew this very well. "Mother had always wanted," Sergei admits, "to be buried beside Father."[1] But at a family council, says Sergei, they "doubted whether that would be the right thing. There might have been awkward, insulting questions." A lame excuse, as Sergei later admitted.

She had discussed this with some of the children as she lay gravely ill in October. "If you don't bury me next to your father, at least bury me next to my children in the village cemetery." These words, Sergei concedes, "served as a pretext rather than a reason for burying her there."

On the wintry day of November 6 they carried her coffin to the village cemetery, where Vanechka and Masha lay buried. The gravediggers, Sergei says, had found as they dug the pit three skulls and some brass buttons which they identified as belonging to an officer at the time of Alexander I, one of the real-life characters in *War and Peace*.

It was very cold and it snowed.

Shortly before her mother died, Tanya, who now lived at Yasnaya Polyana following the death of her husband, had a talk with her about the past.

"Have you thought a lot about Papa all these years?" she asked.

"All the time!" Sonya answered. "I torment myself that I was not good enough for him."

She appealed to the world for understanding. "Let people be indulgent," she wrote in 1913, three years after her husband's death, "to the woman whose strength perhaps was insufficient to bear on her weak shoulders from youth onwards the burden of high destiny, namely to be the wife of a genius."[2]

"Such was the life together of these two beings," Tanya wrote, "as closely linked by mutual love as they were separated by the divergence of their aspirations. Intimately close to one another but also infinitely far apart. A peculiar instance of an eternal struggle between the power of the spirit and the domination of the flesh.

"And who will take it upon himself to call one of them guilty?"[3]

# *Acknowledgments*

A few acknowledgments. My debt to Michael Korda, editor in chief at Simon & Schuster, for his many helpful suggestions and for his encouragement when I most needed it. And to my agent, Don Congdon, who saw this book through many ups and downs. My thanks to the Tolstoy Museum in Moscow; to the curators of the homes of the Tolstoys in Moscow and Yasnaya Polyana, who guided me around those premises; and to the Library of Congress, the Williams College library, the Lenox, Massachusetts, library, and to Ms. Linder Amster, of the *New York Times* archives. I have already acknowledged the help of my wife, Irina Lugovskaya. Irina Petrovna Belenko also helped mightily in Moscow, searching for photographs in the Tolstoy Museum and other archives and keeping me up to date about the latest scholarship on Tolstoy in Russia. Bayara Aroutunova, a Russian scholar who teaches at Harvard, was good enough to read most of the manuscript, catch many errors, and proffer much good counsel. My thanks also to Laurie McLeod for valuable advice, and to Normi Noel for her editorial help and for trying to bring some order to my files.

This is my last book. The first one, *Berlin Diary,* appeared in June 1941, more than half a century ago. Over some fifty-two years my books have been coming out—fourteen in all. That's a long

372   •

span for a writer. I've been lucky. But I shall be ninety early in 1994. Time to quit.


William L. Shirer
Lenox, Massachusetts
June 1993

# Notes

PROLOGUE: *FLIGHT! OCTOBER 28, 1910*

1. Ilya Tolstoy, *Reminiscences of Tolstoy*, p. 397.
2. Sophia Tolstoy, *The Final Struggle*, p. 38.
3. Michael Ignatieff, in *The New York Times Book Review*, August 28, 1988.
4. Martine de Courcel, *Tolstoy*, p. 11. She quotes from *Childhood*.


ONE: *THE TRIALS OF EARLY MARRIAGE*

1. D. S. Mirsky, *A History of Russian Literature*, p. 261.
2. Tatiana Tolstoy, *Tolstoy Remembered*, p. 199.
3. *The Autobiography of Sophia Tolstoy*, pp. 61–62.
4. *Anna Karenina*, pp. 482–90.
5. *Tolstoy's Letters*, letter of August 3–10, 1863, p. 180. Countess Tolstoy quotes it in her diary entry of August 3: *The Diaries of Sophia Tolstoy*, p. 23.
6. Tolstoy's diary, June 14, 1847.
7. *War and Peace*, Book 1, Chapter 7.


THREE: *TWO VERY DIFFERENT KINDS OF LOVE*

1. From Turgenev's correspondence, cited in Henri Troyat, *Tolstoy*, p. 166.
2. From I. Tolstoy's *Reminiscences*, quoted in A. H. Wilson, *Tolstoy*, p. 470.
3. *Confession*, p. 23. It is of little help here to give page numbers, since there are many editions with different translators. I find my own notes come from two different editions, one of which I have lost. Each has its own pagination. My page numbers here are from the edition of *Confession* translated by David Patterson and published by W. W. Norton in 1983.

4. *Tolstoy's Letters*, Vol. I, p. 104.

5. I cannot find the passage in Tolstoy's diary. Martin Green, in *Tolstoy and Gandhi*, p. 48, from whom I've taken it, gives the diary date as June 18, 1858.

FOUR: *A Whirlwind Courtship*

1. Published under the title "L. N. Tolstoy's Marriage," as an appendix to Sonya's diary, pp. 826ff.

2. Louise Smoluchowski, *Lev and Sonya*, p. 35, quotes Tanya's later account in T. Kuzminskaya, *My Life at Home and at Yasnaya Polyana*.

3. *Confession*, p. 18.

FIVE: *Marriage at Last—Despite the Doubts*

1. From Sonya's account of the wedding in appendix, Sonya's diary, p. 840.

2. *Anna Karenina*, Part 5, chapters 1–6.

3. Sonya's diary, p. 843.

SIX: *Yasnaya Polyana, Sonya's Jealousies, and War and Peace*

1. Sonya's diary, Moscow, October 21, 1897.

2. Anne Edwards, *Sonya*, p. 100.

3. This is a quote from Tolstoy's diary, May 10, 11, 12, 13, 1858, in which, as we have seen, he poured out his love for Axinya.

4. Sonya's diary, December 16, 1862.

5. Sonya's diary, June 19, 1866.

6. Tatiana Tolstoy, *Tolstoy Remembered*, p. 22.

7. Ibid.

8. Henri Troyat, *Tolstoy*, p. 295. He quotes the letter from Bartenyev to Tolstoy, August 12, 1867.

SEVEN: *Anna Karenina*

1. Sonya's diaries, editor's notes, pp. 988–1000.

2. Sonya's diary, March 19, 1873, and Tolstoy's letter to Strakhov, March 25, 1873. Tolstoy never mailed the letter to Strakhov because, as he wrote him on April 7, he felt that the news of the new novel was

"premature." Actually, he had written ten different versions of its beginning and tossed them all in the wastebasket.

3. Sonya's diary, November 11, 1873.
4. Tolstoy's letter, November 10, 1873.
5. Tolstoy's letter, November 18, 1873.
6. Tolstoy's letter, June 23, 1874.
7. *Tolstoy's Letters*, Vol. I, pp. 305–6.
8. Tolstoy's letter, May 22, 1887.
9. Sonya's diary, February 24, 1870.
10. Ilya Tolstoy, *Reminiscences of Tolstoy*, p. 145.

EIGHT: *Tolstoy's Great Midlife Crisis*

1. *Confession*, p. 29.
2. D. S. Mirsky, *A History of Russian Literature*, p. 311.
3. Tolstoy's letter, February 2, 1890.
4. Quoted by R. F. Christian in his introduction to *The Diaries of Sophia Tolstoy*.
5. Sonya's diary, October 25, 1886, Yasnaya Polyana.
6. Sergei Tolstoy's introduction to Sophia Tolstoy, *The Final Struggle*, p. 23.
7. Tatiana Tolstoy, *Tolstoy Remembered*, pp. 191–92.
8. Letter to V. I. Alexeyev from Moscow, November 7, 1882. Alexeyev
was a self-educated peasant whom Tolstoy much admired. His opposition
to authority included his refusal to pay taxes.
9. Tolstoy's letter to V. G. Chertkov, July 25, 1884. More about him in the
next chapter and in all those thereafter.

NINE: *The Troubled Saint*

1. Ilya Tolstoy, *Reminiscences of Tolstoy*, pp. 221–22.
2. Henri Troyat, *Tolstoy*, p. 388.
3. Ilya Tolstoy, *Reminiscences of Tolstoy*, p. 222.
4. Tolstoy's letter, October 27, 1878.
5. Tolstoy's letter, November 22, 1878.
6. Ilya Tolstoy, *Reminiscences of Tolstoy*, pp. 216–17. Ilya Tolstoy dates the
letters 1865 and 1866, but this is surely a mistake. In those years there was
no communication between them. They must have been written later,
after the "reconciliation."
7. Ibid., p. 230.
8. Tolstoy's letter, January 10, 1884.
9. Tolstoy's letter, December 5, 1883.

10. Tolstoy's letter, February 5, 1881.

11. Rozanov, *Visit to Yasnaya Polyana*. Quoted in Henri Troyat, *Tolstoy*, p. 400.

12. Maxim Gorky, *On Literature*, p. 333.

13. Tolstoy's letter, March 8, 1881.

14. Tolstoy's letter, March 15, 1881.

15. Pobyedonostev's letter, June 15, 1881. Quoted in Henri Troyat, *Tolstoy*, p. 406.

16. Sonya's diary, November 19, 1878.

17. Sonya's letter, January 30, 1880, quoted in Henri Troyat, *Tolstoy*, p. 416.

18. Tolstoy's diary, March 30, 1884.

19. Tolstoy's letter, quoted in Henri Troyat, *Tolstoy*, p. 466.

20. Sonya's diary, December 10, 1890.

21. Sonya's diary, January 2, 1891.

22. Tolstoy's diary, April 14, 1891.

23. Quoted in Anne Edwards, *Sonya*, p. 271.

24. Tolstoy's diary, July 7, 1884.

TEN: *The Advent of Chertkov*

1. As Sergei Tolstoy remembered him. Sergei Tolstoy, *Tolstoy Remembered*, p. 191.

2. Tolstoy's letter, Moscow, March 17, 1884.

3. Sergei Tolstoy, *Tolstoy Remembered*, p. 192.

4. Quoted in Louise Smoluchowski, *Lev and Sonya*, p. 145.

5. Sonya's diary, Yasnaya Polyana, October 25, 1885.

ELEVEN: *The Kreutzer Sonata*

1. Sonya's diary, December 14, 1890.

2. Sonya's diary, February 12, 1891.

3. Tolstoy's diary, August 18, 1889.

TWELVE: *Conflict and Good Works*

1. Tolstoy's diary, September 11, 1889.

2. I am indebted to R. F. Christian, editor of *Tolstoy's Diaries*, for telling what happened to most of these projects. Vol. 1, pp. 388–89.

3. Tolstoy's diary, March 3, 1891.

4. Tolstoy's diary, June 2, 1891.

5. Tolstoy's diary, June 13, 1891.
6. Sonya's diary, February 7, 1891.
7. Ibid. (This part of the diary entry from Henri Troyat, *Tolstoy*, p. 505, is omitted in *The Diaries of Sophia Tolstoy*.)
8. Tolstoy's diary, June 2, 1891.
9. Tolstoy's diary, October 24, 1891.
10. Sonya's diary, September 10, 1891.
11. Sonya's diary, September 19, 1891.
12. Tolstoy's diary, October 24, 1891.
13. Tolstoy's letter, February 28, 1892.
14. As recounted in Henri Troyat, *Tolstoy*, p. 501.
15. Tolstoy's letter, November 2, 1891.
16. Tolstoy's letter, November 23, 1891, quoted in Henri Troyat, *Tolstoy*, p. 497.
17. Henri Tróyat, *Tolstoy*, p. 500, quotes from the letter but gives no date for it, and I cannot find it in my edition.
18. Sonya's diary, February 20, 1891.
19. Tolstoy's diary, August 21, 1892.
20. Tolstoy's diary, June 14, 1894.
21. Ibid.
22. Tolstoy's diary, May 22, 1890.
23. Tolstoy's letter, May 23, 1890.
24. Sonya's diary, November 20, 1890.
25. Sonya's diary, August 4, 1894.
26. Sonya's diary, February 5, 1895.
27. Tolstoy's diary, February 7, 1895.
28. Tolstoy's diary, February 15, 1895.
29. A footnote to Sonya's diary.
30. Sonya's diary, footnote 26, p. 896.
31. Sophia Tolstoy, *The Final Struggle*, p. 120.
32. Sonya's diary, p. 865. Her account of the death of Vanechka.
33. Louise Smoluchowski, *Lev and Sonya*, p. 183.


THIRTEEN: *SONYA'S STRANGE INFATUATION*

1. Sonya's diary, August 15, 1891.
2. Tolstoy's diary, April 18, 1889.
3. Tolstoy's diary, October 25, 1895.
4. Tolstoy's letter, October 25, 1895.
5. Sonya's letter, October 26, 1895.
6. Tolstoy's diary, May 28, 1896.
7. Tolstoy's diary, Moscow, November 22, 1896.

8. Sonya's diary, June 5, 1897.

9. Sonya's diary, June 6, 1897.

10. Sonya's diary, July 4, 1897.

11. Sonya's diary, July 13, 1897.

12. Sonya's diary, July 15, 1897.

13. Sonya's diary, July 21, 1897.

14. Sonya's diary, July 22, 1897.

15. Sonya's diary, July 23, 1897.

16. Sonya's diary, November 15, 1897.

17. Sonya's diary, December 10, 1897.

18. Ibid.

19. Sonya's diary, February 22, 1898.

20. Ibid.

21. Sonya's diary, March 4, 1898.

22. Sonya's diary, May 26–29, 1898.

23. Sonya's diary, May 30, 1898.

24. Sonya's diary, May 31, 1898.

25. Sonya's diary, July 28, 1898.

26. Sonya's diary, July 30, 1898.

27. The editor of the English edition of Tolstoy's diaries published the dialogue at the end of the entries for 1898. It probably was written at the beginning of August, a few days after the blowup. Tolstoy intended to send it to Tanya Kuzminsky but changed his mind. It was found in his papers after his death.

28. Sonya's diary, September 27, 1898.

29. Sonya's diary, June 6, 1901.

30. The two letters are quoted in Sophia Tolstoy, *The Final Struggle,* pp. 183–85.

31. Quoted in Sonya's diary, p. 899, note 6.

32. Sophia Tolstoy, *The Final Struggle,* pp. 184–85.

FOURTEEN: *No Rest, No Peace for the Writer at Seventy*

1. Tolstoy's letter, December 18, 1896.

2. Tolstoy's letter, January 12, 1897.

3. Tolstoy's letter, December 30, 1986.

4. Tolstoy's diary, July 16, 1897.

5. Tanya's diary, March 7, 1897, in Tatiana Tolstoy, *The Tolstoy Home,* p. 283.

6. Tolstoy's letter, October 14, 1897.

7. Sonya's diary, December 31, 1899.

8. Tolstoy's diary, November 20, 1899.

9. Tolstoy's letter, Moscow, March 11, 1897.

10. Tolstoy's letter, February 26, 1897.

11. Tanya has left a lengthy and amusing account of this interview in her diary of February 4, 1897.

12. Tolstoy's letter, July 14, 1898.

13. Sonya's diary, September 13, 1898.

14. I have used the translations of Simmons, *Leo Tolstoy;* Henri Troyat, *Tolstoy;* and A. N. Wilson, *Tolstoy.*

15. The chief source for this initial reaction in St. Petersburg and Moscow is Sonya's diary, Moscow, March 6, 1901.

16. I have used the translation of Henri Troyat, *Tolstoy,* pp. 563–64.

17. Sonya's diary, July 3, 1901.

18. Ibid.

19. Sophia Tolstoy, *The Final Struggle,* p. 121.

20. Maxim Gorky; *On Literature,* p. 302. Gorky's translator used gentler words in the English-language edition. Wilson, *Tolstoy,* p. 466, translates a little more literally from the Russian.

21. Gorky, *On Literature,* p. 305.

22. Ibid., p. 312.

23. Tolstoy's letter addressed "To the Emperor Nicholas II," Gaspra, January 1, 1902.

24. Sonya's diary, Gaspra, January 17, 1902.

FIFTEEN: *War and Revolution, Illness and Death*

1. Alexandra Tolstoy, *The Tragedy of Tolstoy,* pp. 112ff.

2. Alexandra Tolstoy, *Tolstoy: A Life of My Father,* p. 450.

3. Ilya Tolstoy, *Reminiscences of Tolstoy,* p. 373.

4. Ibid., p. 374.

5. Tolstoy's letter, December 22, 1903.

6. Ilya Tolstoy, *Reminiscences of Tolstoy,* pp. 377–78.

7. Ibid.

8. Quoted in Ernest J. Simmons, *Leo Tolstoy,* p. 646.

9. Tolstoy's letter, November 19, 1905.

SIXTEEN: *The Return of Chertkov*

1. Alexandra Tolstoy, *The Tragedy of Tolstoy,* p.108.

2. Ibid., pp. 199–200.

3. Tolstoy's diary, March 27, 1895.

4. Tolstoy's diary, Yasnaya Polyana, August 11, 1908.

5. Sophia Tolstoy, *The Final Struggle,* p. 30.

6. Sonya's diary, October 10, 1902.

7. Tolstoy's diary, Yasnaya Polyana, August 11, 1908.

8. The account of the birthday celebration in 1908 is based mostly on Sonya's diary of September 7, 1908, and Alexandra Tolstoy's recollections in *The Tragedy of Tolstoy,* pp. 183–86.

9. Sonya's diary, March 9, 1887.

10. I have omitted Chertkov's use of the patronymics of Tolstoy and his wife, which Russians always use in addressing one another. The Chertkov note is from Anne Edwards, *Sonya,* pp. 404–5.

11. Alexandra Tolstoy, *The Tragedy of Tolstoy,* pp. 161–65.

12. Tolstoy's diary, June 6 and 11, 1909.

13. Alexandra Tolstoy, *The Tragedy of Tolstoy,* pp. 189–92.

14. Dr. Makovitsky's diary, quoted in Henri Troyat, *Tolstoy,* p. 627.

15. Ibid.

16. Alexandra Tolstoy, *A Life of My Father,* p. 481.

17. Ibid., p. 482.

18. The account of Tolstoy's will thus far has been largely taken from Sergei Tolstoy, in his remarks in the autobiography of his mother. Also from his story of the will in his introduction to *The Final Struggle,* and in his book *Tolstoy Remembered.*

SEVENTEEN: *The Beginning of the End*

1. Sergei Tolstoy, *Tolstoy Remembered,* p. 132.

2. Extracts of Tanya's letter to her mother of June 14, 1910, are from a footnote of Sergei Tolstoy in *The Final Struggle,* pp. 98–99, and from Ernest Simmons's *Leo Tolstoy,* p. 733.

3. Valentin Bulgakov's diary, June 16, 1910, from his book *The Last Year of Leo Tolstoy,* p. 142. The book consists of Bulgakov's diaries for 1910.

4. Bulgakov's diary, June 21, 1910 (*The Last Year of Leo Tolstoy,* p. 146).

5. Tolstoy's diary, June 20, 1910.

6. Tolstoy's letter, June 14, 1910.

7. Varya's diary, June 1910. Noted in Sophia Tolstoy, *The Final Struggle,* footnote to p. 101.

8. Alexandra Tolstoy, *The Tragedy of Tolstoy,* p. 210.

9. Valentin Bulgakov, *The Last Year of Leo Tolstoy,* footnote to p. 149.

10. Bulgakov's diary, June 3, 1910.

11. Sonya's diary, June 26, 1910.

12. Chertkov's letter, June 28, 1910; text in Sophia Tolstoy, *The Final Struggle,* footnote to pp. 117–18.

13. Sonya's diary, July 1, 1910. Alexandra Tolstoy, *The Tragedy of Tolstoy,* pp. 216–17.

14. The chief sources for this nightmare of a night are the diary of Varya

Feokritova, and Leo Lvovich Tolstoy in *The Truth About My Father,* both quoted in Sophia Tolstoy, *The Final Struggle,* pp. 143–44.

EIGHTEEN: *THE LAST MONTH*

1. Bulgakov's diary, July 12, 1910 (*The Last Year of Leo Tolstoy,* pp. 157–59).
2. Varya Feokritova, quoted in Sophia Tolstoy, *The Final Struggle,* footnote to p. 158.
3. Letter quoted in Sophia Tolstoy, *The Final Struggle,* footnote to p. 241.
4. Sonya's diary, July 19, 1910.
5. Bulgakov, quoted in Sophia Tolstoy, *The Final Struggle,* footnote to p. 173.
6. Alexandra Tolstoy, *The Tragedy of Tolstoy,* pp. 228ff.

NINETEEN: *THE LAST WEEKS*

1. The dialogue is from Sonya's diary for August 15, 1910, at Kochety.
2. Alexandra Tolstoy, *The Tragedy of Tolstoy,* p. 234.
3. Tolstoy's diary, September 12, 1910.
4. Chertkov's letter to Countess Tolstoy of September 1, 1910, and her reply dated September 11–18, are published in Sophia Tolstoy, *The Final Struggle,* pp. 384–92.
5. Chertkov's letter to Tolstoy is in Sophia Tolstoy, *The Final Struggle,* p. 220. Tolstoy's answer is dated August 12, 1910.
6. Alexandra Tolstoy, *The Tragedy of Tolstoy,* p. 237.

TWENTY: *THE LAST DAYS*

1. Sonya's diary, Moscow, September 21, 1910.
2. Tolstoy's diary, September 22, 1910.
3. Bulgakov's diary, September 22, 1910.
4. Alexandra Tolstoy, *The Tragedy of Tolstoy,* p. 240.
5. The scenes described here are based on the testimony of Bulgakov's diary of September 26, 1910, and Alexandra Tolstoy, *The Tragedy of Tolstoy,* pp. 239–42.
6. Tolstoy's letter, September 25, 1910.
7. Dosev's and Chertkov's letters from Sophia Tolstoy, in the introduction to *The Final Struggle,* pp. 28–29. Tolstoy's diaries, October 22 and 23, 1910.
8. The illness Tolstoy suffered is recounted in the diaries of Countess Tolstoy and Bulgakov for October 3, 1910, in Alexandra Tolstoy, *The*

*Tragedy of Tolstoy,* pp. 243–45, and in Tatiana Tolstoy, *Tolstoy Remembered,* p. 235.

9. Sonya's diary, October 7, 1910.

10. Tolstoy's diary, October 7, 1910.

11. Tolstoy's diary, October 14, 1910.

12. Sonya's diary, October 16, 1910.

13. Novikov's account of his talk with Tolstoy is given in Sophia Tolstoy, *The Final Struggle,* footnote to pp. 329–31.

TWENTY-ONE: *FLIGHT!*

1. From the unpublished notes of Dr. Makovitsky, quoted in Sophia Tolstoy, *The Final Struggle,* p. 348.

2. Alexandra Tolstoy, *The Tragedy of Tolstoy,* p. 251.

3. Sonya's reaction to her husband's departure is told in Valentin Bulgakov, *The Last Year of Leo Tolstoy,* diary of October 28, 1910, and in Alexandra Tolstoy, *The Tragedy of Tolstoy,* pp. 254–56.

4. Isaiah Berlin, *Russian Thinkers,* p. 81. The quote comes from his most famous essay, "The Hedgehog and the Fox"—to my mind, the most brilliant piece, at least in English, ever written about Tolstoy.

5. The main source of Tolstoy's journey from Shamardino to Astapovo is Alexandra Tolstoy, *The Tragedy of Tolstoy,* pp. 264–75.

6. Sophia Tolstoy, *The Final Struggle,* footnote to pp. 360–61.

7. Tanya Tolstoy gives two slightly different versions of this encounter. See her *Tolstoy Remembered,* p. 240, and see also *The Final Struggle,* footnote to p. 359.

8. Sophia Tolstoy, *The Final Struggle,* footnote to p. 364.

9. Ibid.

10. Tatiana Tolstoy, *Tolstoy Remembered,* pp. 241–42.

EPILOGUE

1. Sophia Tolstoy, *The Final Struggle,* p. 152.

2. Sonya's diary, p. ix.

3. Tatiana Tolstoy, *Tolstoy Remembered,* pp. 243–44.

# Bibliography

PRIMARY SOURCES

Bulgakov, V. F. *The Last Year of Leo Tolstoy.* (A diary.) Translated from the Russian by Ann Dunnigan, with an Introduction by George Steiner. New York: Dial, 1971.

Chertkov, Vladmir. *The Last Days of Tolstoy.* London: Heinemann, 1922.

Gorky, Maxim. *On Literature.* (Including his reminiscences of Tolstoy.) Translated from the Russian by Ivy Litvinov. Seattle: Washington University Press, 1973.

Makovitsky, D. P. *u Tolstogo 1904–1910: Yasnaya Polyanaskie zapiski.* ("At Tolstoy's 1904–1910: Notes from Yasnaya Polyana.") Moscow: Izdatelstvo Nauka, 1979.

Tolstoy, Alexandra. *The Tragedy of Tolstoy.* Translated by Elena Varneck. New Haven: Yale University Press, 1933.

———. *A Life of My Father.* Translated from the Russian by Elizabeth Reynolds Hapgood. New York: Harper & Brothers, 1953.

———. *Out of the Past.* New York: Columbia University Press, 1981.

Tolstoy, Ilya. *Reminiscences of Tolstoy: By His Son Ilya Tolstoy.* Translated from the Russian by George Calderon. New York: Century, 1914.

Tolstoy, Leo. *Leo Tolstoy's Last Diaries.* Translated by Weston-Kesich. Edited and with an Introduction by Leon Stillman. New York: Putnam, 1960.

———. *Tolstoy's Diaries.* Edited and translated by R. F. Christian. 2 volumes. New York: Scribners, 1985.

———. *Tolstoy's Letters.* Selected, edited, and translated by R. F. Christian. 2 volumes. New York: Scribners, 1978.

Tolstoy, Sergei. *Tolstoy Remembered: By His Son Sergei Tolstoy*. Translated from the Russian by Moura Budberg. New York: Atheneum, 1962.

Tolstoy, Sophia. *The Final Struggle: Being Countess Tolstoy's Diary for 1910. With Extracts from Leo Tolstoy's Diary of the Same Period*. Preface by Sergei L. Tolstoy. Translated and with an Introduction by Aylmer Maude. New York: Octagon Press, 1980.

———. *The Diaries of Sophia Tolstoy*. Edited by O. A. Golinenko, S. A. Rozanova, B. M. Shumanova, I. A. Polroyskaya, and N. I. Azanova. Translated by Cathy Porter, with an Introduction by R. F. Christian. New York: Random House, 1985.

Tolstoy, Tatiana. *The Tolstoy Home: The Diaries of Tatiana Tolstoy*. Translated by Alice Brown. New York: Columbia University Press, 1951.

———. *Tolstoy Remembered*. Translated from the French by Derek Coltman, with an Introduction by David Giles. New York: McGraw-Hill, 1977.

### Works by Tolstoy

*War and Peace*. Translated from the Russian by Constance Garnett. New York: Dodd, Mead, 1920. A better edition was published in 1968 in paperback by New American Library and translated by Ann Dunnigan from the definitive Russian edition brought out in Moscow by the State Publishing House for Literature in 1963, with a brilliant Introduction by John Bayley.

*Anna Karenina*. Translated and with a Foreword by David Magarshack. Paperback. New York: New American Library, 1961.

*Resurrection*. Translated and with an Introduction by Rosemary Edmunds. New York: Penguin, 1966.

*Confession*. Translated and with an Introduction by David Patterson. New York: Norton, 1983.

*The Kingdom of God Is Within You*. Translated from the Russian by Constance Garnett. Foreword by Martin Green. Lincoln: University of Nebraska Press, 1984.

*Great Short Works of Leo Tolstoy*. New York: Harper & Row, 1967.

*The Portable Tolstoy*. Selected and with an Introduction by John Bayley. New York: Penguin, 1978.

### Books About the Tolstoys and the Background of Their Life

Asquith, Cynthia. *Married to Tolstoy*. Boston: Houghton-Mifflin, 1961.

Berlin, Isaiah. *Russian Thinkers*. New York: Viking, 1978. The book includes Berlin's famous essay on Tolstoy "The Hedgehog and the Fox" and also "Tolstoy and Enlightenment."

Chekhov, Anton. *Letters of Anton Chekhov*. New York: Viking, 1973.

Courcel, Martine de. *Tolstoy: The Ultimate Reconciliation*. Translated from the French by Peter Lévi. New York: Scribners, 1988.

Edwards, Anne. *Sonya: The Life of Countess Tolstoy*. New York: Simon & Schuster, 1981.

Green, Martin. *Tolstoy and Gandhi*. New York: Basic Books, 1983.

Mann, Thomas. *Three Essays*. New York, 1929.

Mirsky, D. S. *A History of Russian Literature*. New York: Viking, 1958.

Pares, Bernard. *A History of Russian*. New York: Knopf, 1944.

Pipes, Richard. *The Russian Revolution*. New York: Knopf, 1990.

Polnder, Tikhon. *Tolstoy and His Wife*. New York: Norton, 1945.

Simmons, Ernest J. *Leo Tolstoy*. Boston: Atlantic Monthly Press, 1946.

Smoluchowski, Louise. *Lev and Sonya: The Story of the Tolstoy Marriage*. New York: Paragon House, 1988.

Steiner, George. *Tolstoy or Dostoyevsky*. New York: Vintage, 1959.

*Tolstoi v Moskve*. ("Tolstoy in Moscow.") Moscow: Izdatelstvo "Planeta," 1985.

Troyat, Henri. *Tolstoy*. New York: Doubleday, 1967.

Wilson, A. N. *Tolstoy*. New York: Norton, 1988.

# Index